Time Out

Beijing

timeout.com/beijing

Published by Time Out Guides Ltd, a wholly owned subsidiary of Time Out Group Ltd.
Time Out and the Time Out logo are trademarks of Time Out Group Ltd.

10 9 8 7 6 5 4 3 2 1

This edition first published in Great Britain in 2007 by Ebury Publishing
Ebury Publishing is a division of The Random House Group Ltd,
20 Vauxhall Bridge Road, London SW1V 2SA

Random House Australia Pty Limited 20 Alfred Street, Milsons Point, Sydney, New South Wales 2061, Australia
Random House New Zealand Limited 18 Poland Road, Glenfield, Auckland 10, New Zealand
Random House South Africa (Pty) Limited Isle of Houghton, Corner Boundary Road & Carse O'Gowrie, Houghton 2198, South Africa

Random House UK Limited Reg. No. 954009

For further distribution details, see www.timeout.com

ISBN 10: 1-904978-74-6
ISBN 13: 9781904978749

A CIP catalogue record for this book is available from the British Library

Printed and bound by Firmengruppe APPL, aprinta druck, Wemding, Germany

The Random House Group Limited makes every effort to ensure that the papers used in our books are made from trees that have been legally sourced from well-managed and credibly certified forests.. Our paper procurement policy can be found on www.randomhouse.co.uk.

Temple of Heaven. *See p76.*

Time Out Guides Limited
Universal House
251 Tottenham Court Road
London W1T 7AB
Tel + 44 (0)20 7813 3000
Fax + 44 (0)20 7813 6001
Email guides@timeout.com
www.timeout.com

Editorial
Editor Chris Moss
Deputy Editor Edoardo Albert
Consultant Editors Tom Pattinson, Dominic Fitzsimmons
Listings Editor Lauren Mack
Listings Checker Sarah Keenlyside
Copy Editor Ros Sales
Proofreader John Pym
Indexer Jonathan Cox

Managing Director Peter Fiennes
Financial Director Gareth Garner
Editorial Director Ruth Jarvis
Deputy Series Editor Dominic Earle
Editorial Manager Holly Pick

Design
Art Director Scott Moore
Art Editor Pinelope Kourmouzoglou
Senior Designer Josephine Spencer
Graphic Designer Henry Elphick
Junior Graphic Designer Kei Ishimaru
Digital Imaging Simon Foster
Ad Make-up Jodi Sher

Picture Desk
Picture Editor Jael Marschner
Deputy Picture Editor Tracey Kerrigan
Picture Researcher Helen McFarland

Advertising
Sales Director Mark Phillips
International Sales Manager Fred Durman
International Sales Executive Charlie Sokol
International Sales Consultant Ross Canadé
Advertising Sales (Beijing) CIMG
Advertising Assistant Kate Staddon

Marketing
Group Marketing Director John Luck
Marketing Manager Yvonne Poon
Sales and Marketing Director North America Lisa Levinson

Production
Group Production Director Mark Lamond
Production Manager Brendan McKeown
Production Coordinator Caroline Bradford

Time Out Group
Chairman Tony Elliott
Financial Director Richard Waterlow
Time Out Magazine Ltd MD David Pepper
Group General Manager/Director Nichola Coulthard
Time Out Communications Ltd MD David Pepper
Time Out International MD Cathy Runciman
Group Art Director John Oakey
Group IT Director Simon Chappell

Contributors
Introduction Chris Moss. **History** Tom Pattinson. **Beijing Today** Tom Pattinson (*Scaling the Great Firewall* Jenny Niven). **Beijing 2008** Dominic Fitzsimmons. **Where to Stay** Sarah Keenlyside *Additional reviews* Helena Iveson. **Sightseeing Introduction** Tom Pattinson. **The Centre** Sarah Keenlyside. **Houhai & the North** Dominic Fitzsimmons. **Chaoyang** Tom Pattinson. **South Beijing** Tom Pattinson. **Financial District** Sarah Keenlyside. **The North-west** Poppy Toland. **Restaurants** Eileen Wen Mooney (*Beijing bites, On the wild side* Dominic Fitzsimmons; *New Beijingers* Tom Pattinson; *More than a cuppa* Nancy Pellegrini). **Bars & Pubs** Tom Pattinson, Dominic Fitzsimmons (*Firewater and fakes* Gabriel Suk). **Shops & Services** Sarah Keenlyside (*Hairy monkeys and serious trees* Nancy Pellegrini; *Nothing is real* Chris Moss). **Festivals & Events** Helena Iveson. **Children** Poppy Toland. **Film** Eriko Miyagawa. **Galleries** Stacey Duff (*Growing up in private* Karen Smith). **Gay & Lesbian** Dinah Gardner. **Mind & Body** Vanessa Mulquiney. **Music** Tom Pattinson. **Nightlife** Daisy Darvall. **Performing Arts** Nancy Pellegrini. **Sport & Fitness** Dominic Fitzsimmons. **Getting Started** Nancy Pellegrini. **Ming & Qing Tombs** Helena Iveson. **The Great Wall** Chris Moss. **Inner Mongolia** Vanessa Mulquiney. **Xi'an** Dinah Gardner. **Pyongyang** Nancy Pellegrini. **Directory** Dinah Gardner (*Etiquette and customs* Nancy Pellegrini; *Slow berth to China* Chris Moss). **Further Reference** Jenny Niven. **Chinese Translations** Yue Xu.

Maps john@jsgraphics.co.uk

Photography by Ben McMillan, except: page 12 AP/Empics; page 15 Mary Evans/Grosvenor Prints; page 16 Getty Images; page 17 Pierre Colombel/Corbis; page 19 New China Pictures/Magnum Photos; page 20 AP Photo/Xinhau; page 21 Tim Sloan/AFP/Getty Images; page 27 Pu Feng; pages 51, 53, 202 Carolina Gryngarten; page 54 Private Collection/The Bridgeman Art Library; pages 63, 74, 81, 83, 146, 200 Yang Yaoxin; pages 66, 123 (top right), 168, 178, 180 Chen Chao; pages 68, 69 Lu Bin Photography; pages 100, 101 Wang Wei; page 148 Yang Wen; page 154 Xie Meng/Courtesy of Colordance Pictures; page 155 Fortissimo Films; page 159 Xu Ruotao; page 160 Courtesy of Red Gate Gallery, Beijing/Zhu Wei; page 174 Courtesy of Mao; page 190 quiksilver.cn; page 205 Vicky Sotriffer; page 208 Gavin Hellier/Robert Harding; pages 210, 212 Koryo Tours.
The following images were provided by the featured establishments/artists: pages 34, 37, 41, 164, 204.

The Editor would like to thank Peter Cheng, Simon Cockerell, Carolina Gryngarten, Gissing Liu, Sara Liu, Ben McMillan, Vicky Sotriffer, Josh Wenger, Yue Xu, and all the editorial staff and freelance writers at Time Out Beijing magazine.

The Editor flew to Beijing with British Airways (www.ba.com; direct, daily flights from Heathrow).

Contents

Introduction

Beijing is a fitting capital for the most populous country on earth. It doesn't merely sprawl; it pullulates, it erupts, it teems. Flyovers get raised above flyovers, railway lines are laid down on top of highways and every new skyscraper seeks to belittle its lofty neighbour.

This presents problems for tourists and Beijingers alike. How do you combine sightseeing, eating out and drinking – not to mention working and living – when each activity seems to have been allotted to a separate district? Come the Olympics – and sometimes the whole city seems to be saying 'Come the Olympics!' – it will be fascinating to see how the estimated 500,000 visitors and 10,000 athletes and 20,000 members of the press get around.

Fortunately, there are some unmissable one-stop experiences and moments of peace and tranquility amid all this mayhem. The cranes and bulldozers haven't been allowed near the superlative Forbidden City or the Temple of Heaven. Imperial grandeur, dusty old hutongs and senior citizens dancing and singing opera are a welcome break from the aching aspiration to be modern that is besetting Beijing's emerging middle-class. Contemporary culture is renascent, as art, music and film strive to keep pace with the economic juggernaut that shows no sign of slowing down.

As the political, historical and cultural centre of China, Beijing is a world away from the glitz and glamour of the business capital Shanghai. Beijingers don't care so much about pleasantries or looks. The grit of the city is its beauty, and the grit of its people underlies a quiet confidence that a new 1,000-year-old city is being created on top of the ancient foundations of the old one.

If there is one overriding emotion that any traveller is bound to note during a stay, it is the sense of expectation in Beijing – among Chinese residents as well as expatriates and regular business visitors. The Mings and Qings may be long gone, and the latest empire-building experiment – Maoism – has had to be 'revised', but many Beijingers really do expect that the 21st century will be theirs – just as the 20th belonged to New York, Bonn and Tokyo and the 19th century to London and Paris.

This could go either way: Beijing could become a botched, rather soulless city where Occidental consumerism squeezes out the last drop of Eastern mysticism; or it could evolve into a world-class capital combining Hong Kong's trading nous, Taipei's internationalism and the tiniest hint of Shanghai's shazam. Hedge your bets and you might miss something; go now and you'll catch a city on the verge of something new and exciting.

ABOUT TIME OUT CITY GUIDES

This is the first edition of *Time Out Beijing*, one of an expanding series of Time Out guides produced by the people behind the successful listings magazines in London, New York, Shanghai and Beijing. Our guides are all written by resident experts who have striven to provide you with all the most up-to-date information you'll need to explore the city, whether you're a local or a first-time visitor.

THE LOWDOWN ON THE LISTINGS

We have tried to make this book as easy to use as possible. Addresses, phone numbers, transport information, opening times and admission prices are all included in the listings. However, businesses can change their arrangements at any time – and Beijing is in the thrall of a construction boom that wipes away well-known residential areas, bars and even hotels on an almost daily basis. Before you go out of your way, we'd strongly advise you to phone ahead to check opening times and other particulars. While every effort and care has been made to ensure the accuracy of the information contained in this guide, the publishers cannot accept responsibility for any errors it may contain.

THE LIE OF THE LAND

Beijing is gargantuan, but many sights are concentrated in the city centre and around the Houhai lakes and lanes, while Chaoyang is the indisputable hub for eating and drinking. We have divided the city down into six fairly navigable areas – explained on page 48.

Exploring the city on foot can be very tiring. Even car-free spaces such as the Forbidden City and Tiananmen Square are huge and you'll be glad of your taxi when you've tramped through

a hundred arches and across the cement deserts of Beijing's 'plazas'. The parks and palaces are pedestrian-friendly, however, and provide a much-needed breath of fairly fresh air.

Street signs in Beijing are in both English and Chinese. For an explanation of the Chinese names for 'street', 'road' and 'avenue' and further details of the city's geography, *see p48.*

The metro service is risibly limited for a city of this size, but should be far more useful by mid-2008, when a further five lines will have opened for the Games. This guide provides a metro stop where possible – but either be prepared to walk several blocks after exiting the subway, or catch a cab. For information on getting around and transport options, *see p214-215.*

ESSENTIAL INFORMATION

For all the practical information you might need for visiting the area – including visa and customs information, details of local transport, a listing of emergency numbers, information on local weather and a selection of useful websites – turn to the Directory at the back of this guide. It begins on page 214.

PRICES AND PAYMENT

We have noted where venues accept the following credit cards: American Express (**AmEx**), Diners Club (**DC**), MasterCard (**MC**) and Visa (**V**). Many may also accept travellers' cheques, and/or other cards.

Prices in this book are given in Chinese *renminbi* (RMB), often referred to as *yuan* or the slang term *kuai*. At the time of going to press the exchange rates were around RMB 8 to the dollar or RMB 15 to the pound sterling.

The prices we've listed in this guide should be treated as guidelines, not gospel. If prices vary wildly from those we've quoted, ask whether there's a good reason. If not, go elsewhere. Then please let us know. We aim to give the best and most up-to-date advice, so we want to know if you've been badly treated or overcharged.

TELEPHONE NUMBERS

The country code for China is 86 and the area code for Beijing is 10. The latter need only be dialled when you're phoning from outside the city; when inside, just dial the 8-digit nuber given in our listings. For more details, *see p225.*

MAPS

The map section at the back of this book includes street maps of Beijing, a map for the Trips out of Town and a plan of the metro. The maps start on page 238 and pinpoint specific locations of hotels ❶, restaurants and cafés ❶, and bars and pubs ❶.

LET US KNOW WHAT YOU THINK

We hope you enjoy *Time Out Beijing* and we'd like to know what you think of it. We welcome tips for places that you consider we should include in future editions and take note of your criticism of our choices. You can email us at guides@timeout.com.

Advertisers

We would like to stress that no establishment has been included in this guide because it has advertised in any of our publications and no payment of any kind has influenced any review. The opinions given in this book are those of Time Out writers and entirely independent.

There is an online version of this book, along with guides to more than 100 international cities, at **www.timeout.com**.

Time Out
Miami
Milan
Mumbai & Goa
Naples
New Orleans
New York
Paris
Patagonia
Prague
Rome
San Francisco
Seville & Andalucia
Shanghai
Singapore
South of France
Stockholm
Sydney
Tokyo 東京
Turin
Venice
Vienna
Washington, DC
Amsterdam
Athens
Bangkok
Barcelona
Beijing
Boston
Brussels
Budapest
Buenos Aires
California
Cape Town
Chicago
Copenhagen
Croatia
Dublin
Edinburgh
Florence
Havana
Hong Kong
Istanbul
Las Vegas
Lisbon
London
Madrid
Mallorca
Marrakech
Miami
Milan
Mumbai & Goa
Naples
New Orleans
New York
Patagonia
Prague
Rio de Janeiro
Rome
San Francisco
Seville & Andalucia
Shanghai
Singapore
South of France
Sydney
Tokyo 東京
Toronto
Turin
Venice
Vienna
Washington, DC
Amsterdam
Athens
Barcelona
Beijing
Berlin
Boston
Brussels
Budapest
Buenos Aires
California
Cape Town
Copenhagen
Croatia
Dubai
Dublin
Edinburgh
Florence
Havana
Hong Kong
Istanbul

In Context

Features

The Forbidden City. *See p51*.

Communists forces enter Beijing in May, 1949.

History

From dust-blown frontier town to global capital of an emerging superpower.

China's history spans 5,000 years, something the Chinese are proud to point out, and many of the country's defining dramas have unfolded in Beijing. It's been the capital since 1279 and locals are often accused of having a superiority complex as a result. But over the centuries ordinary Beijingers have been oppressed, ejected, castrated and conquered, so perhaps it's time they revelled in their splendid past.

Tucked away in the northern corner of China, or Zhongguo (Middle Kingdom) in Chinese, Beijing is distant from both the coast and major waterways. With the Gobi desert just to the west (the cause of the phenomenal dust storms that plague the city each spring), incredibly hot summers and freezing winters, it is an odd location for a capital city.

But Beijing has always been a frontier town, from where the emperor would defend the lush green plains to the south from northern invaders such as the Hun, Mongol, Manchu and Jurchen. As far back as the eighth century BC walls were put up just north of Beijing to keep these barbarians out of China, but they were hardly a success. The first dynasty to make Beijing their capital were the Mongols. The native Han Chinese won the country back during the Ming Dynasty, but it wasn't long before the northern Manchus invaded to found the Qing Dynasty.

WALLS AND WARLORDS

Far earlier traces of life are present in the area, which has an important prehistory. In 1923 archaeologists came across two human-like teeth while excavating a site 50 kilometres (31 miles) south-west of Beijing. These teeth, along with several skull caps found at the site, shocked the world by revealing that the area had been home to Peking Man from the Pleistocene period – half a million years ago. Along with Java Man, Peking Man was the oldest fossilised Homo erectus found in the world and the site turned out to be where Peking Man had called home for around 260,000 years, from 500,000 BC to 240,000 BC.

However it was some time before anyone made Beijing their home – settlements of agricultural people have been found just west of the city that date back to 3000 BC. The first records of Beijing townships date from the

Western Zhou Period (1050-256 BC), when two territories then known as Ji and Yan (both in the south-western Xuanwu district in present-day Beijing) were captured by marauding Zhou forces that were expanding their reach east from their home in Shaanxi. The city expanded between the eighth and fifth centuries BC and grew in importance as Yan conquered its neighbour Ji to become the capital. To this day Beijing is sometimes known as the Yanjing – The Yan Capital – most notably on the local beer bottles.

Between 221 BC and 206 BC the Qin Dynasty led by Qin Shihung subjugated the Yan and five other states to unify China for the first time. This semi-mystical period has become the subject of many recent Chinese films such as the box office hit *Hero*, which tells the story of the assassination attempt on the Qin king by the Yan king. But Qin survived the attempt on his life and China's first emperor joined together the separate walls the states had built for protection, to start what we now know as the Great Wall of China.

After the fall of the shortlived Qin Dynasty, Beijing fell under the dominion of dozens of tribes, dynasties and empires for the next thousand years. The city became a military staging post for missions into the north for most dynasties, including the famously artistic Tang, which had its capital in modern day Xian. Emperor Taizong (626-649) built a temple for troops that fell in battle, which still exists as Fayuan Temple in modern-day Beijing. The Tang Dynasty eventually fell, in part due to a military rebellion that originated in Beijing, and another era of warlordism erupted.

'As the Jin pushed south the formidable Mongols were advancing in the same direction from the steppes.'

The Late Jin Empire, which ruled over northern China from 936 to 947, began to lose control over large parts of its territory to the Khitai, a Turco Mongolian tribe from the north, which was steadily spreading its nomadic ways south. By 947 the Khitans (or Qidans as they were called in Chinese) had reached Beijing and burnt it to the ground. They rebuilt the city and named it Nanjing – Southern Capital – forming the Liao Dynasty and ruling the north of China, while the Song Dynasty controlled the south of the country. When Marco Polo reached China nearly three hundred years later, he called the country Cathay from the word Khitai – the name the West would use for China for the next six hundred years.

The Han Chinese Song Dynasty was keen to push further north and send the Liao back over the Great Wall. It formed an alliance with the Tungustic Jurchen tribes of the far north – past

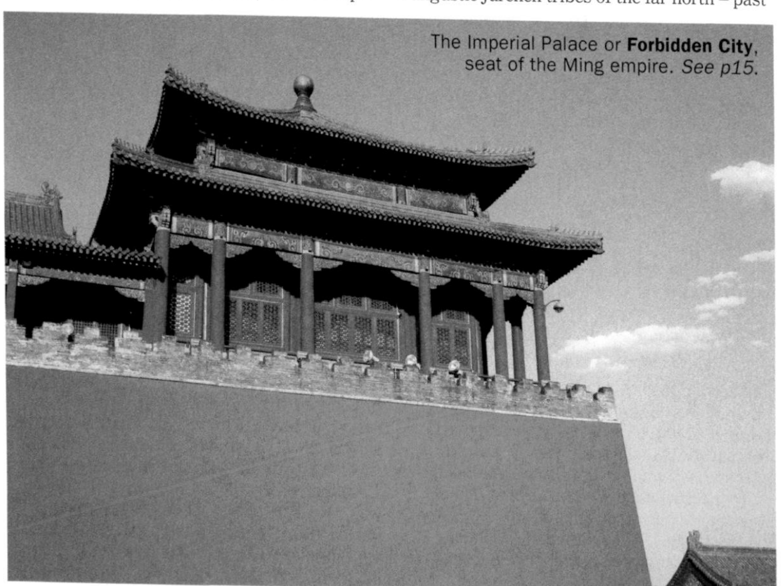

The Imperial Palace or **Forbidden City**, seat of the Ming empire. *See p15.*

The Tiananmen incident

For the vast majority of the world's population, Tiananmen Square means just one thing: the events that took place from 15 April to 4 June 1989 – the 50-day occupation of the square that was forcibly ended by Chinese troops, resulting in hundreds and possibly thousands of deaths.

After the death of the pro-democratic reformist Hu Yaobang on 15 April 1989, students and intellectual supporters of liberal reform marched along the streets of Beijing to Tiananmen Square to mourn the death of the denounced former leader. The mourning led to protests for an increase in the pace of reform and an end to corruption. Days turned to weeks and hundreds of protesters turned into hundreds of thousands. Joining the students, whose main concerns were corruption and reform, were factory workers alarmed at the rise in inflation and concerned about unemployment.

By mid May, many of the protesters occupying Tiananmen Square had begun a hunger strike. The visit of reformist Soviet leader Mikhail Gorbachev meant that not only were global TV networks on hand to record what was happening, but that the crowds were spurred on, hoping that China could reform following the Soviet Union's example.

Some within the government elite sympathised with the students' issues. There were disagreements over how to handle the situation and fears that both protesters and government figures were using the demonstration as part of a power play. Such was the suspicion that when Secretary General Zhao Ziyang, fearful of military involvement, pleaded with the protesters to go home, he was removed from office and never again seen in public. The next day, 20 May, Deng Xiaoping declared martial law.

On 4 June tanks and troops from outside Beijing were brought in to end the occupation, as local troops refused to fight. (The 38th Army set fire to their trucks and joined the protesters, so the story goes.) Instead, war-hardened soldiers who had been fighting border wars in the south were among those arriving in the capital. At 10.30pm on 4 June 1989 tanks rolled into the Tiananmen Square, crushing occupied tents as they passed. The troops fired into the crowds and cut off many escape routes, shooting at those who fled. Many soldiers were also killed – some burned to death in their trucks as Molotov cocktails rained down.

The total number of deaths is still unknown. Estimates vary from 36 civilian deaths – the government figure – to over 3,000 deaths, a total covering both the incident and the subsequent purges and executions.

Many people claim that the students and intellectuals were ready to leave the square by the time martial law was imposed on 20 May, and that out-of-town factory workers had taken up the fight. Students claim it was these workers who became violent against the troops, giving the soldiers reason to open fire. But the government's handling of the incident changed the Western world's view of China from that of a reforming Communist state to a repressive regime, which led to a slowing of international commitments to the country and the imposition of an arms embargo.

Ironically, the 4 June incident put the democracy movement in China back by many years – throughout the '80s the government had been on a slow path to reform, which almost ground to a halt after the incident, and didn't gain momentum again until almost a decade later.

Discussion of a multi-party state is still taboo and press freedom has only marginally increased, meaning that today many young Beijingers are completely unaware that so many people lost their lives in the capital less than two decades ago.

modern day Harbin – and easily overthrew the now-Buddhist Khitans. By 1153 the Jurchen tribes – called the Jin Dynasty – had moved their capital to the former Nanjing, around present day Tianning Temple in west Beijing, naming it Zhongdu – Central Capital. The Jin, however, carried on pushing south, deep into Song territory, but the formidable Mongols were hot on their heels, advancing in the same direction from the steppes.

STRIVING FOR UNITY

In 1215 the Mongols passed through Zhongdu, razing the city and taking very few prisoners. Hundreds of thousands were killed and little was left standing – some Jurchen made it south to Kaifeng where they built a new capital but it was only a matter of time before the Mongols finished them off. The Mongolian army began building the new city just to the north of Zhongdu, with the Mongol palace in present-day Beihai Park and the centre where the North Third Ring Road lies today. Their new Capital was named Dadu in Chinese, meaning Great Capital, and Khanbaliq (known as Cambuluc in the West due to Marco Polo's accounts) meaning Great Residence of the Khan in Mongolian. By 1267, the Mongols, led by Ghengis Khan's grandson Kublai, had overthrown the Jin Dynasty, and a decade later they finished off the Southern Song Dynasty, united China, and formed the Yuan Dynasty (1279-1368). For the first time, Beijing was the capital of all China.

Dadu's planned city structure followed a rectangular shape with a palace in the centre, surrounded by temples and gardens – a structure that remains to this day. The Mongolian Empire stretched all the way to Europe and was the most extensive continuous empire in the history of the world. As the capital of this enormous kingdom and also the starting point for the Silk Road, Dadu became incredibly rich. It was during this period of immense wealth that Marco Polo came to the city and worked in China. He describes the palace as 'so rich and so beautiful that no man on earth could design anything superior to it'. Travellers from all over the world came to trade and visit the magnificent palaces of Dadu – the White Dagoba Temple in the west of Beijing can still be seen today.

The Mongolian horsemen were exceptional warriors who occupied large areas of the known world; however they lacked the administrative know-how to control a population of hundreds of millions. Unlike their subjects, the nomadic Mongols were tradesmen and not farmers. Inflation, due to over-circulation of paper currency, led to poverty and after widescale flooding of the Yellow River, rebellious farmers led by Zhu Yuanzhong started war. The farmers won and Zhu became the first emperor of the Ming Dynasty.

RISE OF THE GREAT DYNASTIES

After Zhu Yuanzhong sent the Mongols packing back to the steppes of Mongolia he moved his capital south to present day Nanjing, changing the name of Dadu to Beiping – Northern Peace. However by 1403, the third and most famous of all Ming emperors, Yongle, began preparing to move the capital back to the north.

Much of Dadu had been destroyed and construction work began to create the city we see today. The north–south axis of the city – with the Imperial Palace at the centre and the Temple of Heaven to the south – was built, as well as the city walls; an auspicious nine gates enclosed the criss-cross road pattern of the new city. Small alleyways and courtyard homes, given the name *hutong* by the Mongols, sprung up inside the walls around the Imperial Palace.

The last Ming swings, 1644. *See p17.*

'In 1421, the city became the capital again, and was given the name Beijing. Five years later, it was the largest city in the world.'

In 1420 the palaces, temples, roads and walls were ready. The following year the city became the capital again, and for the first time was given the name Beijing – Northern Capital. Five years later, it was the largest city in the world. The Ming Dynasty was a prosperous one that saw the creation of a vast navy with ships capable of displacing 1,500 tons, and a million-strong army. It also presided over major advancements in commercial iron production and printing. Thanks to an evolved administrative system, scholars flooded the city and made it the cultural centre it still is today.

With continual and increasing pressure from northern invaders – the Mongolians and the Manchurians were both pushing on the Ming borders – the Great Wall was expanded to some 6,430 kilometres (4,000 miles) in length and reinforced with cannons and watch towers. After firing an arrow into a Chinese general's

Foreign Devils 1

Marco Polo

One of the first foreigners to get to Beijing, Marco Polo first arrived in the Mongol capital – known as Khanbaliq, the great city of Khan – with his father in 1272. A favourite of the emperor, he worked for Khublai Khan for 17 years as an envoy and traded freely. He chronicled his experiences in a book, *The Travels of Marco Polo*, bringing the mystical Orient to the Western world.

Matteo Ricci

The Italian Jesuit, mathematician and cartographer learned classical Chinese in Macau before making his way to Beijing. Ricci petitioned for several years to gain residency in Beijing and to preach Christianity. Finally in 1601 Ming Emperor Wanli granted him access to the city, making him the first Westerner to ever see inside the Forbidden City. He was Beijing's first foreign resident, and he remained in the city until his death in 1610. Ricci brought Catholicism to Beijing, drew the first map of the world in Chinese and translated the Confucian classics.

George McCartney

In 1793 George McCartney, a cousin of King George III, led the first British diplomatic mission to Beijing. His demands to establish the first embassy in China, relax trade restrictions and to take possession of a 'small unfortified island near Chusan for the residence of English traders, storage of goods, and outfitting of ships' were all denied by Qing Emperor Qianlong. McCartney refused to observe court traditions and referred to a gift of jade as a worthless rock. This was just the beginning of bad relations between the two nations that led eventually led to the Opium Wars.

Edgar Snow

The American journalist, Edgar Snow, came to China in 1928 and chronicled the early years of the Communist Revolutions. The first Westerner to interview Mao, Snow's book *Red Star Over China*, published in 1937, launched Mao on to the world stage. Snow's portrayal of Mao as an intelligent and skilled leader helped him to victory.

Richard Nixon

After the US table tennis team took up Mao's invitation to play in China in 1971, President Nixon sent Henry Kissinger on a secret mission later that year to pave the way for one of the most high profile state visits of the century. Nixon's visit in February 1972 not only led to Mao's China taking the UN seat from Taiwan, but the fear of a Sino-US alliance caused detente with the Soviets at the height of the Cold War. As one of the first non-Communist leaders to meet Mao, Nixon inaugurated the links between China and the outside world.

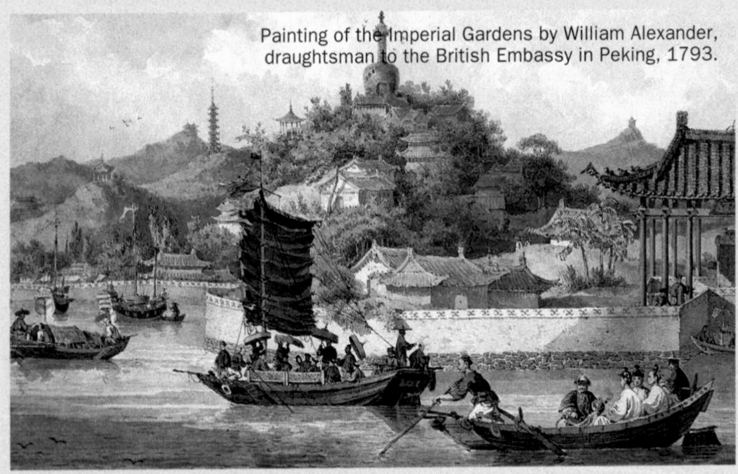

Painting of the Imperial Gardens by William Alexander, draughtsman to the British Embassy in Peking, 1793.

Manchu-Qing emperor **Kangxi**, who united China in the late 17th century. *See p18.*

camp in 1549 to warn of an imminent invasion, the Mongols the following year broke through the Great Wall but never made it to the capital. After this incursion an outer city wall was built in 1553, and the old city wall was expanded to the south.

But the Ming Dynasty continued to face threats. Japanese invasion attempts, although not successful, put continual pressure on the already stretched army, and corruption on the part of eunuchs and palace officials led to large-scale disaffection from the peasant population, which culminated in a rebel leader named Li Zicheng marching on Beijing without opposition in 1644. With peasants overrunning the capital and the Manchus fast approaching, the last Ming emperor walked up Jingshan Park tied a noose around his neck and hanged himself from Crooked Neck Tree.

Manchu forces had already taken Korea and were at the northern borders by 1644. The peasant Li Zicheng presented himself as the new emperor, whereupon Ming General Wu Sangui opened the gates of the Great Wall at Shanhaiguan to let through the Manchu army.

'For the first time the Chinese realised they were not the superpower they had believed.'

The Manchurians forcibly evicted all Chinese from the city proper and relocated them to the south of the city – outside of the old city wall and south of present day Changan Avenue. The newly founded Qing Dynasty took up residence in the expanded Imperial Palace and started building gardens and palaces including the Old Summer Palace. The Qing Manchus also forced people to wear traditional Manchu dress and their hair in a queue style – shaved at the front with a long pigtail down the back. To unite the empire, Qing emperor Kangxi personally led invasions of Tibet and Russia. But for the first time the Chinese nation was about to realise it was not the superpower it had believed itself to be as it came face to face with other empires. Relations with the 'barbarians', specifically the British, had started badly after the emissary of King George III had his request for increased trade and a permanent trade representative turned down in a patronising letter from Emperor Qianlong before he even arrived in 1793. The relationship did not improve.

Two opium wars and disputes over foreign legations led to significant military action from the British and the eight Alliance Powers – such as the destruction of the Old Summer Palace in 1860 – and increasing concessions from the Qing Court, culminating in Britain's acquisition of Hong Kong and the creation of a Legation Quarter in Beijing.

The Qing Court was in trouble. It took major foreign intervention to quash the 13-year Taiping Rebellion in which 50 million died, and 50 years later, in 1900, an anti-foreign movement called the Boxer Rebellion attacked the foreign legations. This uprising, which was first covertly and later overtly supported by the Empress Dowager Cixi, led to fighting between foreign and imperial troops as well as the Boxers, and finally foreign occupation of the city. By this stage all faith in the Qing Court had collapsed, an increased foreign presence combined with calls for serious reform led to the evolution of a republican movement.

EMPERORS' NEW CLOTHES

Sun Yat-sen, a forward thinking and republican politician, led a military uprising in October 1911, ending thousands of years of Imperial rule in China. Beijing remained the capital, although the Republic of China was announced and officially managed from Nanjing in 1912. Sun Yat-sen could not take full control of the nation as the power was in the hands of Yuan Shikai – the man responsible for negotiating between the last emperor and the republicans. It turned out that Yuan had lofty ambitions and after becoming the president of the Republic declared himself emperor in 1915 when he prepared to undertake the Temple of Heaven ceremonies. It didn't last, and the unpopular Yuan Shikai died the following year. The power vacuum in Beijing left by his death was filled by numerous warlords and military commanders creating another unstable warlord period.

In 1919 the Treaty of Versailles allowed Japanese forces to take control of former German territory in China. This led to a student uprising in Tiananmen Square known as the May Fourth Movement, which targeted its ire at China's domestic situation. There followed a rise in nationalism and anti-imperialism, as did an interest in democratic ideas. It was during this time that the sciences and arts flourished as the next generation of academics and literati formed a cultural consciousness to end the old Confucian values and take up modern science.

The following year Sun Yat-sen died of cancer and Chiang Kai-shek took over as the leader of the Nationalist Party known as the Guomindang or KMT. At the same time the Chinese Communist Party was gaining strength and a young library assistant at Peking University named Mao Zedong was showing a strong interest in the Party. The strengthening Nationalist Party based in the south declared Nanjing the capital of the Republic of China in 1928, and Beijing was once again renamed Beiping. But the country was far from unified. Warlords still held large parts of the country and the Communists were recruiting widely. By 1933 the Japanese were coming down from Manchuria, preparing to invade Beijing. That year, 19,557 crates of valuable treasures from the Imperial Palace were taken to Shanghai for safe keeping. By 1949, 13,484 of these crates had ended up in Nationalist Taiwan.

In 1937 Japanese troops, who had already taken Manchuria and much of Inner Mongolia, were massed at the Marco Polo Bridge just outside Beijing. After claiming to have been fired on, they occupied Beijing where they stayed until the end of World War II.

'In the 1950s, more changes took place in China than in the previous 500 years.'

At the end of the war (known in China as the War Against Japanese Aggression), the Japanese left Beijing just as a major civil war broke out between the Communists, who had been strengthening their army with Soviet aid, and the Nationalists, who had been seriously weakened after fighting the Japanese. Mao Zedong led the Communists to victory, taking Beijing in January 1949 and forcing the Nationalists to retreat to Taiwan.

BUILDING A PEOPLE'S CAPITAL

On 1 October 1949 Chairman Mao Zedong stood on Tiananmen Gate and declared the People's Republic of China. Over the following decade, more changes – both physical and social – would take place in China than had taken place during the previous 500 years. Initially greeted with joy, the Communist Party managed to

Holy Mao

Thirty years after his death Chairman Mao Zedong, the man who was directly responsible for the deaths of tens of millions of people and the almost complete destruction of China's ancient culture, is still revered in the country he devastated.

The cult of Mao began in the 1960s when Mao made himself the face of Communism to rival Stalin and Marx. Traditional culture and entertainment were replaced with a whole new mindset known as Mao Zedong Thought. Everyone had to carry and memorise his quotations – collected in the *Little Red Book*. Posters and slogans were daubed in red paint in every commune, factory or school, reading: 'Mao – Saviour of the People', 'The red sun in the centre of our hearts' or 'May Chairman Mao live ten thousand years'. Children were taught to love Mao – to love him more even than their parents.

The cult of Mao worked so well that thousands would flock to see him, people would not wash a hand that touched him and many would provide him with anything he wanted. Now, although Maoism has ended and the Great Helmsman has died, the cult lives on – TV shows still document and broadcast Mao's heroic deeds, while books and websites critical of Mao are banned on the Mainland. Many still say that Mao ended a century of foreign humiliation and that he improved living standards, literacy rates and women's rights in China. The official line (from the party that Mao brought to power and which still holds government) is that Mao's policies were 70 per cent right and 30 per cent wrong. Even today hundreds of people queue daily to see Mao's body resting in his mausoleum, statues can be seen in universities, while posters of the dictator are on display in some homes and even in taxis.

The postmodern take is that the Chinese (people and government) are ironic in their reverence – but while many have not forgotten the famines caused by Mao's collectivisation nor the purges and humiliation of the Cultural Revolution, there are few people living in China who would openly criticise him.

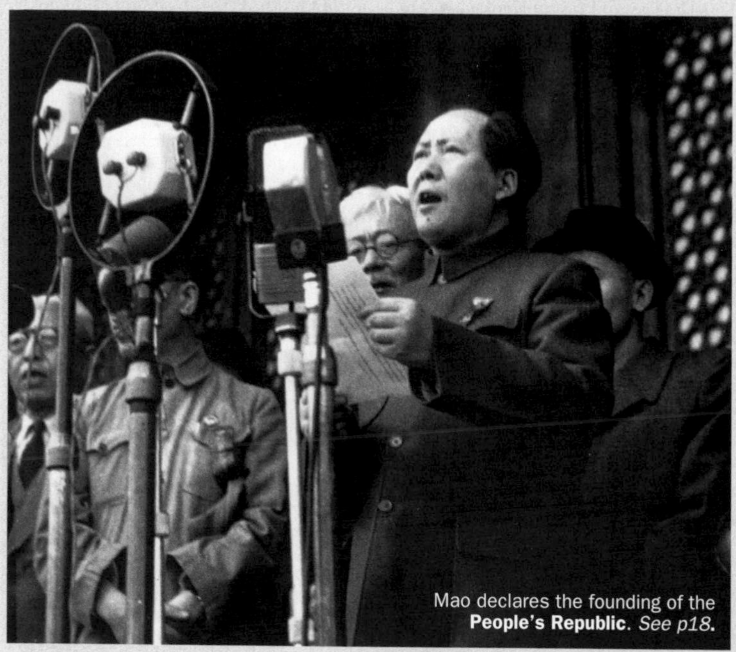

Mao declares the founding of the **People's Republic**. *See p18.*

clean up some aspects of the city and deal with the 'evils of the past' such as drug addiction and prostitution. But the revolution focused on building the new, rather than protecting the old. Temples were pulled down or converted into factories, barracks and store houses; courtyards, once the home of nobles, were split into small residencies – each housing hundreds of peasants who had moved to the city to help with industrialisation; and the Ming Dynasty city walls were torn down to make way for the second ring road – although cars were still a rare sight in the city.

After making his inaugural speech on Tiananmen Gate, Mao decided to use the old city as the new home of communism rather than a more practical western location. Thus the old town was ripped up to make way for factories, infrastructure and other industry. Tiananmen Square itself was expanded in 1949 from the long rectangular walkway leading from the Forbidden City to the Temple of Heaven to become the largest square in the world (beating Moscow's Red Square), flanked by the Great Hall of the People and the National Museum of History.

THE GREAT LEAP FORWARD?

Mao's first campaigns in the early 1950s began with land reforms – the forcible redistribution of land from wealthy landowners to the poor. The farmers were put into *danwei*, or work units, that would work collectively in cooperatives of up to several hundred families and would have production targets to meet.

The centralised system that Mao introduced meant that food was bought by the government, sold by the government and distributed by the government. Rice and grain was sold abroad – often to Moscow – to finance the industrialisation and militarisation programmes that he had envisioned for China. By 1956 this had proved a massive failure as millions were plunged into the misery of famine.

The following year Mao launched the Great Leap Forward, a project to radically increase both agricultural and industrial production. He saw steel as a cornerstone of development, and aimed to increase steel production to rival that of the UK within 15 years. Local backyard iron furnaces were developed so every commune could smelt its own iron and produce enough for mass export. All metal objects – from bikes, pots and cutlery to doornails and hairpins – were put into backyard furnaces only to produce useless pig iron that had almost no value. Mao eventually realised that steel could only be produced using large factories but refused to back down, claiming that the workers would lose faith in the Great Leap.

At the same time, many peasants had been pulled off the fields to work on the industrialisation projects, which left crops unharvested. It's estimated that the terrible administration and economic planning of the Leap cost the country around 30 million lives due to famine.

Deng Xiaoping in 1938, during the war of resistance against Japan. *See p18.*

CLASSES FOR THE MASSES

After the catastrophe of the Great Leap Forward, Mao lost a lot of support within his government. Party official Liu Shaoqi was beginning to challenge him as a potential leader, so to retain control of his government as well as a massive population of starving peasants, in 1967 Mao began the Great Proletariat Cultural Revolution – an enormous project to purge counter-revolutionaries, which also allowed Mao to consolidate his power. Many major party officials were removed from their positions and sent to labour camps or put under house arrest. Anyone Mao regarded as a threat or a potential supporter of any breakaway group was arrested under the label of being counter-revolutionary – or working against the revolution.

Hundreds of thousands of students left their classrooms to become Red Guards, a militia of children rampaging through the streets looking for enemies of the state and enemies of Mao. Academics, teachers, landowners and people associated with foreigners, as well as those who were simply caught in the crossfire or who tried to defend a colleague, were ritually humiliated and brutally, often fatally, attacked. Many artists and writers were either killed, forced into re-education camps or committed suicide during

World leaders: **Hu Jintao** meets George W Bush at the White House, 20 April 2006.

this period. Red Guards set fire to temples, burned books, and smashed works of art and religious relics. Those found trying to save a rare musical instrument or book were classed as rightists and sent away for re-education.

Education came to a complete halt as schoolchildren denounced their teachers. Children were even encouraged to denounce their parents for anything they said that could possibly be interpreted as negative by the Communist regime or slanderous of Mao. In 1968, at the height of the Cultural Revolution, the Red Guards were disbanded and the cult of Mao swung into full force. The whole nation was forced to recite from Mao's *Little Red Book*. Posters and images of Mao adorned every home as Mao took on a god-like persona among the people of China. *See also p19* **Holy Mao**.

The Cultural Revolution continued with its purges, and intimidation techniques didn't end until the death of Mao in 1976. Outside China, historians agree that Mao's policies were responsible for millions of deaths and compare the excesses of his regime with those of Hitler and Stalin. Today he rests in his mausoleum in Tiananmen Square, where every day hundreds of people queue to visit him.

THE NEW BEGINNING

After a brief power struggle following Mao's death, Deng Xiaoping eventually became leader of China, and remained so until his own death in 1997. Although a veteran in the struggle for the control of China and one of the earliest members of the Communist Party, Deng was eager to make changes. 'Reform is China's second revolution,' he said. 'Poverty is not socialism. To be rich is glorious.' Deng's open door policies of the early 1980s led to the economic success of the country today.

However, Deng's economic freedoms were not matched by his political thought. After the death of a moderate but disgraced official in 1989, students took to the streets of Tiananmen to mourn his death and to protest the lack of transparency and increased corruption of the government. After 50 days of protest that saw over a million people camp out in the square, Deng Xiaoping gave the order for troops to clear the area. Hundreds of people were killed and it is thought that many more were killed or imprisoned after the incident.

The '90s saw China truly open up, with a massive influx of foreign companies. In 2001 China finally got the international recognition it had been seeking for so long. Entry into the World Trade Organisation and winning the 2008 Summer Olympic Games were a double chance to show the world how far China has come in such a short time. Current president Hu Jintao embodies the historic transition from a government of ageing party figures to one of younger technocrats; an arch-conservative, known for his iron will while serving as Party Chief in Tibet, Hu seems set on taking China forward to become *the* global superpower.

Beijing Today

Smash it up and start again.

If Hong Kong's decade in the spotlight was the 1980s and Shanghai's the '90s, then the present is all about Beijing. Compared to the glitz, glamour and bright lights of Shanghai, Beijing is a lot grittier – in every sense of the word. It's among the most polluted cities in the world, but it's earthier, and has more character and attitude than anywhere else in China. Beijing is the heart of the country, where the passion of its people can be seen everywhere from a dive bar in the University district to a gallery in the burgeoning 798 Art District. Beijing is the cultural and political centre where decisions are made and where fringe movements, punk music, contemporary art and underground scenes begin.

All over the world, everyone is trying to keep up with the changes afoot in China. People running businesses supplying everything from mobile phones to sex toys are reading books with titles like *One Billion Customers* in an attempt to get a foothold in the biggest market on the planet. But Beijingers are struggling to keep up too. China is changing fast and the changes affect every aspect of life – nowhere is that more evident than in its capital city.

RESHAPING THE CITY

Beijing today looks like one big building site and, outside the very centre and the Forbidden City, there is little to indicate that you are in the capital of historical China.

Beijing's physical design changed hardly at all for 500 years until the 1950s when Mao Zedong tore down much of the old city to make way for the functional buildings and industrial development of the People's Republic. Nevertheless, in the 1980s, the highest building in the city was the 17-storey Beijing Hotel. The '80s and '90s put Beijing on a long, steady path to gradual change, but today it seems the brakes are off and that change has become an unstoppable juggernaut almost out of control. Literally thousands of cranes can be seen on the skyline of Beijing, helping hundreds of hotels, skyscrapers, office and apartment blocks to spring up across the city.

'The perfect restaurant you found one week is turned to rubble the next, with no sign that it ever existed.'

This causes a few problems with navigation. Thanks to the enormous army of workers from the countryside working around the clock, a building, a landmark, an entire road even, may disappear without notice in a matter of hours. New malls and skyscrapers emerge from the ground with lightning speed. The perfect restaurant you found one week is turned to rubble the next, with no sign that it ever existed. The development is all-encompassing and that's in no small part due to the Olympics.

The negative effects are clear and well documented, in particular the demolition of the old traditional courtyards and narrow alleyways, called hutongs (*see p75* **Out with the old**). But while there may be less character to the new Beijing, the quality of buildings and in turn the quality of living is on the rise.

The new face of Beijing will go down in history as being on the cutting edge of 21st-century architecture, with buildings such as the Rem Koolhaas-designed CCTV building, the 'Bird's Nest' Olympic Stadium and the 'Egg' – the $600 million National Theatre and Opera House – becoming new landmarks. Ironically, just as the town planner whom Mao snubbed in the 1950s recommended, Beijing has now expanded. It has a financial centre in the west, the central business district in the east, a technology centre in the north and new commercial centres in the south, with little further development occurring within the old city. In fact, numerous conservation projects have been implemented to protect the temples and what remains of the old city.

The entire Central Business District did not even exist a decade ago. Now, with the clutch of home-office-building schemes currently being developed by real-estate giant Soho China, as

Scaling the Great Firewall

Press freedom is a sensitive subject in China, with small steps forward often followed by huge backward leaps from the government. In the 2006 Press Freedom Index, China was number 163 out of a possible 168, narrowly beating North Korea, Cuba, Turkmenistan, Eritrea and Myanmar (Burma).

Domestic news is heavily censored, particularly items related to 'state secrets', civil unrest, democracy, press freedom, corruption, Tibet, Taiwan, and religious and spiritual groups such as Falong Gong. Xinhua News, the state-run news agency, maintains the sole right to distribute and release foreign news content in China, including the lucrative financial news sector.

Journalists, film-makers and writers are still arrested or detained for indefinite periods with disturbing regularity. In January 2007 restrictions on foreign journalists were nominally relaxed ahead of the 2008 Olympics, and Reporters Without Borders made its first-ever official visit to the country, raising hopes of a policy change. However, the moves were followed in February with the announcement that another eight books by Chinese authors were to appear on the 'banned' list, and a delegation of 20 Chinese journalists to the International PEN conference in Hong Kong were stopped at the Chinese border and their papers and visas removed.

China's internet is also massively monitored, with the 'Great Firewall' or 'Golden Shield' currently blocking anything between 20,000 and 100,000 sites. Sophisticated filtering systems are in place to detect the use of prohibited key words on sites and in web searches, and an estimated 30,000 police are employed to monitor how China's citizens make use of the internet.

Nonetheless, the increase in internet use in China has continued to defy all expectations, with the number of people surfing the web leaping from 300,000 in 1997 to a staggering 111 million in 2006. Blogging is also a massively popular activity, with 52 per cent of white-collar workers in Beijing apparently regular bloggers. The Chinese appetite for instant communication isn't limited to internet use alone – 12 billion SMS messages were reportedly sent during 2006's Chinese New Year Spring Festival.

Another day, another flyover...

well as the World Trade Centre, China World Mall and 300 other buildings under construction, it could almost match New York for its number of awe-inspiring tall buildings. Thanks to the Olympics, by 2008 the city's infrastructure will rival that of any Western city. By 2020 Beijing will have the biggest metro system in the world.

THE GIANT AWAKES

China is the fourth largest economy in the world after the US, Japan and Germany. Where wealth was something punishable – even by death – during Mao's era, it's now not only socially acceptable, but a sign of success that should be flaunted. The country is undergoing an industrial revolution comparable to the UK's in the late 18th century, or the US in the 19th century. Known as the factory of the world – and producing more textiles, computer parts and trainers than the rest of the world combined – China is finally and slowly beginning to create its own brands to market abroad as Japan did so successfully in the '80s.

At the end of 2006 it's estimated there were 15 US$ billionaires and 320,000 US$ millionaires in China – 500,000 including property millionaires. This ranks China as sixth in the global league table of millionaires. Not bad considering that a generation ago, outside government HQ, there wasn't one legal Chinese millionaire. Beijing has a very high proportion of the country's millionaires – partly due to the government's involvement in the sell-off and management of state industries.

But as the rich get richer, the poor aren't keeping up, creating a wealth divide not only between the rural and urban areas but also within Beijing. Although inflation is well controlled, prices continue to rise. The wages of teachers, factory workers and labourers have hardly risen over the last decade. The era of the 'iron rice bowl' – with state allocation of employment and housing, which meant that a job was for life – is ending.

POWER, CORRUPTION AND LIES

The increase in wealth has led to corruption and backhanders at every level of business. In 2006 Beijing Vice Mayor Liu Zhihua was sacked for corruption after demanding bribes to sell land to a private developer. He was one of 97,260 party members who were disciplined that year for corruption, which included accepting bribes, gambling with public money and abusing land rights.

The capital's society is certainly shaped by the government being based here. There is more self-censorship among the people and the media – the general rule being the further from the capital, the more you can get away with. Therefore local papers in Beijing have an extra element of nationalism and are certainly less risqué than in smaller cities. However, blogging, gossip and the traditional Chinese attribute of reading between the lines means that Beijing is far from ill-informed.

Beijing is going through a sexual revolution as Shanghai did in the '90s. A recent survey of Beijing schoolchildren found that the average age for them to lose their virginity was 15 – over two years lower than the global average of 17.3. Half the students thought that a one-night stand was all right, and a visit to the nightclubs of the Workers' Stadium can reveal evidence of that: the sexualisation of Beijing's young people is visible on the dancefloor as they bump and grind to hip hop beats.

'Whereas Shanghai has had almost a century to adjust to wealth, champagne and parties, Beijing seems to be guiltily asking "Is this OK?"'

Less than a decade ago, it was almost impossible to find young Beijingers who could be described as stylish by Western standards, but many today look as if they've stepped out of the pages of *Vogue*. Yet for all the glitz and glamour and sex on show, there is still something lacking in Beijing's nightlife. The champagne, the trendy lounge bar, even the cocaine and international DJs are all here, but you may find the coolest bar empty on a

Saturday night. A film premiere may have the red carpet, stars and flashing cameras all present and correct, but there is a staged feeling and a lack of pizzazz. Perhaps this is best attributed to the lack of evolution – as if modernity has been dumped on the city and it's not quite sure how to handle it. Whereas Shanghai has had almost a century of glam – from the roaring '20s to the present day – to adjust to wealth, celebrity, champagne and parties, Beijing seems to be guiltily asking 'Is this OK?'. The game has begun but no one really seems to know what the rules are.

BAD AIR DAY

Beijing is a land of opportunity and money, but it is sliding down the league table of desirable cities to live in. And that is due to one factor: pollution. Admittedly the smog has reduced since the dirty days of the late '90s, in no small part due to the government's concerted effort to clean up air quality by 2008. One of the first projects was to relocate Beijing's biggest polluters outside the city, which has made a difference, but still 70 per cent of all the energy Beijing uses comes from coal-burning power stations, and there are days when Beijing – now the world's most polluted city – reaches dangerous levels of air pollution, with warnings to stay inside being sent out by text message.

The 2007 target for blue-sky days – that means days when you can see the sky – has risen from 238 in 2006 to 245. Officials promised to reduce sulphur dioxide, nitrous dioxide and ozone to within World Health Organisation accepted levels to win the Olympic Games, and are still aiming to get there. However, summer pollution levels still reach two or three times the US safety standard.

Increased wealth brings environmental costs. As well as more air-conditioning units, and offices and hotels using vast amounts of energy, water is being siphoned off to irrigate 30 golf courses and the city's many fake ski slopes. The water table is dropping and only one reservoir remains, prompting academics to claim that if something isn't done soon, Beijing will be unsustainable within 20 years.

Another main cause of pollution, and the city's main gripe, is the number of vehicles on the road – currently 2.5 million. And with 1,000 extra cars on the road every day, that figure is expected to reach three million by the time the Olympics come round. A decade ago cars were still outnumbered by bikes; today the cyclist is being killed off – literally and figuratively.

BEIJING ON A GLOBAL STAGE

Beijing has become an international city that sees DJs from London and New York performing in mega clubs. Designers like Philippe Starck come to deck out the latest top-notch restaurant. Film stars such as Nicole Kidman and Daniel Craig might be spotted in Rui Fu or Bed Bar, and bands such as Placebo and Sonic Youth make sure Beijing is on their tour diary as China comes under the world media's spotlight in the run-up to what will be the biggest coming-out party of the century, the 2008 Olympics Games.

But what will happen after the Olympics? Will there still be the same interest in Beijing that there is today, and will the building ever be finished? Hosting the Olympics is just the opportunity to invite everyone to the opening party. By 2020, if present trends continue, China will be the number one tourist destination in the world and, after having its old identity wiped away, Beijing's new buildings, fresh culture and new history will be in place to create a Chinese capital the next generation can – perhaps – come to know and love.

Beijing by numbers

53 The distance in miles between the Armani store on Wangfujing and the village of Dagucheng, Hebei Province, where average annual income is RMB 2,000 ($250).
2020 The year by which, according to the Communist Party, the goal of a 'harmonious society' will have been achieved in China.
440,000 Size in square metres of Tiananmen Square.
9,000 Number of rooms in the Forbidden City.
10,000,000 Number of bicycles in Beijing.
600 Approximate number of people killed every day in road accidents in China.
15,112,000 Number of mobile phone users in Beijing.
15,244,000 population of Beijing.
6,000 Number of hutong (historic alleyways) in Beijing in 1985.
459 Number of hutongs in Beijing in 2006.
3,573,000 Conservative estimate of Beijing's unregistered migrant population.
15 Percentage of Beijing land currently being used for construction.
RMB 500,000 Expected sale price of a phone number featuring a high incidence of the lucky number 8.

Olympic mascots: Nini, Huanhuan and Yingying.

Beijing 2008

Let the Games commence.

At 8.08pm on the eighth day of the eighth month of August in 2008 the XXIX Olympiad opens in Beijing, the first time the Olympic Games has ever been held on Chinese soil and an event that is being touted as transcending mere sporting competition and being of huge political and historical significance.

With 10,500 athletes competing in 302 events across 28 sports, an unprecedented number of journalists and countless spectators due to descend on Beijing for the 17-day Olympic carnival, much of the ancient city infrastructure has had to be ripped out and rebuilt. As well as the grievances of the city folk who have had to make way for the reconstruction there are protests from home and abroad that China, for all the hype, is still under the Communist yoke.

Every precaution is being taken to make sure politics does not overtake sport and divert attention from China's moment in the spotlight. Desperate to showcase the 'new' China, no expense is being spared to try to earn Beijing the coveted 'Best Olympics ever' tag, to change the perception of this often misunderstood nation and to put the host nation at the top of the medals table, challenging the US dominance of world sports. Whatever happens, it's going to be worth watching and with a projected television audience of 4.5 billion, most of the world will be doing just that.

REBRANDING BEIJING

Beijing campaigned for its Olympic bid under the banner 'New Beijing, Great Olympics', a deliberate ploy to disconnect the Games from China's recent past and advertise the country's glittering future potential. Like any would-be Olympic host city, Beijing wanted to hold the event to promote economic growth and was prepared to invest heavily in infrastructure, knowing that a successful bid wins the city not only the Games itself, but the world's focus.

A city badly in need of urban renewal, Beijing's bid emphasised how the Olympics would see the capital remodelled, with the then mayor, Liu Qi, telling the IOC: 'More than 90 per cent of the Chinese people support Beijing's bid, because they believe it will help improve their quality of life,' adding that it would promote economic and social policies as well as 'further help develop our human rights cause'. With memories of Tiananmen Square still relatively fresh in the minds of many in the West, and the Free Tibet and Falun Gong lobbies vocal opponents of the Chinese regime, Liu's speech was an invitation for the IOC to engage with China in the hope that it will bring about positive changes in the country. He Zhenliang, China's IOC member, echoed this sentiment with a plea to pick Beijing for the sake of 'global unity'. As well as physically redefining the city and its social order for generations to come, Beijing also promised to break from its industrial past and be reborn as a greener city. By 2000, Beijing had invested US$3.6 billion of a US$12 billion environmental plan, with the rest due to be spent by 2008.

As well as improving Beijing's image abroad, the process of bidding for the Games also generated a sense of patriotism that helped

The stadiums

Capital Indoor Stadium

Baishi Bridge, Xizhimenwai Dajie, Financial District.

This venue has held everything from ice hockey to stage magician David Copperfield. It will host the Olympic volleyball events and go back to being one of the city's top multi-purpose indoor venues after the Games. The area around the stadium has basketball and badminton courts, open to the public, offering any Tom, Dick or Harriet the chance to boast that they've played at an Olympic stadium.

China Agricultural University Gymnasium

China Agricultural University (East Campus), 17 Qinghua Dong Lu, Haidian, North-west (6273 7264).

This gym is the perfect example of how the city is using the Olympics as an excuse to equip itself with infrastructure that will live on after the Games. During the Olympics it will be the venue for the wrestling events, but after the Games it will become the usual stadium for large indoor events such as badminton, table tennis, gymnastics, volleyball, basketball, handball and even indoor football.

National Aquatics Centre

Olympic Green, Chaoyang, Houhai. Metro Olympic Center or Olympic Park.

Dubbed the 'Water Cube', this purpose-built venue will be where all the Olympic swimming, diving, water polo and synchronised swimming events take place. After the Games it will continue to serve as China's premier water sports venue.

National Stadium

Olympic Green, Chaoyang, Houhai. Metro Olympic Center or Olympic Park.

The main stadium and home to athletics, some of the football, and the opening and closing ceremonies. After 2008 the Bird's Nest (*photo below*) will stage national and international sports events, and concerts.

Workers' Indoor Arena

Gongti Bei Lu, Chaoyang (6501 6300). Metro Dongsishitiao.

Also known as the Workers' Gymnasium, the arena has seen everything from international badminton tournaments to Deep Purple. After the Olympic boxing it will go back to being a multipurpose venue.

Workers' Stadium

Gongti Bei Lu, Chaoyang (6501 6655). Metro Dongsishitiao.

Until the National Stadium came along, this was the home of Chinese sport. It has been refurbished to host some of the Olympic football matches.

Games schedule

SPORT	VENUE	Fr 8	Sa 9	Su 10	M 11	Tu 12	W 13	Th 14	Fr 15	Sa 16	Su 17	M 18	Tu 19	W 20	Th 21	Fr 22	Sa 23	Su 24
Opening	NS	O																
Closing	NS																	O
Archery	AF		O	O	O	O	O	O	O									
Athletics	NS								O	O	O	O	O	O	O	O	O	
Athl. Marath.	NS																	O
Badminton	UA		O	O	O	O	O	O	O	O	O							
Baseball	WCA						O	O	O	O		O	O	O		O	O	
Basketball	WCA		O	O	O	O	O	O	O	O	O	O	O	O	O	O		O
Beach Volleyball	CPB		O	O	O	O	O	O	O	O	O	O	O	O	O	O		
Boxing	WIA		O	O	O	O	O	O	O	O	O	O	O	O		O	O	O
Canoe & Kayak	SOR				O	O	O	O				O	O	O	O	O	O	
Cycling	LBM													O	O			
	LV								O	O	O	O	O					
	LMBC															O	O	
	UCRC		O	O			O	O	O	O								
Diving	NAC			O	O	O	O		O	O	O	O	O	O	O	O	O	
Equestrian	ZBEI		O	O	O	O	O	O	O	O	O	O	O	O				
Fencing	OG		O	O	O	O	O	O	O	O	O							
Football																		
Beijing 1	NS																	O
Beijing 2	WS								O	O		O	O		O			
Beijing 3	OSCS		O															
Gymnastics																		
Artistic	NIS		O	O		O	O	O	O		O	O	O					
Rhythmic	UA														O	O	O	O
Trampln.	NIS									O		O	O					
Handball	NIS														O	O	O	O
	OSCG		O	O	O	O	O	O	O	O	O	O	O	O	O	O		
Hockey	OG			O	O	O	O	O	O	O	O	O	O	O	O	O	O	
Judo	UA		O	O	O	O	O	O	O									
Pentathlon	OG														O	O		
Rowing	SOR		O	O	O	O	O	O		O	O							
Sailing	ZBEI		O	O	O	O	O	O	O	O	O	O	O	O	O			
Shooting	WCA		O	O	O	O	O	O	O	O	O							
Softball	WCA					O	O	O	O	O	O	O		O	O			
Swimming	NAC		O	O	O	O	O	O	O	O	O							
Sync. Swim.	NAC										O	O	O	O		O		
Table Tennis	UA						O	O	O	O	O	O	O	O	O	O	O	
Tae-kwon-do	UA													O	O	O	O	
Tennis	OG			O	O	O	O	O	O	O	O							
Triathlon	NSA											O	O					
Volleyball	WCA		O	O	O	O	O	O	O	O	O	O	O	O	O	O	O	O
	UA		O	O	O	O	O	O	O	O	O	O						
Water Polo	OG			O	O	O	O	O	O	O	O	O	O	O		O	O	O
Weightlifting	UA		O	O	O	O	O		O	O	O	O	O					
Wrestling	UA					O	O	O		O	O		O	O	O			

VENUE LIST

AF	Archery Field
CPB	Chaoyang Park Beach
FH	Fencing Hall
LBM	Laoshan Bicycle Moto Cross Venue
LMBC	Laoshan Mountain Bike Course
LV	Laoshan Velodrome
OG	Olympic Green
OSCG	Olympic Sports Centre Gymnasium
OSCS	Olympic Sports Centre Stadium
NAC	National Aquatics Centre
NIS	National Indoor Stadium
NS	National Stadium
NSA	North Scenic Area
SOR	Shunyi Olympic Rowing
UA	University Area
UCRC	Urban Cycling Road Course
WCA	Western Community Area
WIA	Workers' Indoor Arena
WS	Workers' Stadium
YTN	Ying Tung Natatorium
ZBEI	Outside Beijing

COLOUR KEY

Quarter Final

Semi Final

Final

bolster the position of a Chinese government uneasy with domestic change. In the same way the ruling order had in the past used the likes of Japan, the Nationalist Party, capitalists, Taiwan and the West as common enemies to divert people's discontent, the Olympics was now used as a common good, a patriotic cause everyone could fight for. This sense of nationalism was even displayed in the city's failure to win the competition to host the 2000 Games – which the government spun as being the result of anti-Chinese feeling and IOC corruption, and nothing to do with the city's shortcomings or Sydney's better suitability as a venue.

ON TOP OF THE WORLD?

To most, the Olympic Games are the biggest sporting event in the World – but to China they're more than just that. After decades of self-imposed global exile, China is now taking its place as an industrial and political superpower, with the Games as the coming of age party. With events such as the violent crackdown of the Tiananmen protests, the annexation of Tibet and the suppression of the Falun Gong religious cult ensuring that China was in the headlines for all the wrong reasons, many see this as a chance to put the record straight and show what a vibrant and hospitable place the country is.

With the World Tourist Organisation estimating that China is poised to become the world's number one tourist destination by 2010 – a position buoyed by current world events leaving many tourists wary of visiting the Muslim world – the Olympics should serve as the perfect sales pitch. The Beijing Municipal Tourism Administration Bureau predicts that some 500,000-550,000 foreigners will visit Beijing during the 17 days of the Games.

China's Olympic history is a chequered one that until recently had done little to reflect that it is, population-wise, the biggest nation on earth. As the country started to emerge from the chaos that filled the vacuum left by the collapse of imperial rule, it sent one athlete to the 1932 Los Angeles Olympics. Four years later, China sent a team of 140 athletes to the notorious Berlin Games, hosted by Nazi Germany, the Axis allies to their local foe and soon to be occupying power, Japan. The country's next significant footnote on Olympic history came when the Chinese team boycotted the 1956 Games in protest of the inclusion of a team from Taiwan, the island Nationalist forces retreated to at the end of the civil war, when Communist forces swept to power in 1949. It was not until US president Richard Nixon's brokered 'Ping Pong Diplomacy' of 1971 that the nation stepped back into the world sporting arena and renewed international competition. At odds with one-time ideological ally the USSR, China was one of a few Communist countries to break with the Moscow-led boycott of the 1984 Los Angeles Summer Olympics by 14 Eastern Bloc nations. The Soviet no-show was officially due to security concerns, but was what many saw as a direct retaliation for the US-led boycott of the 1980 Moscow Summer Olympics over the Soviet invasion of Afghanistan in the previous year.

> **'China came fourth in Atlanta, third in Sydney and second in Athens. Where will it be in 2008?'**

Though China's Los Angeles gold haul was trumpeted as a national triumph, in truth they owed much of their success to their former ally and the adoption of the strict Soviet training methods, which hot-housed athletic talent. By building from the ground up, the Ministry of Sports has focused on how to make athletes who stand a better chance of winning medals. With many of the initial fruits of this programme now coaches and training the stars of tomorrow in purpose built sports schools, this production line of talent forms the backbone of China's continued sporting success (*see p189* **Beat or be beaten**). One only has to look at the final medal tally of the 2006 Doha Asian Games in Qatar to see that China's programme is working: Chinese athletes won 165 gold medals, ten more than the next six nations combined. In Olympic terms, China came fourth at Atlanta 1996, was third in Sydney 2000 with 28 Gold medals; second in Athens 2004 with 32 top finishes (three behind the US). It doesn't take much to guess where they plan to be when the event is on home soil.

DISABILITY AN ADVANTAGE

Since the Seoul Olympics in 1988, the Paralympics have always been held on the sidelines of the main Games. But for 2008, the bidding countries were asked for the first time to submit a combined brief for both events. The Paralympics will be held three weeks after the main Summer Games, between 6-17 September. China has come a long way to accepting the disabled, considering that not long ago anyone with a disability was regarded as *feiren*, literally 'waste people'. Though Beijing is short on disabled access to buildings and transport, it is taking the Paralympics very seriously – treating disabled athletes in the same way as their able-bodied counterparts and fielding the biggest national team of all competing nations.

WE ARE THE CHAMPIONS

Despite projecting the prerequisite image of global harmony that every Olympic slogan seeks to do, Beijing's Olympic motto of 'One World, One Dream' rings hollow in a world torn by political, social and religious divisions. With the awakening of this sleeping giant forcing a shift in the world power balance, maybe the dream and world it refers to are China's desire to fulfil its potential as superpower-in-waiting.

During the Ming Dynasty, China was the most powerful nation on earth and after centuries of internal strife and foreign dominance it now looks likely to return to the forefront of world affairs. With sport a tidy metaphor for international conflict, it is easy to see how toppling the US from pole position on the Olympic medal table is being seen by some as a portent of a Chinese-dominated world.

Is the Beijing Olympics about the pursuit of sporting excellence, or is it a crystal ball into global politics? It's going to be a photo finish.

Practicalities

Getting around

Beijing's travel infrastructure has been gearing up for the Games for nearly a decade so is on course to run smoothly. All Olympic venues will be well served by bus and metro links – capital residents will be encouraged to leave their cars at home to decrease pollution, fleets of new greener buses have been put into operation and the capital's warren of new underground lines will all be open. Those with Olympic tickets get free travel to and from the main Olympic site on the Olympic tube line.

Accommodation

All the smartest hotels – including every four- and five-star hotel in our Where to Stay chapter – are already fully booked for the Olympics, the majority having already been assigned a certain sponsor or national team. The full list of accredited hotels is at http://en.beijing2008.com/68/72/column211717268.shtml.

It's therefore advisable to try the smaller, courtyard style and mid-range hotels which can provide another 290,000 rooms or so. See the Beijing Tourism Administration's website (http://english.bjta.gov.cn) or www.beijing-hotels.net for more hotel options in Beijing.

Tickets

So far tickets have only gone on sale to Chinese residents, but nearer the Games expect things to open up to everybody.

Tickets to the opening and closing ceremonies are going to be tough to get hold of, with officials, sponsors, expensive tour groups and those with good connections landing all the prime seats – and that's before you even factor in public demand in the world's most populous nation. If you just have to go to an event, pick a niche sport or one with a huge capacity for spectators, such as football. Bear in mind everyone can watch the marathon, which takes place on the city streets. See www.tickets.beijing2008.cn for details of how you can land that elusive golden ticket.

Venues

The Yuan Dynasty shaped Beijing along two axes (east-west and north-south) and, though the Ming and Qing dynasties left their mark, the city is still laid out along these lines. It is fitting that the Olympic development sits along the horizontal axis, to the north of Ditan Park, as it is in keeping with the city's ancient design. This nod to tradition is of little consolation to the estimated 300,000 people whose homes were knocked down to accommodate the main site, the **Olympic Forest Park** (Metro Forest Park), now the city's biggest green space. As well as acting as an ecological buffer to the city's pollution, the park will house the two showpiece venues: the National Stadium and National Aquatics Centre.

Nicknamed the 'Bird's Nest', the **National Stadium** will seat 91,000 spectators (80,000 post-Olympics), cost 3.5 billion RMB to construct and will host athletics, football events as well as the opening and closing ceremonies. After the games, it will host sporting events and concerts. Designed by Swiss architecture firm Herzog & de Meuron, with input from Chinese contemporary artist Ai Weiwei, its structure contains 36km of steel and weighs 45,000 tonnes. Dubbed the 'Water Cube', the **National Aquatics Centre** seats 17,000 spectators (6,000 post-Olympics), cost over a billion RMB to build and will host all of the swimming, diving, water polo and synchronised swimming events. Designed by Australia's PTW Architects it is contained by a bubble-like membrane that allows in more light and heat than glass, resulting in a 30 per cent decrease in energy consumption. Around 85 per cent of the cost (17 billion RMB) of constructing the six main venues will be met by private investment.

There are a total of 31 Olympic venues in Beijing, 12 of them new, the rest existing venues refurbished for the Games. A full list and map can be seen by clicking 'venues' on the official website's home page: http://en.beijing2008.cn. *See p27* **The stadiums**.

Where to Stay

Features

Peninsula Beijing. *See p35.*

THERE IS NO ADDRESS LIKE ST.REGIS BEIJING
ST. REGIS
HOTEL
BEIJING
北京国际俱乐部饭店
21 JIANGUOMENWAI DAJIE BEIJING 100020, CH
中国北京建国门外大街 21 号 邮编：10002
86 10 6460 6688
STREGIS.BEIJING@STREGIS.COM
STREGIS.COM/BEIJING

Where to Stay

The Olympic hotel spirit is all high-rise and high-end – but the city barely gets a bronze for good, affordable rooms.

It seems that nothing is reaping the benefits of the 2008 Olympic Games and China's economic boom more than the Beijing hotel industry. High-rise hotel after high-rise hotel appears on the skyline, and the constant construction shows no signs of abating.

Up until the late 1970s, very few hotels were built in Beijing – during this period any display of luxury of the sort touted by hotels was explicitly banned. Visitors were expected to stay in distinctly unglamorous dorms or *zhaodaisuos* (accommodation centres). It wasn't until China began modernising in the 1980s that any effort was made to attract foreigners and businesses to the city. With plenty of gaps left in the Chinese market and projections that China will overtake the US as the world's number one tourist destination by 2020, investing in the Beijing hospitality business suddenly makes a lot of sense.

Beijing's range of accommodation varies from courtyard homes and restored royal palaces to design hotels and hutong hostels. In spite of the growing numbers, however, most hotels in Beijing are geared towards business travellers and the number of cutting-edge or boutique hotels are few. For most travellers, the quality of service can also niggle. The absence of any service culture in China, coupled with a shortage of people with the experience and language skills required means this is one area where even international hotels struggle – the pace of progress has been so fast that education and training can't catch up. Things are changing, though, and the situation is improving.

The best hotels unsurprisingly gravitate towards the centre near Tiananmen and the Forbidden City, while Qianmen, Gulou and Houhai provide more authentic accommodation in a less touristy setting, perfect for students or those on a budget. Anything in the Chaoyang district will be near a good bar, restaurant or shop of some kind and Financial Street now has three stylish international chain hotels perfect for business travellers. Those afraid their hotel isn't very central shouldn't worry too much, since getting from A to B anywhere in this sprawling city requires a 20-minute or so taxi ride. It's also worth bearing in mind that even five-star hotels have no qualms about hailing an old banger of a cab off the street, so be sure to take along a piece of paper with your destination written on it in Chinese characters just in case.

Hotels

For pampering yourself while on business

From the moment you get off the plane and are offered a facial in the limo, the **Westin Beijing, Financial Street** (*see p45*) makes life easier.

For an authentic but cheap courtyard experience

The great value **Si He Hotel** (*see p38*) has just the ticket, complete with traditional *kang* beds and red lanterns.

For location, location, location

Walking distance from Tiananmen Square, the Forbidden City, the night market and Beijing's most famous shopping street, the **Peninsula Beijing** (*see p35*) is perfectly positioned.

For communist apparatchiks

If you want to immerse yourself in Mao, the **Red Capital Residence** (*see p42*) is the place. The five-room guesthouse decked out in antique furniture and Communist Party memorabilia is a rare treat.

For your pocket

Located inside Beijing's most fun and famous hutong, the **Peking Downtown Backpackers Accommodation** (*see p43*) can't fail to please.

For young hipsters

After a complete makeover in 2006, the birdcage-inspired Zeta Bar, chic boutique rooms and cool vibe make the **Hilton Beijing** (*see p41*) a great and reasonably priced hotel.

It really is grand at the **Grand Hyatt**. *See p35.*

HOTELS TO LOOK FORWARD TO

The rate at which new hotels are arriving in Beijing means that when you read this, several new ones will have popped up. The ones to look for include the potentially spectacular **Park Hyatt**. Currently towering above all others in the area and due to open by the end of 2007, it will feature Beijing's highest restaurant, fine views of the city and outdoor terraces and bars. Marriot International will have a remarkable four more hotels by the Olympics, including the large high-end **Ritz Carlton** and **JW Marriot**. Hilton Garden Inns and China's own budget chain Jinjiang are also boosting the number of mid-range hotels in the city.

BOOKING INFORMATION

Given the high occupancy rates of most hotels, booking a room in advance is recommended. Hotels in the budget category, and even in the mid-range hotels, may not have a competent English-speaking reservation line, so always make sure you have some sort of written confirmation by emailing or faxing ahead of time. Alternatively, for ease of booking and some genuinely good deals on accommodation rates, try www.english.ctrip.com.

➊ Green numbers given in this chapter correspond to the location of each hotel as marked on the maps. *See pp238-249.*

In this guide the listings are divided into the following categories: **expensive** (above RMB 1,600, around $200); **moderate** (RMB 400-RMB 1,600, $50-$200); and **budget** (under RMB 400, $50). However, it's important to remember that prices given by hotels are their published rates, which are often 50 per cent higher than what rooms actually go for. It's also worth bearing in mind that prices fluctuate greatly throughout the year. Discounts will almost always be given, so haggle hard, whether it's the Grand Hyatt or the Lusongyuang. Rates listed are for basic rooms or suites; something like a 'deluxe room' or 'presidential suite' will be more expensive. For nearly all hotels in the moderate and expensive categories, room rates are subject to a 15 per cent surcharge.

Note that the 120-odd smarter hotels in Beijing (including the yet-to-be-built ones) are already booked solid for the duration of the Olympic Games, having been assigned to a national team and/or sponsor by the authorities.

The Centre

Expensive

The China Club

51 Xi Rong Xian Hutong (west of the Marco Polo Hotel) Xicheng (6603 8855/fax 6603 9594/www.thechinaclubbeijing.com). Metro Xidan. **Rates** RMB 1,900 members; RMB 2,550 non-members. **Credit** AmEx, MC, DC, V. **Map** p241 H10 ➊

Set in a 400-year-old palace built for the 24th son of Emperor Kangxi, and one-time favourite haunt of Communist Party leader Deng Xiaoping, the China Club is for those with money to burn and a penchant for all things authentically Chinese. A series of five courtyards is surrounded by 14 private dining rooms, a bar and banquet hall. The eight guest rooms are housed in a relatively new three-storey pavilion. The rooms (available to non-members for the first couple of visits and during low seasons in particular) are crammed with Ming and Qing dynasty furniture, *kang* beds, stand-alone baths, shocking pink towels and the Club's trademark bulbous Chinese lamps. The private dining rooms are located in what were once the concubines' living quarters and an opium room. The Club's chefs are renowned. A fascinating, intimate and nostalgic experience from start to finish.

Bars (1). Internet (high speed). Parking. Restaurants (2). Room service. TV.

Grand Hyatt

1 Dong Chang'an Jie, Dongcheng (8518 1234/ fax 8518 0000/www.beijing.grand.hyatt.com). Metro Wangfujing. **Rates** RMB 1,250 single/double; RMB 2,250 suite. **Credit** AmEx, DC, MC, V. **Map** p241 L10 ❷

The sweeping crescent-shaped building with a splendid fountain frothing away out front is set on elevated ground above Chang'an Avenue and accessed via a grand staircase running between the malls of the Oriental Plaza. Rooms, decorated in various shades of brown, are simple and spacious. However the hotel's real highlight is the impressive array of restaurants and bars, including the famous Made in China and popular Red Moon Bar; and the fantastic, tropical oasis-style swimming pool, complete with waterfalls, coves and starry night sky. Staff are helpful and professional. **Photo** *p34*.

Bars (1). Business Centre. Concierge. Disabled-adapted rooms (2). Gym. Internet (high speed). No smoking floors. Parking. Pool (1, indoor). Restaurants (3). Room service. Spa. TV.

Peninsula Beijing

8 Jinyu Hutong, Dongcheng (8516 2888/fax 6510 6311/www.beijing.peninsula.com). Metro Wangfujing. **Rates** RMB 2,850 single/double; from RMB 3,800 suite. **Credit** AmEx, DC, MC, V. **Map** p241 L9 ❸

The only hotel in Beijing with its own car fleet (including two Rolls-Royces and 12 Mercedes), the Peninsula also houses an unrivalled collection of more than 50 designer brands in its split-level shopping arcade. Fully refurbished between 2001 and 2005, rooms are all clean lines and modern furnishings, with occasional splashes of colour. Bathroom products are Molton Brown despite their Peninsula logos. Amenities in the rooms are state of the art, from dual voltage plug sockets, free wireless internet and silent fax machines in every room, to a hands-free phone and TV in the bathroom (the latter automatically mutes itself if a call comes through). Even the regularly updated DVD library is standard. The gym, massage room and swimming pool (in a bright atrium with rose petals in the foot-bath) aren't open to non-guests, providing an element of exclusivity most other hotels don't offer. A full spa is due to open in spring 2008.

Bars (1). Concierge. Business Centre. Disabled-adapted rooms (1). Gym. Internet (high speed, free). No smoking rooms. Parking (free). Pool (1, indoor). Restaurants (2). Room service. TV.

Raffles Beijing Hotel

33 Dong Chang'an Jie, Dongcheng (6526 3388/ fax 8500 4380/http://beijing.raffles.com). Metro Tiananmen East. **Rates** RMB 3,800 single/double; RMB 5,600 suite. **Credit** AmEx, DC, MC, V. **Map** p241 K10 ❹

Constructed in 1901, this building has one of the longest and most colourful histories in the city and thanks to a full renovation by the world-famous Raffles brand in 2006, now has the comfort and luxury to match its heritage. The hotel has four new restaurants, including the exquisite Jaan and the modern One East on Third, and an impressive central atrium with a modern twist in the form of 13 huge brightly-coloured lanterns. It's true that some of the rooms don't quite match the promise of the exquisite

State-of-the-art luxury: **Peninsula Beijing**.

lobby, but all are of a very high standard and most – in particular the nine Personality Suites – are beautiful. The ballroom and Writers Bar both hark back to the hotel's heyday, with black-and-white photos of Mao and Sun Yat-sen on display. **Photo** *p37.*
Bars (1). Business centre. Concierge. Disabled-adapted rooms (1). Gym. Internet (high-speed, wireless, dataport). No smoking floors. Parking (free). Pool (1, indoor). Restaurants (4). Room service. Spa. TV.

Regent Beijing

99 Jinbao Jie, Dongcheng (8522 1888/fax 8522 1818/www.regenthotels.com). Metro Wangfujing. **Rates** RMB 1,200 single/double; RMB 1,440 suite. **Credit** AmEx, DC, MC, V. **Map** p241 L9 ❺
The Regent aspires to compete with the likes of the Peninsula and Grand Hyatt in the busy Wangfujing shopping area – and with regards to the rooms, it makes a good job of it. Each is equipped with flatscreen TV, DVD player, luxurious bed with brown faux fur throw and deep purple cushions and modern bathroom with glass walls and super-fluffy white mats and towels. The rest of the hotel's design doesn't quite live up to the rooms' standard. The lobby is unfortunately large with a rather pointless flat rockery water feature in the centre, and the lobby bar is disappointing. Head upstairs, however, for the lively restaurants, popular with non-residents. The lengthy and stylish infinity swimming pool and in-house spa are other pluses. The Regent's only real drawback is the view: surrounded by several other buildings, and located at a busy crossroads, there's not much to be inspired by when you glance out the window.
Bars (2). Concierge. Business centre. Disabled-adapted rooms (2). Gym. Internet (high speed). No smoking floors. Parking. Pool (1, indoor). Restaurants (4). Room service. Spa. TV.

Moderate

Crowne Plaza Hotel

48 Wangfujing Da Jie (5911 9999/fax 5911 9998/www.ichotelsgroup.com). Metro Wangfujing. **Rates** RMB 980 single/double; RMB 1,580 suite. **Credit** AmEx, DC, MC, V. **Map** p241 L9 ❻
Fans of this highly rated chain will not be disappointed by the Beijing edition. Completely renovated in 2006 in plenty of time for the Olympics, it is set at the north end of the capital's busiest shopping street. Some of the 360 rooms overlook the striking and lavish atrium lobby; luckily sound-proofing is excellent. Sleek bathrooms come with a huge showerhead and all the fluffy thick towels, bathrobes and toiletries you could need. If that wasn't enough, you'll enjoy possibly the most comfortable beds in the world, and to help combat jet-lag all rooms come with sleep and relaxation CDs.
Bars (2). Business centre. Concierge. Disabled-adapted rooms (1). Gym. Internet (high-speed). No smoking floors. Parking (free). Pool (1 indoor). Restaurants (2). Room service. Spa. TV.

Kapok Hotel

16 Donghuamen Dajie, Dongcheng (6525 9988/fax 6523 1056/www.hotelkapok.com). Metro Wangfujing. **Rates** RMB 1,280 single/double; RMB 2,380 suite. **Credit** AmEx, DC, MC, V. **Map** p241 L9 ❼
One of Beijing's small but burgeoning band of boutique hotels, the Kapok appeared in 2006 and was nicknamed 'the Blur' even before it opened, thanks to its 'glowing' grid-like exterior. Designed by local architects Studio Pei Zhu (also responsible for the Olympic technical command centre, Digital Beijing), the hotel also has the advantage of a prime location on the tree-lined street between Wangfujing and the Forbidden City. Inside you'll find a predominantly white reception area that surrounds a central courtyard filled with bamboo that reaches up through the floors to the sky. The lobby bar is minimalist, kitsch and cosy (though rather clumsily put together); a library stocks Chinese books. The rooms are on the stark side but still usually manage to be warm and inviting, with some looking incredibly cool, although others border on being a new page in the Ikea catalogue. In-room facilities are superior throughout, however: all are equipped with flatscreen TVs, generous wardrobe space and decent toiletries. A small gym, sauna, business centre and a chic Western restaurant also feature. **Photo** *p38.*
Bars (1). Business centre. Concierge. Gym. Internet (high-speed). No smoking rooms (10). Parking (free). Restaurants (1). Room service. TV.

Raffles Beijing Hotel. *See p35.*

Park Plaza

97 Jinbao Street, Dongcheng (8522 1999/fax 8522 1919/www.parkplaza.com/beijingcn). Metro Wangfujing. **Rates** RMB 1,784 single/double; RMB 2,839 suite. **Credit** AmEx, DC, MC, V. **Map** p244 L9 ❽

The Park Plaza is a great choice for anyone looking for modern, reasonably priced accommodation in a good location. Rooms are intimate and cosy and the whole place feels a lot more personal (largely thanks to the excellent service) and has more character than some of the bigger, more expensive hotels that you can find in the area. Each of the guest bedrooms features decor in earthy tones of brown, cream and orange, and good-quality bathrooms. Other perks such as a pool and vast array of restaurants are absent, but free wireless internet for guests, a gym and massage rooms aren't, meaning all the important things are accounted for. A solid choice.

Bar (1). Business Centre. Concierge. Disabled-adapted rooms (1). Gym. Internet (high speed, free). No smoking floors. Parking (pay). Restaurants (2). Room service. TV.

Si He Hotel

5 Deng Cao Hutong, Dongsi Nan Jie, Dongcheng (5169 3555). Metro Dongdan. **Rates** RMB 500 double; RMB 1,088 suite. **Credit** DC, MC, V. **Map** p241 L9 ❾

It may have been built for a Qing dynasty warlord, but the Si He Hotel is now a peaceful rather than a warlike place to lay your head in the capital. The name of the hotel comes from *siheyuan*, Mandarin for the courtyard dwellings once common in Beijing. However, due to the city's development, *siheyuans* are being knocked down at an extraordinary rate, so stay here while the place is still standing. The newly repainted courtyard makes an excellent place to kick back, especially at night, when it's lit by lanterns and the only sounds come from bicycles ambling up the hutongs. The hotel's 12 rooms have new spacious and stylish bathrooms. Attractive dark wood furniture includes traditional *kang* beds. Excellent value for money.

Business centre. Internet (high speed). Parking (free). Restaurants (1). Room service. TV.

Budget

Tangyue Hotel

54 Donghuamen Dajie, Dongcheng (6525 2510/ fax 6525 2591). Metro Wangfujing. **Rates** RMB 399 single/double; RMB 680 suite. **Credit** MC, V. **Map** p241 L9 ❿

This zany little hotel is just the thing for students or young people looking for somewhere central, who don't mind staying in a place with stains on the carpet and brightly coloured walls if the price is within budget. More characterful than even the neighbouring Hotel Kapok (*see p37*), the Tangyue can't help but make you smile. Each room is individually decorated, from the garish red room (complete with round bed) to the windowless basement with psychedelic ceiling and walls. They're not all quite so tacky; some rooms are done out in earthy tones or with more subtle furnishings. Despite the aforementioned carpet stains, the rooms are in fact generally clean and all have a modern shower or bath. Staff don't speak English, but are helpful and accommodating. Don't take the Tangyue too seriously and you'll have a whale of a time.

Internet (high-speed, free). TV.

Kapok Hotel. *See p37.*

Chaoyang

Expensive

China World Hotel

1 Jianguomenwai Dajie (6505 2266/fax 6505 0828/www.shangri-la.com/beijing/chinaworld/en). Metro Guomao. **Rates** RMB 4,100 single/double; from RMB 5,100 suite. **Credit** AmEx, DC, MC, V. **Map** p245 O10 ⓫

In a city where modern is king, China World's lobby is a rare treat. The size of a football pitch and filled with gold bamboo panels, shiny red pillars, crystal chandeliers, over-the-top white flower displays and white marble Indian elephants, its opulence knows no bounds. On Sundays the excess continues, with a full orchestra playing for those enjoying a coffee or cocktail in the relaxed lounge bar. A proud purveyor of luxury service, the hotel was first in the city to introduce an airport butler service: guests are escorted from the aircraft gate and through immigration before being popped in a limo and whisked to the hotel. The rooms aren't quite as grand as you might expect but all are elegant and smart. The Italian restaurant Aria is renowned, as is the tennis club and Beijing's only oxygen bar. There is also access via an escalator to Beijing's swankiest shopping mall. What more could a visitor want?

Bars (2). Business centre. Concierge. Disabled-adapted rooms (4). Gym. Internet (high-speed, wireless). No smoking floors. Parking (pay). Pool (indoor). Restaurants (4). Room service. Spa. TV.

Jianguo Hotel

5 Jianguomenwai Dajie (6500 2233/fax 6500 2871/www.hoteljianguo.com). Metro Yong'anli. **Rates** RMB 2,210 single/double; RMB 2,890 suite. **Credit** AmEx, DC, MC, V. **Map** p244 O10 ⓬

Jianguo Hotel was Beijing's first joint-venture hotel, built in 1982, and it has an exterior design redolent of '80's Holiday Inns. But there is one point very much in its favour: the hotel is set between the shopping delights of the Silk Market and Guomao. The 450 rooms vary greatly – some haven't seen a revamp since the 1980s, but there's a well-established garden, so try for a room on the first floor to enjoy the view. As for entertainment, mention Charlie's Bar to any long-term expat and watch them get all nostalgic: the bar was a popular haunt a couple of decades ago and the only place in Beijing open after 8pm. It doesn't seem to have been updated since then, but it's still a pleasant place for a cocktail, perhaps before dining at Justine's, the hotel's French restaurant.

Bars (1). Business centre. Concierge. Gym. Internet (high-speed). Parking (free). Pool (1, indoor). Restaurant (4). TV.

Kempinski Hotel Beijing Lufthansa Centre

50 Liangmaqiao Lu (6465 3388/fax 6462 2116/www.kempinski-beijing.com). **Rates** RMB 2,950 single/double; RMB 3,010 suite. **Credit** AmEx, MC, DC, V. **Map** p245 O7 ⓭

A reputable hotel close to the Airport Expressway and adjacent to the Lufthansa department store, the Kempinski struggles to compete with other international brands in Beijing like the Peninsula or Shangri-La. Aside from the funky Chinese-style black wardrobes, rooms are fairly forgettable, but the hotel as a whole has a cosy, warm and relaxed vibe. Four rooms are specially kitted out for female travellers, though the awful frilly shower curtain and selection of women's products (which you pay extra for) are laughable. The Kempinski is popular with European travellers thanks to two good German restaurants (Kranzlers and Paulaner Brauhaus) and a quality Italian (La Gondola). The Kempi Deli is also a lifesaver if you prefer a *pain au chocolat* to traditional Chinese congee in the morning.

Bars (1). Business centre. Concierge. Disabled-adapted rooms (6). Gym. Internet (high-speed, pay terminal). No smoking floors. Parking (free). Pool (1, outdoor). Restaurants (4). Room service. TV.

Kerry Centre Shangri-La

1 Guanghua Lu (6561 8833/fax 6561 2626/www.shangri-la.com). **Rates** RMB 3,000 double; RMB 5,000 suite. **Credit** AmEx, DC, MC, V. **Map** p245 O9 ⓮

One of three Shangri-La-run hotels within a few hundred metres of each other, the Kerry Centre is without doubt the most cosmopolitan. Its relaxed atmosphere and famous Centro Bar have contributed greatly to its success in recent years. The fitness centre has extensive facilities used by many locals as well as guests, including basketball and tennis courts and an outdoor running track, on top of the usual pool and gym. Those who return to the Kerry Centre for a second time automatically become 'members' and enjoy complimentary fruit, biscuits and chocolate the next time they check in. Hey, if it's good enough for the entire Manchester United football team, it's good enough for us…

Bar (1). Business Centre. Concierge. Disabled-adapted rooms (2). Gym. Internet (high speed). No-smoking rooms (22). Parking (free). Pool (1, indoor). Restaurants (3). Room service. TV.

St Regis

21 Jianguomenwai Dajie (6460 6688/fax 6460 3299/www.stregis.com/beijing). Metro Jianguomen. **Rates** RMB 3,600 single/double; RMB 4,400 suite. **Credit** AmEx, DC, MC, V. **Map** p244 M10 ⓯

With the scarcity of grand old hotels in Beijing, the St Regis steps in to fulfill the role of secure fortress where politicians, film directors and business moguls can meet their opposite numbers in the emerging superpower. Up until 2007, it was the only hotel in mainland China that could take on the likes of Hong Kong's Peninsula. But competition in Beijing from the refurbished Raffles and others has forced the owners – Starwood and the Chinese government – to knock down walls to make rooms bigger and more modern. These are the most expensive beds in town, but for your money you'll get a personal butler, top restaurants, the lovely, low-lit Press

Bar, vast 24-hour gym and big pool, and beautiful garden. Staff speak the best English in town, and are attentive but generally discreet. The St Regis has its own bowling alley, cigar humidor and lots of private rooms for Chinese-style dining; in fact you need never leave the hotel.
Bars (3). Business centre. Concierge. Disabled-adapted rooms (3). Gym. Internet (high-speed). No smoking floors. Parking (free). Pool (indoor) Restaurants (5). Room service. Spa. TV (DVD player, pay movies).

Medium

Hilton Beijing

1 Dongfang Lu, Dongsanhuan Bei Lu (5865 5000/ fax 5865 5800/www1.hilton.com). **Rates** RMB 950 single/double; RMB 1,650 suite. **Credit** AmEx, DC, MC, V. **Map** p243 O6 ⑯
Since the group fully renovated the property in 2006, the Hilton has become the coolest hotel in the city. Boutique rooms at great prices, a varied and original selection of restaurants and the signature Zeta Bar draw a fun-loving crowd. The staff, dressed in fawn-coloured suits with Mandarin collars, are just one aspect of the careful design, which features little Chinese touches here and there to remind you which country you're in. Rooms are all stylishly decorated, with sleek bathrooms, funky old black-and-white photographs with digitally imposed colours and a shiny green 'apple a day' carefully placed on each glass desk. Rooms on the Executive Floor are equipped with widescreen TV, DVD and CD players. A tri-level ringed atrium serves as a lobby and also houses the hotel's Western and pan-Asian food and beverage outlets. The Executive Tower extension is due for completion by the spring of 2008 and will add another 125 rooms, and the gym, pool and spa will soon be finished too.
Bars (2). Business centre. Concierge. Disabled-adapted rooms (2). Gym. Internet (high-speed, pay terminal, wireless). No smoking floors. Parking (free). Pool (indoor). Restaurants (2). Room service. Spa (by spring 2008). TV.

Holiday Inn Lido

6 Jiangtai Lu (6437 6688/fax 6437 6237/ www.lidoplace.com). **Rates** RMB 2,300 single/ double; RMB 4,150 suite. **Credit** AmEx, DC, MC, V. **Map** p243 Q4 ⑰
A true mid-range hotel in a city that is desperately short of them, this branch of the Holiday Inn is situated in the rapidly expanding Lido area (pronounced 'Li-doo') and, at 25 years old, is one of the oldest hotels in the city. Its proximity to the airport makes it a good choice for short-stay guests (you often see pilots and airline staff buzzing around the lobby), but there's plenty to attract those on holiday too. It's attached to an extremely useful one-level shopping mall; food is perfectly adequate; rooms are clean, well kept and provide all the basics, and staff speak good English. A swimming pool and gym are added bonuses, as is the hotel's proximity to the exciting 798 Art District (*see p163*).

Bar (1). Business centre. Concierge. Disabled-adapted rooms (1). Gym. Internet (high-speed). No smoking floors. Parking (RMB 1/hr). Pool (1, indoor). Restaurants (4). Room service. TV.

Swissôtel

2 Chaoyangmen Bei Dajie (6553 2288/ fax 6501 2506/www.beijing.swissotel.com). Metro Dongsishitiao. **Rates** RMB 1,000 single; RMB 1,100 double; RMB 2,500 suite. **Credit** AmEx, DC, MC, V. **Map** p244 M/N8 ⑱
From the outside, the Swissôtel fits in perfectly among the huge, grand buildings on this stretch of the Second Ring Road. However, those expecting anything too exciting from this 15-year-old hotel will be disappointed when they step through the doors. The general colour scheme and the truly awful carpet in parts of the waiting area lend the place an unfortunate '80s feel. But, lack of cool aside, a well-used gym and excellent location mean it is a good choice for holidaying guests who are keen to enjoy the world outside their hotel rather the one within it.
Bars (1). Business centre. Concierge. Disabled-adapted rooms (30). Gym. Internet (high-speed, wireless, pay terminal). No smoking floors. Parking (free). Pool (indoor). Restaurants (4). Room service. Spa. TV.

Trader's Hotel

1 Jianguomenwai Dajie (6505 2277/fax 6505 0838/ www.shangri-la.com/beijing/traders/en). Metro Guomao. **Rates** RMB 900 single/double; RMB 1,600 suite. **Credit** AmEx, DC, MC, V. **Map** p245 O10 ⑲

Hilton Beijing.

Stay at **Red Capital Residence** for a taste of old Beijing.

Business people who have an eye on the bottom line stay at Trader's Hotel, the younger and cheaper sister to the more glamorous China World next door. However, included in the price is access to some of the China World's facilities, including its swanky fitness centre, so you can take in some the glamour. Don't expect anything too personal or stylish – it's a purpose-built 1970s block with 570 rooms, after all – but staff do an excellent job and you tend to get a lot of bang for your buck. Rooms lack atmosphere and are geared towards the business traveller, with broadband internet access and plenty of desk space, but if cleanliness and home comforts are more important to you than character, Trader's is for you.
Bar (1). Business centre. Concierge. Disabled-adapted rooms (20). Gym. Internet (high-speed). No smoking floors. Restaurant (2). Room service. TV.

Budget

Friendship Youth Hostel (Poachers Inn)

43 Bei Sanlitun Nan Lu (behind 3.3 Mall) (6417 2632/fax 6415 6866/www.poachers.com.cn). **Rates** RMB 70 dorm; RMB 180 single/double. **Credit** MC, V. **Map** p244 O7 ⑳

If you like to party and you're on a budget then Poachers is the place for you. Located in the heart of Sanlitun's bar area, British fish and chips at Fish Nation, a Belgian pub and several shooter bars are but steps away. The downside to being at the heart of the action is that in summer this busy backstreet is riddled with beggars and drug dealers. Rooms are either twin-bed or dorms consisting of four bunk beds. The private rooms are of a perfectly decent quality for the price, but dorms are old and haggard, with flimsy mattresses and frosted windows. Daily breakfast and laundry are included in the price and a squat toilet (with toilet roll) and four showers per two rooms are relatively clean. Rough and ready all the way.
Bars (1). Internet (shared terminal). No smoking floors. Restaurants (1). TV room.

Zhaolong Youth Hostel

2 Gongti Bei Lu (6597 2666/fax 6597 2288/ yhzl@zhaolonghotel.com.cn). **Rates** RMB 60 dorm; RMB 180 double; RMB 350 double en-suite. **Credit** AmEx, DC, MC, V. **Map** p245 O8 ㉑

Tucked behind the Zhaolong Hotel proper down a nondescript alley is this two-storey grey-brick youth hostel. It has standard facilities, with the added bonus that guests are able to use the main hotel's gym. The place has been around for a while and it shows as its utilitarian dorms, rooms and reception areas demonstrate, but the sunny restaurant and bar (which serves up a RMB 15 breakfast) with trellises and plants tumbling down give the place some charm. Staff will also arrange Chinese classes if you are that way inclined. Really though, it's all about location: despite being in a very quiet back-street, the hostel is stumbling distance from party central, aka Sanlitun, with its cheap and cheerful bars and restaurants, but beware: doors close at 1am to prevent unruly revellers.
Bars (1). Business centre. Internet (high-speed). Restaurant (1).

Houhai & the North

Expensive

Red Capital Residence

9 Dongsi Liutiao, Dongcheng (8403 5308/fax 8403 5303/www.redcapitalclub.com.cn). **Rates** RMB 1,162 single; RMB 1,548 double. **Credit** AmEx, DC, MC, V. **Map** p244 M8 ㉒

Like Marmite, guests who stay at Beijing's most exclusive boutique courtyard hotel either love it or hate it. Some rave about the historic atmosphere and five themed rooms around a central courtyard – one named after a famous concubine and fittingly decked out in red – but others complain about the uncomfortable beds and non-English-speaking staff. So don't go to the Red Residence expecting five-star comforts: it's a singular experience, but you pay a premium for it, as rates are out of whack with the level of service and facilities. But, then again, where else can you go and have a drink in a bomb shelter bar with Chinese opera on the stereo? Breakfast is included in the price, and the restaurant, which serves up Communist Party cadre favourites, is two alleys away – the Residence's very own pedal-taxi will whisk you there. **Photo** *p42.*

Bar (1). Internet (high-speed). Restaurant (1). TV.

Moderate

Bamboo Garden

24 Xiaoshiqiao Hutong, Xicheng (6403 2229/fax 6401 2633/www.bbgh.com.cn). Metro Gulou Dajie. **Rates** RMB 380 single; RMB 480 double; RMB 1,200 suite. **Credit** AmEx, DC, MC, V. **Map** p241 K7 ㉓

Eunuchs may have had to go through some occupational discomfort, but there were compensations: they got to live in beautiful courtyards like this one. The former home of a Qing dynasty head eunuch, the Bamboo Garden's rooms are laid out around – you guessed it – a bamboo garden, which is at its best in summer. One of the perks is that it's in walking distance from the many dining options around Houhai. Simple, typically Chinese rooms are easy on the eye, and clean and smart enough to be good value for money.

Business centre. Parking (free). Restaurant (1). TV.

Beijing Qianyuan International Commercial Hotel

19 Dongzhimennei Dajie, Dongcheng (8400 1999). **Rates** RMB 488 single/double; RMB 788 suite. **Credit** AmEx, DC, MC, V. **Map** p244 M7 ㉔

Situated near the Second Ring Road, this hotel is in the heart of all the action. Rooms are spacious with bright interiors, comfy bed linen and flat screen TVs. All the in-room comforts of luxury hotels are here at a fraction of the cost, including internet access, cable TV, in-room safe and in-room refrigerator.

Business centre. Concierge. Internet (high-speed). Restaurant (2). TV.

Hejingfu

7 Zhangzi Zhong Jie, Dongcheng (6401 7744/fax 8401 3570). **Rates** RMB 400 double; RMB 800 suite. **Credit** AmEx, DC, MC, V. **Map** p241 J7 ㉕

This hotel may be stumbling distance from one of Beijing's hippest new clubs, Rui Fu, but don't lower the tone by crawling in drunk: you're staying in a Qing Dynasty princess's dwellings after all. Well, sort of. The actual rooms are in a modern block just behind the grey stone courtyard complex, but the old buildings are an impressive sight to behold from your hotel window. The hotel mainly caters to Chinese tour groups – probably because of the budget price and good location between Houhai and Beihai Lakes and the sights in the east of the city.

Bar (1). Business Centre. Gym. Internet (high-speed). Restaurants (1). TV.

Budget

Lusongyuan

22 Banchang Hutong, Kuan Jie (6404 0436/ lsyhotel@263.net). Metro Dongzhimen. **Rates** RMB 300 single; RMB 490 double. **Credit** DC, MC, V. **Map** p241 K8 ㉖

Originally built in the Qing Dynasty for General Zeng Ge Ling Qin, his pad now attracts tourists who want to stay somewhere with character. Some guests gripe about the slightly shabby rooms, but relaxing in the Qing-style courtyard, complete with caged birds, more than makes up for it. Rooms come with their own bathrooms, but the quality and size of the rooms varies enormously, so ask to take a look before opening your wallet.

Business centre. Internet (shared terminal). No-smoking rooms. Restaurant (1). TV.

Peking Downtown Backpackers Accommodation

85 Nanluoguxiang, Dongcheng (8400 2429/ downtown@backpackingchina.com). **Rates** (incl breakfast) RMB 50 dorm; RMB 150 single. **No credit cards. Map** p241 K7 ㉗

This cheerful hostel in a converted courtyard home opened in 2005 and filled the gaping hole for cut-price, well-located rooms. This is a great place to stay, in the city's funkiest hutong, with many bars and boutiques nearby. The English-speaking staff cater to guests' needs with charm: rooms are clean and basic, and there's a welcoming coffee shop and Western restaurant where you can borrow and swap books.

Internet (shared terminal). No smoking rooms. Restaurant (1).

Red Lantern House

5 Zhengjue Hutong, Xinjiekou, Xicheng (6616 9477). **Rates** RMB 60 dorm; RMB 120 double; RMB 160 double with en-suite. **No credit cards. Map** p241 H7 ㉘

This homely place around a converted courtyard is a challenge to find, but persevere if you want the hutong experience at a cut-price rate. The owners, keen to give visitors a good impression of Beijing, go that extra mile in helping you arrange tours or onward tickets. The traditional Chinese décor doesn't extend to the bedrooms, but they are acceptable and well-heated, something that's important during the winter months.

Bar (1). Restaurants (1). TV room.

The South

Moderate

Jianguo Qianmen Hotel

175 Yong'an Lu (6301 6688/fax 6301 3883/ www.qianmenhotel.com). Metro Hepingmen. **Rates** RMB 900 single/double; RMB 1,500 suite. **Credit** AmEx, DC, MC, V. **Map** p241 J11/12 ㉙

There can't be too many hotels around the world where every night Peking Opera actors get dolled

up in the bright and airy foyer, but that's one of the perks of staying at this mammoth four-star hotel. Also, for an up-market hotel, the standard of English is surprisingly poor. The free breakfast buffet gets good reviews as do the spacious and well-lit rooms but the whole place, built in the 1950s, could do with a revamp to bring it into the 21st century.
Bar (1). Business centre. Concierge. Internet (high-speed). Parking. Restaurants (3). Room service. TV.

Budget

Far East International Youth Hostel

90 Tieshu Xie Jie, Xuanwu (5195 8811/fax 6301 8233/www.fareastyh.com). Metro Hepingmen. **Rates** RMB 60 dorm; RMB 328 double. **Credit** DC, MC, V. **Map** p241 J11 ㉚
Run by the two-star Far East Hotel opposite, this converted courtyard hostel is – gasp! – efficient and well aware of the needs of budget travellers. There's free access to a washing machine, book rental and half an hour of free internet access every day, and the staff stuff your pockets with useful maps – useful because the hostel's location down a hutong near Qianmen can be tricky to navigate. (The whole area is something of a building site at present.) The four-bed dorms are basic but clean – the ones overlooking the courtyard are much nicer than those in the actual hotel, just be prepared on chilly mornings for the gallop across the courtyard to the bathrooms. If you feel like upgrading to your own bathroom, the small doubles are just about worth it, but if it's the courtyard experience you want, stay in the dorms. By the time you read this, the Traveller's Bar and restaurant should be fully renovated.
Bar (1). Internet (free, high speed). Restaurants (1, due to re-open July 2007).

Holiday Inn Temple of Heaven

1 Ding'an Dong Li, Fengtai (6762 6688/fax 6761 1616/www.hitemple.holiday-inn.com). Metro Chongwenmen. **Rates** RMB 325 double; RMB 799 suite. **Credit** AmEx, DC, MC, V. **Map** p247 L13 ㉛
The hotel's school-gym style exterior with a high-rise behind it isn't going to win any architectural prizes, but inside guests are rewarded with very comfortable, bright rooms, a decent health club complete with pool and free high speed internet. Here's the catch: given Beijing's traffic purgatory, you have to weigh up whether the excellent prices are worth the hour spent in traffic getting to and from any sight in the city other than the Temple of Heaven and Panjiayuan Market.
Bar (2). Business centre. Concierge. Disabled-adapted rooms (2). Gym. Internet (high-speed). Pool (indoor). Restaurant (3). Room service. TV.

Home Inn

13 Xijing Lu, Xuanwu (8315 2266/www.homeinns.com). **Rates** RMB 179 double; RMB 300 deluxe double. **Credit** AmEx, DC, MC, V. **Map** p241 J12 ㉜
Since 2002, China's biggest hotel chain has filled the massive hole in the market for budget-conscious hotels in good locations. This one, within walking distance of the intriguing Qianmen backstreets, is one of their newest. The mauve and yellow exterior may not be to everyone's taste but who cares with some of the best room rates in town? For RMB 179, you get a brand-new double room complete with a sparkling clean bathroom (with tub). As a treat to soothe those weary feet, the hotel offers cut-price foot massages for just RMB 30 an hour.
Bar (1). Business centre. Internet (high-speed, free). Parking (free). Restaurant (1). TV (pay movies).

Rainbow Hotel

11 Xijing Lu, Xuanwu (6301 2266/fax 6301 1366/www.rainbowhotel.com.cn). **Rates** RMB 180 single; RMB 300 double; RMB 680 suite. **Credit** AmEx, DC, MC, V. **Map** p241 J12 ㉝
As Judy Garland almost said: 'Somewhere over the rainbow… are much, much better-looking hotels.' Despite its colourful name, this is quite possibly one of the most charmless buildings in Beijing, and in a town that hosts Chairman Mao's Mausoleum, that's saying something. Looks can be deceiving, however, as rooms are well worth the money if – and this is a big if – you get one of the newly renovated doubles. The hotel is about 10 minutes walk from the east gate of the Temple of Heaven, but the street it's on is dull and drab. If saving money is key, the newer Home Inn next door is a better option. If it's full, the Rainbow is a good second choice.
Bar (1). Business centre. Concierge. Gym. Internet (high-speed). Parking (free). Restaurants (3). Room service. TV (pay movies).

Financial District

Expensive

InterContinental Financial Street

11 Financial Street, Xicheng (5852 5888/fax 5852 5999/www.intercontinental.com/icbeijing). Metro Fuchengmen. **Rates** RMB 1,300 single/double; RMB 3,500 suite. **Credit** AmEx, DC, MC, V. **Map** p240 G9 ㉞
Despite being the oldest of the big three on Financial Street, the InterContinental is still barely two years old. Most people who stay here are on business, but the complimentary toddler kit in every room on the Club Floor (including Johnson's baby products and a cuddly toy) and the cool X-Change bar with band playing suggests the hotel is keen to cater to other guests too. The interior is dark and sleek, with amber and yellow box lamps dotted around and a bevy of men and women dressed in black silk *qipaos* and suits waiting to greet you. Rooms still look new and have big squishy beds, brown marble bathrooms and flatscreen TVs; views aren't bad either. InterContinental's own brand I.Spa offers a range of massages and treatments.
Bars (1). Business centre. Concierge. Gym (24 hr). Internet (high-speed). No smoking floors. Parking (free). Pool (1, indoor). Restaurants (5). Room service. Spa. TV.

The Beijing Hotel

When Mao wanted to throw a lavish banquet to celebrate the inauguration of People's Republic in 1945, there was only one possible venue – the **Raffles Beijing Hotel** (*see p35*), the grandest and most famous in the city. Joined at the feast by Liu Shaoqi, Zhou Enlai, Zhu De, Dong Biwu and others, Mao's merrymaking is just one of many fascinating episodes in the hotel's illustrious but chequered history.

From being 'the only hotel de luxe in the Far East' to a hostel for American troops after the surrender of the Japanese in the 1940s, the hotel has enjoyed good times and bad. The journey from its humble beginnings under two French proprietors in the city's Legation Quarter to today's management under the Raffles brand has taken over 106 years. During that period the building has welcomed many other distinguished characters, from George Bernard Shaw to Charles de Gaulle and Henri Cartier-Bresson.

It was the growing popularity of luxury cruises and ocean liners during the early 20th century that caused tourism in China to take off, and it wasn't long before the Grand Hotel de Peking – as the Beijing was then called – became the talk of the town. The height of luxury, with 'steam heating, private baths and flush toilets throughout', the hotel was renowned for its gourmet food and dining terrace overlooking the Forbidden City. 'Unexcelled cuisine, with French chef. Banquets a specialty, wines of the best districts of France,' read one advertisement. The hotel's European-style dancefloor was another hit. The building even housed the headquarters of the Thomas Cook Travel Agency and kept two private limousines to meet guests at the railway station.

Despite knock-backs in the form of Japanese occupation in 1937 followed by World War II, the hotel continued to play an important role in Beijing's social scene and, until the opening of the Great Hall of the People in 1958, was the venue for nearly all major political functions. The hotel continued to expand during the 1970s and for a short time, thanks to an additional 20 storeys, was the only authorised building in the centre of the city tall enough to overlook the Forbidden City. Later, during 1989, it was from the hotel's sixth floor that journalist Charlie Cole took the famous photo of a protester in front of tanks on Tiananmen Square.

As Beijing grew more tourist-friendly again, the hotel was forced to build a new wing to cope with the increased demand, and in September 2005 the respected Raffles brand took on the task of restoring it to its former glory. After nine months of renovation, the building now has new carpets and leather chairs and staff even sport uniforms designed by Benny Ong. Guests are still encouraged to take high tea – a popular tradition at the hotel since the '20s – and the ballroom has been fully restored, complete with its original grand piano. Let's hope Beijing is willing to kick up its heels once more, because this hotel will be around for a while.

Ritz Carlton Beijing Financial Street

1 Jingchengfang, Xicheng (6601 6666/fax 6601 6029/www.ritzcarlton.com/hotels/beijing_financial). Metro Fuchengmen or Fuxingmen. **Rates** RMB 4,000 single; RMB 4,165 double; RMB 6,500 suite. **Credit** AmEx, DC, MC, V. **Map** p240 G9 ㉟

The Ritz Carlton Beijing Financial Street made its debut in October 2006. Condoleezza Rice was the hotel's first high-profile guest and the hotel's location on the edge of 'Beijing's Wall Street' means she probably won't be the last. A touch more modern than other hotels associated with the brand, the hotel aspires to be as Chinese as possible, with oriental screens surrounding the lobby, a courtyard-shaped entrance and 'lucky' animals guarding the door of each room. Rooms are simple, slick and equipped with most amenities, including a widescreen TV, DVD player, electronic blinds and internet connection, and the modern and elegant bathrooms feature a rather exciting selection of mini-Bulgari products. Each day there is a tea ceremony at 3pm, where a selection of Chinese dim sum or traditional English treats are served by women in yellow *qipaos*.

Bars (1). Business centre. Concierge. Disabled-adapted rooms (1). Gym. Internet (high speed, wireless, pay terminal). No smoking floors. Parking (free). Pool (indoor). Restaurants (3). Room service. Spa. TV.

Westin Beijing, Financial Street

9B Financial Street, Xicheng (6606 8866/fax 6606 8899/www.westin.com). Metro Fuchengmen or Fuxingmen. **Rates** RMB 1,100 single/double; RMB 2,100 suite. **Credit** AmEx, DC, MC, V. **Map** p240 G9 ㊱

With 486 rooms, the Westin is too big to be a boutique hotel, but it follows the clever brand theme of earthy hues, arty decor, sumptuous beds and IP phones in the spacious bedrooms. There are incense

burners in the lobby and little gifts (chocolates, games, fruit) left in your room for when you get back from the office… which is where most of the clients will be all day. The cool of the lobby bar, stocked with fine (if pricey) European wines, is mitigated by a guy doing t'ai chi at sunset and evening shows starring Filipina covers singers. The smaller Buzz bar is where to go for chilled music and a cocktail. The hotel specialises in wellness treatments – with a spa, facials in the limo from the airport and a complimentary 'bathologist' sent to your room to draw a bath and give you an aromatherapy session.
Bars (2). Business centre. Concierge. Disabled-adapted rooms (4). Gym. Internet (free high-speed, wireless in rooms, restaurants and public areas). No-smoking rooms (370). Parking (free). Pool (indoor). Restaurants (3). Room service. Spa. TV.

The North-west

If you're on a budget and looking to stay for the long term in Beijing, particularly during the summer months, it's worth considering lodging at a university dorm. Beijing Normal University (overseas students office 5880 6000, 5858 5151) has twins from RMB 240.

Expensive

Shangri-La Hotel

29 Zizhuyuan Lu, Haidian (6841 2211/fax 6841 8002/www.shangri-la.com/beijing). **Rates** RMB 1,850 single; RMB 2,010 double; RMB 2,640 suite. **Credit** AmEx, DC, MC, V. **Map** p248 D7 37

The Shangri-La chain is a major player in Beijing, and this, their flagship hotel, has a great reputation among business travellers. Because it's not in the centre of town, it can afford to be set among lovely landscaped gardens. The rooms may not be particularly imaginative but they are luxurious and come with complimentary broadband internet. Guests rave about the exceptional service.
Bar (3). Business centre. Concierge. Disabled-adapted rooms (10). Gym. Internet (high speed, free). No smoking floors. Parking (free). Restaurants (3). Room service.

Moderate

Friendship Hotel

1 Zhongguancun Nandajie (6849 8080/fax 6849 8825/www.bjfriendshiphotel.com). **Rates** RMB 1,200 double; RMB 2,730 suite. **Credit** DC, MC, V. **Map** p248 E5 38

Comrades! For historic interest alone, a stay here is your patriotic duty. Built in the 1950s for visitors sympathetic to the Communist cause, guests would immediately have felt at home in the Stalinist-style architecture. While the main building is something of an eyesore, most of the 1,700 rooms are in small blocks dotted around a very attractive tree-lined campus. With a swimming pool and tennis court, this hotel makes a good base to relax after frantic sightseeing. It's doubtful if anyone actually pays the advertised rates: make sure you don't. Haggle.
Bar (1). Business centre. Concierge. Gym. Internet (high-speed). Pool (indoor, 1). Restaurants (2). Room service.

Executive perks aplenty at **Westin Beijing, Financial Street**. *See p45.*

Sightseeing

Features

Jingshan Park. *See p58.*

Introduction

China's vast capital is anxious to impress visitors with a new, modern face – but Beijing's alleyways, museums and parks are filled with imperial memories.

Beijing is a fast changing city – a mixture of the imperial old town and the Olympic new – with the new encroaching on the old at an incredible pace. The capital is home to many of China's major tourist sites, including the Forbidden City (*see p51*), the Temple of Heaven (*see p76*) and the Summer Palace (*see p85*) – as well as a great number of ancient temples, the best of which is perhaps the Lama Temple (*see p62*). The proximity of the Great Wall (*see p201*) is also a draw, even for those with an aversion to cities.

A stroll around the winding lanes, collectively known as hutongs, in the south of Beijing is one of the city's great pleasures, but one that may not be around much longer due to the continual development of the area. It's not all bad news though: the functionalist, Soviet-style architecture that dominated until recently is no more. Instead, scores of the world's best architects have been allowed to use Beijing as their drawing board and the new CCTV tower, the 'Bird's Nest' Olympic stadium and 'Water Cube' swimming pool will go down as some of the early 21st century's greatest achievements.

Although Beijing is not as chic as Shanghai, a stroll around the city's flea markets – in particular Panjiayuan – is far more enjoyable than an afternoon at Louis Vuitton. And don't forget the food – Peking duck reaches its apotheosis in the capital, but try the hot pot, too.

BEIJING GEOGRAPHY

Beijing is split into numerous districts, but to make it easier to navigate we have divided the city into six areas, as follows:

- **The Centre** – the heart of the city, including the Forbidden City and Tiananmen Square.
- **Houhai & the North** – where old hutongs and beautiful lakes meet Olympic modernity.
- **Chaoyang** – encapsulating the Central Business District (CBD) and most of the shops, restaurants and bars.
- **South Beijing** – the old commercial district and traditionally the poor part of the city is also home to the beautiful Temple of Heaven.
- **Financial District** – the revamped fiscal centre, currently gaining a clutch of new bars, restaurants and malls.
- **The North-west** – where you'll find Beijing's prestigious universities and the Qing-era Summer Palace.

GETTING AROUND

Beijing is not a very walkable city, but its metro system is clean, inexpensive and easy to use, costing just RMB 3 per journey. At present the only draw back is that the ground it covers is tiny, only really ticking off the main points on the Second Ring Road. However, by 2008 further lines will have been introduced which should make life a little easier (see the map on p256). And, while buses are even cheaper, they can be complicated to use, unless you speak at least some Chinese, and they get incredibly crowded during rush hour. See page 216 for three public routes that serve as tour buses.

Taxi fares are among the cheapest in the world and cabs can be found 24 hours a day, therefore making them the best option for visitors. Fares start at just RMB 10 and go up RMB 2 per kilometre after the first four – in fact all journeys within the city proper rarely cost more than RMB 30 ($3.80)

There are a couple of points about the names of roads that will make navigating the city easier. Many roads are preceded by their geographical position – therefore take note that *bei* is north; *dong* east; *nan* south; and *xi* west. The word *lu* means road, and *xiao* means small – therefore 'Xiaolu' means small road or side street. Another helpful word to remember is *jie*, meaning 'street', which is often given to secondary roads. *Dajie* – literally 'big street' – means avenue and is given to the older streets leading into the city.

Many of the roads inside Beijing are incredibly long and are therefore further broken down into inner (*nei*) and outer (*wai*). The inner roads are normally within the Second Ring Road – the location of the original city wall – while outer roads usually lead from the Second Ring Road out to the third – beyond the original city limits.

You'll also notice that many roads have the word *men*, meaning 'gate', at the end, which indicates that the road led through one of the nine original city gates. Therefore you might have Dongzhimennei Dajie – which literally means Inner Avenue to the East Gate.

► For all the key sights and streets in **Chinese script**, *see pp252-255.*

Essential Beijing

...in one day

Get up at dawn and head straight for the **Temple of Heaven**, starting at the south gate, where as well as the 500-year-old temple itself, you'll get to see local old folk doing t'ai chi, singing traditional songs and writing calligraphy on the ground in the temple's **parks and pavilions**.

Exit the temple's north gate and head first west, then north up Qianmen Dajie, until you hit the clusters of **hutongs** around Qianmen and Dazhalan, taking the time to explore and check out the shops still selling the same **Chinese medicines** they were touting in the Qing Dynasty. Grab some noodles from one of the local stalls before continuing north to **Tiananmen Square**. Pass through the middle and towards Chairman Mao's portrait. It was from this rostrum that the Communist leader declared the People's Republic in 1949.

Pass under the portrait and into the **Forbidden City**, the magnificent Imperial Palace of the Ming and Qing Emperors. At the north end, hop in a cab to the beautiful **Beihai Park,** or walk if your legs are still up for it. Stroll around this imperial playground before heading north again via Gulou Dajie for a pre-dinner drink on **Houhai Lake**. Try the No Name bar for pleasant views and a cosy atmosphere. Rested? Then jump in a cab to **Guijie** – the 24-hour food street laced with red lanterns – and pick one of the hundreds of restaurants serving hot pot before settling down to eat and drink your way into the night.

...in two days

Day one as above, and if the hangover's not too bad get up as early as possible to negotiate with a cab to take you out to the **Great Wall**. Despite being a little further away than most, the Simatai section of the Wall is one of the most undisturbed and beautiful, and worth the extra half hour getting there. Spend an hour or two climbing the steep steps and see how far you can get before (if you've got the guts) swinging down on the zip wire over the lake to the bottom again.

Make your way back to the city. As you re-enter the Beijing, stop off at the **798 Art District** near the Fifth Ring Road where you can eat before seeing if there are any paintings you (or your wallet) like the look of.

From here, take another cab back to Gongti Bei Lu (near the Workers' Stadium north gate) and stop off at **Yashow Market** – yes, we know its full of tourists, but cheap clothes and DVDs make it a great place to stock up on gifts before heading out to dinner. Getting in a taxi again, tell the driver to take you to **Ritan Park** and the Temple of the Sun's south gate. As the evening draws in, spot the young lovebirds kissing and cuddling in the park's quiet corners, and head north toward the main altar. Continuing north-east you'll stumble across one of the coutyard-style restaurants. If it's a warm evening, make straight for the balcony where you can enjoy a meal of authentic, delicious **Peking Duck** overlooking the park.

GUIDED TOURS

Beijing without Mandarin is a challenge, so hiring a guide is an option if you want to meet a Chinese person and know why the hutongs are grey, why men drink firewater with lunch and why Mao is still admired. Try these agencies.

Beijing Fantasy International Travel Service

(6026 7631). **Cost** RMB 200-RMB 400/half-day tours in Beijing. **Credit** MC, V.

A solid English-speaking agency, used by some UK tour operators; it can take care of bookings for Peking Opera, acrobatics and kung fu shows.

Chinese Culture Club

(6432 9341/www.chinesecultureclub.org). **Cost** RMB 50-RMB 120/classes; RMB 100-RMB 250/day tours in Beijing; RMB 1,100-RMB 5,300/tours outside Beijing. **Credit** MC, V.

This local NGO cooks its tours with a little culture – check out their t'ai chi classes at the Temple of Heaven, Peking Opera school trips and, if you've got the balls, a look inside Zhihua Eunuch Temple.

China eTours

(6716 0201/http://beijing.etours.cn). **Cost** US$20-US$160/day tours in Beijing. **Credit** MC, V.

A quirky agency that offers customised tours for women (shopping for dresses $30), the disabled (special vans $40-$550), seniors (meeting Chinese seniors to do t'ai chi $40), relaxation (spas $50) and families (zoo and aquarium $50).

Cycle China

(6402 5653/www.cyclechina.com). **Cost** RMB 150-RMB 350/day tours in Beijing; RMB 300-RMB 370/one day Great Wall trips; RMB 1,000-RMB 13,000/travel tours outside Beijing. **Credit** MC, V.

China by bike: the small group tours run the spectrum from the hutongs to the Great Wall.

The Centre

Welcome to the historic heart of the universe.

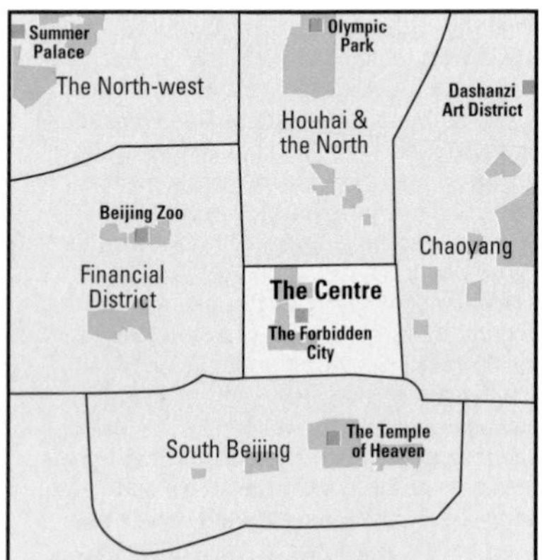

Most people think of two Beijings; the ancient one full of emperors, grand palaces and imperial intrigue, and the modern one being constructed – literally and metaphorically – under the auspices of a government striving to come up with a workable capitalist-friendly communism.

The focal points of both these worlds lie within a few square miles of each other, quite literally at the centre of the city. Tiananmen Square and the Forbidden City today are visited by more than 8 million people a year as well as locals flying kites, hawkers selling Olympic merchandise and Chinese tourist groups on the trip of a lifetime, not to mention the legions of fake 'art students' trying to convince you to visit their galleries (that is, to buy some second-rate art for exorbitant prices).

The Forbidden City, officially called the Palace Museum – though the name hasn't caught on – has remained largely in its original form. By contrast, Tiananmen Square has changed considerably. Dating back to the Ming dynasty in the 15th century, it was originally a T-shape. Rather than an area of particular political or social significance with an identity or name, it was more of a functional space between the east and west Chang'an gates of the Forbidden City (to the left and right of where Mao's portrait now is) and the Qianmen gate in the south – formerly one of the nine gates at Beijing's city walls. The 'I' of the 'T' was lined with the various government departments of state officials during the time of the emperors, while the horizontal bar of the 'T' stretched to the Chang'an gates – gates that had strong associations with the celebrations of scholars who passed their imperial exams to become officials on one side and with imperial trials at which people were sentenced to death on the other.

After the last emperor left the Forbidden City and China became a republic in 1911, it was common for the Chinese to celebrate or demonstrate against various events in this part of the city – from the Allied Forces' victory in the First World War to the subsequent decision to hand over Chinese land to the Japanese.

It wasn't until 1949, when Chairman Mao declared the new People's Republic, that the dynamic of the area changed forever. His vision of what the space should become was ambitious. He knew it was vital to harness the power of the area for his own benefit and to attempt to control the (by that time) highly political space by moulding it into one in keeping with his own values.

Many of the original city gates were demolished at this point in a bid to accommodate Mao's vision of a square 'big enough to hold an assembly of one billion' and for the first time in history, it was permissible to construct buildings taller than those in the Forbidden City. An official architect explained, 'The Chairman's mind, broad as the ocean, flies beyond the confines of the old walls and corridors and penetrates into the future. It is his vision that reveals the direction for construction of the new square.'

Mass demolition was carried out to make way for a flat, open plaza that, despite the planners' best efforts, could only accommodate 400,000 people. (Ironically, it was only after Mao's death that the square was expanded further, and it's now believed that it can hold a million people). Several monuments and Soviet-style government buildings were erected soon after, including the **Monument to the People's Heroes** and the **Great Hall of the People**, then later, **Mao's Mausoleum**, apparently built in an astonishing six months.

Under the new leadership of Deng Xiaoping in the '80s it was only a matter of time before

▶ For key sights and streets in the Centre in **Chinese script**, *see pp252-255.*

the surrounding area began to modernise too. Nearby Wangfujing has become the city's main shopping street, and is dominated by neon signs and foreign brands. Similarly, the east side of Tiananmen now sports a clock ticking down to the Olympics and the south east is in the process of gaining a swanky new restaurant and retail hub in the former Legation Quarter, not to mention that ordinary folk can now frolic inside the once 'Forbidden' City.

The Forbidden City

The jewel in Beijing's crown, the historic axis and the centre of the universe as far as the Chinese were concerned, the Forbidden City is now a UNESCO World Heritage Site and contains the largest collection of preserved ancient wooden structures in the world.

Comissioned in 1406 by Ming emperor Yongle, it reportedly took over one million skilled labourers nearly 14 years to complete. First officially occupied by the court in 1420, it went on to house 24 emperors of the Ming and Qing dynasties over 500 years.

These days familiar to many thanks to China's 'opening up' and the 1987 film *The Last Emperor* (the first feature ever authorised by the government to shoot inside the palace), the Forbidden City was for much of its existence unknown to anyone besides the emperor, his officials, concubines and eunuch servants. Normal citizens were not allowed to enter and even most of those allowed through the initial gates of the city were not permitted to enter the Inner Court. So protected was the 'son of heaven' that the city was encompassed by a ten-metre (32-foot) high wall and a five-metre (16-foot) wide moat, with the layout strictly designed in harmony with the laws of feng shui to ensure the emperor's prosperity.

In its entirety, the palace is 961 metres (3,153 feet) long and 760 metres (2,493 feet) wide, and has a total of 9,999.5 rooms covering an area of 730,000 square metres (180 acres). The site could easily have been destroyed on several occasions. Its walls were breached by British troops in 1860, its occupants were evicted in 1924 during the establishment of the republic, and the Red Guards were on the verge of storming the complex 40 years later.

Most visitors to the Forbidden City start at the south end, passing beneath Chairman Mao's portrait on Tiananmen Square, and through the Meridian Gate. You'll walk several hundred metres past this point before you come to the ticket booths and the place where you can borrow an audio guide, should you want to. Sadly, the sultry tones of Roger Moore no longer explain the City at a pace of your choosing. Instead a helpful Chinese woman senses where you are in the grounds and begins rabbiting on whether you've actually reached the particular spot she's talking about or not, without a pause button. It's therefore only advisable to use the audio guide while you're

No longer the **Forbidden City**, now it's Beijing's biggest tourist attraction.

alone, or if you have particularly large ears (to prevent the ear piece continually falling out). If you do, the guide costs RMB 40 plus a RMB 100 deposit and does have a handy electronic map printed on it.

● **Hall of Supreme Harmony** The first building you will encounter as you enter the nearly 600-year-old City is also the biggest. A purely ceremonial hall, it was used for enthronements, wedding, winter solstice and New Year ceremonies. It is believed to have burned down seven times since it was first built in 1416, hence the huge bronze water vats dotted around the outside.

● **Hall of Complete Harmony** This is the smallest of the three buildings in the 'outer court' where the emperor met officials, prepared for ceremonies in the Hall of Supreme Harmony, and read books and examined documents.

● **Hall of Preserving Harmony** In Imperial times, you could be a doctor, a mathematician or a popular performer, but only those in government jobs earned any real respect. But to become a government official you first had to pass a series of Imperial exams, and the Hall of Preserving Harmony would have been your examination hall. Note the couplet inside that reads: 'teaching should be remembered so it can be told to the next generation'.

● **Gallery of Clocks and Watches** After passing down the rather grand white stone platform from the Hall of Preserving Harmony and into the 'inner court', bear right before you go through the Gate of Heavenly Purity for the museum of imperial clocks and watches (8.30am-4pm in summer, 8.30am-3.30pm in winter, RMB 10). Not desperately exciting, but great emphasis is placed on the clock collection here because their movements, colours, chimes and auspicious symbols were said to be a source of great amusement to the emperors.

● **Gate of Heavenly Purity** Flanked by two lions (the female carries a baby under her paw, the male a ball) in order to ward off evil spirits, it's worth noting that this gate, like many others, has animals marching on its eaves – the number determines the importance of the building and the people within it.

● **Hall of Heavenly Purity** This is where grand banquets were held and where a piece of paper with the Crown Prince's name written on it was secretly hidden behind a plaque to be checked at a later date in order to name the emperor's successor.

● **Palace of Earthly Tranquillity** This is the Palace where the empress stayed on her wedding night, and you can just about make out the marital bed, though sadly it appears that no one has yet bothered to restore it. During the Qing dynasty, the building was split in two and was where pigs were slaughtered for various ceremonial purposes.

● **Hall of Union and Peace** The empress would receive officials and the other concubines here on her birthday and during the Spring Festival. It also contains a 200-year-old-bronze clock and boxes for the 25 imperial seals.

● **Imperial Garden** When you reach the end of the Forbidden City, there's a pleasant surprise in the form of the Imperial Garden. Much prettier in the summer months thanks to the blooming flowerbeds, there are also a number of pavilions and small halls, including the Hall of Study and Cultivation in which the last emperor Pu Yi was educated by Oxford grad Reginald Johnston.

● **West Six Palaces** These are accessible from the imperial gardens if you head left and then back on yourself as you enter, and are the parts most people fail to visit. It can become quite confusing so there's not much point attempting to follow any particular path, but there are several corridors, beautiful doorways and small courtyards to get lost in. These palaces were the residential halls for concubines during the Ming dynasty and later they where the last empress, Ci Xi, spent most of her time.

● **East Six Palaces** are equally maze-like but contain six more buildings sometimes used for exhibitions – concubines, calligraphy and painting have been recent themes.

● **Hall of Jewellery and Treasure Gallery** The far eastern corridor of the Forbidden City is well worth a visit because this is were the majority of the real treasures lie – highlights include the well that concubine Zhen was drowned in by order of the last empress, peaceful courtyards and gardens, and Qing dynasty gold, jade, silver, and pearl treasures made by the imperial workshops. There's even a highly elaborate and colourful Chinese Opera stage with adjoining museum showing theatrical playbills, costumes and even Qing Court vinyl.

● **Nine Dragon Screen** The glazed wall screen, 25 metres (82 feet) wide, was created during Emperor Qianlong's palace renovations. It's impressive, but could do with a clean. The dragon represented the emperor in ancient China – Beihai Park (*see p58*) has one similar.

Forbidden City

North of Tiananmen Square, Dongcheng (6513 2255/www.dpm.org.cn). Metro Tiananmen West or Tiananmen East. **Open** *16 Apr-15 Oct* 8.30am-5pm (4pm last entry) daily; *16 Oct-15 Apr* 8.30am-4.30pm (3.30pm last entry) daily. **Admission** *1 Apr-31 Oct* RMB 60; free children under 1.2m. *1 Nov-31 Mar* RMB 40; free children under 1.2m. Clock Gallery & Treasure Gallery additional RMB 10. **No credit cards. Map** p241 K9.

Don't be too disgruntled if the first thing you see on entering this magnificent space is scaffolding. Between now and 2020 at least one or two of the palaces will be out of action at any one time, but there's still enough of the complex open to be worth visiting. It's also worth noting that people often emerge at the north gate having walked the Palace from end to end and complain that they thought there would me more to see. In fact there's plenty, you just have to know where to find it. Once you've walked the length of the City and reached the gardens, take the opportunity to go back on yourself and explore the East and West Six Palaces and the Hall of Jewellery, Treasure Gallery or Clock Museum, since this is where most of the Museum's artefacts are kept.

Things to look out for in and around each hall include the animals marching on the eaves of each roof, denoting the rank of the person inside (the emperor's sleeping quarters in the Hall of Heavenly Purity is the only building with the maximum number of animals – nine). The roofs themselves are all yellow glaze, since yellow was the symbolic colour of the royal family. It's also interesting to spot the huge bronze vats outside some of the bigger halls that were filled with water (heated from underneath in the winter) to serve as ancient imperial fire extinguishers. If you're really observant, you'll also notice the Starbucks here. Though it's been inside the Forbidden City for years, a recent campaign by a local TV presenter highlighting its controversial location caused the sign to be taken down, so now you have to venture into the souvenir shop to balk at it (or get a cup of coffee). One final tip: don't be confused if you hear people talking about the 'Palace Museum' in relation to the Forbidden City, they are one and the same thing. The Palace Museum was the official name given to the complex when it first opened to the public in 1925 – the name refers to the fact that this is China's biggest collection of ancient art and artefacts – but it hasn't really caught on.

Inside Tiananmen Square

Measuring 440,000 square metres (4.8 million square feet) or, to put it another way, about 63 football pitches, the largest public square in the world isn't difficult to find. All taxi drivers and hotel staff will know how to get you there, and it's only a short metro ride to either Tiananmen East, Tiananmen West or the Qianmen underground stops (though note that the latter will deposit you at the southern end of the square). When you arrive the temptation is to head straight for its centre to get a sense of just how huge it is. If you do, be sure to go via one of the underpasses scattered around the edges for quickness and to avoid the general danger that is never too far away on Beijing's roads.

Tiananmen Square today has a joyful atmosphere, full of red-capped Chinese tourists, kite flyers, and even the odd Buddhist monk or performance artist. If you visit during one of the public holidays, you might also get to see an over-the-top flower display. However, the space itself is surprisingly flat and featureless, save for two interruptions in the form of the Monument to the People's Heroes and Chairman Mao's Mausoleum.

Tiananmen Square.

The royal chop

To anyone living outside of the Imperial city in ancient times, the 'Great Within' was the pinnacle of existence. Housing the emperor and his harem, it was a place of immense wealth and power. For a poor boy living outside the Palace walls, the only hope of gaining access to this world, and increasing his family's chances of a better life, was to become a eunuch.

Often sent forward by their parents, boys as young as eight or nine were submitted for inspection to prove they were 'clean' before undergoing the operation that would end with their 'precious' pickled in a jar. Often, several thousand eunuchs were required to wait on the palace residents at one time, so older men were accepted too, as long as someone could vouch for their good character and they went through with the obligatory castration.

The operation usually took place at the back gate of the Forbidden City, carried out by 'knifers' who were paid 6 taels for each surgical procedure they performed. The patient was asked if he was likely to have any regrets about becoming a eunuch one last time before being strapped to a semi-reclining bed, with legs held down firmly to prevent any movement. The area was numbed by dipping it in a bowl of hot pepper water, before the knifer swiftly chopped off both penis and testicles. A metal plug was inserted into the urethra and the wound bandaged. The boy was expected to thirst for three days so he wouldn't urinate. If they survived this stage of the procedure (and it is believed many didn't), they could enter the Forbidden City proper and, due to the fact that they now posed no threat to the Imperial bloodline, the emperor could rest easy. When eunuchs died, their 'precious' was removed from the jar and placed on the body so they could enter the afterlife whole again.

The last eunuch to serve an emperor in the Forbidden City died in 1966.

Built in 1958, the Monument to the People's Heroes was the first large-scale monument commissioned by Mao to be built in the New China. Get up close and you'll see that it depicts stars, flags, cypress trees and other revolutionary symbols to commemorate the masses that died rising up against the country's oppressors. However, as art historian Simon Leys put it, the Monument to the People's Heroes might also be viewed as being the equivalent of 'a good sneeze' in 'a concert hall at just the most exquisite and magical point of a musical phrase', thanks to its insensitive position on the central axis of the old Beijing.

The huge flat-roofed building in the middle-south of the square, with boy-soldiers standing guard at various points around its generous perimeter, is the **Chairman Mao Memorial Hall**, the place to go if you want to catch a glimpse of the Great Helmsman himself. Be warned, in the morning the queues are very long and once you're inside you'll be hurried past the casket at top speed, but it's still worth getting a look at the now slightly waxy-looking founder of the People's Republic of China if you have time. Dominating the front and rear of the hall are three heroic and quintessentially socialist sculptures. The one north of the building represents the achievements the Chinese people made under Mao's leadership, while the two south of the hall embody the slogan 'Carry the cause of our revolution through to the end.'

Further south is one of the remaining gates of the old city. The Qianmen Gate (or Zhengyangmen), which formerly divided the Imperial City from the suburban area of Beijing, now affords good views of the Square and contains a nice exhibition of old photos (8.30am-4pm, RMB 2). The enormous grey brick Arrow Tower was once equipped with cannons. It has withstood many a battle, including the violent Boxer Rebellion.

To really soak up the nationalist spirit of the Square though, it's a good idea to be there at daybreak or sunset to watch the Five Star Red Flag raising ceremony that takes place at the far north end of Tiananmen. It's easy to underestimate just how many people watch this ceremony every day, so take into account that there will be large crowds. The guards march at exactly 108 steps per minute at 75 centimetres per step and the cars on Chang'an Avenue are all obliged to stop in their tracks.

Chairman Mao Memorial Hall

Tiananmen Square (right in the middle), Dongcheng (6513 2277). Metro Tiananmen East or Qianmen. **Open** 8-11.30am; 2-4pm Tue, Thur; 8-11.30am Wed, Fri, Sat, Sun. Closed Mon, July, Aug. **Admission** free. **Map** p241 K10.

Allegedly built in just six months by the Chinese people in a propaganda-heavy show of dedication to their deceased leader (in defiance of his wish to be cremated), the Memorial Hall contains the embalmed corpse of Mao in a crystal coffin which is raised and lowered from an underground freezer every day. A respectful, even holy atmosphere exists inside, with Chinese people buying gaudy plastic flowers to lay at the bottom of his statue and others praying. Visitors are allowed relatively close to the corpse, but unfortunately not for long enough to work out which one of his ears was supposed to have fallen off. Bags and cameras must be checked in before entering, and it's advisable to get there early. In summer 2007, short-term renovations to the hall were due to be completed by September – but call in advance to double-check.

Around Tiananmen Square

When Tiananmen Square resembled a T-shape and imperial ministries and government buildings ran down either side, the east strip was made up of the Board of Personnel, the Board of Finance, the Board of Imperial Family Affairs and the Board of Commerce. In their place now lies the **National Museum of China**, an amalgamation of the two museums that previously stood on this site; and on the opposite side of the square, the even bigger Great Hall of the People. Built in just 10 months, it is here that the Communist Party and People's Congress convene to discuss legislation and hold ceremonial events, though the majority of the government's day-to-day business takes place in the buildings inside the off-limits Zhongnanhai Park.

Surveying the square from on high is Chairman Mao's portrait. Situated atop the Tiananmen Gate (literally the 'Gate of Heavenly Peace') at the entrance to the Forbidden City, the portrait is flanked by two slogans, the left reading 'Long Live the People's Republic of China', the right, 'Long Live the Unity of the Peoples of the World'. It was in February 1949 that Mao's portrait first appeared, only to be replaced by a more flattering one a few months later, where it has remained for more than fifty years. The two-ton painting is cleaned annually and on the eve of National Day is replaced temporarily by a copy.

For something a little less well known, head toward the south-east corner of Tiananmen Square for the **Beijing Police Museum**, which houses several bilingual exhibits on the history of the Beijing police force, or directly south-east to what used to be the former Legation Quarter (best accessed by heading south down Tiajichang Dajie from the Oriental Plaza). Up to 13 foreign governments were represented here between 1861 and 1959 and a number of European-style buildings still remain. During the 1960s embassies were built in the Sanlitun area.

By the end of 2007, the old American Embassy compound will have been transformed into a slick, international brand complex housing a collection of top restaurants, an art gallery, repertory theatre and even a Bouji nightclub (23 Qianmen Dong Dajie, south-east corner of Tiananmen square, opposite the Beijing Planning Exhibition Hall, Doncheng).

Overseeing the Legation Quarter redevelopment is American lawyer-cum-lifestyle guru Handel Lee, the brains behind Shanghai's Three on the Bund – siting a temple of culture and hedonism right on the corner of Tiananmen Square is a clear indication that the capital is squaring up to its frivolous rival.

Beijing Police Museum

36 Dongjiaominxiang, Dongcheng (8522 5018). Metro Qianmen. **Open** 9am-4pm Tue-Sun. Closed Mon. **Admission** RMB 5; free children. **No credit cards. Map** p241 K10.

Though any reference to the sensitive subject of modern-day police corruption and keeping law and order during the Cultural Revolution are (unsurprisingly) absent, there are still a good number of crime scene exhibits and 'cultural relics' to make this lesser-known museum well worth a visit. Built on the site of what was once the National City Bank of New York, the Police Museum displays over 1,500 artefacts. Some of the more memorable include a cracked skull, Qing dynasty torture and execution instruments, declassified investigation material and interactive shooting games for children.

Great Hall of the People

West side of Tiananmen Square, Dongcheng (6309 6156). Metro Tiananmen West. **Admission** RMB 30; RMB 15 students. **Open** 9am-5pm daily. **No credit cards**. **Map** p241 K10.

Containing 300 meeting halls, a 10,000-seat auditorium and a 5,000-seat banquet hall as well as more than 50 reception and conference lounges spread over different levels, the Great Hall of the People is truly enormous. Organised trips take place regularly and grant access to most rooms so long as nothing major is going on when you visit. And, as long as you don't ask any awkward questions, the tour guide is happy to explain what goes on where, from the impressive Great Hall itself to the dining hall in the north of the building and the 34 halls named after the country's 34 provinces and regions; all decorated or designed by artists and architects from that part of the country. Tickets can be bought from the East Gate. Visiting times vary greatly depending on the time of year, so call ahead.

Ancient Observatory. *See p57.*

National Museum of China

16 Dong Chang'an Jie (east side of Tiananmen Square), Dongcheng (6513 2801/www.nationalmuseum.cn/en). Metro Tiananmen East. **Closed** until 2010. **Map** p241 K10.

The museum is shut for renovations until 2010.

Chang'an Avenue

Chang'an Avenue not only runs through the heart of Beijing, ticking off important building after important building on its route east to west through the city, but its promotion to the capital's main traffic route in the 1930s completely altered the primary direction of movement within the city.

In ancient China, the main road into the Imperial City (through the Tiananmen Gate under Mao's portrait) passed under the gateways you see in and around Tiananmen Square, from south to north. By the time the first tram was installed on the east-west road passing in front of Tiananmen, however, Chang'an Avenue was well on its way to replacing the traditional route. It wasn't until the rapid expansion of the road in the years following the creation of the People's Republic that the avenue began to resemble a modern thoroughfare. The Party cleared a number of ancient and historical gates and wooden archways in order to expand the road, and by 1959 it was 80 metres (262 feet) wide and stretched 40 kilometres (25 miles) in either direction – perfect for all those National Day Parades and mass expressions of support for Mao during his heyday.

Starting a few kilometres west of Tiananmen is Xidan, an increasingly modern shopping area popular with Chinese people. The Capital Time Square and Zhongyou Malls have the usual selection of Western, Hong Kong and Chinese brands and the 77th Street Mall is a magnet for young and trendy Chinese, with scores of clothing boutiques and quirky shops. Not so easy to find, the entire mall is underground so you have to enter via one of the entrances on the Xidan Culture Square. Continuing east along the Avenue, past Tiananmen Square and various ministries, are a number of five-star hotels. Just beyond these Chang'an Avenue turns into Jianguomenwai Dajie. Where it meets the equally busy Third Ring Road, you'll come across the **Ancient Observatory**. Over 500 years old, the grey bricked building looks like a fort from the outside and its several bronze astronomical instruments are visible on the roof.

National Art Museum of China. *See p58.*

Ancient Observatory

2 Dongbiaobei Hutong, Jianguomenwai Dajie, Dongcheng (6512 8923). Metro Jianguomen. **Open** 9-11am, 1-4pm Tue-Sun. Closed Mon. **Admission** RMB 10; RMB 5 students. **No credit cards. Map** p244 M10.

Relying on astronomy to dictate everything from planting crops, to when religious ceremonies should occur, the Chinese have been gazing at the stars for centuries. Appointed by the emperor to help him rule the country and advise on auspicious dates, it was the court astronomers who made some of the greatest advances in pre-telescopic astronomy. When Jesuit priests arrived in China in the 17th century, Eastern and Western methods combined and many of the results can be seen here, including the 8 bronze instruments on the roof. Other exhibits in the observatory's museum explain the all important lunar calendar (the word for 'month' in Chinese is still the same as the word for 'moon') and the Shadow Observation House, where Ming and Qing dynasty astronomers would make sun-shadow observations and therefore be able to tell the time accurately. **Photo** *p56.*

Wangfujing

Happening upon the perpetually crowded Wangfujing Street from whichever direction you come can give you a real sense of the modern China – neon lights, international brands, bustling street food stalls, and McDonald's and KFCs galore.

Largely pedestrianised in 2000, the area is now the city's main shopping street and in the late 1980s began to attract a number of international hotel chains such as Hong Kong's Peninsula, the Hyatt and Novotel. However, Wangfujing's history as a commercial area actually stretches back hundreds of years, having always been known for its quality goods and services; its proximity to the Forbidden City meaning that for centuries, many royal and wealthy families took up residency here, in particular several of the emperor's brothers. The name 'Wangfujing' derives from the site being a so-called 'sweet water' well, a rare commodity in ancient times, leading to the name 'Wang Fu' (aristocratic residence) 'Jing' (well). The now sealed well is marked by a round plaque on the ground just below the neon Olympus sign and in front of a Jessica clothes shop at the north end of the street.

A number of the goods once sold in the area are still in abundance, including jade, tea, roast duck, silk, cloth, calligraphy brushes and ink. Some of it can be found in the Art Mansion, though most Westerners will find the shopping centre gaudy and overpriced. Much better to visit the real deal; the Shengxifu Hat Store's quality headgear have been a favourite of Chinese officials for years (156 Wangfujing Dajie 6525 1196) and the Wuyutai Tea House (*see p139*) is over a hundred years old, still selling the fresh tea that made it famous during the Qing dynasty. The Yong'antang Medicine Shop (a block east on 118 Dongsinan Dajie) has an even longer history, first opening for business in the late 15th century.

Turning on to south Wangfujing from Chang'an Avenue, the first thing you'll see as you start on the city's main shopping street is the Oriental Plaza on the right, one of Beijing's premier shopping malls, which houses a good range of designer and international brands, one or two high end restaurants and even an underground cinema and a Sony Explora Science Museum. Keep on walking until you come to the far north end of Wangfujing street, passing the Century Square Mall, where it meets Dongsi Xidajie, and bear left on to Wusi Dajie where there are a number of extremely good value framing shops and opposite them, the **National Art Museum of China**. The traditional Chinese tower-style gallery houses more than 60,000 art works, most of them modern, including papercuts, pottery, painting, sculpture and ceramics among other things.

Heading back toward the pedestrian part of Wangfujing, where it meets Donganmen Dajie, turn right and opposite the giant Hong Kong Food City you'll find the Donghuamen Night Market. Open from 4pm to 10pm every evening, it's a shocking but absolutely wonderful strip of 88 red lantern-lit food stalls that gives creedence to the idea that the Chinese will eat literally anything. From skewered seahorses to scorpions, starfish, crickets and chicken foetuses on sticks, there's plenty to pull faces at (or dare your friends to eat). The smell of offal in places can be gut wrenching, but there's plenty for the yellow bellied traveller too, including noodles, banana fritters, fresh oysters, dumplings and chicken skewers.

National Art Museum of China

1 Wusi Dajie, Dongcheng (6401 7076/6401 2252/ www.namoc.org). **Open** 9am-5pm (last entry 4pm) daily. **Admission** RMB 20. **No credit cards.** **Map** p244 L8.

NAMOC shows a combination of traditional Chinese art exhibitions and contemporary art shows, although any edgier art work that might offend mainstream visitors is still more likely to be found in the 798 Art District. The museum's director, Fan Di'an, has done a great job of balancing the exhibition programming at NAMOC of late – before his arrival, the museum was known for stale shows that left modern art completely out in the cold. More recently it has begun to exhibit foreign classical and contemporary art works too. **Photo** *p57.*

Temples & parks

Though they aren't immediately visible the centre of Beijing has a number of beautiful parks. Most surround the Forbidden City and one or two are off limits, but without exception they are all quintessentially Chinese and a joy to be in. Don't expect them to have Hyde Park-like expanses of grass for you to picnic on. Chinese parks are more about quiet contemplation than playing footie with your mates or feeding the ducks.

Beihai Park

1 Wenjin Jie, Xicheng (6403 1102). **Open** *Apr, May, Sept, Oct* 6am-9pm daily. *June-Aug* 6.30am-10pm daily. *Jan-Mar, Nov, Dec* 6.30am-7.30pm daily. **Admission** RMB 5. **No credit cards.** **Map** p241 J8.

The favourite of most Beijingers, Beihai Park has a wonderful atmosphere all year round and is one of the biggest and most picturesque in the city. Over a thousand years old, it served as an imperial pleasure ground during five dynasties. Its 69 hectares (170 acres) are filled with halls, pavilions, gateways, gardens and general greenery in the summer. Its main feature is the Tibetan White Dagoba temple on the lake's central Qiong islet. You can take a boat on to the lake when it's not frozen and the park is also popular with old people exercise here in the mornings.

ChangPu River Park

Nanheyan Dajie/Nanchizi Dajie (where they meet Chang'an Jie), Dongcheng (no phone). Metro Tiananmen East. **Admission** free. **Open** 24 hours daily. **Map** p244 K10.

This narrow but vibrant park was 'recreated' in 2003 because in the 1960s it had become a warehouse of sorts, holding equipment for the pageants that took place in Tiananmen Square. Despite its small size (510m – or 1,673ft – in length), its pavilions, rockeries and stone bridges make it one of the most beautiful and colourful parks in Beijing during the summer months and if you're lucky you'll catch one of the weddings that often take place inside. Best reached via Nanchizi Lu or Nanheyan Dajie, just off Chang'an Jie.

Jingshan Park

1 Jingshan Qian Jie, opposite the Forbidden City North Gate, Dongcheng (6404 4071). **Open** 6.30am-8pm daily. **Admission** RMB 2. **No credit cards.** **Map** p241 K8.

Also known as Coal Hill (because coal used to be stored at the foot of it), most people come here after visiting the Forbidden City to take in the great views from Prospect Hill. The hill itself is a 'fake', having been constructed from the earth dug up from the Imperial Palace's moat. It's also where the last emperor of the Ming dynasty hanged himself from a scholar tree as rebel troops invaded. Several pavilions with wonderfully contrived names like Pavilion of Admiring the Surroundings and Pavilion of Accumulated Fragrance provide great viewing platforms, but head for the central Wanchun Pavilion first, where tourists make offerings to the Buddha housed inside and admire the city.

Zhongshan Park

1 Zhonghua Lu, west side of Tiananmen Square, Dongcheng (6605 5431). Metro Tiananmen West. **Open** *Winter* 6.30am-8pm daily; *Summer* 6am-9pm daily. **Admission** RMB 3; RMB 1.5 students; free children under 1.2m. **No credit cards.** **Map** p241 K9.

A few hundred metres to the west on the other side of the Tiananmen rostrum is Zhongshan Park. The former Altar of Land and Grain during the Ming and Qing dynasties, the emperor would come here to offer sacrifices to the God of Earth and the God of Grain in the hope of ensuring a good crop and prosperity for his people. Inside you'll find a flower garden (an additional RMB 5), worth visiting when the Chinese roses and orchids are in season; the celebrated (but unpretentious) Lai Jin Yu Xuan restaurant serving traditional dishes from famous Chinese novel *A Dream Of Red Mansions*; the Sun Yat-sen Memorial Hall (an additional RMB 2 for entry); a concert hall, children's playground, and several broad and elegant walkways and pavilions.

Houhai & the North

Onwards and upwards.

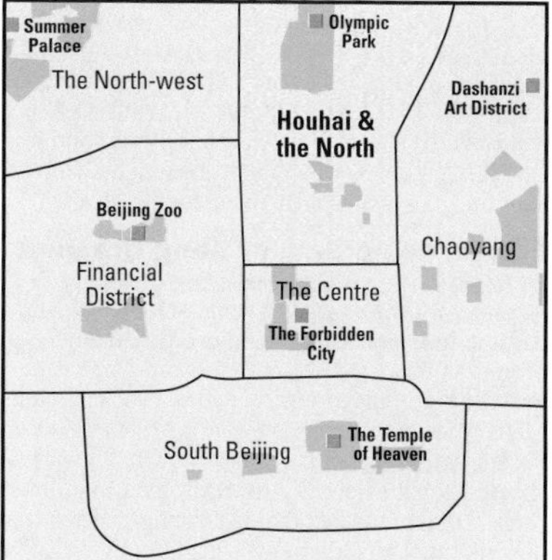

From the ramshackle old-world charm of Houhai to the sleek modernity of the Olympic developments, a journey due north of central Beijing is a trip through time.

This area contains many of Beijing's second-tier sights that rank just below the Great Wall, the Forbidden City and the Temple of Heaven on most visitors' itineraries. Buildings that deemed how the country worshipped and thought – the Lama Temple and Confucius Temple – stand a short way from the former homes of people that shaped this giant's imperial, political and literary history. The narrow streets around the lakes contain some of the city's best-preserved hutongs or 'alleyways', a rapidly shrinking part of the city that looks unmistakably Chinese (*see p75* **Out with the old**).

Where once court officials got up and went to bed to the sound of the Drum Tower and Bell Tower, time is now measured in how long it takes to get served at the growing number of trendy (and tacky) bars, restaurants and cafés that have come to define its modern role as a nightlife district. The Houhai effect has been repeated to the east in Nanluoguxiang – which has been transformed from an ordinary hutong into a remodelled and repaved strip of cafés, bars and backpacker hostels.

As you head north up through the orbital ring roads that serve as strata, roughly marking periods in the city's history, you come across the ugly 'Communist block' buildings that have come to define contemporary Chinese architecture. Beyond this mass of faceless white tile lies the city's immediate future: the National Stadium and the National Aquatics Centre – examples of cutting-edge design that can comfortably compete with the most striking structures anywhere in the world (*see p27*).

GETTING THERE

The best way to get to places of interest in this area is to hop on the metro – the north of the city has the best underground links. Beijing's answer to London Underground's Circle line (Line 2) runs alongside the Second Ring Road, making sites like the Drum and Bell towers and the Lama and Confucius temples just short walks south of their designated tube stops (Gulou and Yonghegong, respectively). Houhai itself is a ten-minute walk south of Gulou or north of Tiananmen. Yonghegong is also served by the handy Line 5, which runs north-south and connects with the east-west axis, Line 10. It is from the Panda Roundabout (Asian Games Village) stop on this line that trains run direct to the Olympic stadium.

If you have a little time and are in the south of this district, it is best to forgo all motorised transport and hop on a bike.

The Lakes

Collectively referred to by most people as Houhai, but officially known as Shichahai – the man-made lakes of Qianhai, Houhai and Xihai snake out northwards from the expanses of water around which the Imperial playground, Beihai Park, and the latter-day seat of power, Zhongnanhai, are built.

These artificial lakes once served as the terminus of the canal network that used to run through the city, some of which can still be seen running alongside the second ring road (*see p82* **Slow boat**). Being so close to the Forbidden City, this area was populated by court officials and the city's elite after the capital was remodelled under the Yuan Dynasty. These former residents include the father of Puyi, the last Qing Emperor, who hung

▶ For key sights and streets in Houhai & the North in **Chinese script**, *see pp252-255*.

his hat in **Prince Gong's Mansion**, and the widow of Sun Yat-sen, who spent her twilight years living in a very stately mansion, now converted into a museum called the **Former Residence of Song Qingling**; there is also a museum to a revolutionary author at **Guo Morou's former residence**.

China's middle class now hold sway as the area revels in its new role as a white-collar bar zone. It all started with No Name Bar (*see p122*) and the Han Cang Hakka restaurant (*see p102*), neither of which have been topped, despite new boozers opening up every month. During the Sars scare of 2002 the area really took off, as outdoor seating was seen as less risky.

Houhai boomed as a nightlife district on the back of the Lotus Lane development – a traditional façade for a row of big money bars and restaurants, the best of which are Lotus Blue (*see p122*) and Buffalo Bar (*see p121*). Wander up Yandai Xijie (the street that leads diagonally to the east of Yinding Bridge) for lots of hutong theme bars with rooftop seating, as well as a few good jewellery and nick-nack shops. Cycle rickshaw trips are available around the area – it is important to agree a price before getting on: expect to pay upwards of RMB 60 for an hour, and be prepared to haggle. The paved area at the south end of Lotus Lane has outdoor ballroom dancing every evening – great people watching and, if you aren't shy, a giggle to join.

To the north and east of the lakes, in what was once the centre of this affluent district, stand the Drum and Bell towers. Around the square which lies between them are a number of trinket shops aimed at parting tourists from their cash as well as a cosy pub, the Drum and Bell (*see p121*). Delve into the hutongs further north, or further east for Beijing's backpacker strip. To the west is Xinjiekou, one of the city's great shopping streets, full of small, cheap and cheerful shops, and a world away from Wangfujing's big name glitz.

Drum & Bell towers

North end of Dianmenwai Dajie, Dongcheng (8402 7869). **Open** 9am-5pm daily. **Admission** *Bell tower* RMB 15; *Drum tower* RMB 20. **No credit cards**. **Map** p241 K7.

These two structures sit at the north end of Imperial Beijing's central axis and have been telling the time since the Yuan Dynasty, though they have been rebuilt many times since then. At 7pm every evening the striking of the drum and then the bell marked the official bedtime; the bell then chimed at two-hour intervals throughout the night until 5am when the drum and then the bell sounded the wake-up call.

Dating from 1272, the Yuan Dynasty Drum Tower was originally made of wood and used to house 25 drums, of which only the large main drum still survives. The stone-built Bell Tower was added in the Ming Dynasty but was rebuilt in the 18th century after it was destroyed by fire. It contains one huge bell, said to be the heaviest in China, which was still rung at 7pm until 1924, when Emperor Puyi left the Forbidden City. The first attempt at casting this huge ringer failed and the Emperor threatened that if the next one was not made perfectly all the bell makers would be executed. They duly forged another bell – but when it failed to set, the daughter of the bell-maker, believing that she too would die, leapt into the molten bronze, leaving just her embroidered shoes. The bell set and everyone was saved, but it is still said that on quiet nights you can hear the ghost of the girl calling for her shoes.

Former residence of Song Qingling

46 Houhai Beiyan (on the northeastern shore of Houhai lake), Xicheng (6404 4205). **Open** 9am-4pm daily. **Admission** RMB 20. **No credit cards**. **Map** p241 J7.

Prostitution, stage musicals and fascism aside, Madam Song is China's answer to Argentina's Eva Perón. After the death of Sun Yat-sen, his widow showed some sympathy towards the Communist cause. Despite the fact that her younger sister was married to Nationalist Party leader and arch-foe, Chiang Kaishek, Mao Zedong gave Song this beautiful lakeside compound in 1963 to reward her loyalty. She lived here until her death in 1981, devoting much of her time to the education of the city's children. Generally regarded as a secular saint by the establishment, her residence now functions as a popular museum honouring her life, and includes all of her material possessions.

Guo Morou's former residence

18 Qianhai Xijie, Xicheng (6612 5392). **Open** 9am-4.30pm Tue-Sun. **Admission** RMB 20; RMB concessions. **No credit cards**. **Map** p241 J8.

This revolutionary author's home has been turned into a museum exhibiting many of his works as well as his household objects. Guo was very popular with the Communist clique, meaning that the residence hasn't found much of an audience among young Chinese people and has little to offer foreign literati.

Prince Gong's Mansion

14 Liuyin Jie (from Pingan Dadao walk north on Qianhai Xidajie and follow signposts), Xicheng (6618 0573). **Open** 8.30am-4.30pm daily. **Admission** RMB 20 (includes guide and Peking Opera performance). **No credit cards**. **Map** p241 J7.

This is probably one of the best-preserved examples of a courtyard house in the city, though its size makes it anything but typical. The nine courtyards and landscaped gardens were originally built for Heshen, a member of the Imperial guard who rose to great power under Qing Emperor Qianlong. Responsible for the Imperial finances and the appointment of civil servants, Heshen abused his position to such an extent that he is widely seen as one of the most corrupt officials China has ever seen. Qianlong's

Traditional Beijing Street life

Away from the flash new developments and renovated tourist hotspots of Olympic Beijing lies a city where ordinary folk go about their lives as they have done for decades. Free of traffic, since most people choose to walk or cycle, Beijing's back streets have a slower pace of life. Here, hawkers call out their wares as they slowly pedal their bicycle-cum-roving shops; knife sharpeners drum up trade by clanking chunks of metal strung together; soy milk and tofu sellers summon people out of their homes; while rag and bone men ask for muck to turn into brass.

On busier roads barbers park their bicycles, connect their electric clippers to a car battery strapped to the parcel rack, unfold a chair and are ready to snip passers-by into shape. Though a novel way to get a haircut, don't expect anything more complex than a short back and sides or the military crew cut flat top favoured by local forty-something men.

Across the city pigeons circle overhead, let out for their morning and evening exercise; caged songbirds look on enviously from their perches behind bars or tethered to their owners' bike handlebars. On street corners, keenly contested games of chess are played out on boards roughly drawn on an old box. These kerbside matches inevitably draw a crowd of onlookers, all keen to share their opinion of what the players should have done. Games of mahjong seem to be less of a draw, sedately played in quiet spots – though the recent boom in mahjong clubs has seen many players take their games indoors.

People need neither an excuse nor a court for badminton, with games taking place in the road. With no net, court markings or – usually – scoring, it's just done for the fun of getting a rally going. Pensioners prefer to get their morning exercise on the ubiquitous roadside gyms – the colourful tubular steel machines are a common sight near any housing development. In the evenings look for elderly ladies practising their fan or drum dancing, or couples ballroom dancing in public squares. This can be seen nightly at the southern end of Shichahai lakes.

successor, Jiaqing, had Heshen executed in 1799, confiscated his fortune of 800 million ounces of silver and gave the property to Prince Qing. In 1851, Emperor Xianfeng gave the house to his brother, Prince Gong, the father of Puyi, the last Qing Emperor.

The Lanes

Any trip to Beijing is incomplete without at least one lazy afternoon spent wandering around the old city. The whole point is to get lost in this maze of streets as you rub shoulders with vendors, watch old men exercise their pigeons, and snack on traditional food. If you do lose your bearings, don't worry, just head in one direction for ten minutes and you are guaranteed to come out on a main road. It's a good idea to combine a wander with visits to both Beijing's biggest functioning lamasery, the **Lama Temple**, and the ancient university which was the **Confucius Temple**. Other noteworthy local sights include the **Mao Dun former residence**, now a museum to the life of one of the heavyweights of Chinese contemporary literature.

You can smell the Lama Temple (Yonghegong) long before you get there, the wind carrying the whiff of burning incense on the breeze. Established in the 18th century, it still functions as the state-sanctioned centre of Tibetan Buddhism, but is used as propaganda in China's ongoing feud with the Dalai Lama – something that became all too apparent when China's choice of Panchen Lama was sworn in at this building in 1995, after six-year-old Gedhum Choekyi Nyima, the Dalai Lama's choice for Buddhism's second most holy post, and his family 'vanished'. Politics aside, this is a place of worship, so you may bump into a monk or two as you wander through the five main prayer halls.

The area immediately to the north of Beihai Park and the Forbidden City was where court officials used to live in single-storey courtyard homes (*siheyuan*), built to a traditional plan that has not changed much since Han Dynasty times. A typical house has stones either side of the entrance, used for mounting horses and often carved to depict the rank of the building's occupant. The main door faces south and is shielded by an internal wall, said to protect against evil spirits, but also fulfilling the more practical function of stopping draughts.

The first courtyard has servants' quarters to the left and right, with an entrance to the family compound to the north. Family elders would occupy the north part of this inner sanctum, facing south. Most of the rich occupants of these traditional houses were ejected when the Communists took power in 1949, replaced with ordinary people, living a family to a room.

Only a few of these courtyards have been renovated into single upscale dwellings and many are still home to the city's *laobaixing* (literally 'old hundred names') or working classes. Often without such amenities as basic plumbing, many of these hutong homes were torn down to make way for faceless developments, although Beijing's recent tourist boom has seen some areas around the centre of the city escape the wrecking ball (*see p75* **Out with the old**).

Confucius Temple

13 Guozijianjie, Dongcheng (6404 2407). **Open** 9am-4.30pm Tue-Sun; *Guozijian* 9am-4.30pm Tue-Sun. **Admission** *Kong Miao* RMB 10; *Guozijian* RMB 10. **No credit cards.** **Map** p241 L7.

In the same way that Confucianism's self-centred practical ethics are the antithesis of Buddhism's quest for enlightenment, the Confucius Temple couldn't be more different from gaudy neighbour Yonghegong. Built in 1306, this building is split between a Confucian temple (Kong Miao) and the academy (Guozijian) where civil servants used to train for the exams that would launch them into court life. The two are still split – thanks to a bureaucratic battle for control between the ministries of culture and cultural relics. Now more of a museum, things still get busy at the temple when Beijing students prepare to sit the university entrance exams and come here to ask the sage for a bit of help.

Lama Temple. *See p61.*

Lama Temple (Yonghegong)

12 Yonghegong Dajie (just inside the North Second Ring Road next to Yonghegong metro station), Dongcheng (6404 3769/4499). Metro Yonghegong. **Open** 9am-4pm daily. **Admission** RMB 25. **No credit cards. Map** p241 L7.

Originally built in 1694 as a residence for eunuchs of high rank, it became the official residence of Prince Yin Zhen and most of the complex was converted into a monastery in 1723 when he took the throne as Emperor Yongzheng. After his death the temple was granted imperial status, swapping its turquoise glazes tiles for regal yellow ones and became a lamasery for the 'yellow hat' Lama sect of Buddhism, housing monks from Tibet and Mongolia.

Peek behind the curtains of the third prayer hall, the Pavilion of Eternal Happiness, to see the Buddha getting it on in what was a sex education mural for the regal tenants; there's more erotic sculpture in the fifth (Wanfu) pavilion – where the largest carving made from a single piece of wood stands. The street alongside the temple is full of shops selling incense, Buddhist trinkets and icons.

Mao Dun former residence

13 Yuanensi Hutong (behind Jiaodaokou Nanjie), Dongcheng (6404 4089). **Open** 9am-4pm Tue, Thur, Sat. **Admission** RMB 5. **No credit cards. Map** p241 K7.

Born plain old Shen Dehong in Zhejiang, Mao studied in Hangzhou and published his first work before taking a place at Peking University studying Chinese and Western literature. He couldn't afford to finish his degree, dropping out to take jobs on a variety of cultural periodicals. Penning the Chinese classics *Hong* (1930) and *Midnight* (1933), Shen adopted the pen name Mao Dun, meaning 'contradiction', as a reference to the contradictary revolutionary ideology in 1920s China, though his friend Ye Shengtou later made him change the first character so it read 'thatch' to protect him from political persecution.

A believer in the Communist cause from the start, he was involved throughout their ascent to power and served as the minister of culture until 1964 when he ended up on the wrong end of a persecution during the Cultural Revolution. He was rehabilitated during the '70s and went on to edit a children's magazine. He died in 1981 before he could finish his memoirs, but leaves a legacy in the Mao Dun Literature Prize, which is awarded to outstanding novelists. His old house was made a key state-preserved relic in 1994.

Northern Beijing

It's true what they say; it really is grim up north. Well, maybe that's a bit harsh as there are some great places outside the Second Ring Road, but there's a lot of faceless urban sprawl in between them. Without a doubt, the new Olympic development will do much to rectify this as the stadiums are examples of the most

Traditional Beijing Park life

For many years Beijing's imperial parkland was the preserve of a privileged few. But after the revolution the gates to these previously off-limits green spaces were flung open – and city folk have been taking full advantage of them ever since.

A potter through any city park is to embark on an urban safari through Beijing at play. Some of the activities may at first seem odd, but are just city folk unwinding in a space that, although public, they use as their own private playground. Early risers may catch people practising t'ai chi – either doing 'sticky hands' movements solo or in a group using ceremonial swords.

Other strange sights include shoeless pensioners walking backwards across cobblestones – said to massage the feet – and people practising calligraphy with a mop-cum-brush, splashing water into a line of poetic characters only to watch it evaporate in the summer sun.

As well as the more familiar jogging and walking the dog, some choose to exercise their vocal chords, congregating in groups to sing Peking Opera favourites. These are often beautifully complemented by musicians giving their neighbours a break from hearing them practise, plucking away at violins or the Chinese *erhu*. Head to the park around the Temple of Heaven to hear Beijing's best impromptu orchestral manoeuvres in the park.

Beihai Park. *See p58.*

Spring offers the best winds for kite-flying, and clusters of brightly coloured kites dot the skyline on any day with even a slight breeze. Ditan Park offer good take-off spots, though many kite flyers perch on bridges, some even flying at night with lights attached to kite and line – proof, as if it was needed, that no matter how many hutongs are levelled, you're never going to stop the people of Beijing doing the things they've always loved to do.

striking modern architecture anywhere in the world, while the Olympic Forest Park has taken the title of Beijing's biggest green space away from Chaoyang Park.

Ditan Park – the Temple of the Earth – is at the northern end of the imperial axis of worship, which features the Temple of Heaven (*see p76*) as well as the Temples of Sun and Moon in the east and west of the city. Though defunct as a holy place and lacking the buildings that have made the Temple of Heaven a must, Ditan Park is still a nice place to visit, if just to soak up the atmosphere.

Other honourable mentions go to the **Science & Technology Museum** and the **Chinese Ethnic Cultural Park** – a theme park that clumsily crams all of China's 56 ethnic minorities into one village. To the west, Yayuncun was built for Beijing's hosting of the 11th Asian Games in 1990.

Chinese Ethnic Cultural Park

1 Minzuyuan Lu, Chaoyang (6206 3646/7). **Open** 8.30am-6pm daily (ticket office shuts 4.50pm); Southern Park closed Dec-Mar. **Admission** *both* RMB 90; *either* RMB 60. **No credit cards.** **Map** p242 J3.

This theme park puts the *zu* in *minzu* (ethnic minority), cramming every facet of China's anthropological tapestry into one place, resulting in a jumble of architectural styles and brightly costumed people.

Science & Technology Museum

1 Beisanhuan Zhong Lu, Xicheng (6237 1177). **Open** 9am-4.30pm Tue-Sat. **Admission** RMB 30; RMB 20 concessions. **No credit cards.** **Map** p242 K4.

Lots of corporate bumph masquerading as exhibits, but do go to see China's first space capsule, the giant game of mousetrap, and the funhouse-style wonky room and hypnotic walkway. Also head to the top floor for an exhibition on ancient Chinese science.

Walk 1 Ancient and modern

Start Lotus Lane
Finish Olympic Forest Park
Length Ten kilometres (six miles)

Starting from the southern end of **Lotus Lane**, head anticlockwise around the right shore of Qianhai lake. A few hundred metres along there is a bridge across a canal running to the east – take a few minutes to look at the pair of handsome stone tigers which lie along its banks, pawing a stone ball which appears to be floating at water level.

Head north along the lake shore and turn left to cross the lake on **Silver Ingot Bridge** (Yinding Qiao), then skirt the west shore of Houhai, the middle lake. This part of the route goes past lots of bars, many of which have lakeside seating.

Follow the lake round, to the **canoe hire** bar on Houhai's north shore. If you want to see how Houhai looked before it became a full-blown bar district, then head over the main road to **Xihai**, the northernmost of the three lakes. Here the banks bristle with fishing poles as old men pass the day chatting, drinking and occasionally catching something.

Return to the canoe hire area and carry on clockwise around the lake, back to the eastern shore – here is a small park where people play chess and mahjong, while hardier souls swim all year round, even breaking the ice for a winter dip. The big gates facing the lake are the **Former Residence of Song Qingling**, a popular tourist attraction.

Head back around the lake, turning left at Yinding Bridge and then taking the first right, up **Yandaixiejie**, the street that once housed Beijing's pipe makers. At the end of the alley cross the main road and turn left towards the junction in front of the **Drum Tower**. You can go down either side of this building to gain access to the square that lies between it and the Bell Tower. It is possible to go up both towers but, as the southernmost of the two, the Drum Tower has the best views over old Beijing.

From the Bell Tower head north and then take a right down **Doufuchi Hutong** at the junction in front of a fruit market. Notice the carvings on either side of the doorsteps – these and the door lintels used to indicate the rank of the occupant of each courtyard house in Imperial times. At the second crossroads turn left and then take the second right, along Cheniandian Hutong and follow this alley across the main road, through the ornate arch that marks the entrance into the **Confucius Temple**. A hundred metres from the old academy where the road ends, cross the main road to enter the **Lama Temple**.

From the entrance to the Lama Temple on Yonghegong Dajie head north and cross under the Second Ring Road and go west on the road beside the canal. Just before the road passes underneath the second bridge, go up the ramp on your right and on to the cycle path that runs north alongside **Andingmenwai Dajie**.

After a couple of hundred metres you'll see the West gate of **Ditan Park** on your right. Continue north over the Third Ring Road and onto **Anding Lu**.

Take a left at **Beitucheng Donglu**, skirting the thin green park, and turn north (right) again at **Beichen Lu**.

On your left is the **Chinese Ethnic Cultural Park** – conspicuous by the fact it has crammed every variety of Chinese architecture into one development.

You are now on the edge of the **Olympic Forest Park**, Beijing's biggest green space. You should be able to see the 'Bird's Nest' and 'Ice Cube' – the **National Stadium** and **National Aquatic Centre** – ahead, rising above the trees and Olympic annexes.

The route ends here. The easiest way to return is by retracing your steps and following **Andingmenwai Dajie** south, all the way back to Dianmen Dajie, the road that runs to the south of Houhai; you can pick up Line 2 of the metro at the Andingmen station. By mid-2008 there should also be a metro line serving the Olympic sites.

From start to the Olympic site should take around two and a half to three hours; add at least an hour for stopping at the Lama Temple, and half an hour for other stops.

This is an ideal route for cyclists. For bike hire try Cycle China (12 Jingshan Dongjie, Dongcheng, 6402 5653, 139 1188 6424, www.cyclechina.com), opposite the East Gate of Jingshan Park. They give out a free cycling map.

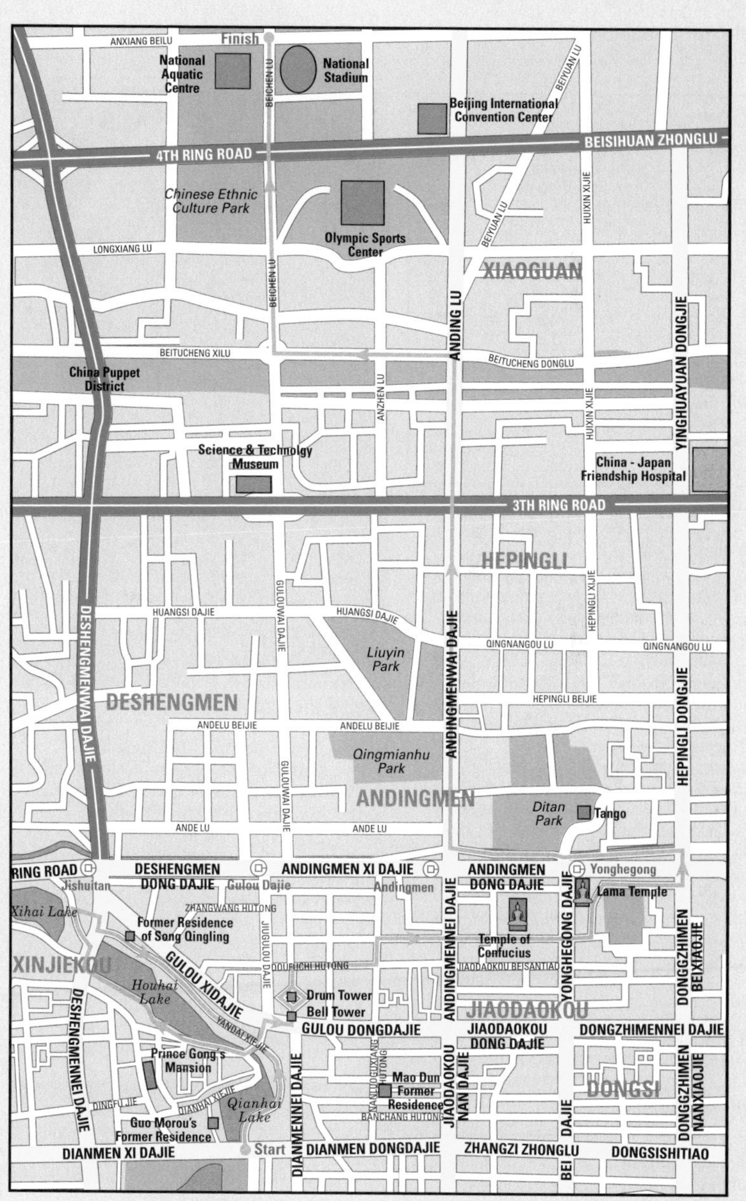

Finish
ANXIANG BEILU
National Aquatic Centre
National Stadium
BEICHEN LU
Beijing International Convention Center
BEIYUAN LU
4TH RING ROAD
BEISIHUAN ZHONGLU
Chinese Ethnic Culture Park
Olympic Sports Center
HUIXIN XIJIE
LONGXIANG LU
XIAOGUAN
ANDING LU
YINGHUAYUAN DONGJIE
BEITUCHENG XILU
BEITUCHENG DONGLU
China Puppet District
ANZHEN LU
Science & Technolgy Museum
China - Japan Friendship Hospital
3TH RING ROAD
HEPINGLI
HEPINGLI XIJIE
GULOUWAI DAJIE
HUANGSI DAJIE
DESHENGMENWAI DAJIE
Liuyin Park
QINGNANGOU LU
ANDINGMENWAI DAJIE
DESHENGMEN
HEPINGLI BEIJIE
HEPINGLI DONGJIE
ANDELU BEIJIE
Qingmianhu Park
ANDINGMEN
Ditan Park
Tango
ANDE LU
RING ROAD
DESHENGMEN DONG DAJIE
ANDINGMEN XI DAJIE
ANDINGMEN DONG DAJIE
Yonghegong
Jishuitan
Gulou Dajie
Andingmen
Lama Temple
ZHANGWANG HUTONG
Xihai Lake
Former Residence of Song Qingling
Temple of Confucius
DONGZHIMEN BEIXIAOJIE
YONGHEGONG DAJIE
XINJIEKOU
GULOU XIDAJIE
JIUGULOU DAJIE
DOUFUCHI HUTONG
JIAODAOKOU BEISANTIAO
Houhai Lake
Drum Tower
Bell Tower
ANDINGMENNEI DAJIE
JIAODAOKOU
YANDAI XIEJIE
GULOU DONGDAJIE
JIAODAOKOU DONG DAJIE
DONGZHIMENNEI DAJIE
DESHENGMENNEI DAJIE
Prince Gong's Mansion
NANLUOGUXIANG HUTONG
Mao Dun Former Residence
DONGSI
DINGFU JIE
JIANHAI XIEJIE
Qianhai Lake
BANCHANG HUTONG
JIAODAOKOU NAN DAJIE
BEI DAJIE
DONGGZHIMEN NANXIAOJIE
Guo Morou's Former Residence
Start
DIANMEN XI DAJIE
DIANMENNEI DAJIE
DIANMEN DONGDAJIE
ZHANGZI ZHONGLU
DONGSISHITIAO

Sightseeing

Chaoyang

Expats, embassies and electronics.

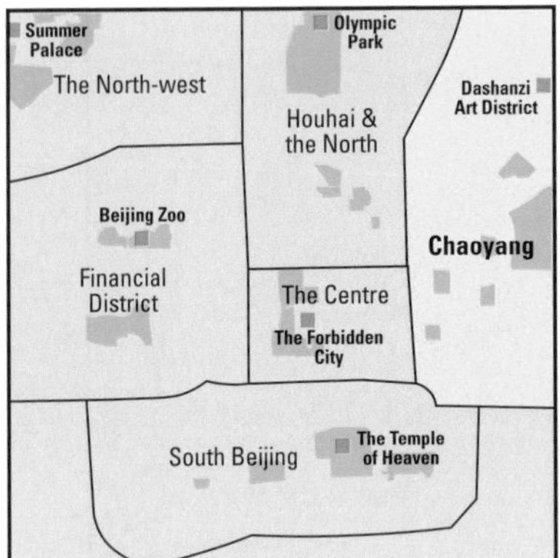

If capitalism is Beijing's new passion, then Chaoyang is its heart. Lying in the north-east of the city, the area is home to most of the international companies, embassies and news agencies that have flooded into the country in pursuit of profit and one billion consumers. As a result, Western-style bars stud Chaoyang, as do occidentally styled locals. This is not the part of Beijing to visit for a taste of the past, but if you want to see the Chinese giving the lie to Kipling's phrase that east and west shall never meet, the place is for you.

Covering 470.6 square kilometres (292 square miles) and having a population of 2.29 million, Chaoyang is the largest and most densely populated urban district in Beijing. The city's new Central Business District, as well as hundreds of skyscrapers, hotels and new technology areas, such as the electronic town in Jiuxianqiao and Wangjing industrial park, make it the base for new industry and commerce.

As new money has washed in, old Beijing has been cleaned out, so head here to shop, eat, drink and party.

GETTING THERE

Chaoyang is the fastest growing part of Beijing and the public transport system is struggling to keep up with growth. Dongsishitiao Metro Station, beside the Poly Theatre, is the nearest station to the Workers' Stadium and the Sanlitun area, and the nearby Dongzhimen Station is a good starting point for the Guijie food street. Chaoyangmen Station stops by the Dongyue Temple, and Guomao Station stops right at the main Guomao Shopping Mall in the centre of the Central Business District.

The airport express road runs from the airport, passing Dashanzi and through Dongzhimen, to the Second Ring Road, making for a useful route through Chaoyang. Not particularly pedestrian friendly, at least this is one part of Beijing where you never have to wait long for a taxi.

▶ For key sights and streets in Chaoyang in **Chinese script**, *see pp252-255.*

Beijing Blue Zoo. *See p67.*

Gongti

Unlike Shanghai, Beijing has never been known as a party city. But you know what? Work hard, play hard could be the capital's new motto, and nowhere is this better shown than in the area around the **Workers' Stadium** (known as Gongti in Chinese, *see p192*). Over the last few years an active nightclub scene has built up on the south and west side of the stadium, and nearly all Beijing's mega-clubs can be found here. Gay club Destination (*see p167*) and several high-end lounge bars such as Face (*see p125*) and the Bank (*see p178*) have ensured the area remains the nightlife king. To keep the clubbers fed there are 24-hour restaurants including Bellagio (*see p104*) and Three Guizhou Men (*see p108*). Daytime brings bus loads of tourists to the stadium's north gate for Yashow Market (*see p131*), all eager to stock up on dubious denims and dodgy DVDs.

The Workers' Stadium itself was built in 1959 as a multipurpose venue and is home to Beijing's Guo'an football team as well as being the venue for major sporting occasions and music concerts. It's currently being refurbished for the Olympics and is due to reopen in August 2007, when it will host the quarter- and semi-finals of the local football cup competition. A block to the west of the Workers' Stadium is the Workers' Gymnasium (Gongti Bei Lu, 6501 6300), a smaller indoor arena that will host the boxing events for the 2008 Olympics.

At the south gate of the Workers' Stadium is the **Beijing Blue Zoo**, the largest walk-through aquarium in Asia.

Beijing Blue Zoo

Gongti Nanmen (Workers' Stadium South Gate) (6593 5263). Metro Chaoyangmen. **Open** 8am-8pm daily. **Admission** RMB 75, RMB 50 students. **No credit cards**. **Map** p244 N8.

Go to see fish from all over the world in China's largest aquarium or, if you call in advance, you can even go swimming with dolphins or sharks. With professional staff and a recent renovation, and over 6,000 sea creatures, the Blue Zoo is a good way to spend an afternoon in Beijing with children. **Photo** *p66.*

Sanlitun

Only a few minutes' walk north of the Workers' Stadium is Sanlitun – Beijing's most famous bar area. Before 1949 the Legation Quarter near Tiananmen Square was the centre of diplomatic activity, but in the '50s it was moved outside the city centre to what is now known as Sanlitun. The large number of embassies and foreigners working in the nearby UN building encouraged entrepreneurs to open the first Western style bars and restaurants and today Sanlitun has become a popular bar street for foreigners as well as locals – Bar Blu (*see p124*) and the Tree (*see p127*) are among the more popular hangouts.

However, much of its original charm has been lost as street hawkers, prostitutes, small time drug dealers and beggars plague the area –

Snap!

Until recently, most people in China had never left the province they were born in. Transport was expensive, and travel was restricted. Now people get around, and to take a picture inside a plane cabin, or at one of Beijing's landmarks – better yet, one featuring a Westerner – is evidence to show people back home that you've made that trip of a lifetime. Barely 20 years ago, most key sights were littered with photo booths. The only way people could preserve their memories was to pay someone else to take a photo. Now many own a camera or camcorder – as a nation used to being part of a group becomes more individualistic, these photos are an expression of that. Chinese albums are full of smiling faces declaring: 'I exist, I went here'.

So put up with the whirring shutters – and if that village woman from Hunan wants you to pose with her baby in the Forbidden City, why not do it: she'll get some kudos and you'll have experienced a real Chinese encounter in a city where tourists often feel disconnected.

Sightseeing

especially in summer months when the tourists are in town. The main bar street is occupied mainly by Chinese-style bars dedicated to separating visitors from their money. Avoid these and head down the back streets for the more entertaining venues.

North of the main strip and on the other side of Dongzhimen, behind the German and Australian embassies, is a quaint quarter of tree-lined shady streets more reminiscent of Shanghai than Beijing. There is a smattering of mid-price Western and Asian restaurants – some with beautiful roof gardens – as well as an increasing number of boutique shops. Further east, where Dongzhimenwai Dajie meets the Third Ring Road, is the **Agricultural Museum**.

Despite the less than family-friendly characters that hang out around Sanlitun Jiubajie – literally Sanlitun Bar Street – it's still the first and main bar area of Beijing and one of the most popular spots to head to for a night out. The New Sanlitun Mall and the 3.3 Shopping Centre (*see p137*) are both worth a visit during the day to pick up some one-off pieces that can't be found at nearby Yashow Market. Nali Market just to the east of the main street is home to some clean and bright cafés and shops selling ethnic jewellery, affordable shoes, bags and clothes.

Agricultural Museum

16 Dong Sanhuan Bei Lu, Chaoyang (6509 6067). **Open** 9am-4pm Tue-Sun. **Admission** RMB 10. **No credit cards**. **Map** p245 P7.

For those interested in ancient agriculture, and farming in China goes back a long way, then this is a must. There are 10,000 artefacts dating from the neolithic age until the 1840s on display. Check before going though, as the museum is closed until 2008.

Nurenjie (Ladies' Street)

Nurenjie, just north of the Third Ring Road and behind the very swish Kempinski and Lufthansa hotels, is a rather confused mishmash of bright lights, dirty streets and a rancid lake. Nevertheless the bars, shops and market here are worth investigating. Far from picturesque, it does house some of the better markets in town, the best of which is **Laitai Flower Market** (*see p130*), in the middle of Nurenjie, just south of the main road – the largest wholesale flower market in the city. Until recently flowers were most commonly given at funerals, but the last decade has seen giving flowers as gifts become popular. Laitai and its smaller neighbour, **Liangma Flower Market** (*see p130*), (continue east along Nurenjie and it's just to the south) are the two places for the best blooms.

Below Ladies' Street is a subterranean market catering to – you guessed it – women. Bags, clothes, nailshops and a variety of other stalls sell everything a girl can need. Nurenjie is home to a string of small private shops selling everything from furniture to clothes, goldfish to car parts.

If you can be bothered to sift through the tat, then you are likely to find a couple of really nice one-off articles. Avoid Super Bar Street (Xinba Lu) – it's got lots of bars but drinking warm beer looking at a fetid lake falls short when it comes to living up to the 'super' bit.

With the **International Exhibition Centre** just down the road and the American and Israeli embassies having moved to the area, speculators have begun to open a couple of fairly decent restaurants and bars. Things can only get better.

Super Bar Street isn't.

Chaoyangmen

Running the entire length of Chaoyangmen Avenue the Chaowai area is all about bright lights and tall buildings. However, among these new temples to mammon there lurks a temple to an older faith: the **Dongyue Temple**, the largest Taoist Temple of the Zhengyi school of Taoism in China. Around 1,000 of the 3,000 statues that it is famous for still stand and the stone tablets – the largest collection in Beijing – give the area a graveyard feel. Of the 90 stones still remaining, the most impressive is the tablet inscribed in 1329 by Zhao Mengfu, one of the 'Four Calligraphers' of the Yuan Dynasty.

South of Chaoyangmen on Guanghua Lu is The Place (*see p129*), the latest shopping mall. Best of all is the huge Chaoyang Park with an amusement park and boating lake, and grass you can walk on.

Chaoyang Park

Chaoyang Gongyuan 1 Nongzhan Nan Lu, Chaoyang (6506 5409). **Open** 6.30am-9pm daily. **Admission** RMB 5. **No credit cards**. **Map** p245 Q7.

Chaoyang Park – the largest urban public park in Asia – is almost unique in allowing people to kick a ball about or picnic *on the grass* in the summer. Plenty of tree cover as well as some wonderful public sports facilities, including dozens of basketball and football pitches, mean this is a great place to hang out in the warmer months. The amusement park and boating lake are great for outdoor fun and Choayang Park is also the venue for many events.

Dongyue Temple

141 Chaoyangmenwai Street, (500 metres east of Chaoyangmen subway station), Chaoyang (6551 0151/6551 4148). Metro Chaoyangmen. **Open** 8.30am-4.30pm Tue-Sun. **Admission** RMB 10. **No credit cards**. **Map** p244 N8.

It was Zhang Liusun, the descendant of the founder of the 'Tradition of the Celestial Master of the Mighty Commonwealth of Orthodox Oneness' sect of Taoism, Zhang Daoling, who first went fund raising to build this temple. He managed to buy the land and was given the title of Grand Taoist Master at the end of the 13th century, but died just as the construction started. The temple was completed and ultimately founded by Zhang's disciple Wu Quanjie in 1319; it was repaired by Ming Emperor Yingzong in 1447, before being further expanded in the late 17th century. After serving as a school, a residential compound and a government office until 1996, it underwent extensive refurbishment in 2002 and the temple now looks a little too new to be taken seriously, with brightly coloured statues looming over the visitor. Death – the theme of the temple – it seems, is as beset by bureaucracy as life. First pass through the 'Department of Suppressing Schemes', before moving on to the 'Department of Wandering Ghosts', and watch out for the 'Department for Fifteen Kinds of Violent Death'.

Ritan Park area

North of Jianguomen and south of Chaowai is the Ritan area – named after **Ritan Park**, the Temple of the Sun and one of the four famous Temple Parks. Also known locally as 'little Moscow' expect to find plenty of tall blond women drenched in fur being ferried around by rickshaw drivers. The Alien Market on Yaba Lu is a great place to find the most obscure items, or to get kitted out for Hallowe'en and mainly sells knock-offs to Russian tourists. The district is also the other main embassy area and boasts a wide selection of markets including the Silk Market (*see p131*) as well as the Russian market on Ritan Lu that predominantly sells furs to those tall blond women.

Making a song and dance of it in **Ritan Park**.

Ritan Park

6 Ritan Bei Lu, Chaoyang (8563 5038). Metro Jianguomen. **Open** 6am-8pm daily. **Admission** free. **No credit cards**. **Map** p244 N9.

Ritan Park – the Temple of Sun – is one of the four royal shrines, and is the altar of the Sun. Built in 1530 it was used by Ming and Qing Emperors to make sacrifices to the gods. But now Ritan is one of Beijing's more peaceful parks. Certainly not as impressive or lively as the Temple of Heaven, Ritan is one of the best spots to see old folk practise t'ai chi, swordplay or twirling napkins in the morning without hordes of tourists flooding the place. Stop in for a rest at the Stone Boat Café (*see p127*) or one of the other restaurants surrounding the park.

Central Business District (CBD)

High-rises, designer shops and five-star hotels are splattered around the hundreds of modern office buildings that make up the new CBD. Beijing's eastern skyline is dominated by the twin towers of the **World Trade Centre** and **Jinwai Soho** (39 Dong Sanhuan Lu). The latter, built by property tycoon celeb couple Pan Shiyi and Zhang Xin, is the fourth mega city of home/offices that takes the Soho name. This one boasts a plethora of shops and fancy restaurants catering for the white-collar workers who live and work in the modern units. Until recently it had a rather ghost town air to it, but as more enterprises open shop the atmosphere has begun to improve. Due to be completed for the Olympic Games, the new **CCTV Building** (32 Dongsanhuanzhong Lu) will be the architectural highlight of the area – architect Rem Koolhaas's 230-metre (755-foot) building is costing US$728 million and will provide some 550,000 square metres (136 acres) of space for news production, broadcasting and administration of the state TV company CCTV. Rather than the standard Asian billionaire's phallic tower, the structure is a Möbius-like loop generating a huge open space beneath it.

The whole CBD area didn't exist a decade ago – building began in 1997 – an amazing feat when you see Beijing's Manhattan staring down at you. Very little remnains of the past except for Tuanjie Lake Park, a mere drop in the concrete ocean. This area is great for fashionistas to pick up the designer goods but offers little for the budget tourist.

Tuanjie Lake Park

16 Tuanjiehu Nanli, Chaoyang (8597 3603). **Open** 6am-9pm daily. **Admission** free. **Map** p245 P8.

Not a patch on the lake areas of Houhai Tuanjie Lake Park is one of ten man-made lakes in Beijing. Built in the Suzhou style of landscape gardening, it is more manicured than many of Beijing's other lakes and worth a romantic evening stroll.

World Trade Centre

1 Jianguomenwai Dajie, Chaoyang (6505 6688). **Open** 9.30am-9.30pm daily. **Map** p245 010.

Slap bang in the middle of the CBD are the twin towers of the World Trade Centre. It is here that China's new millionaires are made, and no doubt some of that money is provided by shoppers in what is also one of Beijing's best malls. A host of restaurants, cafés, bookshops and delis provide sustenance, and the centre is also home to an indoor ice rink.

Lido & 798 Art District

The north-east corridor from the city centre to the airport has been one of the fastest growing residential areas in recent years and the Lido Holiday Inn Hotel is its hub, with new bars, shops, restaurants and spas opening around it. Lido Park, opposite the hotel, has a small lake surrounded by tree-lined gardens with cafés offering a pleasant pit stop, while Si De Park just to the south of the hotel offers great sports facilities and is very family friendly.

Just to the north, and surrounded by new overpasses and the light rail to the airport, is the entrance to the 798 Art District. It looks as inconspicuous as many another compound entrances on the outskirts of Beijing, but guarding the entrance stands a six-metre (20-foot) 'village elder' greeting visitors to China's most avant-garde art district. The graffiti that covers many of the Bauhaus-style buildings juxtaposes with the Cultural Revolution slogans in peeling red paint, wishing Chairman Mao '10,000 years of long life'. The tree-lined streets walled off from the urban sprawl are home to the biggest collection of galleries and studios in China.

Built in the 1950s by the East Germans, the 640,000-square-metre (158-acre) space was a top-secret weapons factory rumoured to be where electronic components for guided missiles were built. Originally called Joint Factory 718 (all military factories started with the number 7) it was split into more manageable sub-factories in the '60s, of which 798 was the biggest and the name it is most commonly known by today. During the '80s, as state-owned assets were sold off, the land was put under the control of the Seven Stars Huadian Science and Technology Group, and by the late '90s many of the huge edifices were empty. During the same time a group of independent artists – unpopular with the communist government – were evicted from their commune at the Old Summer Palace where they had been living for almost a decade. Looking for a new area to call home they came across 798. Dean of Sculpture at the China Academy of Fine Arts, Sui Jianguo, got permission to use the well-lit factories, before opening his studio in 2000. Scores of artists and designers moved in, restaurants and bars followed, and a new living-working-latte-drinking neighbourhood was born.

In 2005, it seemed the area was under threat as the Seven Stars group realised the real estate value of the land. However, lobbyists, persuaded the district and Beijing government to make 798 a cultural showcase in the run up to the Olympics and it was saved from developers – at least until after 2008. But with rising rental costs many artists have been forced to move further out of town and some critics claim that the area has begun to sell out. 798 founder Huang Rui was recently controversially evicted from the district and with Seven Stars Group taking a more proactive role there are fears that the while 798 is only just beginning as a cultural hub, the utopian ideal of an artists' village may be coming to an end.

Beyond the Fifth Ring Road is the blooming Wangjing area – home to a large Korean population. Wangjing's Liquor Factory is fast becoming a new art district and large retail outlets such as Ikea are also springing up here. Beijing continues to grow outwards in concentric rings, but it is the north and east that are growing fastest. Shunyi is like an enclave of California with large villas being built for Western families and affluent Chinese. Songzhuang and Caochangdi are also artist villages, and – with lower rents and less tourists than 798 – are gaining a reputation for more experimental work. See the **Galleries** chapter, and in particular, the map and listings on pp162-163, for more information about the avant-garde art scene.

798 Art District.

South Beijing

Temples of heaven, cranes of hell.

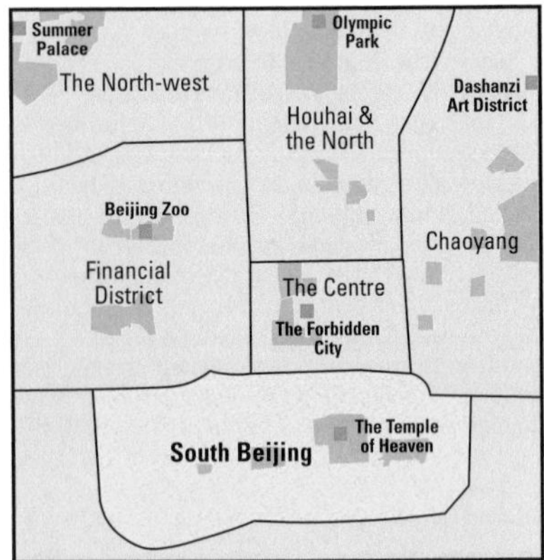

When the Manchurian army invaded Beijing in 1644 to found the Qing Dynasty the Han Chinese residents were forcibly relocated to the south of the city, while the north was reserved for Manchu nobles and hereditary military officials, known as the Banners. This led to the south having a more organic street pattern than the rectangular grid north of Changanjie that the Manchus imposed – and that is still evident. Away from the Imperial Palaces and gardens of the north, the south has always been the poorer side of the city and, unlike the modern north of Beijing, remains comparatively undeveloped.

With a slower pace of life, friendly south Beijing is how the north was a decade ago – don't expect to see glamorous women with designer bags here. People still stop, stare and shout hello at visitors before asking to have their photo taken with the foreigner. The south doesn't have the glitzy modern architecture or the style of the north, but there is an old world charm that offers a glimpse of what life might have been like in Imperial China.

The area is broken up into three main districts: Xuanwu, south-west of the centre, Chongwen, to the south-east and – beyond the Third Ring Road and of no interest to visitors – Fengtai in the far south-west.

GETTING THERE

South Beijing is one of the most pleasant parts of town to stroll around and the main areas of interest can be walked to on foot over several hours. From Tiananmen, keep heading south on foot to get to Qianmen and from there, it is easy to walk through the hutong from Dazhalan to the mosque, taking in Liulichang and Fayuan Temple in just a few hours.

A bike ride makes the same route quicker and just as pleasant and it's easier to reach the further out Tianning Temple to the west. If you are on two wheels, it is only a short ride south-east from Qianmen to the Temple of Heaven, or there are plenty of buses that will take you to the Temple. Qianmen is the starting and ending point for the majority of buses in town, so from here, you can set off in any direction. Take the 803 bus for the temple's South Gate. The Qianmen metro stop is the best place to start journeys into the south-east or south-west or north on to Tiananmen. Chongwenmen station in the east is the nearest to the Temple of Heaven and Hepingli station is only a short walk from Liulichang Market.

Xuanwu district

Xuanwu district has traditionally been the home of the lower classes and trading guilds, shop workers and factory workers. It was the commercial area that existed just outside the original city wall. But just because there isn't a Starbucks on every corner doesn't mean that the area is an unspoilt ideal of old Beijing. Much of the cityscape is dominated by Soviet-style apartment blocks and the wonderful maze of hutongs is being destroyed at an alarming rate (*see p75* **Out with the old**).

However, getting lost amid the remaining hutongs is a wonderful way to spend a morning and a highlight of a visit to Beijing that might not be possible in a few years. You can walk from the Cultural Street of Liulichang, through the former red light district of Bada Hutong, to the famous hutongs of Qianmen and Dazhalan. This is one of the few parts of Beijing where walking is enjoyable rather than a chore, and it's possible to also visit **Fayuan Temple**, **Beijing Mosque** and even **Tianning Temple** within a couple of hours on foot.

From the starting point of Qianmen, the **Laoshe Teahouse** is a great place to soak up some traditional Chinese culture before heading to the **Museum of Ancient Architecture**, where you can catch a glimpse of how the city

Welcome to **Beijing Mosque**. *See p74.*

used to be. Continue south and you will hit Beijing's oldest public park, **Taoranting Garden**. The devotion at Catholic **Nantang Church** to the east of Qianmen shows that, despite the communists' best efforts, religion is not dead in this officially atheist country.

Cultural Street of Liulichang to Qianmen

From Hepingmen Metro walk south down Nan Xinhua Lu to Liulichang.

First built in the Yuan Dynasty (1271-1368) south of the Peace Gate, Liulichang means coloured glaze factory and it was where tiles were made for the palaces and temples of the city. Luilichang became a hangout for scholars preparing for the Imperial exams; to make ends meet they would peddle calligraphy and writings. Soon, stores selling art materials sprang up as other shops opened to sell the works of the impecunious students. It wasn't long before tailors, cobblers, pharmacies and shops made this the main shopping centre of the Qing Dynasty.

In recent years Liulichang has been redeveloped and given the moniker 'Culture Street', meaning that, like so much of Beijing, government tinkering has added a theme park feel to the area and removed much of the organic nature that gave the area charm and attracted visitors in the first place. But the brightly coloured façades of the shops, the paved streets and the low-rise buildings are a great place to browse for Mao memorabilia, tea, jade, books, trinkets, small antiques and Buddhist statuary, as well as calligraphy brushes and wall hangings. As usual, haggling is a must and don't expect the antiques to be genuine, but this is a good spot to pick up souvenirs and gifts. Rongbaozhai Bookshop (No.19, behind the first courtyard as you head north) is China's most famous art supplies store and has a wonderful mix of old Chinese and foreign-language books. Make sure to get off the main strips and into the surrounding hutongs. Nan Xinhua Lu is a good place to get your bearings, and the central point where Liulichang Xi Lu meets Dong Lu.

At the end of Liulichang Dong Lu pass through the hutongs heading south-east and you will come across Dazhalan – another collection of hutongs that is home to the city's oldest commercial shopping district. Here you'll find the same shops selling the same goods that

▶ For key sights and streets in South Beijing in **Chinese script**, *see pp252-255.*

they have been offering for hundreds of years, together with, of course, fake watches, trainers and North Face jackets. Ruifuxiang Choubu Dian at No.5 Dazhalan has been in the silk trade since 1893 and is still a great place to pick up a tailored *qipao*, whereas Tongrentang (No.24 Dazhalan, 6303 1155) is probably the most famous of all. It first began selling Chinese medicine to emperors and public alike in 1669. Just north of Dazhalan is Bada Hutong – literally the eight big hutongs. Bada was Beijing's largest red light district from the 18th century until 21 November 1949 (just over a month after the founding of the Peoples Republic of China), when 3,000 troops marched into the area 'freeing' 1,290 prostitutes. A 1908 survey had earlier revealed 308 brothels in the area, and entertainment ranging from ladies of the night serving the masses to 'flower girls' reciting poetry. Local street-side 'hair salons' still exist, but it is the quiet Old City hutongs that makes the place worth a morning stroll.

Beijing Mosque

88 Niujie Guanganmennei, Xuanwu (6353 2564). **Open** 8am-6pm daily. **Admission** RMB 10. **No credit cards. Map** p241 H12.

Museum of Natural History. *See p77.*

China isn't known for its diverse religions, but there are in fact around 80 mosques in Beijing and the Ox Street Mosque is the largest of them all. Islam has been active in China for over a millennium. Originally built (in wood) by Nasruddin, the son of an Arabic cleric who came to China to preach the Islamic faith in 996, the traditional Islamic architectural style has been diluted over the centuries to such an extent that there is little recognisably Islamic about it any more. If it wasn't for the many white-hatted Muslims who come to pray daily it would be hard to differentiate from a Chinese Temple. Pretty much the only Muslim relics at the mosque on Ox Street are those of two ancient imams dating from the 13th century that lie in catacombs in the east wing. The legend goes that any non-believer who enters the prayer hall will be killed by a hail of ball bearings fired off by the reawakened imams, thus sending the kafir to meet Allah. **Photo** *p73.*

Fayuan Temple

7 Fayuansi Qianjie (walk west down Nanheng Xijie and the temple is just off the main road halfway down), Nanheng Xijie, Xuanwu. **Open** 8.30-11am, 1.30-4pm Mon, Tue, Thur-Sun. **Admission** RMB 5. **No credit cards. Map** p241 H12.

A short walk south-west of Luilichang and hidden down a hutong not far from Ox Street is a quiet and secluded temple famous for its clove trees and numerous ancient gingko trees. The oldest surviving temple in Beijing, Fayuan Temple, was built during the Tang Dynasty in 645 to commemorate soldiers lost in battle. However, it has been destroyed and rebuilt many times since then, falling prey to war, fire and earthquake, and much of what you see today was built in the early 18th century. During the Qing Dynasty it was converted to a Buddhist temple, where in 1956 the Chinese Buddhist Academy was founded.

Fayuan Temple is a gem – it's both wonderfully peaceful and tranquil, yet active, with a lively Buddhist community. Monks dressed in flowing yellow robes pass quietly through the six main buildings as young boys, barely teenagers, sit in the sun, cross-legged in their robes reciting scriptures. It's refreshing to see an active temple with Buddhist worshippers who make their way to pray in front of the huge reclining Buddha in the final temple rather than just another tourist attraction.

Laoshe Teahouse

3 Qianmen Xi Dajie, Qianmen, Xuanwu (6303 6830). Metro Qianmen. **Open** 8.30am-9.30pm daily. **Credit** AmEx, DC, MC, V. **Map** p241 J11.

Although something of a tourist trap, Laoshe Teahouse is worth popping into for a cup of tea and to catch a performance of one of the classic Chinese arts. The massive 2,600sq m (28,000sq ft) teahouse is decked out old-Beijing-style, and aims to give visitors a taste of 'real Beijing' by serving snacks of the type Qing Dynasty patrons would have munched on. Tea comes with a performance of various folk arts, dramas and musicals – prices rise for evening shows.

Out with the old

Beijing has been burnt down, destroyed in war, damaged by earthquakes and ravaged by the changing of each dynasty. More recently the Red Guards of the Cultural Revolution spent their days chopping the heads off Buddhas, burning books and smashing religious relics. Many old buildings, homes and temples were destroyed – even the 500-year-old Ming Dynasty city walls and gates were replaced with the Second Ring Road in the 1950s. Today many of the buildings that give character to the city – the hutongs – are being bulldozed to make way for anonymous skyscrapers and city infrastructure in the run-up to the Olympics.

Beijing's hutongs are intricate maze-like lanes, made up of courtyard houses built with incredible attention to detail in accordance with the principles of feng shui. Hutong is a Mongolian word meaning water well, indicating that homes like these were built around wells since the 13th century. Due to the imperial rule that no building should be higher than the palaces, these low-level buildings spread out from the Forbidden City, creating a large part of the physical landscape of the city. More importantly, hutongs formed the social framework of the city. With several families living in close proximity, using communal courtyards and toilets, the community network and support system was very tight. Still today in the hutongs of south Beijing and around Houhai, men drink beer on the streets while watching the world go by as women gossip and knit, and children chase and kick balls off the walls of the narrow alleys.

But increasingly, sprayed on the wall of a hutong in white paint, is the character 'chai' – demolish. The increase in land prices, combined with the urgent need for further infrastructure, has led to large swathes of hutongs being destroyed to make way for road expansion and new property developments. With almost no legal tenants' rights, combined with the rampant corruption of officials and property developers, land is cleared with almost no concern for either the heritage being destroyed or the people who once lived there. Residents are often offered paltry compensation and have to move outside the city – forced evictions are not uncommon, with families protesting and even using suicide as a tool to be heard.

Records show that there were 3,679 hutongs in the 1980s. That figure has dropped by over 40 per cent, with up to 600 hutongs destroyed each year. Homes, shops and restaurants have all been demolished, most notably in the south of Beijing around Qianmen and Dazhalan – home to some of the most interesting and famous hutongs in the city. Although the government has said it will protect a few dozen of the older hutongs, we can only hope there will be some left by 2008.

There are also daily performances of Peking Opera, drama and acrobatics, with other high profile events held at the venue on occasion.

Museum of Ancient Architecture

21 Dongjing Lu, Xuanwu (6301 7620). **Open** 9am-4pm daily. **Admission** RMB 15. **No credit cards.** **Map** p246 J12.

This fascinating museum features a large model of old Beijing and exhibits traditional architecture – a glimpse of life before the bulldozers came to the city. The museum is at the site of the Xiannong altar where Qing emperors performed ceremonies during the lunar spring equinox.

Nantang Church

141 Qianmen Xi Dajie, Xuanwu (6603 7139). Metro Xuanwumen. **Open** 8.30am-4pm daily. **Admission** free. **Map** p241 H10.

Known also as the Catholic Cathedral, the Cathedral of the Immaculate Conception and St Mary's, Nantang Church was first built in the middle of the 16th century before being rebuilt in 1657 during the Qing Dynasty. A tablet in the grounds reads 'Cathedral Built by Imperial Order', but communist China does not recognise the authority of the Vatican and only accepts priests ordained into the official church, known as the Chinese Catholic Patriotic Association. Catholicism was first brought to China by Italian missionary Matteo Ricci in 1601, who lived just west of this site. The largest church in Beijing, Mass is said daily from 6am to 8.30am in Latin and Chinese, on Saturdays at 6.30pm and five times on Sundays (English at 10am and 4pm) to around 2,000 worshippers.

Taoranting Garden

19 Taipingjie, Xuanwu (6353 5704). **Open** 6am-8pm daily. **Admission** RMB 2. **No credit cards.** **Map** p246 J12.

Until 1911 parks were predominantly the domain of the emperor and his family, but Taoranting Garden was one of the few open to the public. The Taoran Pavilion, from which the park gets its name, is the focal point of the park and where writers, academics and poets would meet. As one of the four famous pavilions (the others being in Changsha, Chuzhou and Hangzhou), it is part of the Cibei Temple (Temple of Mercy), built in the Yuan Dynasty.

Tianning Temple & Pagoda (Temple of Heavenly Rest)

2 Tianningsi Qianjie, Guanganmenwai Dajie, (West bank of Hucheng River), Xuanwu. (6343 2507).
Open 8am-1pm on the 1st and 15th day of Chinese lunar calendar. **Admission** free. **Map** p240 F11.
This beautiful Buddhist pagoda would look more at home in a small southern town than the bustling outskirts of Beijing. The stupa was built during the reign of Emperor Xiaowen of the Northern Wei Dynasty (386-543). That's a whopping 1,600 years old! The 60m (198ft) pagoda was added a mere 1,000 years ago during the Liao Dynasty (907-1125). Wonderful relief sculptures adorn the four sides of the first storey above layers of massive lotus petals that support the 13 tiers of eves that make this a great example of Liao architecture. If it's not open on the day you visit, it's still clearly visible from the road.

Chongwen district

Most famous for the Temple Of Heaven, Chongwen district is also home to two of the city's best markets – China's biggest pearl market at **Hongqiao** and the antique market at **Panjiayuan** (*see p130*). The **Museum of Natural History** has a host of interactive displays while **Longtan Park** (8 Longtan Lu, 6714 4336) is divided by Zuoanmen Dajie, with **Beijing Amusement Park** (1 Zuoanmen Dajie, 6714 3611) taking up most of the western side of the park.

Temple of Heaven.

Temple of Heaven

After the Great Wall and the Forbidden City, the Temple of Heaven is probably the most famous of Beijing's landmarks and arguably the most interesting. The finest architecturally and the most active of all Beijing's temples, a morning spent strolling around the impressive park is a must for any visitor.

Built by the Yongle Emperor in 1420 at the same time as the Forbidden City, the Temple of Heaven was one of the four sacrificial temples of the emperors – the others being the Temples of Sun, Moon and Earth. But it was this temple that was the most important and it was here that all Ming and Qing Emperors performed sacrificial rites at each winter solstice.

Built according to strict religious principles, with perfect symmetry and covered in dark blue tiles representing heaven, every detail of the architecture is built in nines – the number that represented the emperor. Originally the temple was known as the Temple of Heaven and Earth and so a perfect square park was built to the south, and a semicircular park to the north – as earth was symbolised by long and square, heaven was symbolised by high and round. However, during the Cultural Revolution two large chunks were taken out of the south-east and south-west corners of the square, southern half of the park, ruining its symmetry. But this hasn't really affected the park and there's still plenty of space to explore.

The structure is divided into three main parts with the South Gate being the natural starting point of any visit to the temple, that culminates at the incredible Hall of Prayer for Good Harvest – perhaps the most impressive architectural structure in Beijing.

As you enter from the south the Circular Altar is the first building you come across – a massive three-tiered marble terrace first built in 1530 and expanded in 1749. It was on top of the nine balustrades that bulls were slaughtered and burnt in sacrifice. North of the Circular Altar is the Imperial Vault of Heaven where ceremonial stone tablets were kept – sadly these were destroyed in the Cultural Revolution by Red Guards. It is this vault that is surrounded by the circular Echo Wall. Here you can stand diametrically opposed and still hear the whispers of your conversation partner 65 metres (213 feet) away. However, the crowds and railings mean that it is now next to impossible to use, unless you arrive at the crack of dawn before the tourists.

Take a detour to the west of the circular altar to see the Hall of Abstinence, where emperors fasted and prayed for five days, with the last night spent in the Living Hall at the back of the compound. If you look closely you can see rare swastikas – meaning longevity in China – on the doors of the piers. The green tiled compound faces east, which is the best side to enter from before returning to the main strip.

Continue straight over from the Imperial Vault along the main road called Danbi Bridge and you will see the most beautiful building in Beijing: the circular, wooden Hall of Prayer for Good Harvests with its triple-eaved cylindrical blue tiled roof. Built in 1420 it was burned to the ground in 1889 after being struck by lightning – not a good omen for the Qing Emperor – but a perfect replica was made the following year. Impressively, this building, which is 38 metres (125 feet) high and 30 meters (98 feet) in diameter, was made without the use of a single nail. As China lacked timber of such length the 28 pillars were imported from Oregon. The central four timbers represent the seasons, the following 12 the months of the year while the final 12 mark the divisions of a single day. Check out the ceiling that has some of the most intricately painted panels in China.

To the west is the Pavilion of Longevity – a wooden structure built in 1741 by Emperor Qian Long to celebrate his mother's 50th birthday. It is here, and to the east by the Long Corridor, that one can spend several hours watching improvised performances of Peking Opera, huge crowds singing classical Chinese songs from printed song sheets, musicians playing the stringed Erhu, and old folk playing cards and mahjong. Early in the morning the park is packed with t'ai chi practitioners, creating a more authentic Chinese atmosphere than almost anywhere in the city.

Temple of Heaven (Tiantan Gongyuan)

Yongdingmen Donjie (for the South Gate), Chongwen (6702 8866). Metro Chongwenmen. **Open** *Summer* 8am-6pm daily; *Winter* 8am-5pm daily. **Admission** *Summer* RMB 15; *Winter* RMB 10. **No credit cards. Map** p241 L12.

Qianmen

In the heart of the old town Qianmen, meaning front gate, was the doorway to Beijing. The gate itself was built in 1419 and rebuilt with German advice in 1914, but it is the surrounding area rather than the gate that people come to see. A busy shopping area evolved just outside of the front gate. Qianmen is still a bustling part of the city, where shops merge with hutongs, and a good place for a stroll. In recent years most of the hutongs of Qianmen have been destroyed (*see p75* **Out with the old**), but some remain, so catch it while you can. But be warned: this is a prime place for tourists to be ripped off, so make sure you bargain hard and don't end up paying RMB 100 for a bowl of RMB 5 noodles.

You won't be ripped off at Quanjude (*see p114*), Beijing's most famous restaurant, but the food doesn't really live up to its renown. On the other hand, the almost unknown **Underground City** is well worth a visit.

Museum of Natural History

126 Tianqiao Nan Dajie, Chongwen (6702 4431). **Open** 8.30am-4pm daily. **Admission** RMB 30; RMB 15 children. **No credit cards. Map** p241 K12.
Race a bike against your choice of dinosaur, pose for a photo next to a T Rex's foot and put together a dino-bone jigsaw: this museum is full of hands-on fun for children. Only a few of the exhibits sport English-language signs, but the fine displays ameliorate this drawback. The third floor famously houses three pickled human cadavers wearing hoods that look like the victims of a botched kidnapping. **Photo** *p74*.

Underground City

62 Xi Damochanjie, Qianmen (6702 2657). **Open** 8.30am-5.30pm daily. **Tickets** RMB 20. **No credit cards. Map** p241 L11.
Fearing attack by the Russians, Mao ordered 70,000 labourers to build an underground city capable of holding 40% of the city's population. Today, only one public entrance to the underground city remains (there used to be 3), and the short tour led by women in army fatigues gives just a glimpse of this bizarre part of Beijing's infrastructure. It is thought government leaders used it to get around the city during the Cultural Revolution and the army utilised the tunnels during 1989's Tiananmen incident.
Directions: Emerging from Chongwenmen subway station, exit D, take the first left down Qinian Dajie and cross the road where you'll see the China Construction Bank. Take the hutong down the left side of the bank and you'll see the entrance, marked by a traditional wooden doorway and black sign, about 300m (980ft) down on the left hand side. Alternatively, make your way to the Zhangyi Lu intersection, where during the morning you'll find pedicab drivers asking if you want to go to the underground city. Approx cost around RMB 10 for two people.

Financial District

Where flow the old canals and the new money.

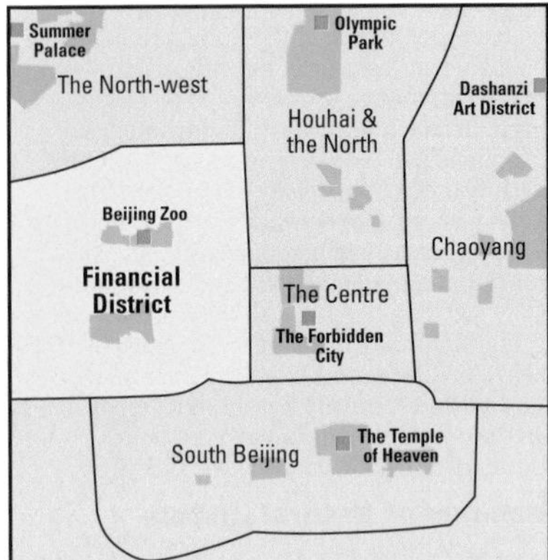

The equivalent of London's Square Mile, Whitehall and Bloomsbury combined (though a lot less dynamic), Beijing's Financial District is the city's economic centre, and also contains several important ministries and a number of academic institutions. An increasing emphasis on the area's modernity doesn't really do justice to its history as the one-time home of princes, government officials, temples, and a network of imperial canals running to the Summer Palace. Wide avenues abound near Financial Street and the enormity of the buildings hammer home the sheer scale of 'New China' as it swallows up what used to be a vast network of hutongs.

The points of interest are not few, but they're certainly far between, so it's best to head here with a destination in mind. Running along the south is Fuxingmenwai Dajie – a continuation of Chang'an Avenue – home to a proliferation of government buildings and offices, as well as a number of museums and a Parkson department store. Further north are several parks, including one that is home to one of Beijing's 'four altars' – Yuetan, or the 'Temple of the Moon' and the tourist-friendly Xizhimen. It's here that you'll find the Beijing Zoo, Wanshousi temple and the Planetarium.

Financial Street itself is currently the subject of a massive RMB 45 billion overhaul, and is in the process of acquiring a high-end shopping mall, a cluster of premium hotels and a new bar street – all befitting a region where the total assets amount to mor than RMB 1,300 billion.

GETTING THERE

Fuxingmen, Fuchengmen, Xizhimen and the Military Museum all have metro stops that will drop you relatively near the action. However, expect to do some walking and take a map with you. By 2008, a metro line going directly to the zoo will also be completed.

Fuxingmen

This major road leading to west Beijing from the centre is flanked by dozens of immense buildings, from the 2,800-square-metre (30,000-square-foot) Cultural Palace of the Nationalities and the sweeping crescent-shaped HQ of the People's Bank of China at the eastern end, to the grand, Soviet-style Ministry of Radio, Film and TV and the **Capital Museum** at the west. A huge neon rainbow frames the road where it meets Fuxingmen Beidajie (there's another at Jianguomen) which is supposed to represent not only a gate, but 'China's bright future' after it was erected for National Day in 1997, the year Hong Kong returned to the motherland.

A block east of Fuxingmen North Road runs **Financial Street** (in Pinyin, Jinrong Jie). During the Yuan, Ming and Qing dynasties, it was the site of several *yinhao* (banks) and *jinfang* (gold shops) and was where rich businessmen and royal families kept their money. During the first year of the People's Republic, the Bank of the Qing Dynasty became the Bank of China, and from then on others began to follow.

Now, with a distinctly slick feel, several major companies line the road, including China Mobile, China Power Investment Corp and, of course, the Bank of China. Where a Chinese courtyard home once stood, a park with several small traditional buildings and rock pools has been reconstructed, perfect for a summer lunch break in 'the City'.

South-east of where Financial Street meets Fuxingmen, buried in a maze of hutongs and currently being renovated, is the former residence of Li Dazhao, one of the founders of the Communist Party who lived here in the

► For key sights and streets in the Financial District in **Chinese script**, *see pp252-255.*

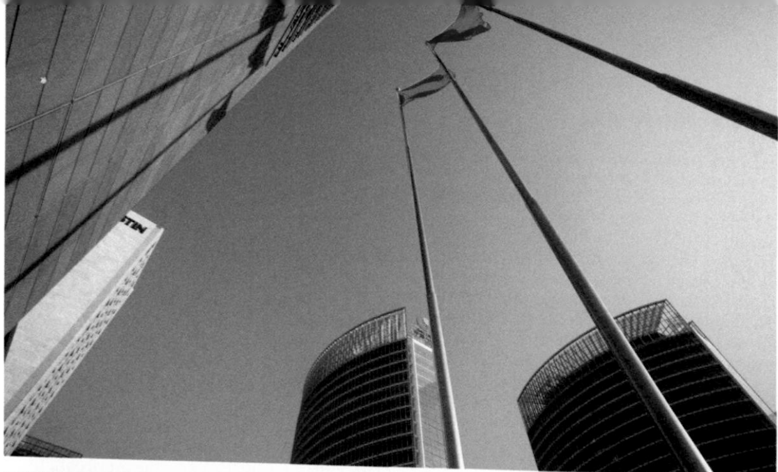

Making money since Yuan dynasty times: Jinrong Jie, aka **Financial Street**.

early 1920s. Further south-west is the Central Conservatory of Music (once upon a time Prince Chun's Mansion, the seventh son of Emperor Daoguang) and returning to and continuing west along Fuxingmen Wai Dajie is the recently reconstructed Capital Museum.

Also on Fuxingmenwai Dajie, just past the Ministry of Communications building, is the **Military Museum of the Chinese Revolution** and a five-minute walk away, the Millennium Monument. Here government officials rang in the year 2000. This odd-looking structure also houses the **Beijing World Art Museum** which has exhibited Leonardo, Titian and other Old Masters. To the west of the monument lies the CCTV centre – China's state-run television service – soon to move to a state-of-the-art Rem Koolhaas-designed building in Chaoyang's CBD area. Then, just north of the CCTV building is the popular **Yuyuantan Park** and a mile or so to the east, Yuetan Park, the 'Altar of the Moon'. The park remains off limits to the public until restoration work is completed, a lengthier process than it needs to be because of the huge television tower plonked right in the middle. It's believed the unsightly structure will be removed in the next five years.

Beijing World Art Museum

A9 Fuxingmenwai Dajie, Haidian (6852 7108/ www.worldartmuseum.cn). Metro Military Museum. **Open** *Summer* 8am-6pm daily; *Winter* 9am-5.30pm daily. **Admission** RMB 30; RMB 20 concessions. **No credit cards**. **Map** p248 D6..

Striving to bring the best of the rest of the world to Beijing, the Beijing World Art Museum has already been the site of several high profile international exhibitions and continues to impress visitors with its hi-tech art centre and digital gallery. Its current exhibition, 'The Great Civilisations', is scheduled to run until October 2008.

Capital Museum

16 Fuxingmenwai Dajie, Xicheng (6337 0491/ www.capitalmuseum.org.cn/en). Metro Muxidi. **Open** 9am-5pm Tue-Sun (last ticket 4pm). Closed Mon. **Admission** RMB 30; RMB 15 concessions. **No credit cards**. **Map** p240 F10.

Second only to the National Museum of China in Tiananmen Square (*see p56*) in terms of size, a successful refurbishment in 2006 now means that the Capital Museum is well worth a visit. Designed by the vice director of the China Architectural Design Research institute, Cui Kai, the building is recognisable by the huge bronze cylinder that can be partially seen from the outside and which houses a number of artefacts inside. The focus of the museum is on traditional Chinese art, as well as exhibits telling the story of Beijing's 850-year history as capital. Ethnic clothing, jade, bronze, sculpture, painting, calligraphy, Buddha statues – it's all there, and these days with the added bonus of English translation.

Military Museum of the Chinese People's Revolution

A9 Fuxingmenwai Dajie, Haidian (6686 6244). Metro Military Museum. **Open** 8am-5.30pm Mon-Sat. Closed Sun. **Admission** RMB 20. **No credit cards**. **Map** p240 E10.

Zhou Enlai's plane, Mao Zedong's limousine, a torpedo boat and a US spy plane are just some of the attractions in this comprehensive collection of China's long military history. Some of the displays border take patriotism into jingoism, but the museum is worth a visit, if just for a look at the ancient weapons exhibit. The Ming Dynasty cannons, rocket launchers and grenades are at the very root of modern war technology.

Yuyuantan Park

Xisanhuan Lu, Haidian (8865 3806). Metro Millennium Monument (south entrance). **Open** 6am-9.30pm daily. **Admission** RMB 10. **No credit cards**. **Map** p240 E9.

This park in west Beijing is best known for its historical *diaoyutai* (angling terrace) because the writer Wang Yu used to fish there during the Jin dynasty. For hundreds of years a favourite scenic spot of the emperors, it's now the site of the Diaoyutai State Guesthouse – a sort of 'Chinese Camp David' for foreign dignitaries. The park itself is also famous for its cherry blossom and is a hit with families thanks to the two huge play areas.

Fuchengmen

Fuchengmen, the next major road north of Fuxingmen, was once one of the nine city gates built during the Ming Dynasty. Coal from the western suburbs was transported by camel through the gate during the winter and it was also here that troops allowed insurgents led by Li Zicheng to pass through in 1644 – the subsequent invasion of the Forbidden City leading to the fall of the Ming Dynasty.

Now what you'll find in the same spot is a perpetually busy overpass (where Fuchengmen meets the Second Ring Road) and just west of here, where Fuchengmen meets Nanlishi Lu, a similarly manic pedestrian footbridge crossed by hundreds of people every second, with fake DVDs being flogged left, right and centre. Head east, however, and a network of hutongs remain, housing several unassuming but beautiful temples and the **Lu Xun Museum**. Best accessed from the main road rather than via the complex alleys, this peaceful quadrangle was the residence of China's best-loved modern author and now houses several thousand items.

Standing at the gate of the museum and glancing to the right, it's possible to see the top of the **White Dagoba Temple**, sticking up like a giant ice cream above the grey rooftops. Head back to the main road where you'll find the main entrance. Inside there's a handful of low-slung, traditional buildings containing a fine collection of Buddhist statues and texts that seem out of place in their current setting.

Back on Fuchengmennei Dajie, on the same side of the road and marked by an ornate gateway and sturdy surrounding red stone wall, is the **Temple of Emperors of Successive Dynasties in China**. This is one of only three imperial temples in the city, built in 1530 for the emperors to worship the gods, powerful ancestors, past rulers and heroes. A further 10-minute walk east will drop you at the door of the **Temple of Great Charity**, a good place to dip into for half an hour, and opposite, the **Geological Museum of China**, not hard to spot thanks to the 5.5-metre (18-foot) dinosaur out front.

Geological Museum of China

15 Yangrou Hutong, on the corner of Xisi Nan Dajie and Fuchengmennei Dajie (6655 7858). Metro Fuchengmen. **Open** 9am-4.30pm Tue-Sun. **Admission** RMB 30; RMB 15 concessions. **No credit cards**. **Map** p240 H9.

A world-renowned research institute once home to the world's first intact, feathered dinosaur, its main attractions now are the varied and colourful crystal collection and a series of interactive simulation machines recreating earthquakes and aerospace missions. Some exhibits have English translation.

Lu Xun Museum

19 Gongmenkou Santiao, Fuchengmennei Dajie, Xicheng (6616 5654). Metro Fuchengmen. **Open** 9am-4pm daily. **Admission** RMB 5; RMB 3 concessions. **No credit cards**. **Map** p240 G8.

Regarded as the founder of modern Chinese literature for writing the way people spoke rather than in the classic literary style of the past, left-wing author Lu Xun was named the country's leading cultural icon by the Chinese in a recent online survey. A key member of the May Fourth Movement, Lu Xun

The old West Gate of the city, **Xizhimen**.

wrote wry commentaries on the country's social problems at the beginning of the 20th century and in particular the Chinese national character. His book *The True Story of Ah Q*, published in the 1920s, later became his most famous work. This museum pays homage to Lu Xun's life as a writer, ideologue and revolutionary and includes some 21,842 items as well as the famed scroll known as the *Self-Mockery Poem*.

Temple of Emperors of Successive Dynasties in China

131 Fuchengmennei Dajie, between the White Dagoba temple and Temple of Great Charity (6616 1141). Metro Fuchengmen. **Open** 9am-4.30pm daily. **Admission** RMB 20; RMB 10 concessions (RMB 60 with English-speaking guide). **No credit cards. Map** p241 H8.

A thoroughly pleasant temple with several magnificent buildings on a par with those in the Palace Museum, the Temple of Emperors is worth a visit. The comparatively small crowds and leafy surrounds lend the place a more reverential feel. Be wary of being told that admission is RMB 60, however – it's not. That's just if you want to make use of the band of enthusiastic English-speaking guides.

Temple of Great Charity (Guangjisi)

Xisi, east end of Fuchengmennei Dajie, opposite the Geological Museum (6616 0907). Metro Fuchengmen. **Open** 9am-10.30pm daily. **Admission** free. **Map** p241 H8.

This peaceful, atmospheric temple is now the headquarters of the Chinese Buddhist Association and is still very much in use, the smell of incense filling your nostrils as soon as you enter. The temple was destroyed several times by fire (an ancient tree and hundreds of Buddhist scriptures no longer survive), it still houses a good number of handwritten sutras, rubbings and stone inscriptions in its library.

White Dagoba Temple (Baitasi)

171 Fuchengmennei Dajie, Xicheng (6613 3317). Metro Fuchengmen. **Open** 9am-5pm daily (last ticket 4.30pm). **Admission** RMB 20. **No credit cards. Map** p240 G8.

First built in 1096 and then restored by a Nepalese architect under Kublai Khan in 1271 and again during the Ming Dynasty, this is one of the two great dagobas in Beijing (the other, smaller one is in Beihai Park, *see p58*). The dagoba itself has been whitewashed lest the pollution cause it to be renamed the 'Black Dagoba', and small bells hang from its canopy to scare away evil spirits.

Xizhimen & the north

Branching off from the north-west Second Ring Road and out to the Third, Xizhimenwai Dajie is always buzzing. Most Chinese come here as tourists to visit the zoo, aquarium or planetarium, or to watch a musical concert or exhibition at the Beijing Exhibition Centre. Western-style consumerism is in evidence: a Carrefour and a plethora of pizza, Japanese and Chinese snack restaurants line the main thoroughfare between the Exhibition Hall in the east and the Capital Gymnasium in the west; and two or three super-cheap wholesale clothing markets sit on the south side of the road, hidden behind the bus station. Countering the modernity, the canals that run north of the zoo are popular with local fisherman and were once the Empress's route to the Summer Palace (*see p82* **Slow boat**).

Just south of Xizhimen proper, down Zhanlangyuan Lu and behind the French Church inside the Beijing Administrative College (6 Chegongzhuang Dajie), is the

Slow boat

Beijing's landlocked state is unusual for a capital city; the static in the air and lack of rain just add to the general feeling of dryness most people notice while here. So it's a nice surprise to learn that there is a network of canals running through Beijing that are particularly beautiful during the summer and perfect for seeing parts of the city other thoroughfares can't reach.

In particular, those just north of the centre lead to the Grand Canal linking Beijing to the much more watery Hangzhou in the south-east, while those in the west run all the way to the Summer Palace (*see p85*) and beyond. The latter network, once connected to the central lake district of Houhai, Beihai, Zhongnanhai and the moat around the Forbidden City, is the one most accessible to tourists. The brainchild of Mongol Emperor Kublai Khan, these canals were constructed during the Yuan dynasty (1279-1368) from the Western Hills to Beijing in an attempt to improve the city's water supply.

Unsurprisingly, the pleasant trip to the Summer Palace via these waterways soon became a favourite pastime of the royal family. However, it was the infamous and extravagant Empress Dowager Cixi who became most associated with the canals due to the fact that she would travel from the Forbidden City to the Summer Palace with her entourage on day-long pleasure cruises, often stopping off at the Temple of Longevity on the way. Here she would apparently touch-up her face (the temple still houses her make-up table), enjoy a meal and get some rest after a tough day being rowed around by eunuchs.

In 1999 the Beijing Water Conservancy Bureau opened the canals to the public, running a passenger boat service from behind the Beijing Exhibition Centre in Xizhimen and from Yuyuantan Park in Fuxingmen to the Summer Palace. Several barges kitted out to resemble the imperial ones (as well as regular ones) currently operate between 1 April and 30 October each year.

From the Beijing Exhibition Center: tours leave every hour, on the hour, from the north-east corner of the complex between 10am and 4pm. *Single trip* RMB 40; *return* RMB 70.

From Yuyuantan Park: boats run from the south gate of Bayi Lake twice in the morning and once in the afternoon. *Single trip* RMB 60; *return* RMB 80.

Jesuit cemetery (open 8.30am-5pm daily, free). Matteo Ricci, the Italian missionary responsible for bringing Christianity and Western mathematics to China, is buried here along with 63 others (*see p16* **Foreign Devils**)

Xizhimen was the 'West Gate' in the old Beijing city wall, through which passed those entrusted with bringing the sweet water from the Jade Mountain in the north to the Forbidden City. This was a daily ritual as the emperor wouldn't sully his lips with water from any other source. The gate was demolished in 1969, however, and now the most recogniseable feature in this area is the trio of finger-like arched office buildings above the train station.

Heading west from the station, the first major building you come across is the **Beijing Exhibition Centre** (No.135 Xizhimenwai Dajie). Humourlessly Soviet in its design, the building's steeple is still emblazoned with the red star of socialism. A couple of hundred metres further west is the infamous **Beijing Zoo**. Still not up to Western standards by any means, today the zoo is notorious for the fact that Chinese tourists feed chips to the bears without being reprimanded and, apart from the giant pandas, most cages are still miserably small.

For a less depressing experience it may be better to head to the back of the zoo where you'll find the more modern and well equipped Beijing Aquarium (*see p151*). Or alternatively, cross over the road to the recently spruced-up **Beijing Planetarium**.

Continue west along Xizhimenwai Dajie and, back on the same side of the road as the zoo, you'll come to the stately China Banknote Printing and Minting Corporation, which sits incongruously side by side with the Babyface West (*see p178*) nightclub.

Turning right and heading up Zhongguancun Nan Dajie, the first building you'll see is the National Library of China (8854 5593, www.nlc.gov.cn, 9am-9pm Mon-Fri, 9am-5pm Sat, Sun, RMB 5/mth). A huge structure, it's the largest library in Asia and is where the majority of ancient Chinese texts are held, as well as the biggest collection of foreign-language books in the country. It also holds over 35,000 pieces of scripted turtle shells and animal bones (so called 'oracle bones') which date from the Yin to the Shang dynasty (16th-11th century BC).

On the east side of Zhongguancun Nan Dajie, almost directly opposite the start of the Library building, is a small road which runs along the canal and leads to the **Five Pagoda Temple**. Once, when the area was surrounded by fields and not construction sites, the temple and its locale were frequented by picknicking locals. Now these are probably the oldest surviving structures in the area.

Back at the crossroads of Xizhimen Nan Dajie and Zhongguancun Nan Dajie, on the opposite side of the road you'll come across the east gate of the Purple Bamboo Park, also known as **Zizhuyuan** (winter 6am-8pm, summer 6am-9pm, free). A peaceful, landscaped park whose traditional arched stone bridges, boating lakes (a third of its area is water), rockeries and stands of bamboo – 50 different types – make it a pleasant way to pass a couple of hours.

To the north-west of the park is the **Temple of Longevity**, reached by exiting the park's north gate and heading west along Wanshousi Lu until you see the canal again and the busy Third Ring Road. The temple, built in 1577, was originally used to house Buddhist scriptures written in Chinese, but is more famous for being the place where members of the imperial family (in particular Empress Dowager Cixi) would stop on their way to the Summer Palace (*see p82* **Slow boat**). The temple also houses the modern Beijing Art Museum.

Beijing Planetarium

138 Xizhimenwai Dajie (opposite the Beijing Zoo), Xicheng (6836 1691/6835 2453/www.bjp.org.cn). Metro Xizhimen. **Open** 10am-3.30pm Wed-Fri; 8.30am-4pm Sat, Sun. **Admission** RMB 15; RMB 10 concessions. *All-inclusive tickets* RMB 105; RMB 75 concessions. **No credit cards**. **Map** p248 F7.

Beijing's pollution means that the planetarium offers the city's best view of the stars. First opened in 1957, it was given a RMB 36 million overhaul between 2001 and 2004, and now houses the best-equipped auditorium in all China and a digital universe theatre, as well as a solar observatory and hundreds of ancient and modern astronomical exhibits.

Beijing Zoo

137 Xizhimenwai Dajie, Haidian (6831 4411/www.bjzoo.com). Metro Xizhimen. **Open** *Winter* 7.30am-5pm daily; *Summer* 7.30am-6pm daily. **Admission** RMB 10; RMB 5 concessions. **No credit cards**. **Map** P248 E7.

Created in 1906 by the Empress Dowager Cixi to accommodate animals bought from abroad by a high-ranking official, it was then called the 'Park of Ten Thousand Creatures'. Despite its bad reputation, it is currently home to over 5,000 animals and boasts an impressive collection of giant pandas, snub-nosed monkeys, 13 different types of crane and the world's biggest indoor aquarium. For Western visitors, its claim to be 'the paradise which links men and animals together' will strike a hollow chord, but enrichment programmes and educational centres are slowly improving conditions.

Five Pagoda Temple (Wutasi)

24 Wutasi Cun, just off Zhongguancun Nan Dajie, Baishiqiao, Haidian (6217 3543). **Open** 9am-4.30pm, Tue-Sun. Closed Mon. **Admission** RMB 20; RMB 10 concessions. **No credit cards**. **Map** p248 E7.

First constructed in 1473, renovated under Emperor Qianlong, but then ransacked by Allied Forces and looted during the Boxer Rebellion, this temple has taken some beatings over the years. Restored once more (though with few original elements), the temple now includes the Stone Carving Museum. The five Buddhist pagodas within the complex are of the Indian 'diamond throne' variety: tall, tiered structures rising from square bases on a heavily engraved 'throne' foundation. The exquisite carvings on the throne depict Buddhist symbols, animals and Sanskrit writings; note the carving of Buddha's feet underneath the central pagoda.

Temple of Longevity (Wanshousi)

Xisanhuan Beilu (6845 6997). **Open** 9am-4pm Tue-Sun. **Admission** RMB 20. **No credit cards**. **Map** p248 D6.

A sort of imperial motorway services during the Ming and Qing dynasties, the beautiful Temple of Longevity is a complex of traditional buildings and gardens. Inside you can still see a statue of the goddess Guan'yin in the likeness of Empress Dowager Cixi, erected in an effort to flatter her by the canny eunuch Li Lian'ying. The temple was also the headquarters of the occupying Japanese army and a PLA kindergarten before becoming the Beijing Art Museum in 1985. It now houses several jade, bronze and calligraphy artefacts, Ming and Qing dynasty paintings and temporary exhibitions by local artists.

Zizhuyuan.

The North-west

Join the emperors and escape to the hills.

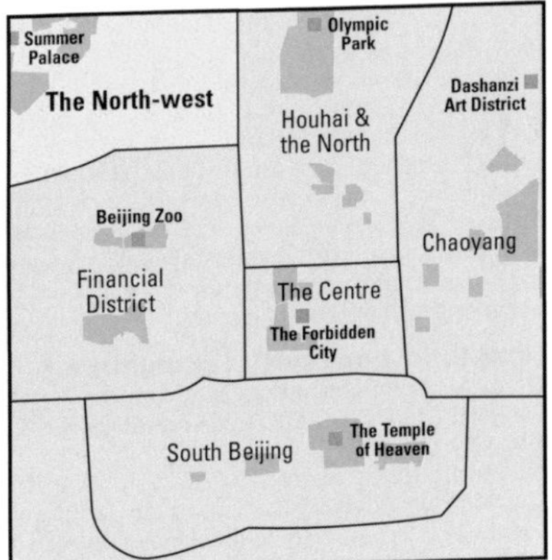

The north-west of Beijing is a very Chinese mixture of electrical, academic and imperial worlds. Starting at the Great Bell Temple, on the Third Ring Road, and heading away from the city towards the Western Hills, you'll pass through the electronic jungle of Zhongguancun, often referred to as Beijing's silicon valley, famous for its masses of stores and markets specialising in computer hardware, software and digital equipment.

Further out is Wudaokou, where the city's universities are concentrated. Epitomising Beijing's student cool, Wudaokou is awash with vibrant cafés, live-music venues and arty shops. The campuses of most universities are open to the public, and those of prestigious Peking and Tsinghua universities are particularly worthy of exploration.

The fantastic scenery of the area at the foot of the Western Hills and its proximity to the city meant that the area enjoyed imperial favour during the Qing dynasty. The Old and New Summer Palaces flourished under the Qings, who enhanced the already great natural beauty with the striking palaces, pavilions, hillside temples and pagodas that climb up to the Botanical Gardens and Fragrant Hills.

GETTING THERE

Taking metro line 13 from Xizhimen to Wudaokou is the easiest way to get to the north-west – Tsinghua and Peking universities are both walking distance from the station. From Wudaokou you can either get buses or catch a taxi onwards to the Summer Palaces, Xiangshan or the Botanical Gardens. There are also regular tour buses running from Qianmen and the zoo to these destinations. A new metro (line four) will be running from Xizhimen directly to the Summer Palace by 2008.

Great Bell Temple

As the Great Bell Temple is the sole sight in this forlorn corner of Haidian, you might be tempted to pass by and continue to the tourist hotspot of the Temple of Heaven. But you can't really understand Beijing – or China – if you don't grasp its bells. From ancient times to the present, the bell has been used as a symbol – and instigator – of social control and cohesion, and as an imperial summons to the masses.

This temple was built in 1733, during the Qing dynasty, and was used by emperors to pray for rain. The bell dates back much further, to the reign of Ming emperor Yongle (1402-1424), who was an enthusiastic student of Tibetan Buddhism. He commissioned the casting of the bell and and ordered 17 whole Buddhist scriptures, a total of 230,000 characters, to be inscribed upon it.

Great Bell Temple (Dazhong Si)

31 Beisanhuan Xi Lu (6255 0819). Metro Dazhongsi. **Open** 8.30am-4pm daily. **Admission** RMB 10; additional RMB 2 for the bell tower. **No credit cards. Map** p249 F5.

The 'King of Bells' refers to the 6.87m- (22.5ft-) high, 3.3m (10.8ft) diameter bronze chimer, weighing in at almost 50 tons, that can be found housed in the temple's Bell Palace. There are many other bells on display inside the temple courtyards and inside the Ancient Bell Museum, which charts both the artistic and mechanical development of bells throughout the dynasties.

University district

A hub of scholarly activity radiates from a cluster of no less than 68 universities that inhabit north-east Haidian District, also referred to simply as the university district.

Among these are two of China's most prestigious academic establishments, **Peking University**, commonly referred to as Beida, and **Tsinghua University**. Tsinghua,

Seek out some breathing space at **Xiangshan**. *See p90.*

renowned for it's engineering, boasts the likes of president Hu Jintao among its former students; Peking, known more for its excellence in the humanities, includes revolutionary writer Lu Xun on its list of famous alumni. Wandering through the beautiful, expansive university grounds you'll get a glimpse of the higher echelons of Chinese student life against the backdrop of campuses which are former Qing and Ming dynasty royal gardens.

The Arthur M Sackler Art and Archaeology Museum (6276 5711, www.sackler.org/china, 9am-5pm daily, admission RMB 5, RMB 1 students) is well worth a visit if you have a spare half hour. Housed in the university's Archaeology Department, not far from the campus's west gate, what started its life off as collection of antiquities used for teaching and research purposes has grown into an impressive and sizeable collection of artefacts spanning 280,000 years and includes contributions from archaeological institutions all over China.

You don't have to go to the museum to see Chinese relics though. On campus there are also plenty of notable objects, many of which used to be housed in the Yuanmingyuan (*see p87*) and were relocated after its destruction. These include the two stone obelisks (*huabiao*) that stand directly in front of the office building. These date from 1742 and used to be in the Yuanmingyuan's Ancestral Temple. The two stone unicorns (*kylin*) guarding the front gates of the office building were also formerly in the Yuanmingyuan.

A short walk east of Peking University, you'll find yourself at the west gate of **Tsinghua University** (also spelled Quinghua), accessible via Yuanmingyuan Dong Lu. Here you'll find the most ancient and picturesque parts of the campus.

Jinchun Gardens (Jinchun Yuan) was the central area of the earliest imperial garden site and a former royal residency, and comprises traditional living quarters, pavilions and gardens surrounded by a serene, clear-watered lake. To the north-east of the gardens is the Palace of the Ancient Moon, a courtyard building, which was formerly used by members of the imperial family as a study, but now functions as university offices.

To the north is Tsinghua Water and Wood (Shuimu Tsinghua). With its lotus flower-filled lake surrounded by weeping willows and rock formations, it is renowned for being the most beautiful place on campus and is often described as 'the garden within the garden'.

Further north is Tsinghua's sprawling student library. The original library building,

▶For key sights and streets in the North-west in **Chinese script**, *see pp252-255.*

located on the east side, was constructed in 1919. Other parts were added in 1931 and in 1991, under the architectural direction of Guan Zhaoye, a Tsinghua engineering faculty member, who designed it to integrate perfectly with the former buildings. The Great Hall, just south of the library, is a stocky Graeco-Roman building, built in 1920 – made up of four different sections, it seats 1,200 people.

Peking University (Beida)

1 Yiheyuan Lu, Haidian (6275 1230/www.pku.edu.cn). Metro Wudaokou. **Open** *Visitors* 8am-5pm Mon-Fri; *students* 24hrs daily. **Admission** free. **Map** p248 D3.

Established as the Metropolitan University in 1898, it wasn't until 1912 that it merged with another institution and was renamed Peking University (aka Beida). In 1952 it moved from a much smaller,

Walk 2 Campus crawl

Start Wudaokou light-rail station
Finish West Gate, Peking University
Length approximately three kilometres (1.8 miles)

From Wudaokou light-rail station head west on Chengfu Lu for about half a mile. If you need a quick breather before entering the campus, pop into the **All Sages** bookshop (123 Lanqiying, Chengfu Lu, 6276 8748) on the right-hand side of the road. It has a good coffee shop upstairs.

Enter Peking University using the **East Gate (1)** and go past the library and bear left. After passing the basketball courts on your left, turn right and enter the **Jing Garden (2)** – flanked on both sides by beautiful, traditional courtyard buildings – which today house university departments.

From here head north-west towards the commemorative statue of **Cai Yuanpei**, former president of Peking University, famous for his liberal thinking and contribution to education in China during the early twentieth century. Walk behind the hill the statue stands on and aim for the **Bell Pavilion** – its huge bell used to chime throughout the day, but now remains silent.

Stroll half-way round **Weiming (Nameless) Lake (3)** – one of the most beautiful, peaceful spots on the campus. to see the **Boya Pagoda**, which was both designed and funded by an American architect in 1924. Continue round the lake and you'll also see a small island that is accessible from the pathway. Stop to rest and take in the **Island Pavilion**.

Follow the small path on to the island where you will see a **stone boat**: during the Second Opium War in 1860, this boat was seriously damaged by the French and British and now the only original part is its base.

Take a right and head straight on. You may wish to take a detour to the right to see the Arthur M Sackler Museum of Art and Archaeology. If not, continue going straight and you'll see **Bei Gonglou**, the University President's office

Take a right to go round the building to see the two *huabiao* or **stone obelisks (4)**. These date from 1742 and used to be located in **Yuanmingyuan** (Old Summer Palace). Walk across the little stone bridge up ahead and exit Peking University through the **West Gate**, also called the Alumni Gate.

Form here you can retrace your steps to Wudaokou station or hail a cab to the nearby Summer Palace, Fragrant Hills of Botanical Gardens. All are no more than a 20-minute cab ride from here.

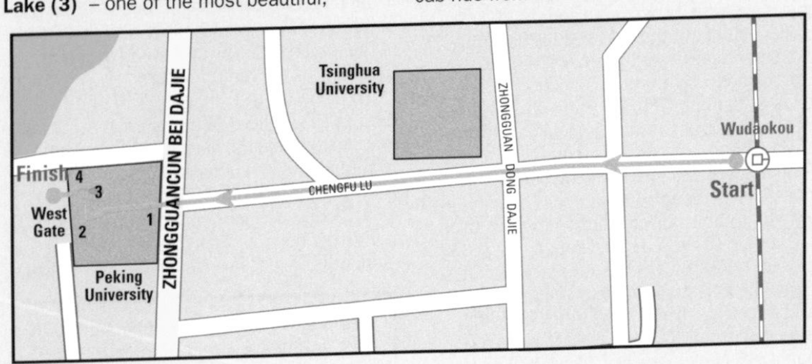

central campus on Wusi Dajie to its current location, engulfing the university previously housed there. With its large lakes, little bridges, meandering paths and pretty pavilions the campus is an exquisite example of Qing dynasty architecture.

Tsinghua University

Chengfu Lu, Haidian (6278 9437/www.tsinghua .edu.cn). Metro Wudaokou. **Open** *Visitors* 8am-5pm Mon-Fri; *students* 24 hrs daily. **Admission** free. **Map** p249 E2.

Founded in 1911 on funds remitted from the Boxer Rebellion indemnities – imposed by the victorious foreign forces that quelled the uprising – Tsinghua was initially used as a preparatory college for students going to study in the United States. Like Peking, Tsinghua's campus is a former Qing dynasty royal park and a lot of consideration has gone into ensuring the new architectural additions to the grounds blend in with the character of the older structures. The campus covers an incredible 3,000,000 square metres (756 acres), so unless you have a full day to wander round, you'll have to prioritise what you want to see.

The Long Corridor at the **Summer Palace**.

The Palaces

A stroll through the grounds of the **Summer Palace** and **Yuanmingyuan** can be extremely pleasant in its own right, and you're not required to know a lot about their history in order to enjoy them. However, some background adds depth, and is particularly fascinating because the palaces were in the foreground of the dramatic transition from ancient to modern China. What remains and what has been lost chart a tumultuous period of the country's history. It's also rewarding to look closely at the gardens and fountains – they are not merely open spaces but are, in a sense, microcosms and metaphors for the imperial spirit (*see p90* **Chinese leaves**).

Summer Palace

Although the Summer Palace is most closely associated with the Qing dynasty, as an imperial site it actually dates back to 1153, when Jin dynasty emperor Wan Yanliang built a palace on Longevity Hill. During the Mongol Yuan dynasty water was channelled from a nearby spring to make the sizeable lake we see today. Qing emperor Qian Long, who was very fond of the southern Suzhou and Hangzhou style-gardens, ordered the palace grounds to be designed in their image. He also created a series of temples and pagodas as a tribute to his mother on her 60th birthday. Sadly, save for the Bronze pavilion and the stone-built Temple of the Sea of Wisdom that resisted the inferno, these edifices were all destroyed when Anglo-French forces besieged the palace in 1860, in retaliation for Chinese acts of defiance during the second Opium War.

In 1880 the Empress Dowager Cixi lavishly rebuilt the palace at great expense, only to have it destroyed by foreign forces again in 1900, who were this time expressing their displeasure at her support for the Boxer Rebellion. In 1902 Cixi, known for her extravagance more than her common sense, painstakingly rebuilt the palace yet again, using funds earmarked for the navy.

Highlights of the palace include the Hall of Benevolence and Longevity (Renshoudian), which is the first building you reach when entering via the east palace gate. This is where Cixi and her nephew, the puppet emperor Guang Xu, used to conduct their official affairs and give audience to visitors, Cixi hidden away behind her famous screen, which has unfortunately not survived. The Hall of Jade Ripples (Yulangtang), the next building you come to, is where Cixi held emperor Guang Xu captive. If that wasn't bad enough, the windows, which used to look out on the lake, were also boarded up and historians speculate this was done at Cixi's command to make her nephew's existence even more pitiful.

The Garden of Virtue and Harmony (Deheyuan), a courtyard complex, houses a three-storey theatre, whose construction took over four years, completed in time for Cixi's 60th birthday in 1895. Directly behind it is the Hall of Nurtured Joy (Yiledian), where Cixi sat on her golden throne to watch Peking Opera performances. The Long Corridor (Changlang) is a beautiful covered walkway, which runs along the lakeside for 700 metres (2,300 feet), its bowers decorated with elaborate landscape paintings and pictures of characters from Chinese history and literature. About halfway along the Long Corridor, you come to a path which leads up to Longevity Hill (Wanshoushan). Following this path you pass a series of pagodas, pavilions, palaces and temples until you reach the peak, and the Tibetan-style Fragrance of Buddha (Foxiangge) tower.

Heading back down the hill and along the lake to the west brings you to the magnificent Stone Boat. Constructed initially by Qianlong in 1755, it was destroyed by Western forces. In 1893 Cixi ordered its reconstruction and the elaborate 36-metre (118-foot) long, two-tier high structure still stands proud, symbolising the stability of the Qing dynasty – however, more commonly it is thought of as a symbol of Cixi's decadence and the demise of a dynasty that fell 18 years later.

Summer Palace (Yiheyuan)

Yiheyuan Lu, Haidian (6288 1610/www.summerpalace-china.com). Bus No.726 from Wudaokou/boat from Beijing Exhibition Centre Apr-Oct RMB 40 one way; RMB 70 return (see p82). **Open** *Winter* 7am-5pm daily. *Summer* 7am-6.30pm daily. **Admission** *Winter* RMB 20; RMB 10 concessions; RMB 50 all-inclusive ticket. *Summer* RMB 30; RMB 15 concessions; RMB 60 all-inclusive ticket. **Map** p248 A2.

It's not hard to understand why the Summer Palace is one of Beijing's most frequented and well-loved sights. It's not just its picturesque setting at the foot of the western hills, surrounded by the expansive Kunming Lake; it also offers beautiful architectural examples from the late Qing dynasty all of which can be enjoyed from ground level, or at a bird's-eye view by climbing up to one of the temples or pagodas dotted across Longevity Hill.

Yuanmingyuan

Not far from the Summer Palace lie the ruins of Yuanmingyuan, which offer time-worn baroque arches jutting from the ground, overgrown wilderness and, thanks to a non-committal attitude to restoration, an authenticity lacking in many of Beijing's tourist sights.

Created during the Qing dynasty and consisting of three gardens, Yuanmingyuan (Garden of Perfection), Changchunyuan (Garden of Everlasting Spring) and Wanchunyuan (Garden of Eternal Spring), the site is collectively known as Yuanmingyuan – and sometimes as the Old Summer Palace.

The work for the first garden was started in 1707 during Emperor Kang Xi's reign and took nearly 150 years to complete. The other two were built under the rule of Emperor Qian Long, who commissioned Italian and French Jesuits to design Changchunyuan with baroque and Renaissance architecture, and a palace to resemble Versailles, along with its fountains. Sadly the palace is long gone, razed to the ground by French and British troops along with the Summer Palace in 1860, although unlike the latter little effort was put into its reconstruction. In 1900 it was plundered again, first by foreign troops and later by local bandits. To this day the ruins remain 'a monument to China's national humiliation', as a sign displayed at the entrance solemnly reads.

Like the Summer Palace, Yuanmingyuan's landscape is largely based on the southern Chinese garden style, and lakes make up a huge proportion of the park's total area. The most prominent of these is Fuhai Lake, which covers over 280,000 square metres (69 acres) and, along with other areas of the park, has become subject to huge restoration projects in recent years. Many of these have met with concern and opposition, both from local environmental groups who want to protect the wildlife that's taken refuge within the overgrown parks, and heritage groups, who think the ruins should be left as they are. This doesn't seem very likely, as RMB 700 million has already been invested in its restoration since 2000.

Yuanmingyuan

Qinghua Xi Lu, Haidian (6262 8501). Bus No.331 from Wudaokou metro. **Open** *May-Oct* 7am-7pm daily. *Nov-Feb* 7am-5pm daily. *Mar, Apr* 7am-6pm daily. **Admission** *all three parks* RMB 15. *Excluding Changchunyuan* RMB 10; RMB 5 children/students. **No credit cards. Map** p248 C2.

Taking up nearly 3.5 million square metres (865 acres), you can easily spend a whole day wandering the grounds of Yuanmingyuan – also known as the Yuangminyuan Remans Park – but if you are pushed for time, Changchuyuan, in the north-east of the park, and its well-preserved fountain ruins and magnificent marble columns, are undoubtedly the best feature. To the west of this there's a fun labyrinth, a reconstruction of the one that was destroyed during the various onslaughts.

Class struggles

With their expansive, handsome campuses and conscientious-looking students milling about, Beijing's universities may appear to be visions of tranquillity, but the reality is quite different. Beijing had a turbulent 20th century, with lots of radical and often violent political and social movements, and these universities have often been at the heart of the action.

Only 20 years after it was established, Peking University became the birthplace of the May Fourth Movement, one of China's most progressive movements. Under the influence of the university's president Cai Yuanpei (whose statue can be found on the campus, just behind the Bell Pavilion) and his revolutionary faculty members, including acclaimed writers and thinkers Lu Xun, Hu Shih and Chen Duxiu, 5,000 of Peking's students, took to the streets on 4 May 1919. They were venting their anger at a weak government that had accepted unfair clauses in the Treaty of Versailles and were calling for change in the form of progressive, scientific Western thinking.

The movement was the start of a continued drive towards modernisation. Under Chen Duxiu and Hu Shih, written Chinese was reformed to make it more accessible to people other than academics and to increase literacy. Calls were made for the emancipation of women and the ending of foot binding and in 1920 Peking became the second university in China to admit female students. May Fourth gave birth to a surge of change within China and many believe that it paved the way for the Communist Revolution thirty years later.

Universities certainly didn't thrive under Mao's leadership. To the side of Peking's Centennial Commemorative Hall, located near the east gate of the campus, you can see a series of bulletin boards and fliers where posters informing students about the start of the Cultural Revolution were stuck. During this time school and university students were transformed into Red Guards and their teachers and professors 'punished' for their rightist ideas and actions, tormented both physically and mentally during so-called 'struggle sessions' put on by these brainwashed student-guards. Red Guard activities began in Tsinghua University in August 1966, or Red August as it is known. Between then and 1969 it is estimated that 48 people died on the campus, mostly due to fighting between Red Guard factions. The most unrestrained and violent period, known as the Hundred Days war, lasted between April and July 1968. The science department, which acted as base for one of the factions, still retains the scars. During this time academic activity in schools and universities virtually halted and did not pick up again properly until after the Cultural Revolution ended in 1977.

During the next couple of decades China opened up to the world and started to reform. The wounds of the Cultural Revolution began to heal, students became emboldened and their calls for democracy grew increasingly louder. On 15 April 1989, ousted political leader Hu Yaobang, a man who had been sympathetic to earlier student protests, died.

Then, 70 years after the May Fourth movement, Peking University again became the site of protest. The students' demands, including free media, the stamping out of corruption, more and equal dialogue with the country's leaders, were met by silence. Student representatives from more than 20 different universities, including one of the protest leaders – Wang Dan, a twenty-year-old Peking University student – met to organise a united student strike. They decided to move the protests to Tiananmen Square.

Western Hills

Beautiful scenery, cool climes, a good source of spring water and easy access from the city have made the Western Hills popular as a place for retreat and relaxation for imperial families over many dynasties.

As is common with positions of elevation in China, the mountainside has attracted the construction of many temples and pavilions, and despite many having suffered depredations similar to the Summer Palace, much beauty – as well as breathable air – remains to be enjoyed. Start by wandering around the gardens and conservatories of Beijing's impressive **Botanical Gardens**, located at the foot of the mountain range. Two kilometres west you'll find **Xiangshan (Fragrant Hills)**, Beijing's nearest mountain. The Botanical Gardens and Xiangshan can be easily visited in one day. Just off our maps, they are a short taxi ride from the Summer Palace and not to be missed.

Sightseeing

Chinese leaves

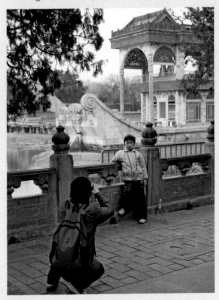

Chinese gardens are designed with precision; nothing is left to chance. The components necessary for any Chinese garden, including expanses of water, little bridges, pavilions, walls and rocks, are positioned not only for their aesthetic value, but for their symbolic meaning: the rocks represent mountains, the bodies of water are seas and lakes, and pavilions and other edifices are the human element.

Compacting all these elements into one small area is akin to creating a microcosm of the universe in one's own backyard. Most of Beijing's private gardens have now been turned into public parks. Formerly owned by royalty and officials these gardens were used as an escape from the stresses and strains of public service. Enclosed by high walls, they provided a haven of serenity and the entrance into a world of flight and fantasy. Obviously each garden reflects the character of its creator and his or her lifestyle preferences and leisure pursuits. It is said that the Empress Dowager Cixi's favourite spot was from within the Kunming Lake, seated on her marble boat.

It is no coincidence that so many royal gardens are north-west of Beijing. At the foot of the Western Hills, this location has not only lovely backdrops, but the yang (masculinity and strength) of the mountains also perfectly complements the yin (femininity and calm) of the water in the lakes and ponds. According to Chinese philosophy yin and yang need to be balanced to create a harmonious environment – too much of one or other could well give way to catastrophe.

Botanical Gardens

Xiangshan Nanlu, Haidian (6259 1283/www.beijingbg.com). Bus No.904 from Xizhimen metro/No.333 from outside Yuanmingyuan Park. **Open** *June-Mar* 8am-4.30pm daily. *Apr, May* 6am-7pm daily. **Admission** *June-Mar* RMB 5; RMB 2.5 children. *Apr, May* RMB 10; RMB 5 children. Hot rooms RMB 50; RMB 40 children (price includes park entrance). Wofosi Temple RMB 5. **No credit cards.**

Within its 4 million square metres (990 acres) of conservatories, hot rooms and outside gardens, Beijing's botanical gardens boast over 6,000 species of plants, including tropical varieties, water plants such as lotuses and lilies, and species used to make Chinese medicines and rarities such as a sequoia that was discovered in China after it had been thought extinct for millions of years. There is a magnificent peony garden, which is best to visit in May, also the time to catch the large number of fruit trees flowering. Blossom-related exhibitions and festivals are held at the gardens at this time of year. Don't miss Wofosi Temple, which hails from the Tang dynasty, set into the mountain cliffs and containing a 5m (16.4ft) long reclining Buddha.

Xiangshan (Fragrant Hills)

Xiangshan Lu, Haidian (6259 1155). Bus No.904 from Xizhimen metro/No.333 from Yuanmingyuan Park. **Open** *Nov-Mar* 8.30am-5pm daily. *Apr-Oct* 7am-6pm daily. **Admission** *Nov-Mar* RMB 5. *Apr-Oct* RMB 10. **No credit cards.**

Just 25km (15.5 miles) from Beijing's city centre, Xiangshan draws crowds of visitors everyday, particularly in autumn, and for good reason. This is when all the leaves on the mountain's smoke trees turn a wonderful shade of red. Xiangshan is also a lovely place to visit during the summer months since, thanks to its elevation and leaf coverage, it offers cooler temperatures and provides a refreshing reprieve from the sizzling city. **Photo** *p85*.

Eat, Drink, Shop

Features

Spin. *See p133.*

Restaurants

Forget celebrity chefs and designer decor – Chinese food is about eating... anything and everything.

Restaurants

Aria
Aria never disappoints in terms of quality, standard and flawless service. The lunch special is best deal in town. *See p110.*

Din Tai Fung
Din Tai Fung's *xiao longbao* has been recognised by foodies as the best steamed bun in the world. *See p104.*

Guo Yao Xiaoju
One of those hidden Beijing gems that you'll only find if you disappear into the hutongs. *See p101.*

LAN
Soak in Philippe Starck's wild design while dining on thrilling, mouth-numbing Sichuan dishes accented with liberal doses of Sichuan peppercorn. *See p106.*

People 8
This sparsely lit, hip restaurant provides an intimate setting for trying innovative Asian cuisines. *See p107.*

South Silk Road
South Silk Road has made ethnic eating fashionable. Wild mushrooms and other exotic ingredients are a hallmark of the food here. *See p108.*

Three Guizhou Men
A variety of lip-smacking dishes smothered in red chillies are on the menu here. *See p108.*

Yuxiang Renjia
Honest, traditional Sichuan dishes with no gimmicks, served in a rustic atmosphere. *See p108.*

Beijing is undergoing a culinary revolution of the most extraordinary kind. Over the past decade, restaurants specialising in cuisines from around China –-and the world – have sprung up across the city. And the venues, from chic, modern dining rooms to hole-in-the-wall eateries hidden in Beijing's ancient hutongs, are a big part of the fun.

The variety is even more impressive when one considers that two decades ago the city was still a culinary desert. In the 1950s, Mao Zedong decided to cut off China's capitalist tails, a move that the closure of private restaurants.

In 1980,**Yuebin Fanzhuang** (43, 31 Cuihua Hutong, opposite main gate of the National Art Museum of China, Dongcheng, Centre, 6524 5322, mains RMB 10-RMB 43) opened in a tiny hutong, becoming the first *getihu*, or private, restaurant to re-open in Beijing. It was nothing special, and has long since been eclipsed by other eateries, but it ended the long hiatus and offered markedly better food and service than the lethargic state-run restaurants. That said, right up to the early 1990s eating in the capital often meant dining out at one of the ubiquitous Cantonese or spicy Sichuan cafés, usually drab affairs with dim fluorescent lighting and plastic garbage bag table cloths that stuck to your forearms. It was not that long ago that huge heads of cabbage were piled up on the roofs of Chinese houses and on street corners, a reminder of the limited fare then available.

The opening of the **Red Capital Club** in 1999 in a restored courtyard house set the trend for quaint hutong restaurants. The beautifully renovated **The Source** offers a set meal of Sichuan dishes; and **The Courtyard**, once an old house next to the East Gate and moat of the Forbidden City, was transformed into a bright space serving fusion food.

▶ Under the 'Chinese' category, the words shown in red refer to the culinary regions – *see p108* **Types of cuisine** for a key.

❶ Purple numbers given in this chapter correspond to the location of each restaurant or café as marked on the street maps. *See pp238-249.*

Restaurants also began moving into the city's parks. Conveniently for tourists many of the best are in Ritan Park. One of the most noteworthy, however, is **Bai Family Mansion,** set in a sprawling garden that dates back to the beginning of the Qing Dynasty.

Gui Jie, or Ghost Street is lined with billowing red lanterns hanging in front of the more than 100 restaurants standing shoulder-to-shoulder on this thoroughfare that stretches 1.5 kilometres (one mile) from east to west along Dongzhimennei Street. The all-night dining boulevard is a night cat's dream. It's best known for its *mala xiao longxia* (hot, numbing crayfish); spicy duck's neck, a specialty of Wuhan; and the hot, sour fish hotpot that made Guizhou famous. Gui Jie was dubbed 'ghost' street because *gui* rhymes with the Chinese word for ghost. Actually, the character for the street name means 'vessel for holding food', but 'ghost' better captures the open-all-hours feel of the neighbourhood.

The most recent trend in restaurants in Beijing has seen the opening of chic restaurants with an ultra-contemporary design. The avant-garde **People 8** is so fashionably dark that you need a flashlight to make your way to what are probably the coolest toilets in the city. Lan, one of the latest additions to Beijing's restaurant scene, was designed by Philippe Starck, who whipped the 6,000-square metre (65,000-square-foot) space into a fairy fantasyland.

The year 2006 saw a foreign invasion as restaurants from all over the world set up shop in Beijing. In addition to American, European and South-east Asian restaurants, the city now offers Iranian, Turkish, Tunisian, Israeli, Cuban and Greek food, all opened by natives of those countries. French restaurants and pâtisseries are at the forefront. **Café de la Poste**, a French bistro set up by a young French chef, serves excellent steaks, while **W dine & wine**, opened by Belgian Geoffrey Weckx, a former chef at several five-star hotels in China, offers a variety of moderately priced continental dishes.

For all the openings, the ancient ritual of the tea house (*see p116* **More than a mere cuppa**) or a dinner at an old *laozihao* (*see p104* **Classic brands**) may still be the best part of your trip. It's difficult to imagine where the next culinary trend will take us, but one thing is certain – dining out in Beijing will never be dull again.

DINING ETIQUETTE

Chinese meals are ordered for sharing, with guests serving themselves from dishes placed in the centre of the table. It is good manners to take from each dish only what can be eaten immediately; don't pile up large amounts of food on your side plate or in your rice bowl.

If there is a serving spoon or serving chopsticks, use them; otherwise it's acceptable to use your chopsticks to take food directly from the communal plate. One custom for serving someone at your table is to flip your chopsticks so you can use the clean ends to take a portion of food to serve guests.

Use your spoon to scoop foods such as tofu or peanuts; after all, your purpose is not to show off your deft handling of chopsticks but to get food onto your plate. For anyone who finds chopsticks awkward, there is no shame in asking for a fork (*chazi*) or spoon (*shaozi*). When you're not using your chopsticks, put them on the chopstick holder – chopsticks sticking up resemble the incense sticks used at funeral services or on ancestral altars.

Cold dishes come first, followed by meat and vegetable dishes, and then fish. Soup comes last. The rice bowl will normally be your soup bowl at the end of a meal.

Chinese friends may try to get you to drink a lot, and you will often hear the toast '*ganbei*', literally 'dry bottom'. If you don't want to down your drink in one you can just say '*suiyi*' or 'as you like', which means either party can drink as little or as much as they choose. And if you don't drink at all, explain that at the beginning of the meal and stick to what you're drinking.

When dining in a more formal setting, guests normally do not drink at will. It is good manners to wait for another guest to toast you before drinking. After a toast, raise your glass with two hands and tip it slightly in the direction of the person who is toasting with you to show that you've taken a drink.

If you are invited to a meal, the person who treats will order the meals. It's rare for Chinese to go dutch, although nowadays some Chinese who understand the go-dutch concept will comfortably split the bill. But reciprocating is the favored Chinese way, taking turns to treat. If you're invited to a Chinese home for a meal bring some fruit or flowers as a gift.

PRACTICALITIES

While most of the restaurants listed in this guide have English menus, some local places will not. Our advice in this case is simply to point to the things you see on other tables. It's what the locals do.

The Chinese tend to eat early by Western standards. Most local restaurants serve lunch between 11.30am and 2pm, and dinner between 5.30pm and 9pm. Some kitchens are now staying open until 10pm, with a few restaurants even venturing into the wee hours. These places are generally not open for lunch. It is advisable to book in advance for the popular restaurants, particularly at weekends.

The Centre

The historical heart is packed with countless inexpensive eateries. Popular choices include authentic **Chuanban**, **Qin Tang Fu**, which specialises in Shaanxi dishes, and the **Red Capital Club**, which serves Zhongnanhai cuisine. For reasonably priced Western dishes, desserts and coffee, go to the **Caribou Café**.

Cafés & snacks

Caribou Café

32 Qianliang Hutong, Dongcheng (8402 1529). **Open** 10am-10pm daily. **Main courses** RMB 22-RMB 62. **No credit cards**. **English menu**. **Map** p241 L8 ❶

The Caribou Café, which you'll find off the beaten track tucked away down a hutong, is cosy, well-stocked with artsy magazines in Chinese, English and French, and decked out in cartoons drawn by customers. The hands-on owner, a former Hong Kong photojournalist who has traded the dark room for the kitchen, turns out simple and inexpensive dishes he mastered while living in Paris. Try salmon steak with mashed potatoes, pasta cooked *al dente* with home-made pesto sauce, or French onion soup. Caribou does a decent cup of cappuccino, as well as strong filtered Vietnamese coffee served with condensed milk; apple tea is a delightful alternative. Scrumptious desserts include crème brûlée, ot brownies and chocolate flan – the volcanic brown goo flows out as soon as your fork breaks into the cake.

Chinese

Chuanban

5 Gongyuan Toutiao, Jianguomennei Dajie, Dongcheng, Centre (6512 2277 ext 6101). **Open** 4.30pm-2am daily. **Main courses** RMB 3-RMB 398. **No credit cards**. **English menu**. **Map** p244 M9 ❷ Southwestern

Hidden in an alleyway just north of the Bright Chang'an Building, Chuanban is always packed. As Sichuan's provincial office it's the place to get cheap and authentic Sichuan dishes. Highlights include pock-marked Chen bean curd, *gongbao* chicken, and twice-cooked fatty pork. Start with the popular appetiser *fuqi feipian*, husband-and-wife meat slices, a mixture of lean beef and ox lung dressed in amazing Sichuan condiments, which warms up your palate for the hot dishes to come. Chuanban doesn't accept reservations, so it's best to arrive either before 6pm or after 8pm. Otherwise, be prepared to wait for at least 25 minutes. The atmosphere is celebratory and raucous rather than romantic; expect loud talking, toasting and clinking of glasses.

Ding Ding Xiang

2/F, Yuanjia International Apartments, 60 Dongzhong Jie, opposite Dong Huan Guangchang (East Gate Plaza), Dongcheng, Centre, (6417 9289). **Open** 4-10pm daily. **Main courses** RMB 100-RMB 688. **No credit cards**. **English menu**. **Map** p244 N7 ❸ Northern

The most comfortable and contemporary hotpot restaurant in town. Each diner has their own individual tiny hotpot, equipped with a small camping-style stove. The cooking here is done by dipping meat and vegetables in the boiling broth. Ding Ding Xiang's dipping sauce – named *jinpai jiang*, or gold medal sauce – is the restaurant's special recipe; this sauce won't get watery until you have finished your hotpot. Hotpots aside, this is worth a visit just to taste the *shaobing*, home-baked bread covered with sesame seeds, served still warm from the oven.

Fangshan Imperial

Inside Beihai Park, 1 Wenjin Street, Xicheng, Centre, (6401 1879). **Open** 11am-1pm, 5-8pm daily. **Main courses** RMB 198-RMB 3,000. **Credit** MC, V. **English menu**. **Map** p244 J8 ❹ Northern

Imperial court food is a style of Chinese cuisine based on the food served to the emperor and his court. It has become a major school of Chinese cooking, adopting both Manchu roasting and grilling techniques and Han braising and steaming. Those who want to experience the lavish 'Man-Han Banquet', need to cough up RMB 10,800 per head, for a minimum of 10 people. The banquet includes 134 imperial dishes, to be eaten over six days.

Huanghe Shui Shaanxi Mianguan

A24, Meishuguan Dongjie, Dongcheng, Centre (6404 4526). **Open** 11am-10.30pm daily. **Main courses** RMB 5-RMB 18. **No credit cards**. **Map** p241 L8 ❺ Northern

A simple place, east of the National Museum of Art and beside the Sanlian Bookstore, which serves Shaanxi-style noodles and dumplings. For RMB 15 you can get a giant bowl of wonderful noodles in chilli sauce, or dumplings in hot and sour soup. *Roujia mo*, the 'hamburger' that made Shaanxi famous, is pork cooked in aromatic broth and stuffed inside a baked unleavened bread. It costs just RMB 6. The place is usually packed with local patrons who know good food and appreciate value for money.

Huang Ting

The Peninsula, 8 Jinyu Hutong, Wangfujing, Dongcheng, Centre (6512 8899 ext 6707). Metro Wangfujing. **Open** 11.30am-2.30pm, 6-10pm daily. **Main courses** RMB 90-RMB 900. **Credit** AmEx, MC, V. **English menu**. **Map** p244 L9 ❻ Southern

Huang Ting' s design is based on the city's rapidly disappearing traditional courtyard houses: the walls are constructed from original hutong bricks taken from courtyard houses that have disappeared to make room for high rises; the pine floorboards and beams are from a large mansion in Suzhou; several carved stones for tying up horses upon arrival are lined up outside the 'house'. And a giant birdcage welcomes you at the door step. This is arguably Beijing's best Cantonese restaurant. Southern favorites, such as steamed scallops and bean curd in blackbean sauce,

LAN. *See p106.*

steamed fish with ginger and scallion, garlic-flavoured spare ribs and sweet and sour pork are wonderful too. Huang Ting's dim sum is delicately prepared and refined: the pan-fried turnip cake in XO sauce, deep-fried taro, spring rolls, steamed pork buns, and steamed rice flour crêpe with *youtiao*, or dough sticks, are not to be missed.

Jingsi Su Shifang

18A Dafosi Dongjie, Dongcheng, Centre (6400 8941). **Open** 10am-10pm daily. **Main courses** RMB 30-RMB 500. **No credit cards. English menu. Map** p241 L8 ❼ Northern/Vegetarian

Soft Buddhist chants hum in your ears in this small and homey restaurant, which serves no meat dishes. Much of the food is prepared to look and taste like meat, though. Try the crispy Peking 'duck', complete with wraps, or a 'fish' (made of tofu skin) that even has scales carved into it. *Zaisu jinshen*, another favourite, has a filling that looks and tastes like pork. It is wrapped in tofu skin, deep-fried, and then coated with a light sauce. *Tongzi baoxiao* ('The crowing of the young chicken') is a tasty cold appetiser made of thinly sliced tofu skin pressed together and served with a tahini-based dipping sauce. The restaurant is clean and cheerful; it's a good choice for a peaceful bite.

Jing Wei Lou

181A Dianmen Xi Dajie, Xicheng, Centre (6617 6514). **Open** 11am-2pm; 4.30-9pm daily. **Main courses** RMB 6-RMB 198. **No credit cards. English menu. Map** p241 J8 ❽ Northern

Jing Wei Lou, or 'House of Beijing Flavors' speciallises in traditional Beijing food, and is always crowded with locals. Dishes include *madoufu* (sauted mung bean pulp), *miancha* (a ground millet-flour gruel), *zha gezi* (Chinese French fries made with mung bean flour), *douzhi* (fermented mung bean juice), as well as a range of mutton dishes. A semi-open kitchen displays plump, honey-glazed ducks roasting in a wood-burning oven. The tables and chairs are made of solid wood, with an interior modelled after the traditional courtyard house to conjure the charm of old Beijing.

Jun Qin Hua

88 Meishuguan Houjie, Dongcheng, Centre (6404 7600). **Open** noon-10pm Mon-Thur, Sun; 9.30am-11pm Fri, Sat. **Main courses** RMB 10-RMB 75. **No credit cards. Map** p241 L8 ❾ Southwestern

Jun Qin Hua is the definitive hole-in-the-wall eaterie, the kind of place you're more likely to pass by rather than enter. But never judge a restaurant by its store front. *Kaili's suantang yu*, fish in tomato-based sour soup, is so fresh the fish was bobbling in the soup for ten minutes after the hotpot came to our table on a recent visit. *Mi doufu* and *juanfen*, rice-based appetisers, drenched in a sour and spicy dressing and a handful of deep-fried soybeans, are mouth watering. The *lazi ji* (à la Guizhou) is fabulous, with bite-sized pieces of chicken smothered in cloves of garlic and crushed chilies – totally different from Chongqing-style *lazi ji*. Stir-fried potatoes cooked with *zaola*, a type of crushed chillies popular in Guizhou, is another instantly likable dish. Another speciality that's not found in many other restaurants is *xiao mizha*, a sweet dish made with glutinous millet, steamed with dates and lotus seeds. This makes for an excellent end to a meal.

Kaifeng Diyi Lou

276 Dongsi Bei Dajie, Dongcheng, Centre (6401 6563). **Open** 10.30am-10pm daily. **Main courses** RMB 8-RMB 48. **No credit cards. English menu. Map** p244 L10 ❿ Central

Kaifeng Diyi Lou specialises in *guantang baozi*, steamed buns, which originate from the city of Kaifeng, capital of Henan province. Housed in a two-storey building where bright fluorescent lighting

Huang Ting. *See p94.*

gives the appearance of a typical state-owned restaurant, it is never going to win prizes for decor. Instead concentrate on the buns, which are served in a stack of bamboo steamers and dirt cheap. They come in pork filling (*chuantong*), vegetarian (*su xian'r*) or a combination of meat and seafood (*sanxian*).

Lei Garden

3/F, Jinbao Tower, 89 Jinbao Street, Dongcheng, Centre (8522 1212). **Open** 11.30am-2pm, 5.30-10.30pm daily. **Main courses** RMB 38-RMB 598. **Credit** AmEx, MC, V. **English menu.** **Map** p244 M9 ⓫ Southern

Don't be intimidated by the lavish menu of shark fin, abalone and bird's nest offered at Lei Garden. There are plenty of typical and reasonably priced Cantonese dishes to choose from, as well as a limited selection of dim sum offered from 11.30am until 3pm. The baked soft-shell crab with egg yolk created by the restaurant's innovative chef, which quickly became a hit, is impressive. A little sweet, a little spicy, just enough to wake your taste buds, and light, crispy and crunchy in texture, it's a delight. With a reputation as Beijing's best Cantonese restaurant, expect it to be packed with locals.

Li Qun Kaoya Dian

11 Beixiangfeng Hutong, Zhengyi Lu Nankou, Chongwen, Centre (6705 5578). **Open** 10am-10pm daily. **Main courses** RMB 10-RMB 100. **No credit cards. English menu. Map** p241 L10/11 ⓬ Northern/Beijing

Package tourists are shipped off to the duck-themed excesses of Quanjude (*see p114*), but this family-run eatery, operated in the Lis' own little courtyard house, is the real thing. Li Qun looks rundown and in need of a fresh coat of paint – and in the winter be prepared to feel chilled because of the poor heating and constant draft coming through the windows. Nonetheless, the place is always full. Photographs of Chinese and international celebrities and statesmen cover the walls, a testament to the quality of the food. Li Qun's ducks – which you'll see lined up in the brick oven on entering – are tasty, roasted to perfection to retain some fat, and the meat is moist and the skin crispy. The restaurant is hidden deep in a hutong neighborhood. It should take about 10 minutes to walk there from Chongwenmen Xi Dajie, although there are several pedicabs in the area that can give you a lift for RMB 5.

Liu Zhai Shifu

8 Meishuguan Dongjie, opposite Sanlian Bookstore, Dongcheng, Centre (6400 5912). **Open** 11am-10.30pm daily. **Main courses** RMB 6-RMB 10. **No credit cards.** **Map** p241 L8 ⓭ Northern/Beijing

This little corner of Lao Beijing is hidden 20 metres down a hutong, the only landmark being the two big red lanterns with the owner's name in characters. In stark contrast to the quiet alleway outside, the place is packed to the rafters nightly – many diners are regulars – and unless you've booked one of the 20 tables, think about dining elsewhere. The Liu family have lived in this courtyard house for over 100 years, but decided to turn it into a restaurant nine years ago, serving classic Beijing cuisine at bargain prices. Don't go if you're on a diet – the trad repertoire includes *madoufu* (pan-fried mung bean pulp), *zha guanchang* (deep fried sausage accompanied by garlic dipping sauce) and *zha gezi* (deep fried fries).

Made in China

Grand Hyatt Hotel, 1 Dong Chang'an Jie, Dongcheng, Centre (6510 9608). Metro Wangfujing. **Open** 11.30am-2.30pm, 5.30-10pm daily. **Main courses** RMB 40-RMB 880. **Credit** AmEx, MC, V. **English menu. Map** p244 L10 ⓮ Southwestern/Contemporary Chinese

When the Japanese design firm Super Potato took on the task of designing a restaurant space in the

Red Capital Club. *See p99.*

Grand Hyatt, there wasn't enough room for a full kitchen and a dining room. The solution: an open kitchen , envisioned as a showcase for the extraordinarily creative cooking talents of head chef Jin Qiang (*see p100* **New Beijingers**) and his staff. The spectacle is enthralling: fires and fumaroles erupt from the giant woks as chefs stir-fry Sichuan-style green beans; sous chefs carefully flip Xinjiang-style pancakes, and stuff and fold dumplings; Peking ducks roast in a brick oven metres away from where diners roll them into soft, tissue-thin pancakes. The performance, far from being a distraction, is a reminder that Chinese food, at its best, is about craftsmanship and colour as well as taste.

My Humble House

W307 Oriental Plaza, 1 Dong Changan Jie, Dongcheng, Centre (8518 8811). Metro Wangfujing. **Open** 6-11pm daily. **Main courses** RMB 200-RMB 1,000. **Credit** AmEx, MC, V. **English menu**. **Map** p241 L10 ⑮ Contemporary Chinese

From décor to dinnerware, there is nothing humble about this fusion restaurant. The main dining area is designed around a pool covered with rose petals, while gingko leaves are scattered in the hallway. My Humble House is one of the few restaurants in Beijing that successfully creates fusion dishes that tap Western ingredients but retain Chinese flavour. The lightly fried crispy prawns glazed with wasabi mayonnaise are unforgettable. For dessert, try the cool lemongrass jelly infused with pandan flavour and served with red wolfberries.

Paomo Guan

69 Chaoyangmennei Nanxiaojie, Dongcheng, Centre (6559 8135). **Open** 11.30am-2pm, 5-10pm daily. **Main courses** RMB 5-RMB 30. **Credit** AmEx, MC, V. **English menu**. **Map** p244 M9 ⑯ Northern

Paomo Guan, as its name suggests, serves up *paomo*, the Muslim dish that made Xi'an famous. First, you break one or two pieces of unleavened bread into small pieces and put them into a bowl. This done, your bowl will be taken to the kitchen where brewed spiced mutton broth is poured over the bits of bread, which expand as the broth soaks in. Side condiments of chopped coriander, chillis and sweet pickled garlic can be added once the bowl is returned to your table. Paomo Guan is often busy, especially at lunchtime, when clients cram themselves into the low chairs to tuck in to the hearty fare.

Qin Tang Fu

69 Chaoyangmennei Nanxiaojie, Dongcheng, Centre (6559-8135). **Open** 5-10pm daily. **Main courses** RMB 5-RMB 30. **Credit** MC, V. **English menu**. **Map** p244 M9 ⑰ Northern

The province's terracotta warriors may get all the publicity, but we think the Shaanxi signature dish of *roujia mo* deserves fame too. Most of Qin Tang Fu's customers are here for the Shaanxi 'hamburger' – pork cooked in aromatic broth and served in unleavened bread. A traditional stove is set by the entrance, producing a constant flow of hot loaves. Framed paper cuts are hung on the wall, handicrafts are dotted around, and there are woven baskets under the table to store your belongings while eating. The low tables and chairs here reflect the lifestyle of Shaanxi folks, who are accustomed to squatting on low stools while slurping their noodles. And it's not just the stools that are low: so are the prices.

Red Capital Club

66 Dongsijiutiao, Dongcheng, Centre (8401 8886). **Open** 6pm-midnight daily. **Main courses** RMB 28-RMB 258. **Credit** AmEx, MC, V. **English menu**. **Map** p244 M8 ⑱ Northern

This finely restored courtyard restaurant is dedicated to the good things in life – fine food and wine and cigars – and to the spirit of Chinese capitalism. So its ironic that the restaurant has turned to the past and Communism, for its theme: *zhongnanhai* ('leadership'). The kitchen produces the kind of food served at official state banquests, and said to reflect the tastes of puritanical senior Communist officials.

There is a story behind each dish. For example, the Marshals' Favourite, large hot green peppers stuffed with minced pork, is said to have been a favoured dish of Party officials during the epic Long March. Deng's Chicken is decorated with small black and a white cats, one carved out of a beet and the other from a turnip, in homage to Deng's statement that 'It doesn't matter whether a cat is black or white, as long as it catches mice.' Don't forget to climb down to the courtyard bomb shelter, which has been turned into a wine and cigar cellar. **Photo** *p98*.

Shaguo Ju

60 Xisi Nan Dajie, Xicheng, Centre (6602 1126). **Open** 11am-10pm daily. **Main courses** RMB 30-RMB 50. **No credit cards**. **English menu**. **Map** p241 H9 ⑲ Northern

Established in 1741, Shaguo Ju serves a simple Manchu favourite – *bairou*, or pork. The first two pages of the menu all the dishes cooked in the *shaguo* (literally 'sand pot', the Chinese term for a casserole dish). The classic *shaguo bairou* is strips of lean and fatty pork neatly lined up concealing the bok choi and glass noodles below. It is accompanied by a pinkish dipping sauce of fermented beancurd, rice wine, chilli oil and sesame seeds. Shaguo Ju has its roots in the ceremonies held by imperial officials and wealthy Manchus during the Qing Dynasty, which included the sacrificial offerings of whole pigs – the meat was given away, and the pork industry boomed in China.

Xiao Nan Guo

2nd Floor, Jinbao Tower, 89 Jinbao Jie, Dongcheng, Centre (8522 1717). **Open** 11am-2pm, 5-11pm (last order 9.45pm) daily. **Main courses** RMB 10-RMB 1,608. **Credit** MC, V. **English menu**. **Map** p244 M9 ⑳ Eastern

Xiao Nan Guo is one of the better restaurants serving 'Shanghainese' cuisine in the capital, a cooking style that favours less oil and a lighter taste. Particularly good appetisers include *malantou xianggan*, finely chopped bean curd mixed with a wild grass that resembles fennel in taste. *Malantou baiye juan* is another variation, in which the vegetables are rolled in a tofu sheet. The food here is rich in vegetables. Among the more unusual, *jicai*, a wild vegetable similar to coriander, is stir-fried with bamboo shoots or stir-fried pea shoots. *Laoya bao*, or duck soup, and braised beancurd with crab roe, are typical Shanghai dishes; for a more energising meal try fried snake meat and stewed turtle. The dark, low-key decor makes for a quiet setting.

International

The Courtyard

95 Donghuamen Donganmen Dajie, Xipei Lou, Dongcheng, Centre (6526 8883). **Open** 6-10pm (9.15pm last order) daily. **Main courses** RMB 125-RMB 245. **Credit** AmEx, MC, V. **English menu**. **Map** p241 K9 ㉑ Western fusion

One of Beijing's most elegant and upscale restaurants, the Courtyard has views of the East Gate and moat of the Forbidden City. Executive chef Rey Lim, who learned his craft at the CIA (the Culinary Institute of America, that is), turns out a version of fusion that relies on French-based cooking with a good sprinkling of Asian ingredients. You might find steamed sea bass with pickled bell pepper; jumbo shrimp with lemongrass-caramel glacé; or grilled lamb tenderloin with ratatouille. Come here to get away from Beijing's crowded streets and sip a good wine, reclining on the brown leather sofa and overlooking the moat that once protected the imperial family from the outside world.

Garden of Delights

53 Donganmen Dajie (by the East Gate of the Wancheng Huafu Hotel), Dongcheng, Centre (5138 5688). **Open** noon-2.30pm, 6-11pm daily. **Main courses** RMB 140-RMB 220. **Credit** AmEx, MC, V. **English menu**. **Map** p241 L9 ㉒ Argentinian

Decorated with scenes of figures frolicking in paradise (à la *Garden of Earthly Delights*), this restaurant is one of a kind. The menu fuses Latin cuisine with a continental twist. Ceviche is a speciality – raw fish or seafood marinated in lime or lemon juice. We like the tuna tartare, a chopped mix of tuna, onions, and the perfect amount of citrus, and the *matambre*, a huge and hearty melt-in-the-mouth steak, prepared with red wine. A warm chocolate soufflé cake with a molten white chocolate centre made an indulgent pudding. Garden of Delights is big on Latin cocktails too – try a minty Mojito or a Caiprihina.

New Beijinger The chef

The main changes in Beijing over recent years have been the increase in living standards. When I was little it was completely different, the city was dirty, but now, the environment, home life, food, everything has got a lot better. Although the changes might not be that different year on year, if you've been living here like I have since I was born in 1964, the changes have been phenomenal. **When I get time off** I try to go to other cities of China that have an interesting food culture, such as Anhui, Guangzhou and Sichuan, so it's more like studying than holidaying. I very rarely go to bars or clubs, but we do go to each others' restaurants and taste different things and see what the atmosphere is like. Unlike when I was young, we now eat for enjoyment rather than just for sustenance. **Transport is something that can be irritating** in Beijing, but the government is working on solutions. The problem is that Beijing is just so big and the speed of development isn't the same. **It's annoying when you find that they are digging up the road** outside your house, but you know that they are only doing this to make the road better eventually. **If I were to take visitors around Beijing**, then of course I would take them to the Temple of Heaven, the Great Wall, the Forbidden City, but I would also take them to the old hutongs of Beijing – there are still thousands. I would also take them to eat *shuanyangrou* (hotpot). **When people meet in China, traditionally they ask 'Are you full?'** but nowadays they ask, 'How's it going?' or 'How are you?' This is because there is no longer poverty and people don't eat to get full, they just eat well. This shows how the quality of life has improved. As more foreigners come to Beijing to see the culture and traditions, there will be an increase in food types, and you will soon see food from every nation. And as the spending power of the Chinese increases they will want to try these new foods. But Chinese people will still always prefer Chinese food. **Although Made In China offers home-style cooking**, it will evolve over time. This year we even cooked Western-style Christmas dinner.

Houhai & the North

The Houhai area was once a quiet and peaceful neighbourhood with a handful of quiet, small bars and restaurants. No longer. The lakeside area is now packed with restaurants and bars serving a wide variety of cuisines. A dozen old restaurants evicted from the Qianmen area have found refuge here in a small hutong at the end of the lake under the collective name **Jiumen Xiaochi**. Nan Luogu Xiang is an upcoming street with a good mixture of coffee shops, bars and restaurants serving Chinese and Western cuisines. Ghost Street – which is lined by hundreds of glowing red lanterns – is famous for its hot and spicy hotpot, spicy crawfish, and tasty duck neck, a specialty of Wuhan; it's also great for snacking as there are dozens of small bars between the restaurants.

Cafés & snacks

Xiao Xin De Dian

103 Nan Luogu Xiang, Dongcheng, Houhai (6403 6956). **Open** 10am-1am daily. **Main courses** RMB 25-RMB 65. **No credit cards. English menu. Map** p241 K7 ㉓

Probably the best coffee shop among the handful located on the memory lane of Nan Luogu Xiang. The walls and book shelves are filled with Beijing memorabilia: an old radio, a kid's bike, old books and magazines. A huge potted plant is the centre piece, and with the goldfish swimming happily in a glass bowl and lots of natural light shining through through the skylight, this is a place to waste a long afternoon. Xiao Xin's famous cheesecake comes in lemon, coffee, and blueberry flavours. Arguably the best in Beijing, cheesecake is baked on the premises, and is fresh, delicious and reasonably priced.

I would love to take real home-style cooking abroad. Not the type of Chinese food you get abroad. It's hard for people to handle *mala* (numbing spice) so it is toned down, so much so that it's not real Chinese food.

The pace of the old people in Beijing is different. They spend their days taking their birds for a walk. Even their language is different and they don't care about modernity. There is an arrogance with Beijing people. The people who still live in the hutongs have shared toilets, but they get migrants (non-Beijingers) to clean them. This is the Imperial City don't forget! Many of the young are only interested in playing. There are more and more playboys. A lot of them are very lazy, their parents pay for everything and they just eat, drink and play. Of course there are young people who work hard, but a lot of people are born into positions. It's like being born into nobility in the UK. This is something unique to Beijing.

My tip for people coming to Beijing is just to be honest. If I'm honest to you, you'll be honest to me. Oh and study the Beijing dialect very hard. That will win you brownie points. Beijing is like a never-finished picture. You paint the picture and think you've finished, but when you come back the next day you need to add to it and readjust as it has changed so much overnight.

Beijing-born Jin Qiang is Chef de Cuisine at Made in China (see p97), in the Grand Hyatt Hotel.

Chinese

Jiumen Xiaochi

1 Xiaoyou Hutong, Xicheng, Houhai (6402 5858). **Open** 10.30am-1.30pm, 5.30-8pm. **Main courses** RMB 2-RMB 15/snacks, RMB 88/hotpot. **No credt cards. Map** p241 J7 ㉔ Northern

Come here for the ancient *laozihao* experience and to sample a variety of cuisines from stalls set up on both sides of the indoor hutong. *See p104* **Classic brands.**

Guo Yao Xiaoju

58 Bei Santiao, Jiaodao Kou, Andingmennei Dajie, Dongcheng, Houhai (6403 1940). **Open** 10am-2.30pm, 5.30-9pm daily. **Main courses** RMB 90-RMB 1,000. **No credit cards. English menu. Map** p241 L7 ㉕ Southern

The Beijing Culinary Association named this small family restaurant as the best for private dining in 2005, and this is no empty accolade. The food prepared here is phenomenal. Chef Guo Xinjun, an expert in Tan cuisine and a former chef at the Beijing Hotel, has prepared state banquets for US Presidents Richard Nixon and Bill Clinton, and Chinese leaders such as Deng Xiaoping. Every dish is in the Tan style, a fusion of Huaiyang and Guangdong cuisine – light and of the utmost delicacy. *Nongtang yudu*, fish maw in rich broth, has a rich stock made from chicken, duck, scallop, and ham by double-boiling on a low flame, a Tan specialty. *Yasi danjuan*, shredded duck with chives rolled in a crispy crêpe, is a perfect marriage of pungent chives and duck: wonderful. For most vegetable dishes only the tender stems are used, and they come poached and lightly seasoned with soy sauce. The sausage is vinous and full of flavour – we've found no similar sausage at any Beijing restaurant. Finish up with freshly ground almond paste or peanut paste, or osmanthus-flavoured red bean paste.

Gu Zhenhuang

3 Qianhai Xijie, Xicheng, Houhai (6613 9641). **Open** 6-9.30pm Mon-Thur; 11am-2pm, 6-9.30pm Fri-Sun. **Main courses** RMB 280-RMB 1,400/set meals only. **No credit cards. English menu.** **Map** p241 J7 ㉖ Southern

Gu Zhenhuang is so proud of its Hong Kong-imported chef, Zhang Jingming, that the owner has put up a plaque with his name on it beside the entrance to this tiny courtyard house, just 200m from the end of Lotus Lane. That owner is a Hong Kong gourmand and writer (Gu Zhenhuang is his pen name), who set up this charming and understated restaurant to showcase the best in Cantonese cooking, in a town that he felt lacked decent Cantonese restaurants. Chef Zhang has been dubbed the 'Young Kitchen God' for his expertise in the southern culinary technique of keeping the inside of food tender and moist while cooking it to a state of crispiness on the outside. Only set meals are available.

Han Cang

Shichahai Dongan, Xicheng, Houhai (6404 2259). **Open** 11am-10.30pm daily. **Main courses** RMB 38-RMB 68. **No credit cards. English menu.** **Map** p241 K8 ㉗ Southern

If you're in the mood for something other than Cantonese or Sichuan fare, try Hakka cuisine, the earthy food of China's Guest People. The specialties here are *sanbei ya*, or three-cup duck, salt-baked shrimp, and baked whole fish wrapped in aluminium foil. If you're in a group, be sure to book one of the tables on the second floor, with a lake view. Han Cang's rustic decor, which features rice paper pasted on the rough cement walls with random calligraphy, lend a chic, rough-around-the-edges look. The bird cage, pig's trough filled with goldfish and thick wooden tables on a granite floor emphasise the peasanty but arty look. **Photo** *p103*.

Kong Yiji

South shore of Shichahai, Deshengmennei Dajie, Xicheng, Houhai (6618 4915). **Open** 24hrs daily. **Main courses** RMB 20-RMB 50. **Credit** AmEx, MC, V. **English menu. Map** p241 J7 ㉘ Eastern

This restaurant, which serves the specialities of Zhejiang province, is named for the down-and-out protagonist of a short story by Lu Xun, the so-called father of modern Chinese literature. Diners pass through a small bamboo forest and the first thing you see upon entering the restaurant proper is a bust of Lu Xun himself.

The antique-looking menu, which is bound in traditional style with thread, features some of the dishes made famous in the popular story, such as *huixiang dou*, aniseed-flavoured broad beans. Other exceptional dishes include *youtiao niurou* – savoury slices of beef mixed with pieces of fried dough, and *dongpo rou* – tender braised fatty pork in caramelised sauce. A wide selection of *huangjiu*, a sweet rice wine, is served in heated silver pots, and sipped from a special ceramic cup with hot water in the bottom to keep the wine warm.

Source

14 Banchang Hutong, Nan Luogu Xiang, Kuanjie, Dongcheng, Houhai (6400 3736). **Open** 10.30am-10.30pm daily. **Main courses** RMB 128-RMB 600. **Credit** AmEx, MC, V. **English menu.** **Map** p241 L8 ㉙ Southwest

Located in a well-renovated courtyard house, the tastefully decorated Source serves a set menu of Sichuan specialties, which changes every two weeks. The menu includes several appetisers, both hot and mild dishes, and a few improvised by the chef. The kitchen always asks if you can take the heat: chefs are prepared to make dishes less spicy by using fewer chillis if need be. The Source's premises were once the backyard of a Qing dynasty general regarded by the Qing court as 'The Great Wall of China' for his military exploits. The grounds have been meticulously renovated; an added upper level of the house overlooks the little garden, filled with pomegranate and date trees. The garden is perfect for al fresco summer dining.

Xi Xiangzi

36 Dingfu Jie, Xicheng, Houhai (1390 136 8036). **Open** 11am-2pm, 5-10pm daily. **Main courses** RMB 10-RMB 88. **No credit cards. English menu. Map** p241 J7 ㉚ Central

Xi Xiangzi is the creation of two people from different countries who share the same passion for good food and authentic Hunan cooking – Aymeric Figureau from France and his Hunan-born wife Liu Jun. A sign outside declares that the restaurant serves 'Hunan food with a French touch'. Actually, there is no noticeable French touch to the Hunan cooking; the French connection is found in the listing of cheese, sausages and other French items at the end of the menu. Instead, the home-style food here will bring back memories of Changsha to any native of the region. *Huiguo rou chao xianggan*, smoked bean curd with pork belly, and *qincai rousi chao xianggan*, smoked bean curd with slivers of celery and lean meat, are typical Hunan dishes, and both are excellent renditions. *Gan doujiao zheng wuhua rou*, steamed belly pork on a bed of pickled green bean, is also flavoursome. *Duojiao yutou*, steamed fish head doused with chillies, is a signature dish.

Zhang Qun Jia

5 Yandai Xiejie, Houhai, Xicheng, Houhai (8404 6662). **Open** By reservation only. **Main courses** RMB 200-RMB 600/set meals only. **No credit cards. Map** p241 K7 ㉛ Eastern

Zhang Qun Jia, or Zhang Qun's Home, was opened three years ago by a Beijing artist as a place where she and her creative friends could hang out, but it soon turned into a one-table restaurant serving the specialties of her native Suzhou. The scattered books, fresh cut flowers, and old furniture, create the welcoming feeling of a friend's home. The aroma and taste of the spring onion in the *yangchun* noodles is captivating. Set meals cost RMB 200 to RMB 500 per person, and include a large number of appetisers, hot dishes and a dessert.

Be the guest of the Guest People at **Han Cang**. *See p102.*

International

Café de la Poste

58 Yonghegong Dajie, Dongcheng, Houhai (6402 7047). **Open** 11am-11.30pm daily. **Main courses** RMB 30-RMB 100. **No credit cards. English menu. Map** p244 L7 ㉜ French

The popular Café de la Poste, not far from the Lama Temple, has a semi-open kitchen where you can watch your steak sizzling in the frying pan. Yannick Gauthier, the 26-year-old chef-cum-owner, says he gave his restaurant the most standard name he could think of – the kind of town meeting point found across France, where patrons pop in for a coffee, a beer or just a simple family meal. The Beijing version is packed nightly with French expats and is a reliable place to come for a decent steak and good wine without having to dig too deep.

Café Sambal

43 Doufuchi Hutong, Jiu Gulou Dajie, Xicheng, Houhai (6400 4875). **Open** noon-midnight daily. **Main courses** RMB 100-RMB 140. **Credit** AmEx, MC, V. **English menu. Map** p241 K7 ㉝ Malaysian

For fine food in totally laidback surroundings, you can't beat Café Sambal. The sambal in the name refers to a sauce made with chillies and, in this case, lots of sambal. Food is authentic and quality consistent; over three years in the business and standards remain high, rare in Beijing's all-too-flaky dining scene. The hutong setting is a delight, as is the layout, with a bar area fronting three distinct dining rooms: formal; not quite so formal, and so completely informal that chairs and tables are dispensed with altogether in favour of wall-to-wall cushions.

Luce

138 Jiu Gulou Dajie, Dongcheng, Houhai (8402 4417). **Open** 1-10.30pm daily. **Main courses** RMB 36-RMB 88. **No credit cards. English menu. Map** p241 K7 ㉞ Italian

Quality Italian food in a quietly upmarket setting is the name of the game at Luce. White walls, pale cream and green furnishings, fresh-cut flowers and light flooding through a skylight set the scene. The menu is reassuringly short and snappy: a starter of orange salad with lemon vinaigrette might be followed by a rich but not heavy potato gnocci with tomato sauce and gorgonzola, or a creamy risotto with Yunnan mushrooms. Steaks are another popular choice. For pudding, a rich cheesecake has a nutty rather than a biscuit base.

Chaoyang

Many upscale Chinese and international restaurants are located in the Jianguomenwai and Sanlitun areas. Ladies Market Street and Lucky Street, in the north-west near the Kempinski Hotel, are on the rise because a new embassy area is being built around here, and there are dozens of restaurants. The 798 Art District has cool coffee shops and restaurants alongside hip art galleries.

Chinese

Anping Gujie

Tower A, No. 106, Jianwai Soho, 39 Dong Sanhuan Zhonglu (south of China World), Chaoyang (5869

Classic brands

Beijing's *laozihao*s – literally meaning 'brand-name' but referring to ancient restaurants of great repute – used to crowd the old Dazhalan section of Qianmen. In pre-Liberation days, residents lived in the lap of luxury and everything was designed for their convenience. There were eateries of every price and stamp, and the borough buzzed with the cries of vendors offering bean curd custard and the raucous clacker of the plum-juice seller, whose aromatic drink mingled with the fragrant smell of Chen's famed speciality – intestines – which drifted down the alleyways.

The buildings and the vendors have, in the main, vanished, but fortunately, some *laozihao*s, including a few of the best, have found refuge in a large traditional courtyard house called **Jiumen Xiaochi** (*see p101*) – or Nine Gates Snacks – down Menkuang Hutong, which keeps alive centuries-old cooking traditions. The best establishments here include:

Baodu Feng

The Fengs, an old Beijing Muslim family, have been making flash-boiled tripe for several generations going back to Qing Dynasty. The tahini-based dipping sauce that goes with the tripe is a secret family recipe.

Niangao Qian

Known for sticky rice layered with red bean paste as well as *ludagun* or 'donkey rolling on the ground', the most popular sticky rice snack made by the Hui, or Chinese Muslims.

Yangtou Ma

Valued for its fine cuts of boiled meat sliced from a lamb's head. This shop used to be located on Ox Street, in the Muslim quarter.

Doufunao Bai

The characteristic of this outlet's soft beancurd is its fine, delicate texture – served topped with braised lamb and mushrooms.

En Yuan Ju

Famous for *chao geda*, stir-fried morsel-sized noodles with veggies and meat.

Yue Sheng Zhai

Serves wonderful *jiang niurou* (braised beef), *shao yangrou* (braised lamb) and *yang zasui* (soup with sheep entrails).

Dalian Huoshao

Makes pan-fried dumplings in the shape of old-fashioned satchels that Chinese once wore over their shoulders. The recipe was devised by the Yao family of Shunyi, who set up shop in the old Dongan Market in 1876.

2083). Metro Guomao. **Open** 9.30am-12.30am daily. **Main courses** RMB 20-RMB 98. **Credit** AmEx, MC, V. **English menu**. **Map** p245 O10 (35) Southern/Taiwanese

Anping Gujie offers the cuisine of Tainan, a small port city in southern Taiwan. Hakka and Taiwanese dishes are integral elements of the menu here: *oa jian*, a Taiwanese traditional oyster omelette dished up in night markets around Taiwan, *caipu dan*, a Hakka turnip omelet, and *kejia xiaochao*, stir-fried celery with squid. Garlic soup (*suantou ji*) is Anping's signature dish. The aroma alone is enticing, and the broth profoundly subtle in flavour. *Sanbei doufu*, or three-cup tofu, seasoned garlic and basil is one of the best mains, while homemade caramelised pineapple topped with shaved ice makes a sweet and refreshing end to a meal.

Bellagio

6 Gongti Xilu, Chaoyang (6551 3533). **Open** 11am-5am daily. **Main courses** RMB 20-RMB 60. **Credit** AmEx, MC, V. **English menu**. **Map** p244 N8 (36) Southern

With a name like Bellagio, you would think this is an Italian restaurant, but it's not. Its Chinese name – Lugang Xiaozhen (the little town of Lugang) – tells you that this restaurant has a connection with Taiwan. The food is a mixture of typical Taiwanese dishes, like *migao*, steamed glutinous rice flavoured with dried mushrooms and dried shrimps; Hakka specialties such as *caipu dan*, a puffed omelette with turnip; and Sichuan dishes with a Taiwanese twist. The shaved ice as high as Mount Tai is mouthwatering and comes in mango, strawberry, kiwi, and peanut flavours; equally tantalising is the traditional crushed ice topped with slightly sweet red beans or mung beans, with lava-like condensed milk dripping over it. Its airy interior, with high ceilings and large windows, comfortable sofa-like armchairs, fresh cut flowers and willow branches in giant vases attracts the capital's young hipsters. Even the staff here look cool, with identical, but fashionable, short haircuts. Bellagio stays open until 4am, which makes it a popular spot for *xiaoye*, late-night snacks that are common in Taiwan. **Photo** *p106.*

Din Tai Fung

22 Hujiayuan, Yibei Building, Dongcheng, Chaoyang (6462 4502). **Open** 11.30am-2.30pm, 5-10pm daily. **Main courses** RMB 20-RMB 158. **Credit** MC, V. **English menu**. **Map** p244 N7 (37) Eastern

The arrival of Din Tai Fung was keenly anticipated by Beijing foodies. This restaurant, which specialises in the delicate dishes of Zhejiang and Jiangsu provinces, has a bright and contemporary design, and subtle food combinations, skilfully prepared. *Xiaolong bao* – juicy buns wrapped in a skin of light unleavened dough and cooked in a bamboo steamer – is the restaurant's signature dish.

They are served with thin slivers of young, tender ginger in a light black vinegar. *Xiaolong bao* come with three choices of filling: ground pork, seafood, and crabmeat. *Cairou zhengjiao* (steamed dumplings), another specialty, are packed with *youcai*, small green-leaf bok choy and a small amount of minced pork with some lard. These are our favourite of all the dumplings served here – and the lard is key to the flavour. Leave some room for *dousha bao*, sweet red bean paste stuffed in almost transparent buns. These tiny desserts melt in your mouth.

Hot Loft

5th Floor, 8 Gongti Xi Lu, Chaoyang (6552 7992). Metro Dongsishitiao; 4 Gongti Bei Lu, Chaoyang (6501 7501) Metro Dongsishitiao. **Open** 9am-2am daily. **Main courses** from RMB 80. **Credit** AmEx, MC, V. **English menu**. **Map** p244 N8 ㊳ Northern

Hot Loft has dragged the bubbling hotpot into the 21st century by increasing the range of soup bases – the menu features everything from a sour and spicy Thai broth to a duck-based broth – and introducing a variety of novel dipping sauces. The set meal at RMB 56 includes the standard hotpot accompaniment: a choice of beef or lamb, a mixture of vegetables, pork or beef meatballs, and a dipping sauce. We love the beef: it is sirloin cut and truly excellent; paper-thin, it cooks instantly in the bubbling broth. Sleek and stylish, the Hot Loft is probably the most comfortable place to eat hotpot in the city. Just getting inside the restaurant is a little tricky. Place your hand above the a pot which functions as like a barcode reader. When you break the beam of light, the door will open just like in an Indiana Jones movie.

House by the Park

China Central Place, 89 Jianguo Lu (On Xidawang Lu) Level 2, Club House, Chaoyang (6530 7770). Metro Dawanglu. **Open** 11.30am-2.30pm; 5.30-10.30pm daily. **Main courses** RMB 38-RMB 498. **Credit** AmEx, MC, V. **English menu**. **Map** p245 P10 ㊴ Contemporary Chinese

Hues of black, white and dark wood in an interior designed by MYU Planning of Tokyo create a feeling of intimacy and exclusivity in the House by the Park, sister restaurant of My Humble House (*see p98*). The two restaurants offer many of the same dishes, though some of the seasonal fare is different. Owner Andrew Tjioe describes the food as 'modern Chinese cuisine' – it creatively blends global ingredients with Chinese cooking methods and flavours, with special attention paid to artistic presentation. Western-style salad tossed in a fusion dressing made from wasabi, peanut and sesame sauce is intriguing and full of flavour.

Sliced roast duck – an interpretation of the classic Peking duck dish made with tasty pieces of meat, melon and crispy tofu wrapped in a silky smooth steamed bun – is spectacular. The roast rack of lamb is another great fusion dish. A scrumptious fried turnip cake is paired with roast lamb so tender it falls off the bone. Crispy roast spring pigeon, marinated with spices and Chinese wine, is another successful dish. For pudding try cubes of almond tofu flavoured with coconut sherbet or cream of mango with a dollop of vanilla. Wine by the glass is limited and expensive. Best to stick to the house Martinis – the apple one is wonderfully refreshing.

Huangcheng Laoma

39 Fengzha Houjie, Dabeiyao, Chaoyang (6779 8801). **Open** 11am-11pm daily. **Main courses** RMB 15-RMB 50. **Credit** AmEx, MC, V. **English menu**. **Map** p245 P10 ㊵ Northern

What is the secret weapon that keeps luring diners into Huangcheng Laoma? Well, the grey building may look like a castle from a distance, but the interior is furnished comfortably enough with traditional tables and chairs. And as soon as you enter Laoma (Old Mum's Place) your lungs are seduced by the aromatic flavour of Sichuan peppercorn and chillies. The intense spiciness at this Sichuan hotpot restaurant is exhilarating. But please be warned: do not, repeat, do not touch or rub your eyes with your fingers or you'll ruin the whole experience with burning eyes. The food works as in all hotpot restaurants: you order a variety of plates of thin sliced beef or chicken, and all the usual veg is available, including spinach, cabbage, potatoes, tofu, mushrooms, and beanstarched noodles. **Photo** *p107*.

In & Out

1 Sanlitun Bei Xiaojie, Chaoyang (8454 0086). Metro Dongsishitiao. **Open** 11am-11pm daily. **Main courses** RMB 8-RMB 76. **Credit** MC, V. **English menu**. **Map** p244 O7 ㊶ Yunnan/Southwestern

Don't let the name confuse you. This Sanlitun eatery is not some sort of Californian hamburger joint, but owner Li Gang's dream of transporting the Dongba culture of the Naxi – who live in the ancient town of Lijiang at the foot of the snow-capped mountain of Meili – to Beijing. The restaurant boasts eight different ethnic cuisines from all around the southwestern province of Yunnan, including the foods of the Bai, Dai, Naxi, and Wa minorities.

Lijiang *baba* (steamed sticky rice cake), flavoured pork skin and beef skin, and deep-fried green moss – all carefully prepared – are popular ethnic dishes that you won't find in other minority restaurants in Beijing. Dongba calligraphy hangs on the grey-brick wall, and beautiful colour photos of Lijiang punctuate the walls along the stairways, providing a colourful glimpse of the Naxi world. To set the theme, staff decked out in Naxi and Dai costumes greet guests at the door with warm smiles.

Don't judge a restaurant by its name. **Bellagio** is Taiwanese. *See p104.*

Jia 21 Zhaodaisuo

Beitucheng Dong Lu, Chaoyang (6489 5066). **Open** 10.30am-10.30pm daily. **Main courses** RMB 20-RMB 180. **Credit** AmEx, MC, V. **English menu**. **Map** p242 M4 ㊷ Southwestern

Jia 21 Zhaodaisuo features Yunnan, Sichuan, and Guizhou specialities with a hint of Thai influence. Located off a small alley near the Sino-Japanese Friendship Hospital, the restaurant's impressive glass-walled exterior is the first indication that this is no run-of-the-mill Chinese restaurant. Sculptures by artist Gao Xiaowu adorn the interior, along with palm trees, funky chandeliers and lounge chairs – a far cry from the usual round banquet tables. *Nami* salad loaded with mint leaves comes in a giant bowl and is tossed with a tangy tomato dressing at your table. Char-grilled aubergine and red peppers with roasted strips of vegetable in a smoky sauce are vibrant and distinctive. Jia 21's seafood soup is a speciality. It comes served in an enormous bowl that contains crab, prawns, mussels and fish, swimming in a clear broth with leek, lemongrass and lime leaves – a good varierty of ingredients and a nice subtle flavour. The restaurant does other standard dishes well, like the nicely spiced *dan dan* noodles, tender steamed fish head, and *midoufu*, strips of steamed rice cake in savoury and spicy sauce.

LAN

4th Floor, LG Twin Towers, B12 Jianguomenwai Dajie, Chaoyang (5109 6012). Metro Yong'anli. **Open** 11am-midnight (last order 10.30pm) daily. **Main courses** RMB 48-RMB 3,000. **Credit** AmEx, MC, V. **English menu**. **Map** p244 N10 ㊸ Contemporary Chinese

LAN's main attraction is not the food on your plate but the wild and eclectic interior by Philippe Starck. Renaissance-style paintings hang upside down from the ceilings; white sculptures of heads decorate one display case; novels line a shelf. And the toilets: individual loos come with mirrored walls, silver armchair, and swan-shaped taps that make them look like a set from a David Lynch film. The menu runs the gamut from raw oysters to Japanese sushi to fanciful Chinese fusion to basic Sichuanese. Several pages of the menu are devoted to Chinese delicacies like abalone, shark's fin and fish maw. The wine list offers an impressive range of European, South American and Australian choices without a Great Wall or Dynasty in sight. When it comes to ordering at LAN, it's probably a good idea to stick to the traditional Sichuan dishes like *shuizhuyu*, fish cooked in a pot of oil, and *kongpao* chicken, where cashews replace peanuts for a richer crunch and the sauce is spicy, sweet, and slightly numbing – made by the traditional textbook method. LAN serves smart desserts, going for an all-Western selection of cakes and mousses. **Photo** *p95*.

Makye Ame

11A Xiushui Nanjie, Jianguomenwai, Chaoyang (6506 9616). Metro Yong'anli. **Open** noon-midnight daily. **Main courses** RMB 30-RMB 100. **Credit** AmEx, MC, V. **English menu**. **Map** p244 N10 ㊹ Southwestern

Opened in 2001, Makye Ame is one of the oldest Tibetan restaurants in Beijing. Colourful prayer flags fluttering in the wind welcome you at the entrance. Paper lanterns and ceremonial brass trumpets are among the other colourful objects. Dishes include a tender and subtlely spicy roast lamb rib with ground chillies and cumin. Balabani is a puréed spinach with cubes of goat cheese, slightly spicy and very appetising. Stir-fried beef with pickled carrots, and mushrooms with tomatoes roasted with bit of yak butter and garlic are classic Tibetan dishes, both featured here. Curried potatoes are excellent, as is the beef and onions sizzled on a hot stone. Try *tsampa* – the hearty grain that grows in the highlands of Tibet – sweetened with honey and butter.

Noodle Loft

20 Xidawang Lu, Chaoyang (6774 9950). **Open** 11am-10pm daily. **Main courses** RMB 8-RMB 60. **Credit** AmEx, MC, V. **English menu**. **Map** p245 P10 ㊺ Northern

The simple noodle dishes of the Shanxi province, which is situated just to the west of Beijing, are the speciality of Noodle Loft. The restaurant is considered outrageously overpriced by locals, but this place is no ordinary noodle stand. It's a huge space with an open noodle bar on the first floor, where fresh noodles are stretched and pulled, and a comfortable dining area on the second floor. *Daoxiao mian*, knife-shaved noodles, are a trademark of Shanxi. The noodles come with a sauce of your choice: minced meat sauce, tomato and egg or vinegar. Try stir-fried cat's ears (just a name, there are no cats involved), with assorted vegetables. **Photo** *p108*.

People 8

18 Jianguomenwai Dajie, Chaoyang (6515 8585). Metro Yong'anli. **Open** 5.30-11pm daily. **Main courses** RMB 25-RMB 200. **Credit** AmEx, MC, V. **English menu**. **Map** p244 N10 ㊻ Japanese Fusion

'Oh no, not this again' was our first thought when confronted with the two doors to the entrance of People 8, recalling a similar dilemma at People 7 in Shanghai, where we once spent 15 minutes trying to work out the special combination of touch-triggers that would open the doors. This a Shintori Group trick, employed in its other seven restaurants and now in this one – its first in Beijing.

Once you've negotiated entry you'll find yourself in a corridor, pitch black, but for a handful of carefully placed spotlights. The bar, with an array of coloured bottles glistening like gems, greets you at the top of the staircase. In the restaurant, the blackness of the space, surrounded by bamboo trees and with shafts of light peeping through here and there, makes you feel as though you're in an enchanted forest. Huge vases of white lilies light up tables amid the darkness. Food is eclectic. The signature Rock and Roll salad is prepared at the table with Italian black olive oil and tossed in bonito fish flakes. An assorted sashimi plate is beautifully presented on a huge green-glazed ceramic bowl filled with crushed ice. Spare ribs in plum sauce are sweet and succulent, and grilled codfish steak with mono miso is delicious. Considering the fantastic setting and outstanding food, it would be hard to find a more exciting and satisfying dining experience.

Shin Yeh

6 Gongti Xilu, Chaoyang (6552 5066). Metro Dongsishitiao. **Open** 11.30am-2.30pm, 5-10pm daily. **Main courses** RMB 20-RMB 430. **Credit** AmEx MC, V. **English menu**. **Map** p244 N8 ㊼ Southern/Taiwanese

Shin Yeh, a top-notch restaurant focusing on refined Taiwanese cuisine, is serious about its food. The menu is extensive, from basic vermicelli noodles topped with fragrant fried shallots to a lavish Buddha Jumping Over the Wall soup, with ten servings per pot of soup. Any *sanbei*, or three-cup, dish is delicious; choose from chicken, mushroom or, more unusually, bull frog. Deep fried *taro*, deep fried oysters and deep fried cuttle fish are light, crispy and flavoursome. *Babao youfan*, steamed glutinous rice served in a small wooden bucket is a classic. Finish your meal with a cold almond tofu, hot sweet red bean soup with tiny balls of *tangyuan* (made with sticky rice), or *mashu*, steamed starched sweet potato cake rolled with ground peanuts.

Huangcheng Laoma. *See p105*.

South Silk Road

3rd Floor, Bldg. D, Soho New Town, 88 Jianguo Lu, Chaoyang (6615 5515). Metro Dawanglu. **Open** noon-midnight daily. **Main courses** RMB 8-RMB 388. **Credit** AmEx, MC, V. **English menu**. **Map** p245 P10 48 Southwestern

China is an immense country that is home to 56 ethnic groups, most of which have little in common with the Han majority. If you're curious about minority cuisine, consider a meal at this trendy restaurant, which showcases food from Yunnan, China's southernmost province bordering Thailand, Vietnam and Laos. South Silk Road, located in a contemporary loft-like space with a glass floor (women be warned – wear trousers), is owned by artist Fang Lijun, whose artwork graces the walls. This is the place that made ethnic eating really chic. Typical (and delicious) Yunnan specialities include smoked ham, wild mushrooms, sausages with cayenne pepper and Sichuan peppercorn, *dai*-style inflated beef skin, fried goat's cheese, the ubiquitous cross-the-bridge noodles, *niugan* mushrooms, and crispy potatoes. A tasty homemade rice wine is the perfect accompaniment to a meal here.

Three Guizhou Men

2nd Floor, 8 Gongti Xilu, Chaoyang (6551 8517). Metro Dongsishitiao. **Open** 24hrs daily. **Main courses** RMB 2-RMB 168. **Credit** AmEx, MC, V. **English menu**. **Map** p244 N8 49 Southwestern

Sour and spicy Guizhou food has gained popularity fast in the capital. In the few short years since the first Three Guizhou Men opened in a hole-in-the-wall place in an alley behind the Jianguo Hotel, four other branches have found niches for themselves. The Workers' Stadium branch is set in a modern environment, and diners are greeted by waitresses decked in jangling Miao silver ornaments. Food is a fusion of dishes from different regions of Guizhou, cooked, according to the chain's owner, with less oil and one notch less spicy than what is typically offered in his home province. Beef on Fire – a favourite with European diners – features pieces of cooked beef placed over chives on a wire grid that sits on a burning bed of coals. Chinese diners particularly like the sour fish soup.

Yang Jinma

29 Zaoying Lu (next to Café Constance on Lucky Street), Chaoyang (5867 0228). **Open** 11am-11pm daily. **Main courses** RMB 100-RMB 998. **No credit cards**. **Map** p243 P6 50 Tibetan/Southwestern

The decor at Yang Jinma is more refined than that at other Tibetan eateries in Beijing, with colourful Tibetan art objects well displayed. There are performances here every night that are among the most professional showcases of Tibetan culture in Beijing. Authenticity continues with the food. Grilled yak rib seasoned with cumin and salt is beautifully presented in a wooden lacquered box accompanied by a Tibetan dagger; this is no ceremonial knife, but sharp enough to slice through the meat. Steamed chicken soup is packed with chicken, snow lotus (a bitter-tasting flower), *juema* (a sweet-tasting bulb-like tiny root) and wolfberries. Snow lotus and *juema* are medicinal plants indigenous to the Tibetan grasslands 3000m above sea-level. Both are unbelievably tasty. *Xiaguo tangjie ban jingu* consists of golden mushrooms mixed with *xiaguo tangjie*, a grassland herb available only in April and May. The distinctive flavour is an acquired taste, but popular with regulars. Beef strips with shredded carrots, a popular Tibetan dish, is a well-balanced combination of sour, spicy, sweet, and salty. Lhasa beer – which describes itself as 'beer from the roof of the world' – is a perfect accompaniment.

Yuxiang Renjia

5th Floor, Union Plaza, 20 Chaowai Dajie, Chaoyang (6588 3841). **Open** 11-4.30am daily. **Main courses** RMB 5-RMB 100. **Credit** AmEx, MC, V. **English menu**. **Map** p244 N9 51 Southwestern

Yuxiang Renjia opened in 1998, and is still going strong, despite the establishment of a slew of new

Noodle Loft. *See p106.*

Types of cuisine

China's vast scale and variety of flora and fauna combined with the fact that many regions were once relatively cut off from one another means that Chinese cuisine is diverse and complicated, with each province and city boasting its own flavours and style of cooking. But Beijing is a gastronomic mecca, and it's possible to do a culinary tour of ancient China without leaving the city.

Northern

It may quietly lie south-east of the capital but the province of Shandong is said to be the foundation of Beijing cuisine, which also includes facets of Manchu (Qing imperial) and Han Muslim dishes. Beijing cuisine is dominated by wheat-based foods as the main staple, including *mantou*, a steamed leavened bread, and *shaobing*, a baked unleavened bread covered with sesame seeds, and often flavoured with tahini paste and a bit of Sichuan peppercorn. No meal is complete without noodles and dumplings. Peking duck, the hallmark of Beijing cuisine, originates in Shandong. Imperial dishes are a collection of traditional Manchu dishes and recipes from Emperor Qianlong's numerous expeditions to the south on his inspection tours. *See p110* **Beijing bites: five to try** for suggestions of what to try while in the city.

As well as Beijing, the north-east includes Tianjin, Shandong, and the three provinces (Jilin, Liaoning and Heilongjiang) collectively known as Dongbei. Generally speaking, northern food is stodgy, hearty and salty. The north-western neighbours, Shanxi, Shaanxi, and Gansu, are known for their extensive use of black vinegar. Noodles of all shapes and forms – stretched, pulled, shaved, snipped and pinched – are the specialities here, often seasoned with chili oil, soy sauce or vinegar.

Eastern

Eastern Chinese cuisine includes Jiangsu, Zhejiang, Fujian and Taiwanese. The food from this area is a tad more delicate and focuses on light, moderate flavours. Many dishes tend to be sweet, but palatable.

Southwestern

The Southwestern region is made up of Sichuan, Guizhou and Yunnan provinces. The food in this region is characterised by the liberal use of chilis which come in different forms – salted, pickled, dried and fresh – and is spicy, sour, and sweet. Sichuan is known for its numbing spices, such as Sichuan peppercorn, which create the most sensational *ma* (numbing) *la* (hot) taste. In the olden days, the same peppercorns were used as a crude local anaesthetic on eunuchs going under the knife.

Southern

The Southern region is home to Guangdong, Guangxi and Hainan. The food here is best represented by Cantonese cuisine – characteristically light, refined and renowned as China's finest cuisine. The Cantonese are obsessed with freshness, clearness and blandness. Anything alive is welcome into the wok – the rest of China jokes about how the only things with four legs that the Cantonese don't eat are the table and chairs.

Central

Central China is made up of two provinces, Hunan and Hubei. Both provinces are fond of using fresh chilis in their cooking, and so the cooking can be more fiery than in Sichuan; fermented black beans are also a common condiment. Chairman Mao put Wuhan on the culinary map when he visited here in 1958 and did his legendary swim across the Yangtze River, turning two local dishes – Wuchang fish (a species of flatfish steamed with chilis and black beans) and *doupi* (beancurd sheets with glutinous rice and minced pork) – into national celebrities.

Xinjiang

The autonomous region of Xinjiang lies south-east of Kazakhstan and Afghanistan, thus the influences on Xinjiang cuisine are more Central Asian than Chinese. Lamb stews and skewers are combined with naan bread, spicy salads, dark beer and live entertainment.

Sichuanese competitors. This restaurant has kept traditional dishes on the menu, unlike many of the newer restaurants that have followed a nouveau approach, which can lead to culinary disaster. As if to emphasise the point, walls are decorated with black-and-white photos of traditional houses, river towns and people in the south, along with strings of dried red chillies and garlic hanging. Waitresses, who wear simple Chinese blouses, are peasantly charming. Pick classic Sichuan dishes like *kongbao* chicken, *lazi* chicken, *mapo doufu*, camphor smoked duck, or twice-cooked pork, and you will not be disappointed.

Beijing bites: five to try

Peking duck likely tops the list of what visitors most want to eat when they come to Beijing. But Peking man does not live on duck alone. The following is a list of some of our favourite dishes in Beijing.

Cairou zhengjiao

This exquisite steamed dumpling comes filled with very finely chopped baby bok choi and minced pork and, what's more, you get served ten in a steamer. Best at **Din Tai Fung** (*see p104*).

Gongbao doufu

This dish is prepared the same way as *gongbao jiding* (*kungpao* chicken), except the meat is replaced with cubes of golden crispy beancurd, and cashews take the place of peanuts. Really good. Best at **Bellagio** (*see p104*).

Hotpot

One of China's most ancient ways of cooking/eatring. Guests dip almost paper-thin slices of mutton – as well as veggies, noodles, mushrooms and more – into a boiling broth which cooks the food quickly. After taking the items out of the soup, dip them in the tahini-based sauce. Best at **Ding Ding Xiang** (*see p94*).

Sanbei Ya

In preparing Sanbei Ya – or Three-cup Duck – which is the signature dish of Hakka cuisine, the duck is braised in equal amounts of soy sauce, rice wine, and water before cooking. Delightfully tasty. Best at **Han Cang** (*see p102*).

Spare-ribs in plum sauce

Tender spare-ribs are braised in sweet and pungent sauce with a hint of sour Chinese plum (*suanmei*). The small cooked plums that garnish the dish are delicious too. Best at **People 8** (*see p107*).

Twice-cooked pork

This all-time favorite consists of thinly sliced pork stir-fried in a delectable sauce made with sweet flour paste, bean paste and black beans, highlighted with crunchy garlic shoots. Best at **Chuanban** (*see p94*).

International

Alameda

Nali Mall, Sanlitun Jiuba Jie, Chaoyang (6417 8084). Metro Dongsishitiao. **Open** noon-3pm, 6-10.30pm Mon-Thur, Sun; noon-3pm, 6-11pm Fri, Sat. **Main courses** RMB 60-RMB 158. **Credit** AmEx, MC, V. **English menu**. **Map** p245 O7 ⓹⓶ Brazilian

Alameda is the place to go for a bit of transcontinental travelling without having to brave the Airport Expressway. We love the layout and airiness of the glass-walled and glass-roofed dining rooms and the smart but minimal decor: very LA, very Sydney. Most of all though, we love the food. It sells itself as Brazilian, but like the decor it's really more of a globe-trotting fusion along the lines of Mediterranean-meets-Pacific. Sheer variety makes choosing difficult: mushroom and shiitake white wine risotto or pan-fried snapper with salsa verde? It's tough.

Aria

2nd Floor, China World Hotel, 1 Jianguomenwai Dajie, Chaoyang (6505 2266 ext 36/6505 3318). Metro Guomao. **Open** 11.30am-3pm, 6-10pm daily, **Main courses** RMB 165-RMB 885. **Credit** AmEx, MC, V. **English menu**. **Map** p245 O10 ⓹⓷ European

Quality is at the core of the cooking at Aria. Add in the creativity of chef de cuisine Nicolas Blair and you get some pretty amazing food. So skilled is this kitchen that the simplest tomato salad – a few slices of tomato with olive oil and mozzarella cheese, and roasted small tomatoes – is incredibly good. Aria's set lunch, with soup, salads, and a choice of main courses followed by coffee, tea or dessert, is, at RMB 128 (Monday to Friday) good value and a favourite with businesspeople. Soft music plays in the background, the atmosphere is relaxed and pleasant, and the service is attentive.

Biteapitta

30 Tianze Lu, (on Super Bar street) Chaoyang (6467 2961). **Open** 11am-10pm Mon-Thur, Sun; 11am-11pm Fri, Sat. **Main courses** RMB 15-RMB 80. **No credit cards**. **English menu**. **Map** p243 P6 ⓹⓸ Israeli

Biteapitta is a little deli-like eatery with a counter space and some tables and chairs. Fresh pitas are baked daily and you can make your own sandwich with a choice of falafel, hummous, tahini, baba ganoush, kebab or chicken schnitzel.

Carthage

Bldg 30, Sanlitun North Street, Chaoyang (6413 0517). Metro Dongsishitiao. **Open** 9am-10.30pm daily. **Main courses** RMB 20-RMB 70. **No credit cards**. **English menu**. **Map** p244 O7 ⓹⓹ Tunisian

As the name implies, the food at Carthage is Tunisian. With six tables packed into a small room, diners have to sit almost elbow to elbow to enjoy dishes such as the Tunisian classic *brik*, a kind of large egg roll with mashed tuna, minced meat, fried egg and coriander wrapped in a crispy crêpe, or *kibbeh* (minced lamb with spices in a bulgar pastry crust). Couscous is a Tunisian staple; served as a main course, it comes with heaps of carrots, turnips, potatoes, courgettes, and chick peas, as well as meat.

La Dolce Vita

8 Xin Dong Lu (north), Chaoyang (6468 2894). **Open** 11am-11pm (10.30pm last order) daily. **Main courses** RMB 52-RMB 260; RMB 120/set menu. **Credit** MC, V. **English menu. Map** p244 N7 56 Italian

Owners Li Baofeng and Liu Yang fell in love with Italian food while working and studying in Italy. La Dolce Vita is the result. Soft lighting, arches and alcoves, and pale yellow walls set the Mediterranean scene; food is classic Italian. Starters include the likes of *insalata di seppia*, with tender squid and shrimp served on a bed of rocket and olives with a drizzle of dressing. Pasta comes with classic sauces such as carbonara, bolognese and pomodoro, and pizzas are baked in a wood-fired oven.

Ganges

B138A, The Place, 9 Guanghua Lu (Dong Daqiao Lu), Chaoyang (6587 2999). Metro Yong'anli. **Open** 11am-11pm daily. **Main courses** RMB 30-RMB 100; RMB 38/lunch buffet Mon-Fri; RMB 48/lunch buffet Sat, Sun. **Credit** MC, V. **English menu. Map** p244 O9 57 Indian

Ganges serves authentic Indian food that is easy on the pocket. Every dish made here, from Bombay-style meat curry to vegetarian curries and chicken tikka baked in a traditional oven, are outstanding. Ganges handles the basics with skill: *jheer jeera* aromatic rice is seasoned with cumin, cardamon and bay leaves and cooked to perfection – almost a meal in itself. Buttered naan is equally successful, baked until golden and crispy, and great for dipping.

Other locations: 160 Chengfu Lu, Haidian, Northwest (6262 7944).

Hatsune

2nd Floor, Heqiao Building C, 8A Guanghua Lu, Chaoyang (6581 3939). Metro Yong'anli. **Open** 11.30am-2pm, 5.30-10.30pm (9.45pm last order) daily. **Main courses** RMB 30-RMB 100. **Credit** AmEx, MC, V. **English menu. Map** p245 P9 58 Japanese

Hatsune is known for its Californian-style sushi (crab meat and avocado), and the '119 roll', bright red tuna rolls topped with spicy-and-sweet sauce – not to be missed. Another favourite is *inari zushi*, a sweet beancurd pocket filled with rice. The design here is unconventional, using glass and metal material instead of traditional bamboo.

Hazara

26 Dongcao Yuan, Gongti Nan Lu, Chaoyang (6551 6788/www.facebars.com/bj/hazara.htm). **Open** noon-2.30pm, 5.30-10.30pm daily. **Main courses** RMB 65-RMB 195 **Credit** MC, V. **English menu. Map** p244 N8 59 Indian

As one of the two restaurants inside the new Face Bar, Hazara certainly lives up to its surroundings when it comes to quality of food and service. As one might expect, decor is stylish: rooms are all dark wood, candlelight, and Indian and Balinese antiques – the place has a romantic air. Food is Indian, cooked to a high standard. Starters include an array of mixed vegetables, chicken pakora and vegetable samosa – the combination platter includes all of the above and is just the right amount for two. Chicken tikka surprisingly comes on the bone; the well-cooked meat comes away effortlessly. Mutton rogan josh is sweet and spicy. There is a large selection of rice and naan. The bar on the first floor, which has a colonial feel, is a perfect place for a drink before dinner. **Photo** *p113.*

Lai Lai Xuan

8 Xinzhong Jie Xi Li, Chaoyang (6467 8719). **Open** 5.30-10.30pm (10pm last order) daily. **Main courses** RMB 12-RMB 48. **No credit cards. English menu. Map** p244 N7 60 Japanese

Japanese expatriates love to come to Lai Lai Xuan for ramen noodles, cooked al dente, with a choice of miso for a stronger broth or *sioyou* for a lighter one. Noodles aside, we also like the salad here, which comes loaded with sesame seeds, and tossed in Japanese dressing. Barley tea is free and there are plenty of *shochu*, Japanese beers and soft drinks available. The place is simply decorated, and furnished with solid wooden tables and chairs.

Mare

14 Xindong Lu, Chaoyang (6417 1459). **Open** noon-2.30am daily. **Main courses** RMB 90-RMB 180. **Credit** AmEx, MC, V. **English menu. Map** p244 O7 61 Spanish

There aren't many places in Beijing serving decent Spanish food, so Mare is a welcome addition to the city's restaurant roster. It has a long tapas menu as well as a dining menu of 'new Spanish cuisine' With its low-key decor and a relaxed ambience, this is a comfortable place for some tapas or a meal. It is also popular for coffee and dessert – try chocolate lava cake with scoops of hazelnut and vanilla ice-cream, or almond cake made with mascarpone.

Ottoman Turkish Cuisine

32 Lucky Street, Chaoyang (5867 0210). **Open** 11am-10.30pm daily. **Main courses** RMB 100-RMB 120. **No credit cards. English menu. Map** p243 P6 62 Turkish

One of the few places in Beijing serving Turkish cuisine, Ottoman refrains from going down the road of over-the-top Turkish decoration and sports just the odd artefact. Food runs the gamut of Turkish cuisine. Lentil soup with a faint hint of mint is warming and hearty; a squeeze of lemon further enhances the flavour. Excellent appetisers include diced peppers and pickled chillies topped with yogurt; and diced tomatoes, potatoes and aubergine. As you'd expect from a Turkish restaurant, grilled meat is a speciality. A mixed grill of baby lamb chops, with spicy minced beef patties and chicken patties shows off grill skills to perfection, and is accompanied by a hot green pepper and sliced tomatoes.

Paulaner

Kempinski Hotel, 50 Liangmaqiao Lu, Chaoyang (6465 3388 ext 5732/www.kempinski.com). **Open** 11am-1am daily. **Main courses** RMB 112-RMB 228. **Credit** AmEx, MC, V. **English menu.** **Map** p243 O/P6 ⑥③ German

This is the place to come in Beijing if you are hit by a sudden craving for real German food. But since a desire for sausage is normally accompanied by a good old-fashioned thirst, the oriental Germanophile will be relieved to know that the fresh-brewed beer – made in its own microbrewery – is served at the perfect temperature and guaranteed not to be flat. It naturally makes the perfect accompaniment for a meal of wurst sausages and sauerkraut. The constant supply of hot pretzels and rolls served with pâté, lard and mustard is a plus. One tip: the pork knuckle is plenty for two.

Shanzhai

Rainbow Plaza, 6 Dong Sanhuan Bei Lu, Chaoyang (6595 1199). **Open** 11am-10pm (9.30pm last order) daily. **Main courses** RMB 58-RMB 880. **Credit** MC. **English menu**. **Map** p245 O7 ⑥④ Japanese/ Chinese Fusion

Shanzhai takes its mission to provide healthy, organic food extremely seriously – the vegetables on your plate are sourced from its own farm, thus guaranteeing their provenance in this land of the fake and the counterfeit. But the restaurant's signature dish, *wugu*, or five grains, sushi, is impressive in its own right. Avocado and crabmeat are encased in seaweed and rolled within the *wugu*, garnished with a little mayonnaise and plenty of caviar.

Other striking dishes include *qinzhi zha doufu*, beancurd served in a lacquered bowl sprinkled with bonito flakes and seasoned with a light soy sauce. The tofu, which sits on a bed of grated *daikon* (giant white radish), is fried to golden brown. However, in contrast to the calm and serene food, Shanzhai's interior verges on the positively surreal. A larger-than-life ice-carved statue of the Buddha sits in meditative pose on a lotus under a giant bell in the middle ofthe restaurant. Translucent, almost glowing, it seems to shift from milky white to red, blue, green, yellow and purple, mysteriously lit from within. Nevertheless, it's not all wacky decor at Shanzhai. Lovers of traditional Japanese eating can choose the loft eating areas at each end of the restaurant, which are equipped with tatami mats.

Tim's Texas Bar-B-Q

44 Guanghua Lu, two blocks west of Ritan Park south gate, Chaoyang (6532 5905/www.timsbarbq.com). Metro Jianguomen. **Open** 11am-11pm Mon-Fri; 9am-11pm Sat-Sun. **Main courses** RMB 20-RMB 98. **Credit** AmEx, MC, V. **English menu.** **Map** p244 N9 ⑥⑤ American

The Lone Star State heads east and finds itself right at home. Unvarnished wooden walls combined with corrugated aluminum panels lend a rural Southern look to Tim's Texas Bar-B-Q, accented with worn cowboy boots, old farm tools, horseshoes, Texas car plates and a bunch of other bits of small-town Texas memorabilia. Tim's specialises in hearty portions of meat cooked slowly over fruit woods, a Texas tradition. Beef brisket, hand-rubbed with a secret blend of spices and smoked slowly to enable the flavours of the meat, smoke and spices to come together, is based on Tim's Texan family's recipe. Served with gravy, this thin sliced beef is great in sandwiches. Side dishes include chuck wagon beans, coleslaw and potato salad. A pint of Guinness or Kilkenny's makes a good accompaniment.

W dine & wine

22-1 Dongzhimenwai Dajie, on the corner with Xin Dong Lu, opposite the Canadian Embassy, Dongcheng, Chaoyang (6416 5499/www.w-dinewine.com). **Open** 11am-10.30pm daily. **Main courses** RMB 78-RMB 180. **Credit** V. **English menu**. **Map** p244 N7 ⑥⑥ French

Owner Geoffrey Weckx, a veteran of the Great Wall Sheraton, Hainan Sheraton, Sofitel Xi'an, and other international hotels, serves European cuisine with a French base, and the odd dash of eclectic flair – take the Middle East-inspired aubergine purée, for example. Pumpkin soup, with a slight curry spiciness, is beautifully flavoured. A cold appetiser of artichokes, avocado and crabmeat with dill is a light, original combination. Among the mains, citrus ossobucco – a variation on a classic theme, with a hint of lime added to the stew – was robust, while grilled tuna was perfectly seared to a crisp and served with sweet potatoes. Indulgent puddings might include a smooth and creamy chocolate tart, with mint leaves and strawberries. For those addicted to work or networking, the restaurant has wireless internet access. But really, would you want to ruin both your meal and your digestion by connecting?

Yotsuba

2 Xinzhong Jie Xi Li, Chaoyang (6467 1837). **Open** 5-11pm (10.30pm last order) daily. **Main courses** RMB 100-RMB 200. **Credit** AmEx, MC, V. **English menu**. **Map** p244 N7 ⑥⑦ Japanese

Yotsuba is a veritable sushi heaven in Beijing, with seafood flown in daily from the Tsukiji market in Tokyo to ensure the requisite freshness. For a full-on sushi experience, park yourself at the counter where the chef does his stuff right in front of you. You can watch as he runs his knife through the fish of your choice. And then, almost faster than the eye can follow, the bite-size squares of rice topped with fish are on a plate in front of you. We particularly like the grilled eels that are prepared here, brushed with warm soy for a slightly sweet taste. Try them with several glasses of warmed saké; you'll keep wanting more. If you're new to Beijing Yotsuba can easily be missed, since it has an unobtrusive shopfront and none of the traditional indicators of a Japanese restaurant such as red lanterns hanging outside. The restaurant is open for dinner only and has limited seating, ie, it's really not very big, so it's one of the few Beijing restaurants where it really is best to make a reservation.

Hazara. *See p111.*

The South

Qianmen is the oldest part of the city but many eateries were shut down to make way for the 2008 Olympics. Tourists are often off-loaded in the south to eat at **Quanjude** (32 Qianmen Dajie, Chongwen, 6511 2418, www.quanjude.com.cn, mains RMB 198). Opened in 1864, its claim to fame is as the first restaurant to serve roast duck prepared by the imperial kitchen to the masses. Fidel Castro, Yassir Arafat and Kim Jong Il have all eaten here, but the duck is hardly first-rate, the pancakes doughy, and the service is far short of imperial. Locals dying for a duck are more likely to eat at **Jing Wei Lou** (*see p96*).

Chinese

Haitang Ju

32 Xi Dajie Hou He Yan, Xuanwumen, Xuanwu, South (8315 8663). **Open** 10am-2pm, 5-10pm daily. **Main courses** RMB 150-RMB 2,000. **No credit cards**. **Map** p246 H11 ⓺⓼ Southern

It may be located in a remote corner of the southern part of the city, but Haitang Ju is worth the trip out here. The vegetarian 'abalone', made with a mixture of seaweed and beancurd, is quite simply amazing – better than real abalone. *Yigen luobo*, white radish, is another outstanding vegetarian creation. with a rich, meaty flavour. Another stand-out dish is stewed donkey, which is rich, robust and slightly spicy. Drinks are original too: fruit from old crab apple trees, grown in the courtyard, are marinated in sorghum wine – the result is a mellow and delicate brew with a wonderful aroma.

Jinyang Fanzhuang

241 Zhushikou Xi Dajie, Xuanwu, South (6354 1107). **Open** 10am-2pm, 5-9pm daily. **Main courses** RMB 8-RMB 110. **No credit cards**. **English menu**. **Map** p246 J11 ⓺⓽ Northern

This restaurant serves standard Shanxi fare, and is famous for its crispy duck and cat's ears (before you get too worried, that's small pieces of pasta shaped like a cat's ear, stir-fried with meat and vegetables). Another signature dish is *guoyou rou* – or rather unromantically 'oil-passing through meat' in which the meat is momentarily dipped on hot oil – paired

On the wild side

The **Night Food Market**, just off Wangfujing, is a one-stop dining experience for people who want to try some of the more exotic Chinese dishes, although this may be a better photo experience than a culinary one. The stalls here,which are open from 4-10pm daily, have much to offer: deep-fried starfish, scorpions on a stick, silkworm or centipede kebabs, bull testicles, grasshoppers, insects and much, much more...

The south-western province of Yunnan is famed for making a meal of just about anything. Bee pupae, cactus and moss are delicacies to the region's numerous ethnic minorities, and these dishes are offered in Beijing restaurants. Dog meat, turtle, snake, bear paw and tiny pink new born mice are not a novelty, but an ancient tradition. These foods are eaten for their purported medicinal properties. It is common to see dried snake, dried lizard and dried seahorse soaked in wine jugs along with other herbs. Frog, on the other hand, euphemistically known as 'field chicken', is not considered exotic to Chinese, but common and popular because it's fat free and the meat is as tender and as smooth as bean curd. For Yunnan food, try **In & Out** (*see p105*) and **Yun Teng Binguan** (*see p115*).

A lot of Beijing restaurants have penis on the menu, but **Guolizhuang** (34B-3 Dongsishitiao, Dongcheng, Centre, 6405 5698, 10am-10pm daily) is probably the first restaurant to specialise in animal sex organs, from bull's penis to horse penis, with the additional delicacy of imported sea-lion penis from Canada.

Covered windows, signs forbidding diners under the age of 18, and private dining rooms give the place the air of an X-rated cinema. Above the urinal in the men's toilet is a picture of a penis-shaped carved log and the caption: 'The hope of all men.'

Pretty female waitresses come and go wielding the penis – *bian* in Chinese. First the raw item is presented for the customer's inspection, the same way that live fish is presented, though with the head pointing upwards at 45 degrees. For a novice diner, they recommend the penis hotpot, a feast of six different penises with herbal broth and a whole turtle in it.

The Chinese eat penis because they believe that it makes men more virile and horny. Folklore claims it has many benefits for women too, enhancing beauty and, thanks to its wad of proteins, it's supposed to be good for ladies skin as well. But some restaurants warn women off eating the penis as they believe it will lead to increased hair-growth and even a full beard.

Food Manchu at the **Bai Family Mansion**. *See p117.*

with fungus and garlic stalks. Jinyang Fanzhuang is attached to the ancient courtyard home of Ji Xiaolan, a Qing dynasty scholar and chief compiler of the *Complete Library of the Four Branches of Literature* during the years 1773-1782. Diners can visit the old residence without an admission fee and see Ji Xiaolan's study where he wrote his famous essays. The crab apple trees and wisteria planted during his lifetime remain in the courtyard.

Yun Teng Binguan (Yunnan Provincial Government Beijing Office)

Bldg 7, Dong Huashi Beili Dongqu, Chongwen, South (6711 3322 ext 7105). **Open** 11am-10pm daily. **Main courses** RMB 4-RMB 100. **No credit cards. Map** p247 M11 ⑩ Yunnan/Southwestern

Yunnan province, located in south-west China, is known for a wide range of mushrooms and exotic vegetables. Yun Teng Binguan. with its adjoining hotel and restaurant, is where visiting representatives stay and dine when they come to the capital on official business – and it's the real thing.

Come here for *qiguoji* (chicken soup stewed in a clay pot) or wild mushrooms such as *niuganjun, jizhong, songrong* – this last is the best, but is only available in autumn. Bee pupa, a Yunnan delicacy, is deep-fried till it puffs up like a balloon; cactus, also dipped in an egg-flour batter and deep fried to a golden color, has more substance. Down your food with rice wine made with black rice, which is especially fragrant and sweet.

International

Manzo

Bldg 11, 1st Floor, Yilongtai Apartment Complex, 28 Panjiayuan Li, Chaoyang, South (8770 8767). **Open** 6pm-12.30am Mon-Fri, 11.30am-2am Sat, Sun. **Main courses** RMB 15-RMB 30. **No credit cards. English menu. Map** p247 O13 ⑪ Japanese

The name of Taka Yamamoto's restaurant-bar Manzo means 'Walk Slowly', and it's worth taking things slowly here to sample the excellent Japanese snacks – grilled fish, boiled duck liver, deep-fried fish cake, roast gingko nuts – that are prepared in the open kitchen. Manzo is probably as famous for its *shochu* as it is for its food. *Shochu* is made from one of several raw materials – sweet potato, brown sugar, fruit or barley. It can be drunk straight, on the rocks, or with a splash of hot water.

Financial District

The Financial District is a fairly new developed area in the west of Beijing that is home to local and international financial institutions. As you'd expect that means that the dining options focus mainly on expense-account cuisines, generally of a Western origin.

In addition to the restaurants that we have listed below, try Prego at the Westin (*see p45*) for excellent Italian cuisine, Qi at the Ritz Carlton (*see p45*) for food from various regions of China, or any of the local five-star hotels.

Chinese

Golden Peacock

16 Minzu Daxue Beilu, Weigongcun, Haidian, Financial District (6893 2030). **Open** 11am-9.30pm daily. **Main courses** RMB 6-RMB 30. **No credit cards. English menu. Map** p248 D6 ⑫ Southwestern

The authentic, inexpensive Dai food served here means that there is always a queue. Savoury potato balls, pungent salad with glass noodles, sour and spicy rice noodles, pineapple rice, deep-fried spare ribs, fish in lemongrass and meat cooked in a bamboo tube, are all skilfully prepared. Generous portions mean you won't leave hungry.

More than a mere cuppa

You've had the watery restaurant tea, you've seen the taxi drivers drinking from glass jars, but having tea at an actual teahouse may just be the highlight of your Beijing visit. Teahouses have been social, political and economic centers of Chinese urban life since the Tang Dynasty (618-907). Drinking tea was for good health and coherent conversation (as opposed to alcohol), and teahouses were for negotiating business, watching performances and discussing societal ills.

Except for cell phones, laptops and wireless Internet, little about today's teahouses has changed – although late-night business meetings are more common than teahouse theatre. All the tea in China comes in many forms, but the most popular are flower tea, green tea, oolong tea and red tea. Flower tea (hua cha) is 'junk food' to Chinese, but Westerners enjoy the light, fresh taste and aesthetic (and olfactory) appeal. Try jasmine (muoli hua cha) or rose tea (meigui cha), or the startling floral variety on Tea Street. Green tea (lü cha) rates highest on the health metre, with the popular Longjing tea hailing from only 120 trees in Zhejiang province.

Da Hongpao, a type of wuyien cha (of the oolong family) is even more selective, hailing from several trees on Wuyi Mountain in Fujian province. According to legend, a Tang Dynasty Emperor was enchanted with this tea/elixir that had cured his ailing mother and threw his da hong pao (big red cloak) over the trees. Today, mere mortals drink Da Hongpao from inferior cuttings or as blends; pure tea from the source costs thousands of dollars and is

International

Cepe

Ritz Carlton Hotel, 1 Jinchengfang East, Xicheng, Financial District (6629 6996). Metro Fuchengmen or Fuxingmen. **Open** 11.30am-2.30pm, 6-11pm (10.30pm last order) daily. **Main courses** RMB 90-RMB 300, RMB 408/set menu. **Credit** AmEx, MC, V. **English menu**. **Map** p240 G9 ⓻⓷ Italian

An upscale Italian restaurant in the ultra-modern Ritz Carlton, the aptly named Cepe has a menu tilted towards Northern Italy that revolves around mushrooms. Diners are left in no doubt of the theme: silver mushrooms hang from the ceiling, and mushrooms are grown in a series of darkened trays in the dining room. A humidor keeps both dried and fresh mushrooms at the ideal consistency for cooking on spec. A selection of antipasti might feature pungent marinated mushrooms alongside the likes of goose liver between leaves of rocket with a balsamic dressing, and prosciutto. Mushrooms crop up in the mains too, in dishes such as ravioli filled with mushroom, aubergine and proscuitto, with a cherry tomato sauce. All the dishes are great with a glass of Angela Viano sparkling wine, which is on the house. Desserts can include novel tastes such as lavender ice-cream. For a real taste of sunny Italy, a glass of chef Giovanni Terracciano's homemade lemoncello is a good way to end a meal.

only for high-ranking government officials. Red tea (hong cha), known as black tea in the west, is the strongest brew, and oolong tea is featured in Cha Li, the Chinese tea ceremony.

Unlike the Japanese Tea Ceremony's rigid rituals, Cha Li is flexible, focusing less on meticulous method and more on emotional connection. For Cha Li at its best, try the **Confucian Teahouse** (28 Guozijian Street, Andingmen Wai Dajie, Dongcheng, Houhai, 8404 8539, 10am-11pm), across from Confucian Temple, and a four-minute walk from Yonghegong Metro Station. Owner Shi Taotao's well-trained servers take guests step by step – in English and Japanese – through the ceremony, enhancing the standard movements with Confucian sayings and Tang Dynasty poetry, and explaining the basics, such as the zi sha hu teapots made from clay only found in Yixing, south China. The clay absorbs the tea's flavour so that eventually, all you need is hot water. Cha Li's thimble-shaped 'smelling cups' symbolize the deep sleeves of ancient costumes – male customers pining after a lovely tea server had to content themselves with the sweet fragrance emanating from her sleeves. Shi Taotao gives tea classes by appointment, if you want to master the art of pouring.

There are many other great tea houses – we recommend **Ming Ren Teahouse** (Room 2, Building 3, Pinganli Xi Dajie, Xicheng, Centre, 6613 2303, 9am-2am), **China Hangzhou Westlake Tearoom** (3rd floor, Building 10, Sanlihe Dong Lu, Xicheng, Financial District, 6805 6387, 9am-2am) and **Xi Hua Yuan Teahouse** (92 Bei Changjie, West Gate of Forbidden City, Xicheng, Centre, 6603 8534, 9am-12.30am). At these, private rooms are usually charged by the hour and the price of tea varies according to quality. Some food is available, but English is rarely spoken. The ceremony only lasts about thirty minutes, but if time is tight, you can buy tea on **Tea Street** (Jing Min Cha, Ma Lian Dao, Xuanwu, South), where there are hundreds of stores, mostly inside 'tea malls'; if you want personal service visit **Jing Min Cha Zhuan** (8 Zhong Lou Wan, Dongcheng, Houhai, 6405 6102, 8am-10pm) near the Drum Tower.

English-speaking Emma and Angie will let you sample any tea in the shop – no pressure, they enjoy the company. They're also that rare tourist-area establishment that has no kickback arrangement with the local guides and can keep their prices fair. Best of all, their tea comes in gift-ready canisters.

The North-west

Chinese

Bai Family Mansion

15 Suzhou Jie, Haidian, North-west (6265 4186). **Open** 11am-10.30pm daily. **Main courses** RMB 50-RMB 1,500. **Credit** AmEx, MC, V. **English menu.** **Map** p248 B2 ⓻⓸ Northern/Beijing

A visit to the Bai Family Mansion is unforgettable, and more than worth the trip from the centre of town. As you step inside, you are greeted by graceful *geges* (the Manchu word for princess) in pink, vermillion red and lime green; they gracefully glide here and there attending to the diners. The ornamented ceiling has the classic colours of green, blue and gold; lanterns hang from the ceilings; calligraphy decorates the walls.

The cooking style is based on Tan Family cooking and imperial cuisine, combining the best of the two schools to create a unique Bai Family style. *Feizi xiao* ('smile of the imperial concubine') – flower petals tossed in a light vinaigrette dressing – and *jiang lurou* – braised donkey meat, a Beijing specialty – are among the appetisers. *Gongbao xiaren* or *kongbao* shrimp is based on a Sichuan recipe that has been modified to make it less spicy. Snacks such as *gongting paigao* and *yundou juan*, made with peas or kidney beans, are known to have been favourites of the notorious Empress Dowager Cixi. **Photo** *p115.*

Bars & Pubs

Beijingers are waking up to late-night drinking.

Beijing's bar scene is still a long way behind that of London, Paris or New York – let alone the vibrant nightlife offered by Shanghai – but there's a great night out to be had here, whether you're looking for a dive bar, a glamorous cocktail lounge or just a cheap beer with a student crowd.

The Chinese have always put the emphasis on eating rather than boozing and traditionally only drink with a meal. This might mean anything from a cola or a couple of beers to a litre of tastebud-annihilating *baijiu* (*see p121* **Firewater and fakes**).

A decade ago, outside of restaurants, you were limited to a drink in one of the few five-star hotels or necking a bottle of beer in the street. But now an increasing number of young white-collar workers with disposable incomes and a Western attitude to drinking and entertainment has meant that local partygoers have become visible on a scene that was previously dominated by older expats and foreign students.

The Sanlitun embassy district became the city's first full-blown drinking hub in the late 1990s. This soon expanded to the area around the Workers' Stadium, which remains the dominant nightlife stomping ground. In summer 2003 fears over Sars pushed Beijing revellers to explore outdoor drinking options and the picturesque lakeside area around Houhai took off as a place to grab an alfresco ale to such an extent that the local government stopped new developments for fear the area might lose its old-world charm. The neigbouring hutong area of Nanluoguxiang soon became an overspill. Chaoyang Park's West Gate has also seen a recent explosion of bars and clubs all within walking distance of each other.

At the turn of the century many of Beijing's best bars were dives with live music, but the rise of DJ culture and the birth of clubs brought an end to these. The last year has seen the rise of the lounge bar with some classy venues springing up around the city, catering for the increasing number of wealthy Chinese and moneyed foreigners. The latter group has also created a market for café-bars and quieter, more bookish environments, the best example of which is the Bookworm (*see p134*).

Although there are now great bars in the city it is still hit or miss whether there will be much of a crowd on any given night, especially in winter, when the city goes into hibernation. It is also anyone's guess whether certain bars will survive the Olympic wrecking ball – at press time, Nanjie was under threat of closure – though in all cases the proprietors are looking at new locations. So find out what's going on – or going under – before venturing out.

The best Bars

Bed, Tapas & Bar
Located down a hutong, this trendy-meets-traditional bar is a wonderful place to enjoy a mojito, either outside in the courtyard or lounging on one of the many beds inside. *See p120.*

Browns
Expect to see girls dancing on the bar and people partying late into the night at this Western-style bar. *See p124.*

Face
Its laid-back, moody atmosphere with antique furnishings makes this the chicest place for a romantic date. *See p125.*

No Name
The first bar to open on Houhai Lake and still the best. This cute little hidden gem has incredible views of the lake, and very friendly staff. *See p122.*

The Tree
Tucked down a back alley in Sanlitun, this proper boozer sells Belgian beers and excellent pizza. *See p127.*

QUIET ZONES

Sometimes Beijing seems dysfunctionally undemocratic in its distribution of pleasures and services. One area has all the temples,

❶ Pink numbers given in this chapter correspond to the location of each bar as marked on the maps. *See pp238-249.*

another gets all the restaurants. And when it comes to drinking, three areas are still pretty much off the map.

● **The Centre** Considering the volume of tourists, it comes as a surprise that there is very little to do when it comes to nightlife downtown. No all night raves in the Forbidden City just yet. The hotels along Wangfujing and Chang'an Avenue all have their own bars, but none worth spending a night in. The Legation Quarter (*see p55*) just to the south-east of Tiananmen Square is currently being converted into an entertainment centre, with bars, restaurants and clubs all enclosed in this walled-off compound due to open at the end of 2007. With Handel Lee, the man behind Shanghai's Three on the Bund, at the helm, great things are expected.

● **The South** Hidden in the hutongs, the only drinking options are cheap beers available at the streetside noodle joints or catching up with a fellow traveller around Dazhalan (*see p73*).

● **Financial District** As the city expands west, it won't be long before bars and restaurants spring up to cater for the new wave of city boys and foreign businessmen. But currently, outside a few hotel lobby bars, there is little to make the trek to the west worthwhile. However, look out for the upcoming bar in the Westin Hotel (*see p45*), which should be on a par with it's sister bars from New York to San Diego.

WINING IN CHINA

Winemakers from all over the world have been rushing to get their latest vintages to the expanding Chinese market. Bear in mind that when you buy wine in China you are paying a 70 per cent tariff levied on all imported wines. A wine that might cost $20 in an American restaurant or £12 in a British one is going to cost three times that by the time you taste it in one of Beijing's finer eating establishments. Domestic winemaking is still in its infancy, but labels such as Grace Vineyards or a higher end Great Wall are definitely worth trying.

Houhai & the North

During the late 1990s, this quaint area in the old city saw a number of little bars – **No Name** was the first and its homey style started a trend – spring up around the picturesque lakes of Houhai. Although it has grown into something of a neon Disneyland, the backstreet venues around the lake and between the Drum and Bell are popular with visitors and locals alike.

Bed, Tapas & Bar

17 Zhangwang Hutong, Jiugulou Dajie, Dongcheng (8400 1554). **Open** 3pm-2am daily. **Credit** MC, V. **Map** p241 K7 ❶

Minimalism is vogue at this little two-in-one venue. The industrial bar is juxtaposed with Qin Dynasty carved wooden beds, while private rooms are offset by communal seating in the courtyard. With an

Bed, Tapas & Bar.

Firewater and fakes

While beer is the most popular alcoholic beverage in China, *baijiu* comes in second as the Chinese (especially northern Chinese) love to down bottles and bottles of this fiery grain alcohol that is to China what vodka is to Russia. Often mistakenly translated as 'white wine', don't go looking for hints of gooseberry as the clear liquid often tips the scales above 100 per cent proof. While you can pick up a gallon of one of the cheaper varieties at the supermarket for RMB 10-RMB 15, bottles do range upwards of RMB 15,000 – with the most expensive bottle ever sold going for a reported RMB 880,000 (£58,000 or $113,000).

Most *baijiu* sold in a restaurant will come in an elaborately packaged bottle that often requires a special key to crack open the bottle top. Don't let the presentation fool you though as *baijiu* smells and tastes awful and is completely unmixable. Also keep an eye out for bottles of *baijiu* in restaurants that are filled with snakes, rats, twigs and herbs and are reported to be tonics for everything from impotence to arthritis.

Asking for a familiar brand of spirits might not be the best solution, either. In early 2007 there was a spate of reports about fake foodstuffs and medicines being sold in China, and alcohol is no exception. As the bar scene has exploded in Beijing over the last ten years so too has the market in fake drinks. Expertly packaged to look authentic, the copycat booze is moonshine and brings with it the same inherent dangers. A good rule to follow when drinking the hard stuff is: if the prices look too good to be true, they probably are. Prices for name brand liquors are not much less in China than they are anywhere else in the world. When in doubt, stick to beer.

adjoining chic eaterie, Bed is far more chic than its neighbours and also serves up underground parties, full moon festivities, cool cocktails and classy DJs.

Buffalo Bar

6 Lotus Lane, 51-14 Dianmenxi Dajie, Xicheng (6617 2242). **Open** 9.30am-2am daily. **Credit** AmEx, DC, MC, V. **Map** p241 J7 ❷

Buffalo Bar is one bar on the Houhai Lake strip where it's worth stopping for a glass of red. Perched on the lakeside, the two floors are traditionally decorated, and either a string quartet or jazz band keeps punters entertained. Head upstairs for a fine view of the lake.

Drum & Bell

41 Zhonglouwan Hutong, Dongcheng (6593 5050). **Open** 10am-1.30am daily. **Credit** AmEx, DC, MC, V. **Map** p241 K7 ❸

The name conjures up an image of a cosy British boozer. There's no log fire, fruit machine or menacing canine, but the Drum & Bell does have the intimate atmosphere of a country inn as well as sofas to slump into, simple grub and a roof terrace that overlooks the square. Across the square, up an alley to the right of the Bell Tower is Ball House, a bar with three good pool tables. Live music is down the square at Jiangjinjiu (*see p176*).

Goldfish Home Bar

5 Lotus Lane, Houhai, Xicheng (6615 8966). **Open** 1.30pm-1.30am daily. **No credit cards. Map** p241 J/K 8 ❹

Occupying prime space in the flashy stretch of bars on Lotus Lane is the opulent expanse of the Goldfish Home Bar. Its sumptuous decor is reminiscent of 1920s opium dens: antique furnishings and paintings line the gilt-print walls along with a latticed iron balcony that takes advantage of the sweeping vista of Houhai Lake. The expensive alcohol means that this is a place for a quick drink before a meal.

Houhai Zoo

Building 2, Qianhai, Xicheng (6403 6690). **Open** 4pm-2am daily. **No credit cards. Map** p241 K7 ❺

On the east shore of the lake, Houhai Zoo is a funky space offering a pleasant outdoor terrace from which to enjoy a cocktail and a cool, softly lit, brightly coloured interior. The drink list, specialising in mojitos – the sign outside proclaims they are 'fucking good' – is very cheap and cheerful, and inside DJs spin crowd-pleasing tracks to a small dance floor.

Huxley's

Yandai Xijie (the small alley that runs diagonally from Gulou Dajie to Yinding Bridge on Houhai), Xicheng (6402 7825). **Open** 5pm-2am Mon-Thur; 6pm-3am Fri-Sun. **No credit cards.**
Map p241 K7 ❻

Their motto reads: Shut up, just drink! – which pretty much sums it up. Not only is this the cheapest bar on the street, it also shows up the other venues as the pretentious wannabes they really are. Cheap drinks and loud, varied music mean that Huxley's is best enjoyed with a group of mates – go alone and you'll meet plenty in there.

La Baie des Anges

5 Nanguanfang Hutong, Qianhai Beiyan (south of Yiningqiao), Xicheng (6657 1605). **Open** 6pm-2am Tue-Sun. **Credit** AmEx, DC, MC, V. **Map** p241 K7 ❼

Located down a hutong away from the surrounding sea of neon Houhai hype, this is a calm refuge from the hawkers on Lotus Lane. The interior is similarly serene: light-blue stucco walls, soft lighting and central glass floor under which lies a Zen-like pebbled feature. Exposed beams and Mediterranean prints give the venue a decidedly French feel.

Lotus Blue

Lotus Lane, 51-56 Dianmen Dongdajie (Shichahai Qianhai Xiyan), Xicheng (6617 2599/2733). **Open** 1.30pm-2am Mon-Fri; 11.30am-2am Sat, Sun. **Credit** AmEx, DC, MC, V. **Map** p241 J/K8 ❽

Lotus Blue is probably the coolest bar on the strip – its mix of Buddhist bric-a-brac and Chinese artefacts, glitz and a vague homage to the Belgian cartoon hero Tintin, somehow works. Eat Thai food or drink inside on two levels, or in summer head to the third-floor roof terrace and gaze over the lake at the hundreds of floating candles that boaters drop into the water for good luck.

No Name

3 Dajingsi Hutong, Houhai, Xicheng (6618 6061). **Open** 11am-midnight daily. **No credit cards.**
Map p241 K7 ❾

The first bar to open around the Houhai Lake is still the best. This tiny former front room of an old hutong home has developed into a cute bar, where you can curl up with the cat and an Irish whiskey in winter or kick back with a beer in the summer. Relaxed and very discreet, the absence of a name on the door keeps the numbers down.

Pass By Bar

108 Nanluoguxiang, Dongcheng (8403 8004). **Open** 9.30am-2am daily. **Credit** AmEx, DC, MC, V. **Map** p241 K7 ❿

Sip in style in the petite courtyard or loll around in the old-world interior, flicking your way through their well-stocked bookshelves. Head up the road for more of the same – the Nanluoguxiang strip is full of small bars, restaurants and shops making it perfect for either a lazy meander or a full-blown bar crawl.

No Name.

Save face by drinking at **Face**. *See p125.*

Rainbar

North shore of Xihai Lake, Dongcheng (6617 3231). **Open** noon-late daily. **No credit cards.** **Map** p241 H7 ⑪

As the northern-most of the Houhai trio of lakes, Xihai doesn't get many visitors, leaving it relatively unspoilt. Rainbar has a bit of an identity crisis, with an interior that is a jumble of traditional Chinese furniture mixed with odd items like a zebra hide hanging on the wall – but it retains a friendly charm that is well worth the journey.

Reef Bar

North of Nanluoguxiang Hutong, Dongcheng (8169 8494). **Open** 3pm-5am daily. **No credit cards.** **Map** p241 K7 ⑫

More of a rock pool than a reef, this tiny bar offers good cheap drinks in a cosy setting. The clientele is a mix of out-of-towners, faithful expats and Chinese regulars. The fact that it is run by a couple who held their wedding reception at the bar and invited all their patrons is testament to its friendliness.

Rui Fu

Zhangzi Zhong Lu, Pingan Dadao, Dongcheng (6404 2711). **Open** 7pm-3am daily. **Credit** AmEx, DC, MC, V. **Map** p244 L8 ⑬

The latest venture by local nightlife guru Henry Lee. On a good night Rui Fu is peppered with the A-list of Beijing; on a bad one you might be propping up the bar alone. There is little else nearby, so find out what's on before heading there.

Salud

66 Nanluoguxiang, Dongcheng (6402 5086). **Open** 1pm-2am daily. **No credit cards.** **Map** p241 K8 ⑭

Set in a hutong house, this well-stocked bar serves great sangria and tapas.

Chaoyang

If you are looking for all-night drinking dens, hedonistic parties or trendy lounge bars, they are all available in Chaoyang. The main nightlife area of the city, this part of town is where the majority of bars have grown up – originally around the embassies, and then near the office and apartment buildings that are home to the majority of foreigners and moneyed Chinese.

Alfa

5 Xingfu Yicun, alley opposite Workers' Stadium North Gate, Chaoyang (6413 0086). **Open** 11am-late daily. **Credit** AmEx, DC, MC, V. **Map** p244 N8 ⑮

This well-run bar has established itself as a prime hangout. The snazzy decor includes a water feature, second-floor extension and DJ booth; the casual outdoor lounge area and an all-night Asian-French restaurant makes it a popular stop après partying.

Aria

1st Floor, China World Hotel, 1 Jianguomenwai Dajie (6505 2266 x36/6505 3318). Metro Guomao. **Open** 11am-midnight Mon-Thur, Sun; 11-1am Fri, Sat. **Credit** AmEx, MC, V. **Map** p245 O10 ⑯

The China World has managed to neatly sidestep this usual hotel-bar ennui by situating Aria Bar through a small door away from their lobby, enclosing it and making it feel separate from the hotel. A great place for an aperitif, before heading upstairs to Aria restaurant (*see p110*), it's also a popular place for an after-work tipple or meeting thanks to the huge wine list and large selection of hors d'ouevres. The bar stepped up a gear in March 2007 when it headhunted star mixologist Bruce Li (*see p126* **New Beijinger**).

Q bar. *See p127.*

Bar Blu

4th Floor, Tongli Studios, Sanlitun Bei Lu, Chaoyang (6416 7567/6417 4124). **Open** 4pm-2am Mon-Thur, Sun; 4pm-4am Fri, Sat. **Food served** 4pm-midnight daily. **Credit** AmEx, DC, MC, V. **Map** p244 O7 ⑰

Bar Blu's outdoor roof terrace overlooks nearly every other bar in the area and offers respite from the often crowded lower level. The mix of DJs, live sports, pub grub and Wednesday quiz nights ensures that it is busy most nights. On the floors beneath are the mellower Taniwha, thirtysomething hangout Cheers and food shops.

Browns

4 Gongti Bei Lu, Chaoyang (6592 3692). **Open** 11am-2am Mon-Thur, Sun; 11am-4am Fri, Sat. **Credit** AmEx, DC, MC, V. **Map** p245 O8 ⑱

One of the city's recent success stories, this spacious bar would not look out of place in London or New York. During the day it's a good place to grab a burger and a quiet pint; by night things get more animated as the ceiling-high set of optics are put to use conjuring up the 500-strong menu of shooters.

Centro Lounge & Bar

Kerry Centre Shangri-La, 1 Guanghua Lu, Chaoyang (6561 8833 ext 42). **Open** 6.30pm-midnight daily. **Credit** AmEx, DC, MC, V. **Map** p245 O9 ⑲

It may be a hotel bar, but it's one where you can guarantee to find a crowd and, quite possibly, visiting rock stars, government ministers and Chinese film directors. Busy every day of the week, this spacious lounge bar serves incredible cocktails and the house jazz singers give the place some character and help dispel some of the hotel ambience.

China Doll

2nd Floor, Tongli Studios, North Sanlitun Lu (6416 7968/6417 4699). **Open** 8pm-late daily. **Credit** AmEx, MC, V. **Map** p244 O8 ⑳

Chinese star Ai Wan opened this new suave three-level club in the heart of the Sanlitun district. Grab a Peachy Jim cocktail in the laidback lounge of the first floor before heading upstairs to dance to some of Beijing's premier DJs. The more exclusive top floor draws some of the city's biggest names in design, music and entertainment.

The Den

4 Gongti Dong Lu (on the junction with Gongti Bei Lu, next to the City Hotel), Chaoyang (6592 6290). **Open** 24rs daily. **Credit** AmEx, DC, MC, V. **Map** p244 O8 ㉑

Open 24 hours a day and the home bar of Beijing's rugby and Australian Rules football clubs, as well as a Scandinavian football team, the Den serves affordable food, has a slightly dodgy upstairs disco, and screens for every assortment of sporting fixtures. Under no circumstances abuse the staff – the bouncers are hard.

Durty Nellies

Basement, Liangmaqiao Flower Market, Chaoyang (6593 5050). **Open** 10.30am-1.30am Mon-Thur, Sun; 10.30am-2am Fri, Sat. **Credit** AmEx, DC, MC, V. **Map** p245 O/P6 ㉒

An underground location near the CBD with, despite the contrived Irish theme, a wealth of private corners, a dartboard and a pool table. Durty Nellies has all the ingredients of a good dive bar, with great Guinness, good food and occasional live cover bands.

Face

26 Dongcaoyuan, Gongti Nan Lu, Chaoyang (6551 6788). **Open** noon-2am daily. **Credit** AmEx, DC, MC, V. **Map** p244 N8 ㉓

With tables, beds and Buddha heads from Tibet, India, Indonesia and China, this is a suitably grandiose setting for a classy drink. The garden's lawn and streams offer a corner of calm away from the noise and pollution in summer, while the beds and sofas are perfect for a romantic evening during the long winter months. With excellent, if expensive, cocktails on offer and a good selection of beers to enjoy over a game of pool, Face has something for everyone is all seasons. **Photo** *p123.*

Jazz Ya

18 Sanlitun Bei Lu (6415 1227). **Open** 11am-2am daily. **Credit** AmEx, MC, V. **Map** p245 O7 ㉔

Jazz Ya is hidden away discreetly behind a subtle wooden slide door off the neon of the main Sanlitun bar street. A perfect place for an after dinner drink, try their lethal Long Island Iced Teas – if you don't have to be up early in the morning.

Latinos

A12 Nanxincang Gucangqun, 22 Dongsi Shitiao, Nanxincang Historical Complex, Dongcheng (6409 6997). **Open** 7pm-late daily. **Credit** AmEx, DC, MC, V. **Map** p244 M8 ㉕

The sprawling Latin venue located in the old Imperial granary corner of Nanxincang isn't easy to find, so follow your ears. The club has a huge dance floor where rubber-hipped clubbers salsa and rumba their way late into the night. Latinos is about dancing, not drinking, something which is proven by the overly long wait at the bar.

Maggies

South Gate of Ritan Park, Chaoyang (8562 8142/www.maggiesbar.com). **Open** 7.30pm-4.30am Mon-Wed, Sun; 7.30pm-5am Thur-Sat. **Credit** AmEx, DC, MC, V. **Map** p244 N9 ㉖

As one of Beijing's longest established bars, Maggies' notoriety has had plenty of time to spread around the globe. Infamous as a place where expat men and out-of-town businessmen come to drink, dance, play pool and make merry with Mongolian working girls, the bar is the only place in Beijing that is as seedy as it pretends to be – making it a great place to people watch. The hot dogs sold outside are best avoided.

Nanjie

Opposite the Workers' Stadium North Gate, Chaoyang (6413 0963). **Open** 10am-late. **No credit cards. Map** p244 N8 ㉗

Though the threat of demolition hangs over it, this bar packs in the young revellers looking for cheap drinks and rowdy times. It can often get extremely crowded and noisy.

Nashville

Haoyunjie (Lucky Street), 29 Zaoying Lu, Chaoyang (5867 0298/www.nashville.com.cn). **Open** 11am-3am daily. **Credit** AmEx, MC, V. **Map** p245 P6/7 ㉘

Here you'll find the unlikely combination of China and country music. It's perfect fodder for a comedy skit, but the pleasant wood interior, good selection of beer and bar snacks, friendly atmosphere and, of course, the music makes it a great place to sink a few brews. A small stage plays host to live acts most weekends with the Rolling Stones (without Mick and the boys) as the pick of the cover bands.

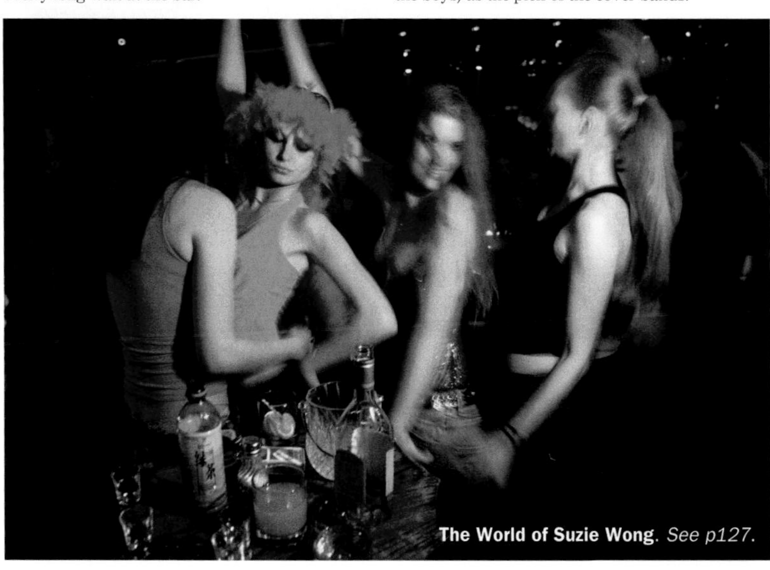

The World of Suzie Wong. *See p127.*

New Beijinger The barman

Beijing is changing with every passing minute. Old pictures of the city bring back memories of gardens, architecture, small alleys, and traditional life and entertainment. Now, the culture-filled city is changing: as well as the rapid expansion of the transport system, the city is now filled with international architecture firms, five-star luxury hotels, and fine residences. Beijing glitters like a youthful and luxurious cosmopolis, yet amid all that, retains its sense of antiquity.

The process of development impacts many areas of life. As more people arrive, native inhabitants relocate to different areas, so ancient courtyard houses and hutongs are becoming rare. However, development, especially transport systems, also creates accessibility to far-flung corners of the city, and helps people keep in touch. Regardless of how much this city develops, its fundamental character remains unchanged for culture comes from within.

I work at Aria (*see p123*). It is a very happening address, with a reputation for being the 'hangout of beautiful people', real cocktails, fine wines, live music and a very good ethnic mix of clients.

I like playing basketball, bonding with friends over karaoke, travelling, watching movies and above all, spending quality time with my family. I have a beautiful wife, and a gorgeous son who is just over three years old.

I love the tension between ancient and contemporary, high culture and fashion, but even more I adore the beautiful gardens and historic sites like the Forbidden City, Summer Palace and Beihai Park.

During the day, I'd recommend visitors head to the beautiful gardens and historic sites, such as the Great Wall. There is a proverb that says 'One is not a hero until he has climbed the Great Wall'. At night, they would have to check out Beijing's sizzling nightlife.

The Beijing bar scene resembles bamboo shoots after a spring rain. They are abundant and strewn across the city from little alleys to high-profile fashionable destinations. More people are developing a taste for bar entertainment, and the bar scene is leaning towards luxurious, fashionable interiors.

Old Beijingers are quite removed from contemporary issues and practise traditional principles that have been handed down through generations. They enjoy a carefree life and show respect to those who they regard worthy of it with sincerity and courtesy.

Most young Beijingers are more confident than their counterparts in other cities. This is evidenced in their comparative eloquence and competitive spirit. They are also polite and hospitable towards others.

Beijing is an icon of striking contrasts where immemorial civilisation and seductive cosmopolitanism coexists.

Bruce Li is an international award-winning cocktail barman and bar manager at Aria.

Nhu

6 Fangyuan Xi Lu, Lido Park South, Chaoyang (6435 6762). **Open** 11am-2am daily. **Credit** MC, V. **Map** p243 Q4 ㉙

Although slightly out of town, the Lido area is growing fast. Nhu lounge is the pick of the place with its excellent sound system playing mellow beats, good cocktail selection and subtle mood. Find out what's on before you go as non-party nights are dead.

Pause

2 Jiuxianqiao Lu, 798 Art District (6431 6214). **Open** 10am-9pm daily. **No credit cards**. **Map** p243 Q4 ㉚

Considering the 798 Art District is a funky area, few bars do it justice, apart from Pause. The single room is simply designed and the food and drink menu is basic, but come to mingle with artists, media darlings and some of the big names in Chinese film.

Pavillion

Gongti Xi Lu, Chaoyang (6507 2617). **Open** 10am-2am daily. **Credit** AmEx, DC, MC, V. **Map** p244 N8 31

Hidden among the trees, this is a venue with the feel of a gentlemen's club – a rarity in Beijing. The clientele is middle-aged Westerners lounging in leather couches sipping pints of bitter. Although a bit of a 19th-hole, it gets rowdy for big football games shown on the big screens. Beat the summer heat with a brunch in their tree-shaded garden or enjoy perhaps the best fish and chips in Beijing.

Q bar

Top Floor, Eastern Hotel, Sanlitun Nan Lu, Chaoyang (6595 9239). **Open** 6pm-2am daily. **No credit cards. Map** p245 O8 32

Concealed on the top floor of a grotty hotel, Q bar is one of the most chilled lounge bars in Beijing. Local cocktail-makers Echo and George mix excellent and affordable cocktails (from RMB 30) which ensures this small venue is packed every weekend evening – especially in the summer when the roof terrace is busy into the small hours. **Photo** *p124*.

Salsa Caribe

4 Gongti Bei Lu (on the street behind Browns and the Bookworm), Chaoyang (6507 7821). **Open** 7pm-late daily. **Credit** AmEx, DC, MC, V. **Map** p245 O8 33

As one of only a few places in the city that specialises in Latin music, Salsa Caribe has built up a healthy following. With dance classes during the week and live music from a genuine Latin band at weekends, the venue is always loud, friendly and fun.

Souk

Chaoyang Gongyuan Ximen, Chaoyang (6506 7309). **Open** 4pm-2am daily. **Credit** AmEx, MC, V. **Map** p245 P7 34

At this trendy bar with in-house DJs, the opium-divan chic offers the perfect place to laze in, or sit outside in the courtyard and graze your way contentedly through the menu of eastern-Mediterranean cuisine.

Stone Boat

Lakeside, southwest corner of Ritan Park, Chaoyang (6501 9986). **Open** 10am-late daily. **No credit cards. Map** p244 N9 35

The Stone Boat is built onto a jetty jutting out into one of Ritan Park's fishing ponds. During the day it is a great place to grab a coffee and watch the fishermen, and by night it is perfect for a romantic drink. Live jazz on a tiny stage on the prow of the boat makes this Beijing's most intimate venue.

The Tree

43 Sanlitun Beijie (100m west of Sanlitun North bar street, at the rear entrance of the Youyi Youth Hostel), Chaoyang (6415 1954). **Open** 11am-late daily. **No credit cards. Map** p244 O7 36

Belgian beers took a while to reach Beijing, and this bar was the pioneer. Drop in for one of their pizzas, cooked in a wood-fired oven – possibly the best slice of pie you'll get in Beijing.

Trio

Jiangtai Xi Lu, west of Rosedale Hotel, Lido, Chaoyang (6437 8399/www.trio-beijing.com.cn). **Open** 10am-2am Mon-Thur, Sun; 10am-late Fri, Sat. **Credit** AmEx, DC, MC, V. **Map** p243 P4 37

The trio concept consists of an upscale sports bar (Frank's) sandwiched between a posh restaurant upstairs (Park Grill) and a wine cellar below (the Cellar). One of the best places to head if you are in the Lido area, Frank's has a good, but pricey, selection of imported beers and pub grub, televised sports and a pool table.

The World Of Suzie Wong

1A Nongzhanguan Lu Chaoyang Gongyuan Ximen, Chaoyang (6595 5049/www.suziewong.com.cn). **Open** 7pm-late daily. **Credit** AmEx, DC, MC, V. **Map** p245 P7 38

Named after the Richard Mason novel, 'Suzie's' is the most famous bar in Beijing. The first port of call for the international jet-set and Hollywood VIPs, the Hong Kong opium-den-style venue is spread over several floors: a nightclub in the basement (*see p180*), divans upstairs, and an open roof terrace in the summer. With an excellent sound selection from some of the city's best DJs, Suzie's is also very popular with singletons. **Photo** *p125*.

The North-west

Student boozing follows a tried-and-tested global format: all-you-can-drink nights, comfort food and RMB 10 beers abound in this part of town.

Lush

Building 1, 2nd Floor, Huaqing Jiayuan, Chengfu Lu, Wudaokou, Haidian (8286 3566). **Open** 24hrs daily. **No credit cards. Map** p249 F3 39

Providing 24-hour booze, food and entertainment, Lush is the hangout of choice for foreign students who crave a taste of home and debates about the relative merits of Qingdao and Yanjing beer. Small, pokey and nothing special to look at, this is the place to find out all the latest goings-on from the student crowd.

Propaganda

Chengfu Lu (100m north of the East Gate of Huaqing Jiayuan), Wudaokou, Haidian (8286 3991). **Open** 8pm-4am daily. **No credit cards. Map** p249 F3 40

Be prepared for throngs of students out for the famous RMB 50 all-you-can-drink evenings. And be warned: if you graduated anytime before 2006 then you're too old for this place.

Zub

Huaqing Jiayuan, Chengfu Lu, Haidian (8286 6240). Metro Wudaokou. **Open** 9pm-3am Tue-Sat. **No credit cards. Map** p249 F3 41

In the depths of the student area of Wudaokou, Zub aims to offer a touch of class compared to its neighbours. The tiny subterranean bar is usually packed and serves passable cocktails at student prices.

Shops & Services

All the pearls, silk, antiques, fakes, clothes – and tea – in China.

Despite the abundance of 'Fendy' bags and 'Nike Air Nax' in China, one of the best things about shopping in Beijing is the markets. Whether you want to buy jeans, Tibetan Buddhas, orchids or a bright orange pashmina, it's hard not to have fun when you get so much for your moolah and a bit of humorous banter with the sales assistant is par for the course. In fact, everything from edible dried seahorses to Chinese Opera masks and bespoke handmade earrings can be found somewhere in Beijing if you know where to look, and a plethora of quirky boutiques abound on some of the city's less frequented streets and in the hutongs.

Though the majority of the Western world associates China with mass production, one of the most refreshing things about shopping in the capital is the sheer range and singularity of most items. In fact, you'll never see two women with the same bag or pair of shoes. If you're willing to overlook the odd tacky sequined cardigan or Chinglish sloganed T-shirt, you'll be shocked at how cheap and funky some of the gear can be. The key things to remember: bargain for everything and carry cash. Outside of the department stores, credit cards are rarely accepted. It's also highly unlikely you'll be given a receipt – a right you give up when you pay RMB 65 ($8) for a winter coat. Nevertheless, if you are unhappy with anything, the quicker you take it back the more likely the shop assistant is to remember you and fix or replace any damaged goods.

If you're a small or medium at home you'll often be a large or XXL in Beijing. In some cases, particularly with shoes, you may find that nothing fits you. But that's where Beijing's legion of expert tailors and cobblers comes in, ready to fashion a copy of your favourite suit or shoes for a fraction of the price.

It's also worth bearing in mind that sales items are marked differently here, showing the percentage of the price you pay, not the percentage of the discount.

China World Shopping Mall. *See p129.*

SHOPPING AREAS

Compared to most cities, Beijing isn't particularly 'joined up', meaning there are few places you can just go for a stroll and discover great little shop after great little shop. The best option is to decide what sort of thing you're after before setting out. Finding international or designer brands is simplest, because all of them can be found inside the more exclusive hotels or in one of the two major shopping malls in Beijing – the China World Shopping Mall (or Guomao, as it's known to locals, *see p129*); and the Oriental Plaza (*see p129*) in Wangfujing. Thanks to a historic reputation as the place to buy quality goods close to the Palace during imperial times, **Wangfujing** has gradually developed into the city's main shopping street.

Walking distance further west is **Xidan**, a shopping district popular with locals and young people in particular, who head straight to the underground 77th Street Plaza for a mix of funky threads and kitsch Chinese toys. For a similar selection of clothes, accessories and fun finds but in a more relaxed and cool setting, head to **Dongsi Bei Dajie**. This road, located just east of the centre, is lined with one-off boutiques and is definitely worth exploring for a couple of hours. For ethnic chic and traditional Chinese arts and crafts, the myriad shops scattered around the periphery of **Houhai Lake** won't disappoint.

For a more modern shopping experience, the **Jianwai Soho** development opposite the China World Trade Centre has a vast but slightly uneven selection of shops. The relatively recent retail boom in the **Lido** area means it's also now worth a visit, especially if you're on your way to or from Dashanzi's 798 Art District. Catering to the large number of expats in the area and dominated by the shops in and around the Holiday Inn Lido hotel, several unique designer-product outlets have sprung up including the wonderful Spin, Jia Na Ma Ni and Kang Deco.

One area that's been around a while and is currently undergoing a mega revamp is **Sanlitun**. Dozens of shops can be found here if you venture off the bar street, including Yashow Market, the 3.3 Fashion Mall, Nali Mall and Tongli Studios. In 2005 residential buildings were cleared to make way for 'New Sanlitun', a major development that's supposed to be Beijing's answer to Covent Garden, housing high-end shops, businesses and even a hotel. Due for completion in October 2007, the whole city is holding its breath. Well, sort of…

One-stop shopping

Malls

It's all very well laughing at the shop claiming to stock Pierre Cardin goods but filled with a strange mishmash of oven mitts and cuddly toys (absolutely true), but if you want the real thing you'll have to head to one of Beijing's many malls. These air conditioned behemoths are currently multiplying out of control in the capital. It's still quite a big event when a mall introduces a new brand to the city, which was why Chinese and foreign women alike swooned over the new bi-level Zara that opened in **The Place** at the beginning of 2007. The most recently opened include the excellent **Gate City Mall** in Zhongguancun (excellent because the area, up in the north-west, had nothing like it until recently); the manageably sized **Ginza Mall** on Dongzhimenwai; and the **Wangjing Mall** set at the boulevard-like crossroads of Guangshun Bei Dajie.

Those set to hit Beijing in the near future include the aforementioned **New Sanlitun**, the **Wanda Plaza** and SOM-designed **Gemdale Plaza** near Guomao, and the **Legation Quarter** – an exciting series of high-end restaurants and shops set in a cluster of buildings that served as the American Embassy compound during the Qing dynasty.

China World Shopping Mall

1 Jianguomenwai Dajie, Chaoyang (6505 2288/www.cwtc.com). Metro Guomao. **Open** 9.30am-10pm daily. **Credit** (some stores) AmEx, MC, V. **Map** p245 O10.

One for the big spenders staying at the adjacent China World Hotel, Guomao has more designer brands per square metre than anywhere else in the city. From Chloé to Louis Vuitton, Salvatore Ferragamo to Chanel, it's all here. For those who don't own small islands in the Pacific, there's a good selection of other, more practical shops too. A Watson's Chemist, Valentino Chocolatier, Sephora and fun Dutch home decor shop Potato & Co. all feature, as do a clutch of mid range men's and women's clothing shops like Esprit and Nine West. **Photo** *p128.*

Oriental Plaza

1 Dong Chang'an Jie, Dongcheng, Centre (8518 6363/www.orientalplaza.com/eng). Metro Wangfujing. **Open** 9.30am-10pm daily. **Credit** (some stores) AmEx, MC, V. **Map** p241 L10.

The mother of all Beijing shopping malls, this is the one most people end up stumbling across when they visit because it's located in the heart of Wangfujing just minutes from Tiananmen Square. Following a fairly conventional but stylish design over two levels, the mall houses brands like Burberry, Mango and Sisley, as well as moderately priced Asian clothing brands Izzue, b+ab and a Sanrio shop for all your Hello Kitty needs.

The Place

9 Guanghua Lu, Chaoyang (8595 1755/8595 1756). Metro Yong'anli. **Open** 11am-9pm daily. **Credit** (some stores) AmEx, MC, V. **Map** p245 O9.

Beijing's funkiest new mall is easy to spot thanks to the digital canopy that sweeps over its central outdoor plaza – the biggest screen in Asia would you believe. However if you find the butterflies and seascapes that flash up on it all a bit much, head straight indoors to the tri-level mall which houses a great selection of mid-range shops like Zara, Aldo, MAC, Adidas, Puma and the English-language Chaterhouse bookshop. Not quite complete at the time of going to press, the west building should be ready by the end of 2007.

Markets

In recent years, a number of Beijing's most famous markets have moved indoors, meaning more regulation but less spontaneity. Even so, the jovial atmosphere and wealth of treasures remain. Aside from the obvious clothing markets, some of the city's food markets are also worth a look. Try **Sanyuanli** (Xinyuan Jie, Xinyuanli, west of Sanyuan Dongqiao, Chaoyang, 5am-7pm daily) or Hongqiao (*see p130*). For lighting, most Beijingers head to **Beisihuan** (Nanhu Liugongzhucun, Laiguangying Xiang, Chaoyang, 9am-5.30pm Mon-Fri, 9am-6pm Sat, Sun), where you can find everything from designer copies of trendy

Mao kitsch

The trinkets and charms emblazoned with Mao Zedong that were once displayed in people's homes as an expression of dutifulness to their leader have now become kitsch souvenirs devoured by Westerners. Despite the, shall we say, failings of the Communist leader, Mao remains the one person who sums up China. Thirty years after his death, the Great Helmsman's portrait still presides over Tiananmen Square and his picture can be found on everything from watches to posters and that sparkly, dangly thing adorning your taxi driver's rearview mirror.

Created throughout the 1950s, '60s and '70s, literally tens of millions of Little Red Books, badges and pins were made, meaning that when you spot one of them at a market such as Panjiayuan or in Liulichang, it could well be an original. Mao lighters that play 'The East is Red' are another favourite with tat-seeking tourists and can be found in places like the Silk Market, the back streets of Wangfujing and Yashow Market in particular. For an unrivalled selection of alarm clocks, key fobs, busts and more, a visit to the Chairman Mao Memorial Hall (*see p54*) is a must, or tour the furniture showrooms inside the entrance to Panjiayuan. More about capitalism than communism, the craze looks set to continue because, for outsiders at least, the grim face of rampant dictatorship is somewhat diffused by a kitsch memento that you can laugh at when you get home.

lamps and crystal chandeliers to the more traditional Chinese bulbous lanterns.

The good news is that the more stuff you buy from a particular stall, the cheaper it becomes. Bargaining is a given and always assume you'll be quoted around three times the real price to begin with (for more on the art of haggling, *see p141* **The ultimate bargaining guide**).

Laitai Flower Market

9 Maizidian Xi Lu (Nurenjie), Chaoyang (6463 6145). **Open** 9am-6pm Mon-Fri; 9am-6.30pm Sat, Sun. **No credit cards. Map** P243 P6.

China's biggest botanical warehouse is a delight to walk through and could be the most greenery you'll see while you're here. Row after row of colourful orchids, peonies, bonsai trees, cacti, Chinese roses, lotus flowers and burgeoning green plants are complemented by the tropical fish shops on the market's periphery. Stalls near the entrance sell dire twisted bark creations and tasteless mystical water features. To keep discovering, head down to the basement from the rear of the market for lamps, ceramics and candle stores galore. **Photo** *p131.*

Liangma Flower Market

On the south bank of the Liangma River, Dongsanhuan Bei Lu (just east of the Lufthansa Shopping Centre), Third Ring Road, Chaoyang (6504 2446). **Open** 8.30am-6pm daily. **No credit cards. Map** p245 P7.

Much smaller than the nearby Laitai market, Liangma is nevertheless much better for flower arrangements and displays, and has a fantastic selection of cheap and cool Chinese crockery upstairs on the first floor. Look out for long, sleek ceramic dessert trays, funky tea sets and dozens of modern, colourful dinner plates.

Panjiayuan Antique Market

Panjiayuan Qiao, South (6775 2405). **Open** 8.30am-6pm Mon-Fri; 4.30am-6pm Sat, Sun. **No credit cards. Map** p247 O13.

We can't recommend strongly enough that you pay this market a visit while you're in Beijing. Though more famous for its (now mostly fake) antiques, Panjiayuan – sometimes called the Dirt Market – is absolutely brimming with everything you could ever want in the way of presents and souvenirs from China's capital city. PLA caps and bags, lanterns, jewellery, Buddhas (real ones as well as repro), books, ancient coins, Mao alarm clocks, old city maps, cigarette cards, ethnic clothing and embroidery, rugs, Cultural Revolution posters, exquisitely painted treasure boxes, vases and traditional leather puppets all feature – and that's just half of it. If it's the antiques you're after, get there at the crack of dawn on Saturday or Sunday to pick up the best deals from the men and women whose trinkets, pottery, statues and even ancient weapons have been collected from all over the country.

Pearl Market (Hongqiao)

Tiantan Dong Lu, Chongwen, South (6713 3354). **Open** 8.30am-7pm daily. **No credit cards. Map** p247 M12.

Another of the 'famous three' markets in Beijing, Hongqiao is just minutes' walk from the Temple of Heaven – which explains the busloads of tourists that flock here and the reason it is often hideously overpriced. Bargain hard, however, and you may get the price down as low as the local Chinese who also visit regularly. Contained inside a more impressive building than most markets, Hongqiao houses the city's biggest fish market in the basement and several floors of stalls selling the usual clothes, shoes, binoculars, cameras – and of course pearls. Look out for the really high quality ones (and good views of the Temple of Heaven) on the market's top floors.

Silk Street Market (Xiushui)

8 Xiushui Dongjie, Jianguomenwai Dajie, Chaoyang (5169 8800). Metro Yong'anli. **Open** 9am-9pm daily. **No credit cards**. **Map** p244 N10.

Almost as popular a tourist attraction as the Forbidden City, the Silk Street Market draws an unbelievable 20,000 visitors a day – 60,000 at weekends – and all you need do is venture inside to believe it. Seven floors packed with clothes, fabrics, jewellery, shoes, bedclothes, souvenirs, MP3 players and much more are the reason people brave the crowds. Fakes can still be found nestling alongside the more traditional Chinese trinkets, shoes and silk scarves.

Tea Street Market

Maliandao, Chayecheng (south of the Beijing West Railway Station), Xuanwu. **Open** 8.30am-6pm daily. **No credit cards**.

For tea lovers everywhere, Malian's 900 plus stalls are testament to just how much tea there is in China. From jasmine to *erlong*, green tea to the expensive *pu'er,* and everything in between, there's almost too much choice. However, vendors help out by inviting you to sit down and have a taste beforehand and the pace is relaxed without any pressure to buy. Tea sets, demonstrations of the tea ceremony and even tea flavoured dumplings can also be found.

Yashow Market (Yaxiu)

58 Gongti Bei Lu, Chaoyang (6415 1726). **Open** 9.30am-9pm daily. **No credit cards**. **Map** p244 N8.

Along with Hongqiao and Xiushui, Yashow is one of the most tourist-heavy markets in the city, but it's also one of the best if you want (fake) jeans, bags, shoes, a good tailor or a gift to take home to your friends. The market spans five levels: there are leather goods in the basement, clothes and DVDs on the ground and first floors, then pashminas, table runners and such, electronic goods and jewellery above that. Paper fans and umbrellas, kites and silk photo albums are all for sale. The blue-shirted girls running the stalls (often no older than 16 or 17) are feisty but fun and if you're polite you should walk away with an armful of bargains.

Yueshow Market (Yuexiu)

99 Chaoyangmenwai Dajie, Chaoyang (6416 8945). **Open** 9.30am-9pm daily. **No credit cards**. **Map** p244 O8.

A five-minute taxi ride away from Yashow and offering almost exactly the same stock, this relatively new market (opened in late 2005) is much quieter, with fewer women screaming 'Hello jeans?!' in your ear than at most other markets.

Zoo Wholesale Market (Dongwuyuan)

Xizhimenwai Dajie, behind the bus station opposite the Beijing Zoo, Xicheng, Financial District (8837 8056). Metro Xizhimen. **Open** 6am-5pm daily. **No credit cards**. **Map** p249 E7.

If you ever wondered where the stallholders at the Silk and Pearl markets get their stock, then ponder

Laitai Flower Market. *See p130.*

Spin. *See p133.*

no more. The Zoo Market (known to locals as Dongwuyuan) is a boxy, heaving little place, crammed to the rafters with dirt-cheap clothes, bags, shoes and coats. If you're looking for a new coat or jacket, RMB 50 should do it, a jumper or top? RMB 20. The lack of foreigners means it's a tough job to get the prices as low as the locals, so it's worth hovering around a stall until a Chinese person comes along to get an idea of the real price – you'll be shocked at how low they are.

Antiques

Due to the sheer number of reproductions masquerading as genuine on the market these days, it's foolish to buy antiques in Beijing without first obtaining some serious know-how. Nevertheless, repros aren't necessarily a bad thing, so long as you know that's what you're buying, and a lot of market sellers are honest about the age of their wares. Relatively modern curios like Mao's *Little Red Book* or Mao buttons or badges will probably be real, because so many millions were made. Whatever you buy, make sure you have a stamp of authentification to show that your antique is legal for export. Anything over 200 years old cannot be taken out of the country.

Panjiayuan Market (*see p130*) has a good selection of genuine antiques mingling with the fakes, you just have to find them; but the most famous area for antiques is Liulichang, a street with an interesting history. Alongside an overwhelming amount of colourless tat, there are thousands of old books (particularly in the western half), along with an abundance of ink slabs, statues, vases, pai... nd other treasures. Try **Ru Gu** ...ılichang East, Xuanwu, South, ...m-6pm daily) for honest service ...ı of old drawings and calligraphy ...owledgeable owner Liu Guo Chu.

Beijing Curio City (Guwan Cheng)

21 Dongsanhuan Nan Lu, South (6774 7711/6773 6018/www.antiquecity.com.cn). **Open** 9.30am-6.30pm daily. **Credit** MC, V. **Map** p247 O13.

Arrive early to make the most of four floors of pottery, Buddha statues, carpets, vases, old time pieces and other cultural relics. While Beijing Curio City is not quite as rough and ready, nor as atmospheric, as nearby Panjiayuan, it's still worth a visit if you're looking for something original.

Gaobeidian

Gaobeidian exit off the Jingtong Expressway from Dongsihuan Lu, Chaoyang. **Open** 8.30am-6pm daily. **Credit** (accepted by larger dealers) MC, V.

For reproduction Ming and the odd genuine piece of Qing Dynasty furniture, Gaobeidian is the place. A handful of dusty, broad streets are lined with showrooms stuffed with tables, chests, opium beds, cabinets, chairs and even drums. Prices can be bargained down a decent amount.

Huasheng Laotianqiao

Shiliheqiao (southeast corner of Panjiayuan), South (6768 8857). **Open** 9am-6pm daily. **No credit cards. Map** p247 O13.

One of Beijing's newer flea markets, Huasheng Laotianqiao is an atmospheric spot marked by a traditional painted gateway and buzzing with locals. Antique furniture and curios are jumbled alongside food and pet stalls; the odd cricket fight has been known to take place too.

Mooi

4 Jiuxianqiao Lu, Chaoyang (8459 9566). **Open** 11am-7pm Tue-Sun. Closed Mon. **No credit cards.**

A retro little boutique inside Dashanzi's 798 Art District, Mooi stocks both European and Chinese goodies from the 1930s through to the 1970s. Space-era tables and '60s Norwegian leather chairs sit side by side with chic Chinese handbags and rugs. The café across the tiny courtyard out back serves quirky snacks including apple cider and cheesecake.

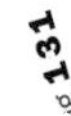

Arts & handicrafts

With thousands of years of history and 55 ethnic minority cultures, China is home to an enormously broad range of traditional clothes, arts and crafts. For outfits and embroidery from China's Miao Minority, as well as Tibetan statues and Beijing Opera masks, the best place is still **Panjiayuan Market** (*see p130*). However, for a more modern take on Chinese arts and culture, the following shops offer a decent selection.

Five Colours Earth

Room 3, 22F, Sky Plaza, Dongzhimenwai Dajie, Chaoyang (8460 8981). Metro Dongzhimen. **Open** 9am-5.30pm daily (later by appointment). **Credit** AmEx, DC, MC, V. **Map** p244 N7.

Clothes designer Pan Xi takes patches of decades-old Miao Minority embroidery and stitches them on to beautiful suits, scarves, dresses and jackets made of silk, wool, cashmere and linen. The style is an elegant combination of East and West. If you're looking for something a little more fitted, she recently began custom-making clothes. Prices range from RMB 800 to RMB 5,600.

Jia Na Ma Ni

6 Fangyuan Xi Lu (on the approach to the Lido Shopping centre), Chaoyang (6437 8812). **Open** 11am-8pm daily. **Credit** DC, MC, V. **Map** p243 Q4.

Unlike the majority of tat-filled Buddhist shops you stumble across, Jia Na Ma Ni is a spacious, colourful setup that sells high quality Tibetan carpets and authentic furniture to boot. Run by a woman and her daughter raising money for a Buddhist school in Qinghai Province, the shop has a great selection of rugs, all handmade from the finest quality materials such as cashmere, silk and yak hair. From traditional, bright designs depicting dragons, to sophisticated zebra print, the selection is extensive. However they don't come cheap; prices range from RMB 14,000 to a whopping RMB 80,000.

Shard Box

1 Ritan Beilu, Chaoyang (8561 3712). **Open** 9am-7pm daily. **Credit** AmEx, DC, MC, V. **Map** p243 Q4.

This unassuming shop sells trinket boxes and jewellery with a difference. Mostly made from shards of smashed Cultural Revolution plates and vases, as well as Ming and Qing dynasty jade, designer Hu Songlin's creations have a twist that distinguishes them from most objets d'art you'll find in Beijing.

Other locations: 2 Jiangtai Lu, Lido area, Chaoyang (5135 7638).

Spin

6 Fangyuan Xi Lu, Chaoyang (6437 8649/www.spinceramics.com). **Open** 11am-9pm daily. **Credit** AmEx, DC, MC, V. **Map** p243 Q4.

Spin features the work of a group of talented young Shanghainese designers and craftsmen from the home of Chinese porcelain, Jingdezhen. There's a huge selection of ceramic art on offer, all of it handmade, singular and delightful. From the lumpy pots collectively known as the Seven Fortunes to the carved Japanese saké bottles and super-square jewellery boxes, the more you look, the more you have to smile. Relatively reasonably priced (a saké bottles cost RMB 70), they make great gifts for those more interested in the new China than the old. **Photo** *p132*.

Three Stones Kite Store

29 Di'anmen Xidajie, Xicheng, Houhai (8404 4505/6403 0393/www.cnkites.com). **Open** *Dec-Feb* 9am-6pm daily. *Mar-Nov* 8.30am-10.30pm daily. **Credit** DC, MC, V. **Map** p241 J8.

For three generations the Liu family has created exquisite, handmade kites, and a visit to their shop just north of Beihai Park will make you feel like a child again. Amazing birds, butterflies, long-tailed fish and dozens of other lucky Chinese creatures hand-painted on to sturdy bamboo frames fill the tiny store, and proprietor Liu Bing, his son and nonagenarian father (who made kites for the Imperial family) will custom-make one for you if you desire something that flies a little higher. **Photos** *p135*.

Jia Na Ma Ni.

Eat, Drink, Shop

Hairy monkeys and serious trees

Every year, visitors descend on Chinese markets, haggling over fake North Face jackets, Prada bags and pirate DVDs. However, for gifts with a story to tell, there's nothing like the extraordinary variety of Chinese traditional crafts to delight people back home.

Consider painted snuff bottles for the friend who has everything. Legend has it that a young monk was watching a Qing Dynasty (1644-1911) official scraping out snuff with a bamboo stick and decided to start painting the bottles – from the inside. Contemporary master Liu Shouben squeezed 108 detailed characters from the Chinese classic *Water Margin* into one tiny bottle. Chinese paper cuts refer not only to ancient torture techniques, but to equally creative artwork done with either knives or scissors. Designs range from the simple to the staggering and are bursting with colour and culture, such as the twelve Chinese zodiac animals or the *shuang an* 'double happiness' wedding symbol. Others are elaborate scenes featuring traditional symbols; pines are 'serious' trees signifying wisdom, bats mean good fortune, peaches symbolise longevity and fish bring abundance.

Most of Beijing's markets (*see p129*) have beautiful basics for sale – embroidery, lacquer boxes and dragon wall hangings. For truly original work, however, try the Bannerman Tang Toys and Handicrafts Shop. Tang Yujie is a fifth generation craft master who has created a showcase for Beijing's other multi-generational craft families, still clinging to a treasured way of life. Look for the exquisite clay figures and the 'hairy monkeys' – delicate creatures crafted from orchid buds and cicada moultings, and arranged in complex dioramas (hand carry them on the plane). The store also stocks handmade kites, model hutong gates, and various miniature figures. The prices are listed and reasonable, and shopping is pleasant and stress-free.

For Tang, it's not about the money, it's about sharing Chinese culture, and she will arrange free craft workshops for those with an artistic bent.

Bannerman Tang's Toys & Handicrafts

38 Guozijian Street, Dongcheng, Houhai (8404 7179). **Open** 9am-7pm daily. **Credit** MC, V. (Some English). **Map** p242 M6.

Beijing Curio City

21 Dongsanhuan Nanlu, South (6774 7711/6773 6018/ www.antiquecity.com.cn). **Open** 9.30am-6.30pm daily. **Credit** MC, V. **Map** p247 O13.

Yellow Earth

28-3 Guozijian Street, Dongcheng, Houhai (6401 1746). **Open** 10am-6pm daily. **No credit cards**. **Map** p242 M6.

Books, movies & music

Obtaining quality books, movies or music in a country where censorship and piracy prevail can sometimes be tricky, but a growing number of shops run by owners who know what the people want are helping to combat that.

The Wangfujing Bookstore (218 Wangfujing Dajie, 6525 2592, Centre) is a good starting place for Chinese books. Most high-end hotels sell the main international magazines.

The Bookworm

Building 4, Nan Sanlitun Lu, Chaoyang (6586 9507/www.beijingbookworm.com). **Open** 9am-1pm daily. **Credit** DC, MC, V. **Map** p245 O8.

A haven for expats, journalists and literary types, the Bookworm isn't just the best place to buy magazines, foreign-language titles and borrow books, but also one of the city's most popular places to relax with a glass of Sauvignon Blanc or catch a talk by an international author. There's free wireless access as well as decent food, and a rooftop terrace to relax on during the long summer months.

Chaterhouse

Shop B107, The Place, 9 Guanghua Lu, Chaoyang (6587 1328). Metro Yong'anli. **Open** 10am-10pm daily. **Credit** AmEx, DC, MC, V. **Map** p245 O9.

At present the only foreign-language bookshop in Beijing to rival the Bookworm, Chaterhouse began in Shanghai and, in its ambience, is a bit more like visiting a typical Waterstones or Borders store in the West. It's not particularly huge, but the shop nevertheless stocks a good selection of bestsellers, literary classics, crime, sport, cooking, history, popular psychology and business titles.

FAB

Inside Oriental Plaza, 1 Dong Chang'an Jie, Dongcheng, Centre (8518 8905). Metro Wangfujing. **Open** 9.30am-9.30pm daily. **Credit** AmEx, DC, MC, V. **Map** p244 L10.

FAB's Chinese music collection is extensive and includes genres from pop to rock and classical. A small foreign music section and hundreds of genuine above board Chinese and Western DVDs all at comparatively cheap prices (around RMB 50) are the best reason to visit FAB rather than more underground music shops.

Fusheng Records

Southeast corner of the Ping'anli intersection (where Ping'an Dadao meets Xinjiekou), Xicheng, Financial District (6613 6182/www.fmusic.cn). Metro Jishuitan. **Open** 10am-8pm daily. **No credit cards. Map** p242 J6.

Fusheng is much frequented by locals looking for Chinese rock, indie or punk, so whether you're looking for a CD by Hang on the Box, the Subs or Brainfailure, this little shop is sure to stock it.

Sugar Jar

2 Jiuxianqiao Lu (opposite Galleria Continua), 798 Art District, Chaoyang (6433 1449/www.sugarjar.cn). **Open** 1-8.30pm Tue-Sun. **No credit cards.**

If you don't mind craning your neck to see what musical delights reside above eye level in this hip underground music joint, you'll be pleasantly surprised by the selection on offer. Purveyor of Chinese indie music Lao Yang opened this, his second, much bigger and airier store last year (the other one, near Tsinghua University, is tiny). His passion for the scene is commendable and he's always happy to make recommendations.

Timezone 8 Art Books

4 Jiuxianqiao Lu, 798 Art District, Chaoyang (8456 0336/www.timezone8.com). **Open** 9am-9pm daily. **Credit** AmEx, DC, MC, V.

Not far from the Sugar Jar (*see above*), Timezone 8 has been around much longer. In fact, the art bookstore's owner, Robert Bernell, was one of the first people to set up shop in the 798 Art District, helping to make it the home of Chinese modern art it is today. Crammed with glossy tomes, this is the place to come for books on contemporary art, architecture, photography and design, as well as books on the history of 798 itself. An extension of the bookshop, Timezone 8 Editions, also serves as café, restaurant and exhibition space, where film screenings and author events occasionally take place. *See p162.*

Electronics

Contrary to popular belief, it's not actually that much cheaper to buy electronic goods in China than it is in the West. Nevertheless, prices have come down considerably in recent years, thanks to a multitude of good-quality local brands, and you can buy MP3 and DVD players to rival any of those made by international companies for a fraction of the price. Buying things like games consoles or Apple computers should probably be given a miss. Be prepared to bargain very aggressively to make it worth your while.

Is it a bird? A plane? No, it's **Three Stones Kite Store**. *See p133.*

Gome

6 Beisanhuan Zhonglu, Xicheng, Houhai (6207 1730/www.gome.com.cn). **Open** 9am-7pm Mon-Fri; 9am-8pm Sat, Sun. **No credit cards**. **Map** p249 H5.
With nearly 30 stores across Beijing, this chain is worth a look for DVD players, mobile phones, cameras and home appliances. Keep an eye out for seasonal sales, particularly around the spring holidays. For similar goods, also try the Dazhong chain, easy to spot thanks to the giant yellow 'D' bell against a red background.
Other locations: throughout the city.

Landao

8 Chaoyangmenwai Dajie, Chaoyang (8563 4422). **Open** 9am-9pm daily. **Credit** MC, V. **Map** p244 N9.
A more central collection of shops selling all the latest mobile phones, a great selection of TVs and DVD players, as well as home appliances, headsets, earphones and the like.

Zhongguancun Electronics City

3 Haidian Dajie, Haidian, North-west. **Open** 9am-9pm daily. **No credit cards**. **Map** p248 D4.
A bit bewildering, but ultimately the best place in Beijing to buy the full range of electronic goods, this massive electronics market in the city's north-west is an experience in itself. Be sure to play the vendors off against each other to get the price as low as possible; you'll need to bargain hard if you don't want to leave feeling disappointed.

Fashion

Refreshingly, China is no slave to Western catwalk fashion and neither is it a huge follower of home-grown trends. After all, if you were just one of 1.3 billion people, would you want to ape the latest style that everyone else is wearing, or might you try for something a little more different? The result is a wondrous mishmash of clothes, some decidedly dodgy, others not. For a collection of funky clothes, shoes and belts made in Beijing or imported from other Asian countries, try Beijing's Nali Mall (Sanlitun Beijie, next door to Alameda restaurant, Chaoyang, 6413 2663, 9am-11pm daily) – not so much a mall as a bazaar-like collection of indoor shops hidden just off Sanlitun Bar Street – and head to Zin (the first shop on your left, 6417 3030, 11am-9.30pm Mon-Thur, Sun, 10am-10pm Fri, Sat). Similarly cool is the Ritan Office Building (15A Guanghua Lu, Chaoyang, 8561 9559, 10am-8pm daily) with its great selection of boutiques selling singular, mostly trendy threads.

For excellent quality cheap brand name clothes, Select inside the Lido Hotel shopping arcade (Lido Place, 6 Jiangtai Lu, Chaoyang, 6430 1005) sells Havaiana flip flops, Ralph Lauren shirt dresses and the like, and Hot Station Factory Outlet (104B, car park level, Building 5, Jianwai SOHO, Chaoyang, 5869 2969, 10am-10pm daily) offers everything from men's Replay parkas to Calvin Klein dressing gowns. Designer fashion can be found in either the Oriental Plaza Mall, Guomao (*see p129*) or the Peninsula Beijing Hotel's shopping arcade (*see p35*) which houses over 50 brands including Wolford, Versace and Chanel.

Plastered T-shirts

42 Nanluoguxiang, Dongcheng, Houhai (134 8884 8855/www.plastered.com.cn). **Open** 1-10pm Mon-Fri; 10am-10pm Sat, Sun. **No credit cards**. **Map** p241 K7.
In fact run by two long-term British expats, this tongue in cheek boutique down the popular and funky Nanluoguxiang hutong produces T-shirts that capture the essence of life in Beijing perfectly. Depicting several Beijing 'in jokes', signs and slogans, the T-shirts come in a reasonable range of sizes and colours, and you can also buy the retro Korean posters and tin robots lying around the store. Not exactly high fashion, but personal and original enough to merit a visit. **Photo** *p137*.

Red Phoenix

Building 30, Sanlitun Bei Jie, Chaoyang (6416 4423). **Open** 9am-6pm daily. **Credit** AmEx, DC, MC, V. **Map** p245 O7.
Ask anyone in the know which local designer the rich and famous go to and they'll tell you Gu Lin. Her modest boutique at the top of the Sanlitun Bar Street houses a small collection of trademark silk embroidered gowns, jackets, tops and dresses and is the perfect place to find modern clothing with beautiful Chinese finishing touches. Her spirited designs incorporate everything from deep purples, bright reds and oranges to embroidered dragons, flowers, fur trim and mandarin collars. Hand stitched and created using fabrics Gu makes personally with traditional techniques, garments cost anywhere between a couple of hundred RMB to tens of thousands.

Shanghai Tang

B1 Grand Hyatt Hotel, 1 Dong Chang'an Jie, Centre (8518 0898/www.shanghaitang.com). Metro Wangfujing. **Open** 10am-10pm daily. **Credit** AmEx, DC, MC, V. **Map** p244 L10.
One of the few Chinese brands that should need no introduction, Shanghai Tang is still the number one purveyor of pop chinoiserie and vibrant, catwalk-worthy clothing in the world. Despite the label's creator, Hong Kong entrepreneur David Tang, refuting claims that the brand is a perfect example of East meets West design, a stroll round the boutique suggests that's just what it is. Hip, sky blue women's trenchcoats with Chinese knot buttons are displayed alongside tangerine-coloured *qipaos* and men's jackets complete with French cuffs, mandarin collar and Tang's signature two-tone double fish motif. Accessories like silk-covered diaries, stationery, candles and handbags also feature. Designed in China they may be, but prepare for Western prices.

3.3 Fashion Mall

33 Sanlitun Beijie, Chaoyang (6417 8886/www.3d3.cn). **Open** 11am-11pm daily. **No credit cards. Map** p245 O7.

If it weren't for the overpricing and snobbish attitude of the shop assistants, this six-storey mall would be the best place in Beijing to browse the city's quirkiest fashion boutiques. 3.3's still worth a visit, however, as its 300-plus stores are crammed with local and imported goods and increasing numbers of local designers are beginning to set up shop within. Look out for China's First Second Hand Clothing Shop at the back of the 3rd floor, Art Space in the basement (B108) for unusual ceramics and Vivienne Lee's cashmere shop on the second floor (2125).

Vivienne Tam

WB101 China World Shopping Mall, 1 Jianguomenwai Dajie, Chaoyang (6505 0767/www.viviennetam.com). Metro Guomao. **Open** 9.30am-9pm daily. **Credit** AmEx, DC, MC, V. **Map** p245 O10.

This Hong Kong-born New York designer's first Beijing boutique opened in the China World Mall only last year – something of a surprise given that Tam made the Mao jacket fashionable and presented her 2002 collection on the Great Wall. The shop features silk dresses, chiffon tops, comfortable trousers and dozens of other versatile creations to suit all ages. Expect to pay between RMB 2,000 and RMB 4,000 for most garments.

Wazzap

Shop 4028, 3.3 Mall, 33 Sanlitun Beijie, Chaoyang (6448 3495/www.wazzap.com.cn). **Open** 1-8pm daily. **No credit cards. Map** p245 O7.

This little store sells locally designed T-shirts popular with punk kids and rock chicks. Prices are relatively cheap (around RMB 90) and designs are all offbeat, eccentric and hip with not a word of Chinglish in sight.

Fashion accessories & services

Dry-cleaning

Fornet

Building H (just along from O Sole Mio restaurant), Xingfucun Zhonglu, Chaoyang (6417 7767/www.fornet.com.cn). **Open** 8am-8pm daily. **No credit cards. Map** p244 N7.

Well established Chinese dry cleaning chain with branches all over town. Offers most services including laundry, shoe, fur and leather garment cleaning, and basic repairs and alterations.

Other locations: S1402 Building C, Xiandai Cheng, 88 Jianguomenwai Dajie, Chaoyang (8580 2080).

Jewellery

Women have been known to turn into magpies when visiting Beijing, finding themselves inexplicably drawn to market stalls dripping with red coral beads, pearls, jade and silver. Of course everything in Beijing that glitters is not gold, but at these prices who really cares? Head to the markets first – in particular Panjiayuan and Liulichang for things like beads, coral and jade, or Yashow (we suggest you try the helpful Cindy on stall 4014) and the Silk Market where you'll find row upon row of stalls selling hairpins, bracelets, cufflinks, necklaces, earrings and other accessories. This is also the location of the majority of Tiffany, Bulgari and Cartier copies. For pearls, make a beeline for the Pearl Market and have a gander at well-established Fanghua Pearls (Shop 4318, 6718 7888, www.fanghua.com, 9am-8pm daily) where you're guaranteed to find the genuine goods.

Plastered T-Shirts. *See p136.*

Made to measure

Imagine an outfit that fits perfectly, is bang on trend and costs less than it would if you bought it off the rack. In Beijing, this is easy to do – with a bit of planning.

First you have to buy the material. Yashow Market (*see p131*) has a good selection of basic silk, shirt and suit material on its third floor, but for a wider variety of prints, colours and materials head to the first floor of the Sanlitun Friendship Store (7 Sanlitun Lu, Chaoyang, 6532 7913, 9am-8.30pm) half a mile up the road. Bargain hard and don't be persuaded to buy reams of the stuff. Look out for dodgy silk – the real thing carries an identification tag featuring five digits beginning with the number '1'.

Unlike the rest of the staff in Yashow Market Sunny's English is near fluent. Expect to pay RMB 65 for a shirt, RMB 800 for a *qipao* and RMB 700 for a suit; she'll also come to your hotel. Tried and tested Lisa Tailor (with stalls in both Sanlitun and the much less crowded 3.3 Mall) can complete garments within 24 hours. Dave's Custom Tailoring is renowned for its Savile Row-quality suits starting at around RMB 2,500.

Dave's Custom Tailoring

104 Kerry Centre, 1 Guanghua Lu, Chaoyang (8529 9433/www.tailordave.com). Metro Yong'anli. **Open** 10am-7pm daily. **Credit** AmEx, DC, MC, V. **Map** p243 P6.

Lisa Tailor

Stall 5011, 3.3 Fashion Mall, 33 Sanlitun Beijie, Chaoyang (139 1079 8183). **Open** 11am-9pm daily. **Credit** AmEx, MC, DC, V. **Map** p244 O7.

Sunny (Huo Youquan)

Stall 3066, Yashow Market, 58 Gongti Bei Lu, Chaoyang (6415 1726/137 0132 0756). **Open** 9.30am-8.45pm daily. **Credit** AmEx, DC, MC, V. **Map** p244 O8.

For young, funky jewellery, the shops inside the Nali Mall (*see p136*) can't be beaten.

It's also worth noting that, particularly outside the clothing markets, Tibetans still tout their wares on the footbridges and pavements, and if you turn a blind eye to the deer feet and wolf skin rugs, their jewellery is often a lot cheaper and more authentic than that sold inside.

Flame Tree

7 Gongti Bei Lu (to the right of the Olive restaurant), Chaoyang (6413 0828). Metro Dongsishitiao.
Open 10.30am-10.30pm daily.
No credit cards. Map p244 N8.
The only traditional-looking building left on Gongti North Road, this tiny shop has a fun selection of colourful bejewelled earrings, necklaces and bracelets as well as some silver pieces. All are hand-made, relatively cheap and singular – think Mikey costume jewellery but for a third of the price.

Hong Julie

Inside the Swissôtel, 2 Chaoyangmen Bei Dajie, Chaoyang (130 5129 8011). Metro Dongsishitiao.
Open 10am-9.30pm daily. **Credit** AmEx, DC, MC, V. **Map** p244 N8.
For something more traditionally Chinese, beautifully crafted and made using the finest materials, Julie designs and oversees a range of jewellery sold from her three outlets in the city. Created with jade from the southern Yunan Province, turquoise from Hubei Province, pearls and lapis lazuli and ranging from RMB 500 to RMB 20,000, it's the perfect place to come for something special.
Other locations: 2 Jiuxianqiao Lu, 798 Art District (by the north entrance), Chaoyang; inside the Kempinski Hotel, 50 Liangmaqiao Lu, Chaoyang.

Things of the Jing

Inside The Bookworm, Building 4, Nan Sanlitun Lu, Chaoyang (6586 9507/6503 2050/www.thingsofthejing.com). **Open** 9am-1am daily. **Credit** MC, DC, V. **Map** p245 O8.
Jewellery designer Gabrielle Harris's creations somehow manage to be both ancient and modern, and Chinese and European, with a dash of tribal thrown in all at the same time. Despite this apparent mish-mash of influences, her jewellery is also unfailingly pretty. A collection of mostly silver items is then accented with pearls, jade, turquoise or amber, and depict everything from ornate doorways to feudal women and Tibetan symbols.

Shoes

Buying shoes can prove difficult in Beijing since Chinese women usually have tiny feet. Most markets sell shoes but only really up to a European size 38 for women or 44 for men. Ask for anything bigger than that and you'll be met with a snort from vendors who will shake their heads in horror at your monstrous feet. Don't be offended. Instead head to the malls for brands stocking a greater number of Western sizes (Nine West, Aldo, Zara) or consider splashing out on a pair of custom-made shoes or boots from one of the city's cobblers.

Lido Shoe Repair
L1 Lobby, Rm206A, Holiday Inn Lido Place, 6 Jiangtai Lu, Chaoyang (6437 6688 ext 3802). **Open** 8am-9pm daily. **No credit cards. Map** p245 Q4.
Whether you're after your shoes polished, heels lowered or replaced, Mr Yu will do it with a smile and even recommend other shoe-related services if he doesn't have the tools to do it himself.

Long.com
Shop 008, Nali Mall, Sanlitun Beijie, Chaoyang (8643 2880). **Open** 11am-9.30pm daily. **No credit cards. Map** p245 O7.
Don't be put off by the first row of shoes you see as you enter Long.com because, while some of the shoes on display are truly awful (the pink bowed espadrilles for example), others are truly fabulous. Silver Kylie-style kitten heels, cute black round-toe pumps and Steve Madden platforms will please the girls, while bigger sized flipflops, casual trainers and shoes will keep the boys happy too.

Pi'erman Maoyi
37 Gulou Dongdajie, Dongcheng, Houhai (6404 1406). **Open** 9.30am-9pm daily. **No credit cards. Map** p241 K7.
If you've never been able to find a pair of boots that compare to the beloved ones you've been traipsing around in, consider having them copied and custom made while in Beijing. For RMB 800 plus (or about half that for shoes) the nice people at Maoyi will do just that, or make a pair from a photograph, but you may have to have them posted to you – most shoes or boots take around 6 weeks to make.

Stall B1-098
Yashow Market, 58 Gongti Bei Lu, Chaoyang (136 4107 6243). **Open** 9.30am-8.40pm daily. **Credit** AmEx, MC, V. **Map** p245 O8.
This lively stall in Yashow Market's basement seems to have a never ending supply of fashionable factory rejects of brands like Steve Madden, Nine West and Michael Kors, all in Western sizes. Heels, boots, shoes and sandals are all jumbled together on the rack and there are a couple of mirrors for posing in. Be polite and friendly and the girls on the stall shouldn't charge you more than RMB 200 for a pair.

Wanzhong Machine Trim Shoe Shop
Yashow Market, 58 Gongti Bei Lu, Chaoyang (136 9121 9943). **Open** 9.30am-8pm daily. **Credit** AmEx, DC, MC, V. **Map** p245 O8.
Chang Yu Lin will charge just RMB 10 to fix your heels, and if you're in a hurry he's been known to whip out his hairdryer to finish the job

Food & drink

For an on-the-go taste of Beijing's more unusual foods, the Donghuamen Night Market (Metro Wangfujing, 4-10pm daily) should be your first stop. Selling everything from noodles to banana fritters and scorpions, traditional snacks abound – the biggest challenge is daring yourself to eat them. Beijing' wet markets are naturally the best place to buy fresh goods, and the basement of Hongqiao Market (*see p130*) is famous for its fish from all over the world as well as its stalls selling fruit and vegetables. It's also fun to browse the shops and carts selling dried fruit, nuts and other Muslim food around the Niujie Mosque in Qianmen, where dates come from Iran and kebabs are cooked by boys from Xinjiang.

For Western food, and in particular pâtisseries and delis, Gourmet Corner (China World West Tower, next to HSBC, 1 Jianguomenwai Dajie, Chaoyang, 6505 2266) sells delicious lunchtime snacks and salads as well as chocolates, bread and pastries; and the Kempi Deli (1F Kempinski Hotel, Chaoyang, 6465 3388 ext 5741, 7am-10pm daily) has a selection of baguettes, cakes and Illy coffee.

Jenny Lou's
Chaoyang Gongyuan Ximen, Chaoyang (6501 6249). **Open** 8am-midnight daily. **Credit** DC, MC, V. **Map** p245 P7.
A godsend for Westerners longing for a taste of home, Jenny Lou's has stores all over town, is open late, has polite staff and even delivers. The majority of the produce is either local or imported from Europe, America or Australia and you'll pay above Western prices for it. Fresh fruit and veg, canned goods, breakfast cereals, hams, cheeses, sweets, biscuits and chocolate are all available.
Other locations: 6 Sanlitun Beixiaojie, Chaoyang (6461 6928); 4 Ritan Bei Lu, Chaoyang (8563 0626); 2 Jiangtai Lu, Hairun International Condo (on the corner of the crossroads), Chaoyang (5135 8338).

Visage Patisserie
26 Dongcao Yuan, Gongti Nan Lu (50m south of the Workers' Stadium South Gate), Chaoyang (6551 6788/www.facebars.com). Metro Dongsishitiao. **Open** noon-2am daily. **Credit** AmEx, DC, MC, V. **Map** p244 N8.
Despite the fact that French pastry chef Eric Perez had a hand in designing the chocolates sold at Visage, the brand is wholly Asian, and is part of the Face chain of bars and restaurants. Available at the small stall in Wangjing Mall and inside the restaurant itself, such delights as creamy raspberry white chocolates and dark chocolate squares laced with the gold 'face' logo are presented in slick black packaging. Look out for a Shanghai-style proper pâtisserie due to open later this year. **Photo** *p140*.
Other locations: 01-17 1F, Wangjing Capital Mall, Guangshun Bei Lu, Chaoyang (8472 8622).

Wuyutai Tea Shop
186 Wangfujing Dajie, Centre (6525 4961). Metro Wangfujing. **Open** 8.30am-9pm daily. **Credit** AmEx, DC, MC, V. **Map** p244 L9.
Over a hundred years old, this store in Wangfujing must have witnessed some serious change on

Visage Patisserie. *See p139.*

Beijing's famous shopping street. Now considered a *laozihao* (time-honoured business) it has expanded to include multiple locations. Not as cheap as the Tea Street Market but the tea leaves are fresh and great quality and the jasmine tea is excellent.
Other locations: throughout the city.

Gifts & interiors

Always start at the markets for the best range of cheap, antique or unusual gifts and interior decoration items. Panjiayuan and Gaobeidian are two of the best and are where you'll find decorated wooden chests, screens, stools, magazine holders, lanterns and jewellery boxes, among other things.

Athena Xu

West of Yashow Market, Sanlitun, Chaoyang (6415 5025). **Open** 11am-9pm daily. **No credit cards**. **Map** p245 08.
A fun, if expensive shop selling handmade accessories designed by Chinese owner Nanan. Her leather cushions studded with jade or decorated with trendy black lace, and hats and berets all embroidered in intricate detail are both fashionable and singular. Necklaces, beaded cummerbunds, silk scarves and pretty corsages are also a winner with locals and tourists looking for a gift to take home. **Photo** *p143.*

DARA

17 Gongti Bei Lu (opposite North Gate of Workers' Stadium), Chaoyang (6417 9365/www.dara.com.cn). Metro Dongsishitiao. **Open** 9.30am-9pm daily. **Credit** AmEx, DC, MC, V. **Map** p244 N8.
Probably the most popular furniture designer in the city, Dara offers those who don't mind paying more a place to splurge on stylish East meets West furniture, mock antiques, lamps and upholstery. Located in several stores around the city, helpful English-speaking sales boys with names like 'Lemon' and 'Snow' will show you bejewelled birdcages, chic hotel-worthy lamps and (expensive) bedside cabinets. Look out for seasonal sales.
Other locations: Boutique 4, Hairun International Apartments, 2 Jiangtai Lu, Chaoyang (5135 7832); 1F Central Park, 6 Chaowai Dajie, Chaoyang (6597 0650).

Kang Deco

Jiangtai Lu (on the approach to Lido Place), Chaoyang (6437 6330). **Open** 10am-8pm daily. **No credit cards**. **Map** p243 Q4.
Serving as the interior design company's showroom, this Lido-based store stocks exciting furniture and accessories that incorporate both modern design and traditional motifs and materials. Qing dynasty-style chests cost RMB 3,000, lamps around RMB 300 – so not particularly cheap – but they also have a wide range of candles, tables, chairs, mirrors and other

accessories including some more unusual, one-off pieces. Kang Deco claim to be a 'complete design platform for the contemporary Asian home' so decorating and design services are also available.

SQ Décor

Rm 216, Holiday Inn Lido Place, 6 Jiangtai Lu, Chaoyang (6430 1199). **Open** 10am-9pm daily. **Credit** AmEx, DC, MC, V. **Map** p243 Q4.
A modern take on traditional Chinese home decorations, SQ Décor stocks a vast selection of sleek, silk, varnished, glazed and perfectly formed accessories such as vases, wine coolers, cushions and crockery.

Health & beauty

All Watsons (*see p143*) supermarkets stock a good selection of Western branded beauty and personal care products, as do all Chinese department stores. The selection isn't bad, though the abundance of whitening products makes finding anything in a regular shade difficult – who needs whitening deodorant for crying out loud?

Cosmetics

Fruits and Passion

NB146 China World Shopping Mall (above the ice rink), 1 Jianguomenwai Dajie, Chaoyang (6505 1538). Metro Guomao. **Open** 10am-9pm daily. **Credit** AmEx, DC, MC, V. **Map** p245 O10.
Since this quality Canadian bath and body chain came to town, it's managed to fill the gap in the market for high quality but (supposedly) mid range products. However, the delicious smelling bubble baths, handmade soaps, body creams and incense have been marked up a good deal in price.

Sephora

NB128 China World Shopping Mall, 1 Jianguomenwai Dajie, Chaoyang (6505 6726/www.sephora.cn). Metro Guomao. **Open** 10am-9.30pm daily. **Credit** AmEx, DC, MC, V. **Map** 245 O10.
The French perfume and beauty emporium has gradually opened more and more stores in Beijing, each one bigger than the last. The China World Shopping Mall branch is the most central and has a decent though limited number of brands to choose

The ultimate bargaining guide

There's no getting away from the fact that in Beijing, bargaining is king. Outside of the department stores (and sometimes even inside) anything can be bartered down to a better price. Visiting China, most Westerners quickly become aware of what goods are really worth without the phenomenal markups imposed by Western retailers, and the sudden realisation can turn even the most frugal shopper into a glutton.

To get the best bargain possible takes practice – but there are a few tricks that can be employed to make sure you get a great deal rather than just a good one:

- Do a little preparation first. If you're going shopping for something in particular, ask the concierge at your hotel, or a local, how much it should cost. And don't dress up – looking like you have lots of money won't encourage the salesgirl to give you a rock bottom price.
- When you get to the market and see what it is you want, mentally decide how much you are willing to pay for it before you start – confidence is key.
- That's not to say that being cocky is, however. All market vendors will tell you that as soon as someone starts giving them attitude, it's over. Remember most stall workers don't get commission so it's not necessarily in their interests to sell you something if they don't want to.
- Don't be put off by the idea that if you're not Chinese or don't speak the lingo you'll automatically be charged more than the locals. 'Everybody gets a good deal these days,' says one vendor, 'because foreigners know the deal now'. More than that, Chinese vendors often favour foreign customers for their ability to decide quickly, buy in bulk and not be too fussy about quality.
- When you approach a stall or vendor, don't head straight for the first thing that catches your eye. Instead, pick up something you don't like and bargain with that first to get the price down. If a vendor knows how much you want something, they'll play on that weakness.
- The old adage that people will initially quote you three times what something's worth is generally true, but remember that it can vary from vendor to vendor. A pair of good quality jeans, that have been bought by the stall owner for RMB 80, will have a hidden lowest price of RMB 100 to ensure that they make at least a 20 per cent profit. You'll be told at first that they're worth RMB 300.

On the other hand, free spending tourists expecting things like Persian rugs to be expensive when they're not means you'll struggle to get the price down more than RMB 500 on a RMB 4,500 rug as stall owners are used to making a 70 per cent profit.

from. Browse Clinique, Shiseido, Dior, and Anna Sui as well as Sephora's own reliable line of products and try before you buy at one of their make-up stations. They provide cotton wool remover pads so you needn't emerge looking like a drag queen…

Hairdressing

Put simply, most local hairdressers are fine if you're not fussy, however, it's best to keep away from the 'hairdressers' with women in short skirts loitering in the window. If you're looking for a 30-minute scalp-stimulating head massage for RMB 10 or a wash and blow dry for RMB 15, local salons can be a real luxury.

Eric of Paris

43 Sanlitun Beijie, behind 3.3 Fashion Mall, Chaoyang (135 0137 2971). **Open** 10am-8pm daily. **Credit** AmEx, MC, V. **Map** p245 O7.

A favourite with local expats for its quality cuts and convenient locations around the city, Eric of Paris also offers a range of beauty treatments such as waxing, tanning, tinting and facials. Started by French coiffeur Eric Constantino in 1996, it's known for its young and funky, foreign and local stylists, and its work on Beijing's fashion shows. The Hilton branch stocks real Kerastase products.

Other locations: Inside the Hilton Hotel, 1 Dong Fang Lu, Dongsanhuan Bei Lu, Chaoyang (137 0118 3307); Shop 123, Kerry Centre, 1 Guanghua Lu, Chaoyang (139 1179 8376); Holiday Inn Lido Place, 6 Jiangtai Lu, Chaoyang (135 0107 5843).

Tony Studio

Villa 9, Jianwai SOHO, 39 Dongsanhuan Zhong Lu, Chaoyang (5869 0050). Metro Guomao. **Open** 10am-9pm daily. **No credit cards**. **Map** p245 O10.

As much a celebrity as the film stars and models whose hair and make up he styles, hairdresser Tony Li's flagship salon is suitably cool and funky. Testino-like snaps of everyone from Gong Li to diving champion Guo Jingjing are dotted around and the Cosy Café on the second floor is just that – an eclectic collection of French and Chinese furniture, as well as memorabilia collected from his photo-shoots. Prices are relatively cheap, with a wash, cut and blow dry from just RMB 180 for a junior stylist.

Vajra

S106, 18 Gongti Nan Lu (next door to the French Cultural Centre), Glory World Apartment, Chaoyang (6551 6461). **Open** 10am-8pm daily. **Credit** AmEx, MC, V. **Map** p244 N8.

Widely believed to be the best salon in Beijing thanks to Brits Martin Harper and Steve Mather who have 40 years of hairdressing experience in China between them. Its accommodating and down to earth style immediately puts customers at ease. Spread over two floors, the bright, white salon has neck-friendly basins, WiFi connection and even a science lab-style colouring table littered with test tubes and fun coloured liquids so the client can oversee the creation of their hair colour. Western prices apply (RMB 400-RMB 1,500 for a cut) but if it's good enough for Zhang Ziyi and Faye Wong, it's good enough for us.

Nothing is real

Business people are wont to regard it as contempt for intellectual property and the sacred rights of 'the brand'. Adbusters, anti-globalisation campaigners and people on tight budgets label it creative genius. Either way, there's no disguising the fact that China is the land of fakes, and Beijing the capital of the simulacrum.

The speed with which fashions are replicated is awesome. If a new line from, say, Zara appears in the shopping malls on a Monday, there'll be faithful copies at the markets by dawn on Thursday. If you meet a Beijinger who buys authentic CDs (to play on his utterly pseudo name-brand hi-fi stack system), take him for a beer. Then again, that might turn out to be bogus too, as might the noodles you tuck into afterwards, and the headache tabs you take the next morning to get over the fake booze-induced hangover.

Everything has its dodgy double. During the past year, there have been reports of silkworm chrysalis 'dietary supplements' that turned out to be a mixture of pig blood and feathers; dried fish laced with insecticide to give it a longer shelf life; gelatine made from rendered leather and fur offcuts. Even staples of the peasant cupboard such as eggs and flour have been found to be unreliable.

Fantasy and horror mix in this specious world where the lure (and saleability) of Western products mingles with Chinese industriousness. Fake antiobiotics killed 11 Chinese people in 2006. There are also stories of dodgy car parts (including brakes that don't stop) and even plane parts (engines that suddenly stop).

At some point during a trip to China, you will have a brush with one fake or another. Chances are it will be one of the friendly 'art students' who hang out on Tiananmen Square preying on potential customers for their 'galleries' where tat is passed off as art. But don't believe every rumour or bit of gossip you hear – some of the more fantastical stories about fakes turn out to be… fakes.

Athena Xu. See p140.

Health stores & pharmacies

There are hundreds of pharmacies and health stores dotted around Beijing. For a 24-hour pharmacy, the Beijing Vista Clinic (B29, The Kerry Centre, 1 Guanghua Lu, Chaoyang, 8529 6618) inside the Kerry Centre can prescribe you what you need quickly and cheaply, and is guaranteed to be of sound quality – something that's important in the land of the fake.

Tongrentang

24 Dazhalan, Xuanwu, South (6301 4883/www.tongrentang.com/en). **Open** 8am-7.30pm daily. **Credit** AmEx, DC, MC, V. **Map** p241 K11.
Beijing's oldest apothecary, Tongrentang was founded in 1669 and still dispenses the same remedies it sold to the Emperor in the Qing dynasty. This original building sells medicines and herbs to 'clear away heat', 'help the five senses and organs' and 'eliminate the wind damp'.

Watsons

SB128 China World Shopping Mall, 1 Jianguomenwai Dajie, Chaoyang (6505 5495). Metro Guomao. **Open** 9am-9.30pm daily. **No credit cards**. **Map** p245 O10.
Western-style pharmacy and personal care store that originated in Hong Kong and now has a branch in almost every mall in Beijing. A great one-stop-shop for medication, basic first aid supplies, shampoo, deodorant, razors and the like. No English spoken.
Other locations: Full Link Plaza, 18 Chaoyangmenwai Dajie, Chaoyang (6588 2145); LG, Oriental Plaza, Dong Chang'an Jie, Dongcheng, Centre, (8518 6426); Holiday Inn Lido Plaza, 6 Jiangtai Lu, Chaoyang (6436 7651).

Sports & outdoor gear

Most malls have a mini sports department store within, usually noticeable by its running track floor. Sport 100 (8518 6740, 10am-9.30pm daily) inside the Oriental Plaza is one example, and carries brands like Reebok, Adidas, Converse and homegrown footwear labels Double Star and Anta. Malls also often have Nike 360*, Puma and Adidas boutiques but, to no one's surprise, places like the Silk Market push knock-offs of all of them.

Decathlon

195 Dongsihuan Zhonglu, Chaoyang (8777 8788). **Open** 9am-9pm daily. **Credit** MC, V. **Map** p245 Q11.
This well known French sports store stocks pretty much the full spectrum of sporting equipment and clothing – and at decent prices too. Decathlon's staff leave you to it, but are helpful and in some cases, English-speaking. Quite simply unrivalled in Beijing in terms of quality and choice.

Demokratic

Upper East Side Complex, No.8, Section A Central Plaza, Dongsihuan Bei Lu, Chaoyang (5130 7173/www.demokratic.com). **Open** 10am-8pm daily. **Credit** MC, V.
This suitably chilled out shop offers a small but quality selection of clothing and kit for men and women, skateboarders and snowboarders who care about looking good. Set up by Vietnamese Canadian Minh Tuan Khuu and managed by Xiao Long – a local trendsetter and veteran of Beijing's skateboarding community – Demokratic is an authorised dealer of Burton snowboards and such brands as Oakley, DC, RED and Coal. They also organise snowboarding lessons and trips to Nanshan ski resort just outside Beijing.

Nice Days Outdoor Gear Store

1-4 Chaoyangmennei Bei Xiaojie, Dongcheng, Centre (8406 9499). **Open** 10am-8pm daily. **Credit** V. **Map** p244 M8.
Friendly, knowledgeable staff and a solid selection of camping, mountaineering and outdoor gear at Western prices. Most of the things that they stock (such as backpacks, breathable shirts and hiking boots) are from quality Chinese and imported brands like Wolverine, Columbia and Montrail.

Arts & Entertainment

Features

Peking Opera. *See p187.*

Festivals & Events

Getting ready for the party.

Long gone are the days when the city shut down at 8pm and festival days were frowned on as superstitious nonsense. Despite the sometimes overwhelming crowds, traditional festival days are a fun time to be in Beijing. **Lantern Festival** and **Spring Festival** see colourfully lit displays and parades throughout the city. Best of all, these events are free and find the Chinese at their most relaxed. Traditional Chinese holidays follow the lunar calendar, meaning that the exact dates change each year. The government usually confirms the dates just a few weeks beforehand.

Apart from traditional holidays, and the increasingly popular religious festivals, you'll find Beijing awash with sports events ranging from the Open China tennis tournament in the autumn to the open snooker competition in the spring, featuring the Chinese prodigy Ding Junhui. Expect plenty more international sporting events as the city prepares for the biggest one of all in 2008.

Despite best intentions, organisation is rarely seamless when it comes to celebrations in Beijing. From over-zealous police guards at pop gigs to concert halls with dire acoustics, attending special events can be a fraught experience. Etiquette isn't the same as in the West: talking, calling out and getting up from your seat are everyday occurrences in theatres and concert halls. But things can only get better and as Beijing aims to raise its profile across the world, expect improvements in the years to come.

PRACTICALITIES

The best way to find out what's going on is to check out the many English-language magazines available, including our own *Time Out Beijing* which lists all the latest concerts, films and festivals. *That's Beijing* (www.thatsbj.com) and *City Weekend* (www.cityweekend.com.cn) are other good sources. Government information websites (www.ebeijing.gov.cn) have got better of late, but still can't be relied upon. Neither can the city's tourist information centres with their grumpy staff. Try speaking to your hotel concierge instead if you are staying at a high-end hotel. For concert, theatre and sports tickets avoid contacting the actual box offices and go to www.piao.com.cn, an English-language ordering service which will deliver tickets anywhere in Beijing for free.

Spring

Lantern Festival

Chaoyang Park and various venues, Chaoyang Park, 1 Nongzhan Nanlu, Chaoyang (6506 5409). **Open** 6am-10pm. **Admission** RMB 5. **Date** 4 Mar 2007; Feb 2008; Feb 2009. **Map** p245 Q7.

Lantern Festival falls on the 15th day of the first moon which varies between February and March. The Festival dates from Emperor Ming Di of the Han Dynasty, when he ordered the lighting of lanterns as a symbolic means of paying homage to the Buddha. Chaoyang Park usually has a big display of beautifully glowing lights, but look out for the paper lanterns being sold and displayed all around the city. Also make sure you try *tangyuan* – rice treats stuffed with black sesame paste.

International Women's Day

Date 8 Mar.

On 8 March China celebrates women's day. All women are supposed to have the day off to relax, but the city seems to have decided it's too busy for that so women usually get a half day off, if that.

Beijing Fashion Week

Various venues (8586 1131/www.fashion.org.cn). **Date** mid Nov 2007; Mar & mid Nov 2008; Mar & mid-Nov 2009.

It may not be Paris or New York, but Beijing's Fashion Week, held twice a year, highlights the work of Chinese designers and their growing influence on the market. See some of China's top designers showing off their collections, with almost 30 catwalk shows, one forum, five design contests and a competition for the best designer and model.

Goddess of Mercy Guanyin's Birthday

Guangji Si (Temple of Great Charity), 25 Fuchengmennei Dajie, Xicheng, Financial District (6616 0907). Metro Fuchengmen. **Open** 7am-4.30pm daily. **Admission** RMB 5. **Date** Mar or Apr. **Map** p241 H8.

The colourful birthday of the Goddess of Mercy, China's most popular deity, falls on the 19th day of the 2nd month of the lunar calendar. The day's festivities are best celebrated in smoky temples full of fervent believers. Guangji Si, in the west of the city, is the most popular place with around 2,000 Buddhists showing up with incense and offerings.

World Snooker China Open

Peking University Student's Gymnasium, 11 Beisanhuan Xi Lu, Haidian, North-west (6275 1230). **Admission** TBC. **Date** late Mar. **Map** p248 D3.

World-class snookers stars such as Ronnie O'Sullivan, Peter Ebdon and Stephen Hendry fly in to compete with China's Ding Junhui and 30 or so others at the Peking University Gymnasium in the west of the city. For tickets, go to www.piao.com.cn or www.emma.com.cn.

Beijing International Kite Festival

Mentougou Sports Centre, Mentougou (64km from Beijing) (6515 8844). **Admission** RMB 10.
Date 1-30 Apr.

Starting with a colourful opening ceremony that involves dragon dances, music and kite displays, the annual kite-flying festival attracts teams from all over the world. Different varieties of kites from the past 100 years are given an airing at this sports centre on the outskirts of the city – just hope that the air is clear enough for you to enjoy the displays.

Tomb Sweeping Festival

Various temples and graveyards in Beijing.
Date usually 4 or 5 Apr.

Many Chinese spend this day visiting cemeteries to clean the graves of their loved ones. The communists discouraged it as superstitious during their ideological heyday in the 1950s and '60s, but the festival is now undergoing a resurgence. Although not an official holiday, hospitals and stock exchanges are noticeably quieter as it's not considered an auspicious day for medical procedures or financial deals with all those spirits floating around.

Zhongshan Park Tulip Festival

Zhongshan Park, 1 Zhonghua Lu, West side of Tiananmen, Dongcheng, Centre (6605 5431). Metro Tiananmen West. **Admission** RMB 3.
Date early Apr. **Map** p241 K10.

Midi Music Festival. *See p147.*

This attractive and peaceful park, right next door to the always-packed Forbidden City, becomes awash with colour in spring with the Tulip Festival. As many as 300,000 tulips in more than 30 varieties planted either in the ground or in pots are displayed in different arrangements around the park.

798 International Art Festival

Dashanzi East, Gaobeidian, Chaoyang (6438 2797/ www.diaf.org). **Admission** TBC.
Date late Apr-early May.

Formally the Dashanzi International Art Festival, the festival presents a lively timetable of visual and performance art, dance, music and theatre. About 100,000 people attend the event each year, roaming the converted Bauhaus-style factory district which is an attraction in itself. A feud between the founder of the original festival and the local landlord has led to breakaway festivals both in Dashanzi, to be held in the autumn, and also at a new site, named Dashanzi East, in Gaobeidian that is planned for 2008.

Summer

May Day

Various venues. **Date** 1st wk May.

May Day is one of China's three Golden Weeks (*see p149* **Golden weeks**), so expect a crowded city in a holiday mood. In the past the actual day was spent celebrating the heroic achievements of the workers with military parades, but now it's much more relaxed and the only parades are those of shoppers in Xidan and Wangfujing taking advantage of the sales.

Midi Music Festival

Haidian Park, 2 Xinjiangongmen Lu, Haidian, North-west (6259 0101/www.midifestival.com).
Admission RMB 30/day; RMB 100/4 days.
Date 1-4 May 2007. **Map** p248 C3.

The much-loved Midi Festival has grown to become the best rock festival in China, attracting fans from across the country to four days of music. In 2006 the jamboree, which is run by the Beijing Midi Music School, featured more than 30 local and 14 overseas bands on the main stage in front of 10,000 rock fans. It's not Glastonbury, but the six-year-old Midi is the longest running annual outdoor rock festival in China – not an easy feat in a country where the genre is still seen as a bit suspect. **Photo** *p146.*

Great Wall Marathon

Great Wall, Tianjin (6858 9496/www.great-wall-marathon.com). **Admission** TBC. **Date** late spring 2008; late spring 2009.

If the idea of running a marathon wasn't exhausting enough, the Great Wall Marathon involves intimidating ascents, steep descents and more than 3,700 stone steps to conquer. Some 800 runners took part in previous years. The first section, which covers approximately nine kilometres (5.5 miles), takes the runners up to, along and down the Great Wall itself, while the second section sends them through picturesque villages and rice fields.

Meet in Beijing Arts Festival

Various venues (6494 1107). **Date** late Apr to late May 2008; late Apr to late May 2009.

The annual Meet in Beijing festival has become one of China's best-known, showcasing 50-plus international acts from more than 20 countries and regions. Guests have included Barcelona's La Fura Dels Baus and director Jürgen Müller.

Children's Day

Various venues. **Date** 1 June.

In a country which follows a strict one-child policy, there was always going to be a celebration for the little 'uns. Schools are decorated and parties thrown, and amusement parks, cinemas and museums usually offer cut-price rates for the little darlings.

Dragon Boat Festival

Taoranting Park, 19 Taiping Jie, Xuanwu, South (6353 2385). **Admission** RMB 2. **Date** 19 June 2007; May or June 2008; May or June 2009.
Map p246 J12.

The Dragon Boat Festival falls on the fifth day of the fifth lunar month and celebrates the memory of the poet Qu Yuan who drowned himself in despair in 278 BC after vainly protesting the corruption of the court. Nowadays, dragon boat racing and memorial services are held on the day and if that's too energetic, you can commemorate Qu's death by eating *zongzi*, a glutinous rice snack stuffed with meat or dried fruit and steamed in bamboo leaves.

Nine-Dragon Cup International Dragon Boat Festival

Ming Tombs Reservoir, Changping (6070 4656).
Admission TBC. **Date** July.

Aside from the actual Dragon Boat Festival day (*see above*), an international dragon boat race takes place every summer on the reservoir surrounding the Ming Tombs (*see p199*). Teams from around the world take part. The nearby Mang Shan National Forest Park is a beautiful spot for strolling before or after the race.

Qi Xi – Chinese Valentine's Day

Various venues. **Date** 19 Aug 2007; July or Aug 2008; July or Aug 2009.

They may not celebrate with chocolates and roses, but the Chinese have an equivalent to the West's day of love. The Qi Xi celebrations fall on the 7th day of the 7th month of the lunar calendar and are based on a Chinese legend about two lovers – a cowherd and a fairy – who fell in love but were separated by a jealous god who created the Milky Way to keep them apart. Only on Qi Xi could the lovers cross the stars to be together for one night.

Autumn

China Open

Beijing International Tennis Centre, 50 Tiantan Dong Lu, Chongwen, South (6714 2374/www.china open.cn). **Date** 10-24 Sept 2007; Sept 2008; Sept 2009.
Map p247 M13.

Chinese New Year (Spring Festival). See p149.

Despite Chinese audiences not always following tennis etiquette (think cameras, talking on mobiles and calling out), it's definitely worth visiting the Open's brand-new high tech stadium. The competition attracts a fair sprinkling of stars: Marco Baghdatis won the men's singles in 2006 and Svetlana Kuznetsova, the women's. Tennis hasn't really caught on yet with the Chinese which means there are no problems getting tickets.

Beijing Pop Festival

Chaoyang Park, 1 Nongzhan Nanlu, Chaoyang (6593 0367/www.beijingpopfestival.com). **Admission** TBC. **Date** early Sept. **Map** p245 Q7.

Unlike the classical Beijing Musical Festival (*see below*), this two-day event is for the pop kids. In 2006, 25,000 fans saw Placebo and Supergrass alongside Chinese punk bands, and the hilarious performance from former Skid Row member Sebastian Bach will never be forgotten by those who witnessed it. The custom-built stage is impressive but don't expect any refreshments: all beer was confiscated in 2006.

National Day

Tiananmen Square and various venues. **Date** 1 Oct.

The last public holiday of the year, National Day celebrates the founding of the People's Republic on 1 October 1949 (*see p149* **Golden weeks**). Every year there are a variety of government-organised festivities, including fireworks and concerts: be sure to check out the lavish decorations at Tiananmen Square where portraits of revered leaders such as Sun Yat-sen are publicly displayed. As for official events, there is a particularly grand flag-raising ceremony at sunrise at Tiananmen Square which attracts around 30,000 people.

Beijing Music Festival

Various venues (6593 0250/www.bmf.org.cn). **Date** mid Sept-end of Oct 2007; Oct 2008; Oct 2009.

The Beijing Music Festival is a significant date for classical music fans. Held in late autumn, the concerts are staged at various venues throughout the capital. In 2007, the festival celebrates its tenth anniversary with an expanded six-week series of concerts. Each year more than 1,000 domestic and foreign musicians take part in approximately 30 performances featuring artists including José Carreras, Valery Gergiev and Julian Lloyd Webber.

Winter

Longqing Gorge Ice Festival

Longqing Gorge, Yanqing County (6919 1020). **Admission** RMB 70. **Date** mid Jan-late Feb.

Can't face the distance, price gouging and Arctic conditions of Harbin's Ice Festival? Well there's an alternative two hours from Beijing at the Longqing Gorge. Expect ice dragons, ice mushrooms as big as a house, a giant ice Chinese chessboard and an ice maze, as well as toboggan rides and ice slides.

Ice Skating Season

Beijing's official ice skating season is set by the government each year. In 2006, the ice at most outdoor lakes was half the thickness of a year ago, so expect the number of official ice rinks to dwindle. Traditional places to skate include the lakes at Peking University, Beihai Park and Zhongshan Park. Expect to pay around RMB 10 to hire skates

Chinese New Year (Spring Festival)

Various venues. **Date** 7 Feb 2008; 26 Jan 2009.

This is the big one: the principal party of the year. After years of official banishment fireworks, which are meant to scare off evil spirits, are again allowed in the capital, and people are enthusiastically making up for lost time. During Chun Jie, families celebrate new beginnings, gathering in homes or restaurants to eat special meals full of auspicious foods like dumplings (for luck) and fish balls (a symbol of harmony). Children receive *hongbaos*, or red envelopes with crisp 100 RMB notes inside. Head to one of the Temple Fairs held throughout the city to see some local colour. The religious aspects of temple fairs have faded – nowadays expect parades, dragon dancing and fairground rides. **Photo** *p148*.

Golden weeks

Opening day of the Macy's sale? Queuing for Wimbledon tickets on a summer morning? You may think you know the meaning of the word 'hectic' but you ain't seen nothing until you've been to China during one of the three Golden Week holidays.

The holidays aren't usually a full week long, but four days each for the Lunar New Year, the May Day celebrations and the founding of the People's Republic. When 1.3 billion people all have their holidays at the same time, it's best to batten down the hatches and watch the hurricane from a place of safety. Train tickets are gold dust, hotel rooms non-existent and tourist attractions crammed to the rafters. Even if you come by that rare and precious ticket, a train carriage may not be the best place to be. According to the *China Daily*, sales of incontinence nappies in Guangdong supermarkets rocket just prior to the beginning of the holidays due to massive demand from passengers anticipating trouble getting to the loo on their long journeys home. And you thought you had problems getting a seat on the 17.58 to Uxbridge...

So, avoid travel at these times and hole up in the capital. Locals often claim that Beijing is the best place to be over the holidays as everyone goes home to the provinces. Suddenly you can get across town without hitting a jam and, because the factories aren't belching fumes, air quality is usually better too. Now that does sound golden.

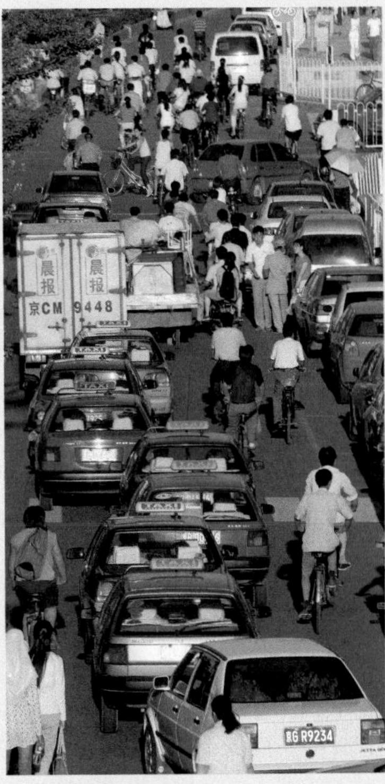

Children

Plan carefully and your tots will thrive in the megalopolis.

Although not the easiest place to travel with little ones, Beijing has enough to keep children fascinated without overwhelming them. Its wide array of activities should keep all age groups happy, particularly in summer when the many parks become useful. A visit to the giant pandas at the Beijing Zoo is a must for most children, as is an evening at one of the acrobatic performances. There are plenty of museums and amusement parks, including the city's newest, Happy Valley, which offers some of the most thrilling rides in the world.

PRACTICALITIES

Although large hotels and Western restaurants offer decent toilet facilities, your child is almost certainly going to have to cope with squat loos at some point. Many of the city's public toilets are cleaner and better maintained than they once were but there are still some undesirable ones. It's a good idea to buy a packet of scented tissues, which children can put over their noses when they find odours too unpleasant. Public toilets often lack soap and good handwashing facilities, so carry a packet of antibacterial wipes or an alcohol-based hand cleaning liquid.

Beijing drivers often pay little consideration to pedestrians and zebra crossings tend to be completely disregarded. Make sure your children know not to cross roads without you and use underpasses or overpasses whenever possible. Seatbelts are few, but when available remind children to buckle up.

Beijingers are welcoming and friendly, and like to make a huge fuss over children. They think Western children are adorable and call them *yang wawa*, or 'little foreign dolls'. Be prepared for attention, especially if your kids have blond hair and blue eyes, as they are likely to find themselves subject to much staring, photographing and even touching.

Remember that English is not widely spoken in Beijing, so in case you and your child get separated, it is vital to make sure they have a note of your hotel address and telephone number written in Chinese, which they must keep with them at all times.

Places to stay

Most hotels are set up to serve the needs of business clientele and adult tourists only. The Kerry Centre Shangri-La hotel and the newly opened Westin are currently the top choices for family travellers – the Kerry Centre with its children's playground area; and the Westin, with its full crèche service, offering daytime art and music classes. Hotels such as the Hilton and the Holiday Inn will add cribs or extra beds to rooms for children and also provide babysitting services upon request.

Hilton 1

1 Dongfang Lu, Dong Sanhuan Bei Lu, Chaoyang (5865 5000/5865 5800/www.hilton.com). **Rates** RMB 950 single/double; RMB 1,650 suite. **Credit** AmEx, DC, MC, V. **Map** p243 O6.

The Hilton provides a babysitting service, cribs and its restaurant has a children's menu and high chairs.

Holiday Inn Lido

6 Jiangtai Lu, Chaoyang (6437 6688/fax 6437 6237/www.lidoplace.com). **Rates** RMB 2,300 single/double; RMB 4,150 suite. **Credit** AmEx, DC, MC, V. **Map** p243 Q4.

The Holiday Inn will equip rooms with extra children's beds on request and offers a babysitting service if you let reception know before 4pm.

Kerry Centre Shangri-La

1 Guanghua Lu, Chaoyang (6561 8833/fax 6561 2626/www.shangri-la.com/beijing/kerrycentre/en). Metro Yong'anli. **Rates** RMB 3,000 double; RMB 5,000 suite. **Credit** AmEx, DC, MC, V. **Map** p245 O9.
This hotel has cribs and extra beds available for rooms, and a babysitting service. There is a playground area for children.

Westin Beijing, Financial Street

9B Financial Street, Xicheng, Financial District (6606 8866/fax 6606 8899/www.westin.com). Metro Fuchengmen or Fuxingmen. **Rates** 1,100 single/double; RMB 2,100 suite. **Credit** AmEx, DC, MC, V. **Map** p240 G9.
The Westin can provide cribs or more beds to take the children, and it also runs a crèche. The hotel's restaurant has a full children's menu, and provides high chairs and child-sized cutlery.

Sightseeing

With so many cossetted only-children out there (*see p153* **Little emperors**) lots of investment is going into child-oriented industries, and museums are top of the list. Many of Beijing's mainstream tourist attractions can also be child-friendly; places such as the Old and New Summer Palaces (*see p85*) and the Forbidden City (*see p51*) all have big grounds that provide a perfect place for children to run around and explore. A rickshaw ride around the hutong and lakeside area of Shichahai (*see p59*) is a must, as is a trip to one of Beijing's awe-inspiring acrobatic performances, such as the one at the Chaoyang Theatre (*see p187*).

Beijing Aquarium

18B Gaoliangqiao Xiejie, Haidian, Financial District (6212 3910/6217 6655 6791/www.bj-sea.com). Metro Xizhimen. **Open** *Aug-May* 9am-5pm daily. *June, July* 7am-10pm daily. **Admission** RMB 100 adult (two children under 1.2m admitted free with each adult); RMB 50 seniors/children; free children under 1.2m. **No credit cards. Map** p249 F7.
Dolphin shows are held at 11am and 3pm daily (included in the ticket price). The Aquarium is within the confines of the zoo and tickets include access to the land animals as well as the aquatic ones.

Beijing Planetarium

138 Xizhimen Wai Dajie, Xicheng, Financial District (6835 2453/6831 2570/www.bjp.org.cn). Metro Xizhimen. **Open** 10am-3.30pm Wed-Fri; 10am-4pm Sat, Sun. **Admission** RMB 15; RMB 10 children. *Exhibitions* RMB 105; RMB 75 children. **No credit cards. Map** p249 F7.
3D and 4D film theatres allow you move through the Milky Way on an exploration of our home galaxy, while experiencing the sensations of travelling through time and space. The show soundtracks are in Chinese only, although they are so awe-inspiring this doesn't have to be a hindrance.

Beijing Zoo

137 Xizhimenwai Da Jie, Haidian, Financial District (6831 4411/www.bjzoo.com). Metro Xizhimen. **Open** *Winter* 7.30am-5pm daily. *Summer* 7.30am-6pm daily. **Admission** RMB 10; RMB 5 students/children; extra RMB 5 for panda hall tkts. **No credit cards. Map** p249 E7.
With over 600 animal species on display, there's not only a chance to meet China's national treasure, the giant panda, but also the golden monkey and other rare species native to China. However, parents be warned: if you've got sensitive children be prepared for the fact that, while the conditions the animals are kept in are steadily improving, they are still not up to Western standards.

China Puppet Art Troupe

1A Anhuaxili, Beisanhuan Lu, Chaoyang (6425 4849/6425 4798/www.puppetchina.com). Bus 300 and 302 to Anzhenli. **Performances** 10.30am Sat, Sun. **Admission** RMB 50-RMB 100. **No credit cards. Map** p242 K5.
Fun shadow puppets and hand puppet performances put on by a theatre group which has toured all over the world. Plays vary between folk tales and modern stories, from China and abroad. All shows are performed in Chinese.

Natural History Museum

126 Tianqiao Lu, Chongwen, South (6702 4439/www.bmnh.org.cn). **Open** 8.30am-5pm Tue-Sun. **Admission** RMB 30; RMB 15 children. **No credit cards. Map** p246 K12.
A large collection of exhibits ranging from fossils to the giant panda, with an interactive dinosaur display aimed at entertaining younger children.

Sony ExploraScience

1 Chaoyang Gongyuan Nan Lu, inside Chaoyang Park, near the South Gate, Chaoyang (6501 8800/www.explorascience.com.cn/english). Buses 115 and 302. **Open** 9.30am-6pm Tue-Fri; 9.30am-7.30pm Sat, Sun. Closed 2nd Mon, Tue of each mth. **Admission** RMB 30; RMB 20 children; free children under 1.2m. **No credit cards. Map** p245 Q8.
With plenty of interactive components, the Sony ExploraScience museum's focus is on exploring the science behind light and sound. On weekends experiments are performed in the laboratory, with competitions and live science shows.

Gardens, parks and playgrounds

Park culture is huge in Beijing, no matter what time of day you go. If your children wake up early in the morning then some entertainment can be provided for them by heading to the Temple of Heaven (*see p76*) or Beihai Park (*see 58*) to see the morning t'ai chi, swordplay and dance displays. For good boating and picnicking locations downtown, try Chaoyang Park (*see 69*) or Tuanjie Lake Park (*see p70*).

Beijing Shijingshan Amusement Park

25 Shijingshan Lu, Shijingshan (6887 4060/ www.bs-amusement-park.com). Metro Bajiao Youleyuan. **Open** *Apr-Oct* 8.30am-5pm daily. *Nov-Mar* 9am-4.30pm daily. **Admission** RMB 10; rides charged individually. **No credit cards.**

A sizeable city amusement park, with a huge selection of fairground rides, including rollercoasters, a Ferris wheel and a Disney-esque Cinderella Castle. You will also find a section called Water World, which features Beijing's first ever outdoor wave machine, water slides, jacuzzis, play pools and boats.

Beijing World Park

158 Fengbao Lu, Huaxiang, Fengtai (8361 3344/ www.beijingworldpark.cn). Special bus 7 from Qianmen. **Open** *Winter* 8.30am-4.30pm daily. *Summer* 8.30am-5pm daily. **Admission** RMB 65; RMB 24 children. **No credit cards.**

This popular Beijing attraction boasts over a hundred models of famous man-made and natural wonders. Traverse the 46-hectare park on foot, or using its little train, motorboat or cars. Jump from continent to continent to explore sights including the Eiffel Tower and the Statue of Liberty. Between May and October there are often lively cultural festivals.

Chaoyang Park

1 Nongzhan Nan Lu, Chaoyang (6506 5409). **Open** 6am-10pm daily. **Admission** RMB 5; RMB 2.5 children. **No credit cards. Map** p245 Q7.

Centrally located, this is one of Beijing's most popular parks and it is perfect for a stroll, a picnic, a leisurely turn on a pedalboat or a fairground ride. Sony ExploraScience, a recent addition to the park, is also well worth a visit (*see p151*).

Chinese Ethnic Culture Park

1 Minzuyuan Lu, Houhai (6206 3646/6206 3647/ www.emuseum.org.cn). **Open** *North Park* Jan-June, Sept-Dec 8.30am-6pm daily; July, Aug 8.30am-6pm Mon-Thur; 8.30am-9pm Fri-Sun. *South Park* Apr-Nov 8am-6pm daily. Closed Jan-Mar, Dec. **Admission** RMB 60 (with one free child under 1.1m) to visit one park; RMB 90 for both North and South parks; RMB 40 seniors/students to visit one park; RMB 65 for both North and South parks. **No credit cards. Map** p242 J3.

All of China's 56 ethnic minority groups can be found represented within this park, along with information on their lifestyles and customs. Explore model villages, and watch song and dance performances.

Happy Valley

Wuji Beilu, Dongsihuan, Chaoyang (6736 0303/ 6738 3333/http://bj.happyvalley.com.cn). **Open** 9.30am-8pm daily. **Admission** RMB 160; RMB 80 children; free children under 1.2m. One ticket lets you on all rides. **No credit cards.**

Divided into six themed regions, Happy Valley's 120 attractions aren't just a series of daredevil rides, although there are these available for the eager thrill seeker. Beijing's newest amusement park also offers exhibits, sculptures, performances and an IMAX theatre. Among the scream-inducing rides on offer is the flying rollercoaster, the single most expensive amusement attraction to be found in China.

Tuanjiehu Park

Tuanjiehu Nanli, Chaoyang (8597 3603). Bus 115. **Open** 6.30am-9pm daily. **Admission** *Park* RMB 5. *Beach* RMB 20; RMB 15 children. **No credit cards. Map** p245 P8.

A third of the area of Tuanjiehu Park is water and it boasts Beijing's largest man-made lake, with little waterfalls. Surrounding a huge swimming pool is an artificial sandy beach for the pleasure of sunbathers and sandcastle builders alike. This park is so centrally located it really draws the summer crowds, so arrive early to bag your patch of sand.

Eating & drinking

Eating with children in China can depend on the likes and dislikes of your child. While Chinese food is quick and cheap, some may find it oily and seasoned with too many strange new flavours. Ordering can be hard, and it makes sense to work out early on a couple of basic dishes your child likes and have them noted down in Chinese. Beijing has enough Western-style restaurants to satisfy children who don't take to Chinese food, but working these into your sightseeing schedule needs extra planning.

As a contingency plan, you can always fall back on ubiquitous fast-food joints like KFC, McDonald's and Pizza Hut. Another point to consider is that many restaurants do not provide children's cutlery, and unless your child is adept at using chopsticks, you're advised to carry a set of cutlery.

Donghuamen Night Market

Donghuamen Jie, Dongcheng, Centre (no tel). Metro Wangfujing. **Open** 4-10pm daily. **No credit cards. Map** p244 L9.

This market offers the more unusual side of Beijing cuisine and gives children a chance to witness people tucking into deep-fried scorpions and locusts. It also offers child-friendly snacks like fried noodles and dumplings.

Fish Nation

31 Nanluoguxiang, Dongcheng, Houhai (6401 3249). **Open** 9am-1.30am daily. **Credit** MC. **Map** p244 K8.

For little tummies craving a taste of home, Fish Nation serves up authentic British fish and chips. There's a toddler's menu with child-sized portions of food like fish and chips, pizza and spaghetti. High chairs are available, as are plastic children's cutlery.

Grandma's Kitchen

Level B, 0103 Jianwai Soho, Dongsanhuan Zhong Lu, Chaoyang (5869 3055). **Open** 7.30am-11pm daily. **Credit** MC, V. **Map** p245 O10.

Little emperors

In the past the Chinese used 'little emperor' for a privileged and pampered child. The term now extends to describe a whole generation of urban Chinese. This phenomenon isn't only due to their sibling-less existence, but also to the fact that this age group are the first to enjoy all the educational, lifestyle and consumer opportunities the recent increase in China's economic wealth have created.

Social psychologists spent the 1980s watching China conduct the 'social experiment' of the One-Child Policy. What impact would such an individualistic generation have on the country and its social structure?

Research into the first generation of only children, currently in their mid-twenties, indicates that they have increased scholarly aptitude and higher academic achievement than their peers from larger families. Chinese parents' desire for their children to become successful means that education is prioritised over learning other life-skills. Parents are willing to cosset their children and do all the housework as long as the children hold up their side of the bargain and excel academically.

This lifestyle of being excessively reliant on their parents also has health implications: child obesity and early-onset diabetes are on the rise as young children are encouraged to give priority to sedentary activities over physical ones.

With many relatives relying on them alone to provide support in old age, these single children will feel the pressure as they grow older. Only time will tell how they'll survive in an increasingly competitive and unpredictable Chinese society.

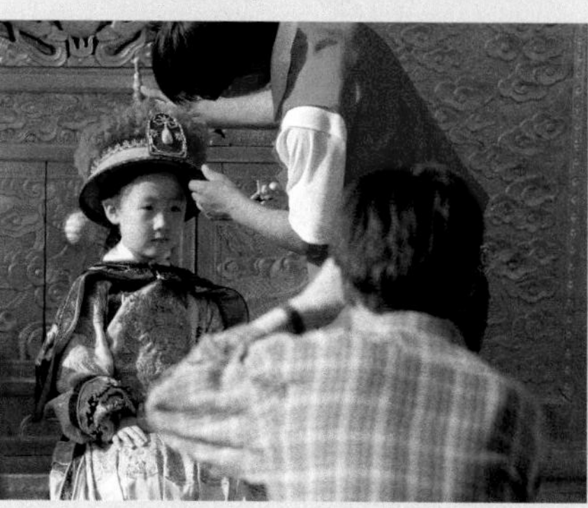

For the child sick of noodles Grandma's, with its American-style comfort food, is the perfect antidote. Its children's menu offers a wide range, such as grilled cheese sandwiches, waffles, pancakes, hot-dogs, pizzas and chicken. High chairs available.

Huajiayiyuan

235 Dongzhimennei Da Jie, Dongcheng, Houhai (6405 1908). **Open** 10am-4am daily. **Credit** MC, V. **Map** p244 M7.

This large and lively courtyard restaurant offers fantastic Chinese food, including great Peking duck. As an added attraction, every Friday evening from 7pm acrobatic performances are held in the main hall. High chairs are available.

Zone de Confort

Building 15, Sanlitun Bei Jie (at nort-hwest corner of 3.3 Fashion Mall), Chaoyang (6500 8070/www.zonedeconfort.com). **Open** 10am-2.30pm; 5.30-10.30pm daily. **Buffet** Sat, Sun lunch RMB 110; RMB 70 children. **Credit** AmEx, DC, MC, V. **Map** p245 O7.

Every Saturday and Sunday this family-oriented French fusion restaurant hosts a buffet lunch and a children's cooking session, where little ones are invited to learn some culinary skills from the chef.

Health

Beijing has a few first-class foreign-run clinics staffed by English-speaking paediatricians – these can be costly, so check your insurance before committing to treatment. *See also p220.*

Beijing Vista Clinic

B29 Kerry Centre, 1 Guanghua Road, Chaoyang (8529 6618/www.vista-china.net). Metro Guomao. **Map** p245 O9.

The Vista Clinic offers 24-hour medical assistance for the whole family and provides home visits and free telephone consultations. The paediatrics department covers all general paediatric conditions.

New Century International Children's Hospital

56 Nanlishi Lu, Xicheng, Financial District (6802 5588/www.ncich.com.cn). Metro Nanlishi Lu. **Map** p240 G10.

This newly opened US-managed hospital provides a full range of paediatric care services via a team of bilingual Chinese physicians. It is a more affordable option than some of Beijing's other clinics.

Film

It's not all kung fu in the film capital of China.

In 1905 the first Chinese film, *Conquering Jun Mountain*, was shot by Ren Fengtai, proprietor of Beijing's Fengtai Photo Studio. It was an abbreviated version of a Peking opera and kicked off the turbulent and dramatic history of Chinese movies. Over a century later Beijing remains an important city for Chinese cinema. This is home to most of the country's filmmakers, it's where they were schooled and it's where they develop their next project.

In earlier days Shanghai was the film capital, and the centre of the Golden Age of Chinese Cinema in the 1930s. Theatres were packed with movies of all genres from around the world. A prolific domestic industry encountered few government restrictions and freely portrayed sex, drugs and violence.

The glorious era was short-lived. When World War II broke out, film became a mere propaganda tool. And Mao emphasised the role of film as a political tool for class struggle to the neglect of its artistic expression. As soon as the Communist Party of China formed the People's Republic of China in 1949, Beijing Film Studio and Shanghai Film Studio were founded to control the industry and produce propaganda. Beijing Film Academy, still the nation's leading film school, was founded shortly afterwards for the same purpose. The industry was effectively shut down during the Cultural Revolution (1966-72). Over 1,400 films were banned, and many leading filmmakers were imprisoned or sent to labour camps.

Since the Reform era, which began in 1978, films have no longer been required to depict workers, farmers and soldiers as their heroes and class struggle as the main theme. Although films released in China today still have to meet the political standard of not challenging the Communist Party, they do not have to sing its praises to pass censorship. The emphasis on cinema's artistic and commercial aspects, and the de-emphasis of the political, has changed the China's film industry dramatically.

Today's post-Reform industry is largely led by graduates from the Beijing Film Academy and the Central Drama Academy. The 'Fifth Generation' of filmmakers – the first students to be admitted to the Beijing Film Academy since the Cultural Revolution – revived Chinese cinema in the 1980s. Zhang Yimou (*Red Sorghum*, *Raise the Red Lantern*) and Cheng Kaige (*Yellow Earth*, *Farewell My Concubine*) changed the way Chinese films were perceived

Beijing's bright young things, in *Waiting Alone* (2004).

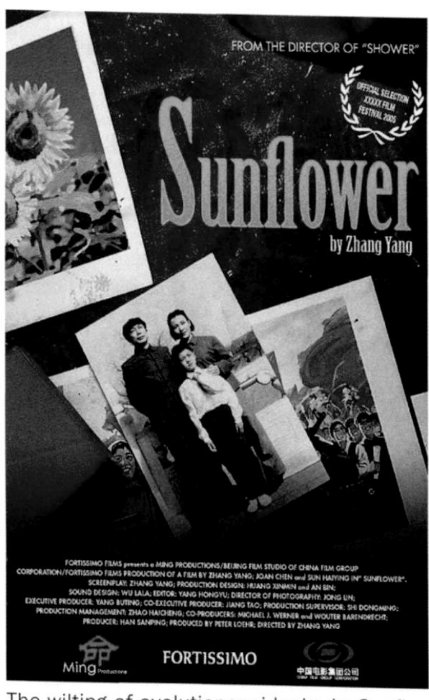

The wilting of evolutionary ideals, in *Sunflower* (2005).

overseas. Gong Li, graduate of Central Drama Academy, and star of all of Zhang's films until 1995, emerged as the first major international star from China. Their successors, the 'Sixth Generation' of filmmakers, among whom are Jia Zhangke and Wang Xiaoshuai, emerged in the aftermath of the 4 June 1989 Tiananmen Square movement. Dark, cynical visions of Chinese urban culture, not exhibitable in China, found success on the international festival circuit.

In 2000 Zhang Ziyi, also a Central Drama Academy alumnus, claimed the hearts of millions in *Crouching Tiger, Hidden Dragon* (shot in Beijing Film Studio), which broke through in the North American market, igniting a gold rush of costume martial arts dramas such as *Hero*, *House of Flying Daggers* and *The Curse of the Golden Flower*.

ON LOCATION

Many westerners associate Chinese films with bamboo, mystical martial arts and ornate palaces, but Beijing has provided a memorable urban backdrop for a handful of contemporary Chinese films. *Waiting Alone* (2004), the first rom-com from mainland China, directed by Chinese American director Dayyan Eng, was a big hit among Chinese audiences for showing young Beijingers as they really are. The film is pretty daft slapstick – with a great soundtrack – the tale of a twentysomething aspiring writer on a relentless pursuit of the 'perfect girl'. Another Beijing-set film is *Sunflower* (2005) by Zhang Yang, an intimate portrayal of the inner dynamics of one post-Cultural Revolution family and their struggle over 30 years. Some memorable scenes were shot at destinations such as the 798 Art District and Houhai Lake.

GOING TO THE FLICKS

Cinema-going is still limited to wealthier urban residents. Ticket prices are RMB 40 to RMB 120, more than a day's wage for many locals. According to the China Film Co-production Corporation (CFCC) there were a mere 65 cinemas with 198 screens in Beijing in 2006, not many for a population of nearly 15 million. In 2005, 280 domestic films were made; in 2006, 330, plus 110 digital films. In 2006 the Municipal Bureau of Culture pledged to set up at least 1,500 digital film screens by 2010 in a bid to reduce the price of film tickets.

In 2006 only 20 foreign films were released in Beijing cinemas. Inevitably most foreign films shown here are profit-generating Hollywood blockbusters: *Titanic* still holds the Chinese box-office record. Most Chinese films are screened without English subtitles, unless they were made with an international audience in mind. Foreign movies get dubbed into Chinese, but most big cinemas will screen the original-language version with Chinese subtitles.

Since joining the World Trade Organisation the government has been actively going after DVD counterfeiters but piracy remains rampant.

FILM FESTIVALS

Beijing lacks a serious and large-scale film festival, but the Beijing Student Film Festival is worth noting for potential surprises. Open to the public, the event features everything from the latest Chinese films to foreign classics, as well as a variety of short films by students. Most screenings are followed by talks with filmmakers (www.filmfestival.com.cn, www.cfa.com.cn).

In North Korea the Pyongyang International Film Festival, which was previously known as the Pyongyang Film Festival of the non-Aligned and Other Developing Countries, is held every two years around September. It showcases plenty of obscure films about Middle Eastern guerilla groups, imperial oppression in Africa and such random international films as *Evita* and *Bend It Like Beckam.*

Cinemas

Besides commercial venues, some embassies and cultural centres offer regular screenings. The **French Cultural Centre** (6553 2627, www.ccfpekin.org) screens French movies with

Foreign devils 2

For many years war, the aftermath of war and censorship discouraged foreigners from filming in China. Hollywood films set in China such as *The Good Earth* (1937), *55 Days at Peking* (1962) and *Shanghai Express* (1932) were either shot in Hollywood studios or on location in other countries.

After 1949 the Chinese government was heavily involved in restricting foreigners from filming in China. The stand-off in relations between China and the West continued until the early 1970s, with Chinese xenophobia being at its height between 1966 and 1976.

So it came as something of a surprise when Michelangelo Antonioni was invited to China by Zhou Enlai in 1972. Zhou believed that China's own documentaries were too strident for Western audiences' tastes and that if a sympathetic outsider were to make a film, China would gain artistic and political credibility. But the result wasn't quite as he expected: Antonioni depicted China as poor and struggling, rather than heroically marching toward the radiant future. Infuriated, the Chinese propaganda machinery – which also launched campaigns at that time against Confucius and Beethoven, among others – stirred up a massive campaign against Antonioni, branding him an 'anti-Chinese buffoon' and an 'accomplice to Soviet revisionism [and] socialist imperialism'. His film *Cina*, was abhorred as of 'venomous intent, despicable means'. For a long time afterwards, Antonioni's was a name that was synonymous with 'traitor', despite the fact that the vast majority of ordinary Chinese had never seen his film.

Times had changed when Bernardo Bertolucci made his Academy Award-winning *The Last Emperor* (1987), a film about the life of the last imperial ruler of China. With a script formally sanctioned by the Chinese government and its full cooperation, there was no campaign against Bertolucci. This was the first feature film authorised to film in the Forbidden City, as well as elsewhere in China.

The government's cage was rattled a couple of times during the 1990s, with *Red Corner* (1997) and *Kundun* (1997). *Red Corner* starred Richard Gere as a lawyer falsely accused of murder, and shot in Beijing for a week without permission. *Kundun*, though not filmed in China, dramatised the life of the Dalai Lama and China's invasion of Tibet. Director Martin Scorsese and his writer, Melissa Mathison, were added to the list of over 50 people banned from entering Tibet.

Since joining the World Trade Organisation in 2001 China has been opening up and loosening restrictions. Quentin Tarantino's *Kill Bill* (2002) was the first non-Chinese film to be shot at the Beijing Film Studio. *Painted Veil* (2005) and *The Kite Runner* (2006) followed. Though scripts still have to pass the censors, there is no doubt the government has warmed to foreign filmmakers. In 2004, *Cina*, along with some other of Antonioni's films, returned to China and received an enthusiastic reception. And 35 years after the 'Antonioni incident' Beijing is giving the 'foreign devils' another chance by inviting world-class directors such as Oliver Stone, Giuseppe Tornatore and Majid Majidi to make promotional shorts for the Beijing Olympics.

Western blockbusters at the **Star City/Oriental Plaza Multiplex**.

Chinese subtitles as well as organising events throughout the year; **Instituto Cervantes** (5879 9666) screens Spanish films with English subtitles on Fridays; the **Italian Embassy Cultural Office** (6532 5015) shows Italian movies with English subtitles on Thursdays; the **Mexican Embassy Cultural Office** (6532 2244) has Mexican films with English subtitles on Wednesdays. For underground local films and other international films, check out **Box Café/Space for Imagination** (5 Xiwangzhuang Xiaoqu, Shuanqing Lu, Haidian, North-west, 6279 1280, www.qfworld.tv) and **D-22** (*see p175*).

Cherry Lane Movies

Inside Kent Centre (east of the 21st Century Theater), 29 Liangmaqiao Lu, Anjialou, Chaoyang (135 0125 1303/1390 113 4745/www.cherrylanemovies.com.cn). **Open** 7pm most Fri, Sat; movie starts at 8pm. **Tickets** RMB 50; RMB 30 students. **No credit cards. Map** p243 P6.

Classic and contemporary Chinese films are shown with English subtitles on a large screen on Fridays and Saturdays and include snacks served from 7.30pm before the 8pm screening.

Hart Centre of Arts

4 Jiuxianqiao Road, 798 Art District, Chaoyang (6435 3570/www.hart.com.cn). **Tickets** from RMB 30. **No credit cards.**

An independent multi-disciplinary arts centre run by an artist couple. The husband is a painter and the wife is a film producer. Independent film and documentary festivals, screenings and workshops are held throughout the year. Call or visit the website for schedules and updates.

Maple Drive-in Cinema

21 Liangmaqiao (1,500m east of Yanshaqiao), Chaoyang (6431 9595/6432 9884/www.drive-in.com.cn). **Tickets** RMB 100 per vehicle, max 6 people. **No credit cards. Map** p243 P6.

China's first drive-in cinema is a fun getaway for locals tired of constantly getting shoved around in the over-populated city. The serene spot has a bar, a hotpot restaurant and a gaming centre.

Star City/Oriental Plaza Multiplex

Oriental Plaza, Basement 1, Dong Changan Jie, Dongcheng, Centre (8518 5399/8518 6778/www.xfilmcity.com). **Tickets** RMB 50-RMB 60. **No credit cards. Map** p244 L10.

Conveniently located in the basement of a major shopping mall, Star City offers comfortable seats, a clean environment and good munchies. Besides showing the latest commercial releases, the cinema often hosts small-scale foreign film festivals.

UME International

Cineplex 44, Kexueyuan Nan Dajie, Shuangyushu Lu, Haidian, North-west (8211 5566/8211 2851/www.bjume.com). **Tickets** RMB 32-RMB 60; RMB 120 VIP. **No credit cards. Map** p249 E4.

Built by Hong Kong filmmaker See-Yuen Ng, this cinema is famed for its huge 430sq m (4,600 sq ft) screen, state-of-the-art equipment (which includes a 3D-enabled projector) and screening of the latest mainstream movies. The fourth floor has a pleasant café.

Galleries

Economic miracle? Building boom? Olympic Games? Who cares – the only real revolution taking place in Beijing is in the art world.

With British collector Charles Saatchi shelling out a cool $1.5 million for a painting by Zhang Xiaogang in 2006, Chinese contemporary art has never been hotter – and Beijing is at its heart. The city is the best place in China to be whether you're an artist, a diehard collector or just like to walk around and enjoy the shows.

Chinese contemporary art was officially born with an unofficial exhibition just outside the China Art Gallery (now the **National Art Museum of China**, *see p57*) by the Stars Group in 1979; it gained momentum with a group of artists frequently referred to as the 1985 New Art Movement and continued to flourish throughout the 1980s when many of today's auction house favourites burst on the scene, including sculptor Wang Guangyi, painter Fang Lijun and video artist Zhang Peili.

The optimism that grew out of the New Art Movement was shattered, though, at a major exhibition in the China Art Gallery in February 1989. After artist Xiao Lu unloaded a firearm into her own installation, authorities closed the show, which would later be reopened only to be shut down again when bomb threats were made to the gallery. The exhibition's failure, and the tragedy at Tiananmen Square later that year, would spur China's next art movement, the Cynical Realists, in the early 1990s, followed soon after by Socialist Pop and Gaudy Art. By early 2000, foreign art collectors had been on the ground in Beijing for almost a decade, and the stage was set for a thriving market.

Red Gate Gallery. *See p161.*

Until recently many established artists rarely showed their work in China, either for political reasons or because of contractual agreements with international galleries. But in 2006, several major artists held their first solo exhibitions in Beijing, including Zhu Wei, Ai Weiwei and Huang Rui. Many younger artists are also basking in the limelight as dealers and gallerists clamour to find fresh work. The artists in one of the strongest groups, collectively known as N12, are all under 30 and include Qui Xiaofei, Song Kun and Wen Ling (*see p164* **New Beijinger**).

ART AREAS

Serious collectors and art students may wish to plan their itinerary by areas. The rule-of-thumb is: head north-east. As the **798 Art District** aka Dashanzi – which opened to visitors in 2002 – is the most important area, both as a centre for new art and for the café-bar culture that clusters around creative folk, we have dedicated listings and a map on pp162-163. The **Chaoyang Brewery**, known as Jiuchang in Chinese, is a newly established commercial art district that lies just to the north of 798. **Caochangi,** a village that lies a few minutes from 798 to the north-east, is far less commercial in presentation.

The National Art Museum of China, though mainly a place to see older, mainstream work, has started to exhibit an ambitious programme of international contemporary and modern art (*see p57*). Peak times for viewing art in Beijing occur in April and May, with several art festivals around the capital, notably the **798 Art Festival** (*see p147*). Around October time, galleries also put up their best work as artists, gallerists and collectors flock to the capital for the China International Gallery Exposition (www.cige-bj.com) and the Beijing Biennale (www.bjbiennale.com.cn).

Growing up in private

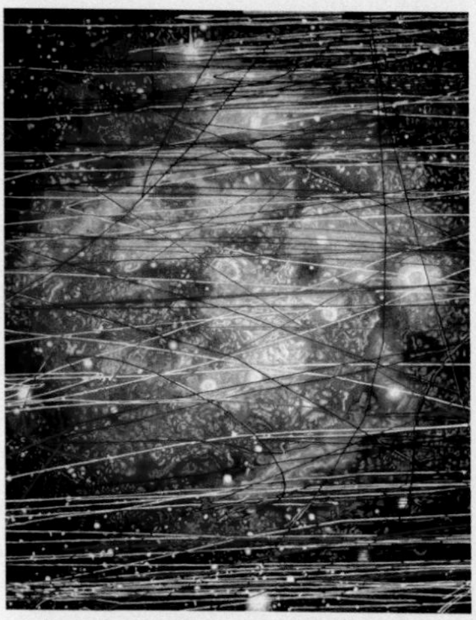

Xu Ruotao's *Heart No.1 Red Moon.*

The Beijing art scene is more complex than suggested by the strings of noughts attached to the prices of works created by a handful of market leaders. The work of many successful artists tends to remain hidden, largely due to the lack of professional spaces in China with which they might want to be affiliated. **Galleria Continua** can be relied upon for quality presentations, though the focus tends to be European rather than Chinese art – something it has in common with the Korean-run **Arario Beijing** at the Alcohol Factory. These, together with the **Today Art Museum** and **White Space Beijing**, are also the most likely places to catch a sight of China's international art stars.

As any kind of reliable system for contemporary art in the public realm has yet to find form, art spaces come and go with alarming speed. Even though contemporary art has achieved a degree of legitimacy, national museums are not the repositories of broad collections that the European public is used to. Nor do they offer permanent exhibitions of art of any modern period except for the impressive cache of Socialist Realist painting and sculpture at the **Military Museum** (*see p79*).

National museums in the capital tend to avoid contemporary art wherever possible, leaving such fare to the growing crop of privately funded museums, and the smattering of spaces that attempt to operate as non-profit centres such as **Platform China** and **Universal Studios-Beijing** in Caochangdi. Shows, many of them themed, are held at irregular intervals, but this is where the real face of creativity and innovation is to be found.

Chinese contemporary art celebrated a youthful twenty-year anniversary in 2006 – and the art scene shifted up a gear. Painting remains the dominant medium, which is more a result of market forces than a reflection of local preferences. But it has become richer in variety, moving beyond the 'emotionally cool', purely figurative and overwhelmingly satirical styles of the 1990s. The 2000s has yet to produce a distinct 'generation' as such, but it can claim some great new artists. In Beijing alone, the work of Unmask, Qiu Xiaofei, Hu Xiaoyuan, Ouyang Chun, Xu Ruotao and Chun Qiulin, to name but a few, is outstanding.

Young or mature, China's artists still have a preference for exploring ornery questions about 'self', individual worth, status, and change. Ironically, Social Realism has never been more popular, and rides high on the rolling tides of urbanisation, redevelopment, rural migration, architecture and the trappings of youth culture.

The money market has had a huge impact, and where some might suggest that keeping commercialism at bay is necessary if an artist is to keep ahead of the game, it is a challenge in a society that has little else to measure success against than the volume of wealth that individual creations command.

This is particularly hard for younger artists who know almost nothing of the hardship endured through the Mao era, which anchors older artists to an ideal of art – rational, conceptual, political and utterly impersonal – and an unshakeable conviction about their chosen paths and direction. Instead, China today awards its artistic youth with uncertainty and insecurity. It all adds up to a paradoxical blend of nostalgia and ambition, both of which are responsible for some remarkable innovations, if you're lucky enough to catch them.

By Karen Smith, author of Nine Lives: The Birth of Avant-Garde in New China *and curator of Tate Liverpool's 'The Real Thing: Contemporary Art from China' in spring 2007.*

Arario Beijing

Chaoyang Brewery, Beihuqu Lu, Anwai Beiyuanjie, Chaoyang (5202 3800/www.arariobeijing.com). **Open** 10am-6pm daily. **Admission** free.

Boasting 3,000 square metres (32,000 square feet) of exhibition space, Arario is huge, even by the capacious standards of Beijing. After the success of his original Seoul gallery, entrepreneur Kim Chang-il opened this space in 2005. Arario combines the best of Chinese and Asian contemporary artists with the work of major figures from Europe and the US.

Beijing Art Now Gallery

Beijing Workers' Stadium, opposite gate 12, Chaoyang (6551 1632/www.artnow.cn). **Open** noon-7pm Tue-Sun. **Admission** free. **Map** p244 N8.

Founded by cultural critic, Huang Liaoyuan, this space maintains a diverse programme of contemporary art from around the country. Many shows explore erotic themes that stop just short of controversy.

CAAW

East End Art district, (down the lane from Zone A and next to the driving school), Nangao Lu, Caochangdi Village, Chaoyang (8456 5152/8456 5153). **Open** 2-6pm Wed-Sun. **Admission** free.

CAAW is the acronym for the Chinese Art and Archives Warehouse, run by one of the country's most influential artists, Ai Weiwei. An ultra-modern yet soothingly simple space, it often features work from China's most cutting-edge young artists.

C5Art

5 Sanlitun Xiwujie, Chaoyang (6460 3950/ www.c5art.com). **Open** 10am-7pm Tue-Sun. **Admission** free. **Map** p245 O7.

Nestled just a block away from the hustle, bustle and noise of Sanlitun bar street, this elegant space often presents some of the youngest artists on the scene.

F2 Gallery

East End Art district (Zone A), Nangao Lu, 319 Caochangdi Village, Chaoyang (6432 8831/134 8870 9596/www.f2gallery.com). **Open** 10am-6pm Tue-Sun. **Admission** free.

An active player in Europe as well as on the New York and Los Angeles art scenes, F2 opened in Beijing in 2005 with a showing of the work of Jean-Michel Basquiat, and while the gallery often treats Beijing to art from the West, most of the exhibits are of Chinese contemporary artists.These can be both established names and others plucked right out of the Central Academy of Fine Arts.

Galerie Urs Meile

104 Caochangdi Village, Cui Ge Zhuang Xiang, Chaoyang (6433 3393/www.galerieursmeile.com). **Open** 11am-6.30pm Tue-Sun. **Admission** free.

Galerie Urs Meile has earned a reputation in Beijing for being one of the most attractive and professionally run galleries in the city. Previous showings have ranged from Ai Weiwei's first solo exhibition in China to Swiss artists Stefan Banz and Carol Bachmann, whose manipulated paintings of famous media figures – including Elvis, former US President Richard Nixon and the Charles Manson women – were the subject of much discussion in 2007.

Imagine Gallery

8 Feijiacun, Cui Ge Zhuang, Laiguangying Dong Lu, Caochangdi Village, Chaoyang (6438 5747/ 139 1091 7965/www.imagine-gallery.com). **Open** 10.30am-5.30pm Tue-Sun. **Admission** free.

French national Latetia Gaudin's Imagine Gallery stands out for actively promoting young international artists. Striking shows in the past have included Japanese performance artist/photographer Megumi Shimizu, whose portraits of herself posing naked with a banana offered a fresh feminine alternative to a local scene often criticised for being too male-driven.

New Pictures of the Strikingly Bizarre, No 5 by Zhu Wei. *See p158.*

The contemporary face of Chinese art: **798 Space**. *See p162.*

One Moon Gallery

Inside Ditan Park, Andingmenwai Dajie, Dongcheng, Houhai (6427 7748/www.onemoonart.com). **Open** 10am-6pm Wed-Sun and by appointment. **Admission** free. **Map** p242 L6.

Tucked away in the evergreen trees and shrubs of Ditan Park, American gallerist Jan Leaming has assembled the country's strongest collection of Chinese abstract expressionism. The gallery, which occasionally holds symposia on art, is also well known for presenting artists who excel in both traditional Chinese genres like ink-and-wash as well as Western oil paintings.

Pekin Fine Arts

241 Cui Ge Zhuang Xiang, Caochangdi Village, Chaoyang (8532 2124/www.pekinfinearts.com). **Open** 9.30am-5pm Tue-Sun. **Admission** free.

Founded by American Meg Maggio, Pekin Fine Arts exhibits many of China's most famous contemporary artists, including world class photographers Liu Zheng and Wang Qingsong.

Platform China

319-1 East End Artzone, Zone A, Caochangdi Village, Chaoyang (6432 0169/www.platformchina.org). **Open** 11am-6pm daily. **Admission** free.

Platform was the location for the city's first experimental art film festival, Borderlines. Previous exhibitions included one artist, Shi Jinsong, who transformed a motorised farmer's cart into an impressive mock Harley-Davidson.

Red Gate Gallery

Dongbianmen Watchtower, Chongwenmen, Chongwen, Centre (6525 1005/www.redgategallery.com). **Open** 10am-5pm daily. **Admission** free. **Map** p247 M10.

Founded in 1991 by Australian Brian Wallace, Red Gate is arguably the best established gallery to be found in China. Located in a 16th-century guardhouse and offering a wide range of contemporary art idioms it is a must visit for any art lover coming to the city. See 798/Red Gate Gallery on p163 for details of its sister location. **Photo** *p158.*

Soka Art Centre/Soka Contemporary Space

Room 101, Building B, Tianhai Shangwu Dasha, 107 Dongsi Beidajie, Dongcheng, Houhai (8401 2377/www.soka-art.com). **Open** 10am-9pm Tue-Sun. **Admission** free. **Map** p244 L8.

This smartly designed venue is divided into two exhibition halls, one presenting traditional Chinese art and a second emphasising the experimental. Although most artists on view are Chinese, SOKA has been known to present some strong Korean artists.

Today Art Museum

Building 13, No.32, Baiziwan Lu, Chaoyang (5876 0452/5876 0011/www.artnow.com.cn). **Open** 10am-4pm daily. **Admission** RMB 10. **Map** p245 P11.

Although Today has been a major player in the Chinese art scene for several years, its current ritzy space only opened in 2006 with a 35m- (115ft-) long canvas from Chinese art star Fang Lijun, the country's most famous painter and the central figure in Cynical Realism, a movement that began in the early 1990s after the initial idealism of the artists was crushed at Tiananmen Square.

Universal Studios-Beijing

A 8 Caochangdi Village, Chaoyang (6432 2620/www.universalstudios.org.cn). **Open** 11am-5.30pm Tue-Sat. **Admission** free.

In the warmer months the gallery's adjacent café and courtyard are frequented by a flurry of collectors, artists and other creative types drawn to the personalities of Pi Li and Waling Boers, co-founders of the space. When Universal Studios opened in 2006 it almost immediately became the centre of Beijing's hip alternative art scene.

Xindong Cheng Space II

Chaoyang Brewery, Beihuqu Lu, Anwai Beiyuanjie, Chaoyang (5202 3868/www.chengxindong.com). **Open** 9am-6pm daily. **Admission** free.

This smart, spacious mezzanine-level exhibition hall is annexed to a mini-café and also offers for sale a generous collection of art books, many of which are published by the gallery.

798 Art District

Also known as Dashanzi, the 798 Art District is north-west of Chaoyang. Founded in the early 2000s on the back of cheap local rents and proximity to the Central Academy of Fine Arts in Wangjing, it's an art and design hub, and, increasingly, a magnet for diners and drinkers. *See p71* for background on the neighbourhood.

As well as the galleries listed below, check out **798 Space** (6437 6248, www.798space.com, *photo p161*), which artists can rent to show off their work; **Timezone 8 Editions** (8456 0336, www.timezone8.com), a combination gallery, restaurant and café attached to a popular bookstore; and **Xindong Cheng Space I** (6433 4579, www.chengxindong.com), a small but strong collection of contemporary artists, and an important publisher. All of these lie on 4 Jiuxianqiao Lu, one of the district's two avenues. See area map on facing page.

Beijing Commune

4 Jiuxianqiao Lu (8456 2862/139 1140 3171/ www.beijingcommune.com). **Open** 10am-6pm Tue-Sun. **Admission** free. ❶

Leng Lin, who founded the space and organizes all of the shows here, is both an international art critic and a curatorial whiz. Most of the shows here revolve tightly around a theme, which is a breath of fresh air in a city in which many exhibitions are thrown up willy-nilly. Shows range from bizarre installation pieces to surreal videos to good old-fashioned oil painting.

Beijing Tokyo Art Projects

4 Jiuxianqiao Lu (8457 3245/www.tokyo-gallery.com). **Open** 10.30am-6pm Tue-Sun. **Admission** free. ❷

The first gallery to set up shop in 798, BTAP's raw space was transformed into its current elegance by renowned architect Ma Yansong. Previous shows have included installations that recreated a rural Chinese landscape with dirt mounds, power-lines and billiard tables; sleek video performances set to lounge room cocktail music; as well as the latest efforts from Chinese and Japanese animators.

China Art Seasons

2 Jiuxianqiao Lu (6431 1900/www.artseasons.com.sg). **Open** 11am-6pm Tue-Sun. **Admission** free. ❸

China Art Seasons is a collectors' favourite, and most of the shows feature the kind of work perfect for the living room. Many of the artists showing in this elegant gallery space end up in the major galleries and auction houses in the West.

Chinese Contemporary

4 Jiuxianqiao Lu (8456 2421/www.chinesecontemporary.com). **Open** 11am-7pm daily. **Admission** free. ❹

Chinese Contemporary originally opened with a space in London – which it still maintains – and recently celebrated its 10th anniversary. One of its more recent claims to fame happened when artist Huang Rui, a famous artistic figure in China, was forced to remove one of the more controversial works from his solo exhibition. Entitled *Chairman Mao Ten Thousand Yuan*, the work featured one hundred RMB 100 notes that formed the words 'Long Live Chairman Mao'.

Contrasts Gallery

4 Jiuxianqiao Lu (6432 1369/www.contrastsgallery.com). **Open** 11am-6pm Tue-Sun. **Admission** free. ❺

Opened first in Shanghai by Hong Kong art collector Pearl Lam, Contrasts is a new addition to the Beijing art scene. Many of the works on show have a strong design element which segues into fine art.

Galleria Continua

2 Jiuxianqiao Lu (6436 1005/www.galleriacontinua.com). **Open** 11am-6pm Tue-Sun. **Admission** free. ❻

Galleria Continua made headlines in May 2005 when it became the first foreign gallery in Beijing to focus almost exclusively on international artists. In addition to its periodic showing of Chinese artists, it regularly shows some of the most renowned names on the global scene, including Daniel Burin, Anish Kapoor, Chen Zhen and Loris Cecchini.

Marella Gallery

4 Jiuxiangqiao Lu, Chaoyang (6433 4055/www.marellabeijing.com). **Open** 10am-6pm Tue-Sun. **Admission** free. ❼

Run by well-known critic and curator Eleanor Battiston, Marella was one of the first foreign galleries to highlight avant-garde Chinese photography with exhibitions like 'Out of the Red'.

New Long March Space

4 Jiuxiangqiao Lu (6438 7107/www.longmarchspace.com). **Open** 11am-7pm Tue-Sun. **Admission** free. ❽

One of the distinguishing features about New Long March Space, run by curator-organiser Lu Jie, is its heavy emphasis on making sure that art makes it to the masses. To that end, it has engaged in a series of projects aiming to make arts education – not just the art market – a topic of hot conversation in the Chinese community. The shows here often feature artists interacting with the people of their home-towns and provinces. Many of the artists who show here, like painter Yang Shaobin and video artist Wang Gongxin, may be educating the locals, but they are fetching hefty prices for their work among international collectors as well.

798 Photo Gallery

4 Jiuxianqiao Lu (6438 1784/www.798photogallery.com). **Open** 10am-6pm daily. **Admission** free. ❾

This cosy gallery is one of the most no-nonsense exhibition venues in Beijing. It is a split-level space with the gallery's permanent collection housed upstairs. Many shows here feature stunning black-and-white portraits of Chinese minorities.

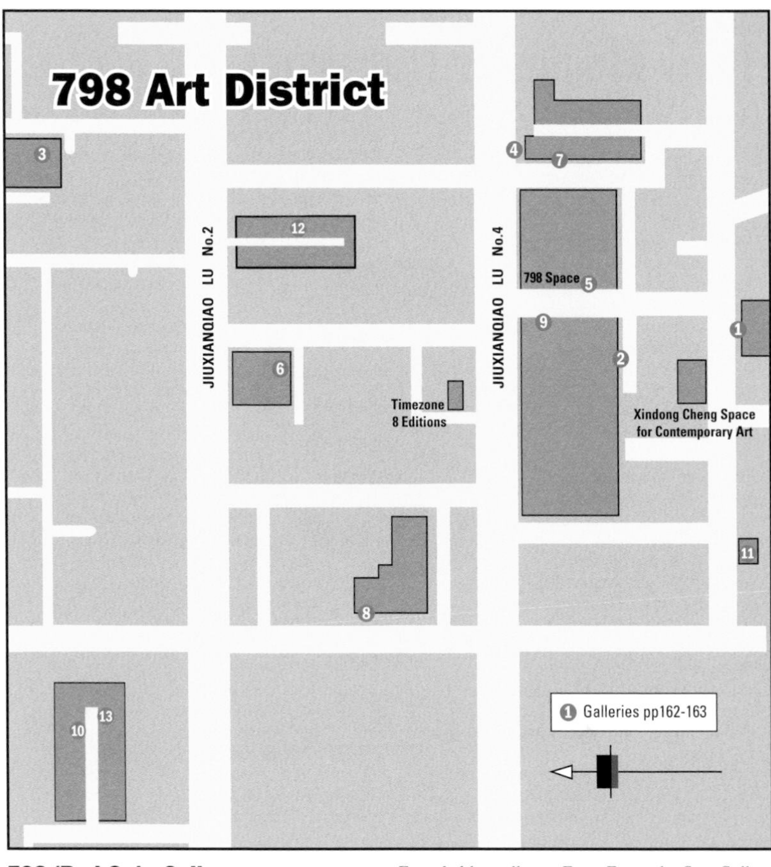

798/Red Gate Gallery

2 Jiuxianqiao Lu (6432 2624/www.redgate gallery.com). **Open** 11am-6pm Tue-Sun. **Admission** free. ⑩

Red Gate was the first art gallery in Beijing. Its 798 location is reserved for riskier and potentially more controversial shows. *See p161.*

798 Red T Space

4 Jiuxianqiao Lu (8911 5762/www.redt.net). **Open** *Apr-Oct* 10am-6.30pm Tue-Sun; *Nov-Mar* 10.30am-5.30pm Tue-Sun. **Admission** free. ⑪

Red T not only exhibits art and organises events but is also proving to be an important force in music, bringing Western bands to Beijing. Brit Tasmin Roberts mixes it up by alternating shows by local artists with a smattering of international types.

Star Gallery

2 Jiuxianqiao Lu (8456 0591/www.stargallery.cn). **Open** 10am-6pm daily. **Admission** free. ⑫

Founded by collector Fang Fang, the Star Gallery focuses on a generation of artists born in the 1970s. Collectively called the Post-70s Generation, these young artists have been criticized for abandoning traditional Chinese symbols in their art and for imitating Japanese animation. Many of the paintings are violent, cartoonish, highly sexual and meant to express the alienation of young Chinese today. These self-styled Kurt Cobains of the Chinese art world have yet to find favor with the Academy, but they are starting to attract the attention of collectors.

White Space Beijing

2 Jiuxianqiao Lu (8456 2054/www.alexanderochs-galleries.de). **Open** noon-6pm Tue-Sun. **Admission** free. ⑬

Founded by German gallerist Alexander Ochs, White Space Beijing is a respected gallery in the city and has become an enviable venue for both established and up-and-coming artists, who are often exhibited in Alexander Och's gallery space in Berlin.

New Beijinger The artist

Beijing is changing super fast: new building projects, automobiles and more and more dog owners. The tragic side of all this advancement is that some nicer aspects of the city, like the hutongs, are being demolished.

I work in a small studio near my home at Jianguomen. When I'm not in my studio, you can usually find me strolling through the hutongs and I actually still love going to the 798 Art District, just to pop my head in some of the galleries and see what other artists are up to.

The thing that really bothers me about Beijing is this great disparity between the rich and the poor. It really is very unsettling. Then there's also the traffic jams and sandstorms that come in every year, as well as really heavy air pollution as of late. There are also big problems with getting food in Beijing – sometimes the food you're eating is actually fake!

If I had foreign friends coming to Beijing I would personally send them to the New Get Lucky Bar (1 Xinba Lu, Nurenjie, Chaoyang, 8448 3335, noon-2am daily) and to a punk performance night at **Nameless Highland** bar (*see p175*). And if they're coming around May, they should try to make it to the annual **MIDI Music Festival** (*see p147*) and the **798 Art District International Art Festival** (*see p147*).

Most Beijingers only get to know art through the mainstream media. They know just a few big-name artists, like Chen Yifei and Chen Danqing. I rarely get to meet old Beijingers, so I don't know much about them.

Young Beijingers are more confident and self-assured. They have a stronger sense of being in control of their lives. Also young Beijingers pay more attention to their appearance, accept new things quickly, and take better care of their health.

Right now I'm working on a lot of separate projects including oil painting, animation works and photography. I hope to make a DVD and films at some point in the future. My works are basically about my repressed and miserable years in middle school.

Wen Ling is one of the most successful young artists in Beijing today. A member of the Post-70s Generation of practitioners that some observers criticise as a generation lacking traditional values (and for that matter, recent historical memory), he is also an important member of the Beijing-based art collective, N12. Check out his photoblog at www.ziboy.com.

Gay & Lesbian

Thirty million queers and counting.

While it's certainly no San Francisco, Beijing has been growing noticeably more gay friendly over the past five years or so. The standard of gay bars and clubs has improved and there are now support groups, helplines, magazines, sporting and social clubs that cater to both queer boys and queer girls in the capital. The government appears not to mind as long as groups stay non-political.

Whence this tolerance? Observers say the main reason for the government support is a need to control HIV infections from unsafe gay sex. Many queer groups expedite or slip past registration procedures by emphasising their work with AIDS. The attraction of the pink dollar and a desire for the outside world to view China as tolerant and modern are also probably powerful incentives.

Even so, changes are gradual. While state-owned media write positive stories on the queer community – China has 30 million homosexuals, they say, and you'd better get used to them – you're unlikely to see gay or lesbian characters on TV shows. Legislators bring up the issue of same-sex marriage, but it will be years before it has a serious chance of becoming law. The government opens a free health clinic for gay men, but is unwilling to advertise it openly. Gays and lesbians experiment in their twenties but are coerced into marriage in their thirties because of family pressures to have a more conventional lifestyle and to produce a grandchild.

On the positive side, there is little or no hate crime. There is also no law against homosexuality – although the police occasionally break up gay parties on anti-prostitution grounds. Gay and lesbian visitors to the city should have a great time – the scene is accessible and hoteliers are unlikely to raise an eyebrow at same-sex couples sharing a bed, although out of respect confine signs of affection to gay venues or your hotel room.

OUT AND ABOUT

The best way to get a taste of gay Beijing is to meet locals in bars and clubs. Men also have the option of scouting out saunas, although be aware that there are some seedy dives on that score. If you want to keep your clothes on, there are several social and sporting organisations where gays and lesbians meet regularly for more 'healthy' activities. Promen, a networking group for professional gay men in Beijing, organises a weekly happy hour bar party and weekend sightseeing trips. Their soirees are a good way to meet English-speaking locals and expats. Visit groups.yahoo.com/group/promen/ for details on how to find them. In early 2007, they were meeting every Thursday night at swanky cocktail lounge, Q Bar (*see p126*), although be sure to check before going. The girls meet for the so-called Lala Salon – tea and talks at Le Jazz Restaurant (4th Floor, 18 Full Link Plaza, Chaoyangmenwai Dajie, Chaoyang, 2-6pm Sat). Note that only a few of the women

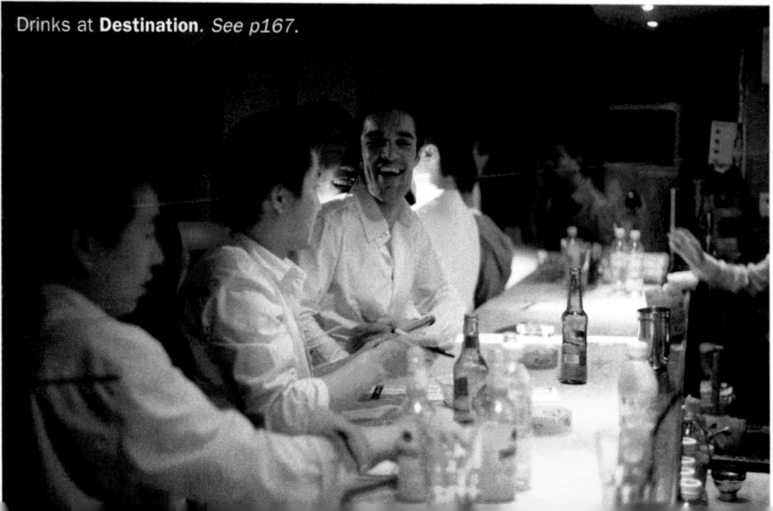

Drinks at **Destination**. *See p167.*

Queen of clubs

Chinese men are used to dressing up like girls. Take traditional Peking Opera for example – until the 1930s men performed all the female roles, which meant going thick on the white face powder and perfecting a convincing mezzo-soprano.

Today's drag queens are no less skilful. Head to one of Beijing's gay bars on your weekend and you are guaranteed to find an oestrogen-charged show. Don't expect glitz; these are no Queens of Las Vegas. Even so, they know how to belt out a song and, in the right light, Asian androgyny is the best ticket to passing the gender test.

There are dozens of drag queens in Beijing, but cream of the crop is 19-year-old Ah Mei, who models herself on a Taiwanese pop star of the same name. Mei Mei, singing Mandarin love ballads in her fetching satin *cheong saam*, has been doing the rounds for at least a decade. And then there's Maobeilin – the Chinese transliteration of US cosmetics brand Maybelline – a short stocky queen in her forties who favours black cocktail dresses and a saucy repartee. Members of the audience shout their support, as Maobeilin belts out a pop song and flexes her biceps.

Most of the drag bars keep themselves hidden, tucked down alleys away from the nightlife district. They are small, intimate places with a loyal crowd – you can tell from the rapport that the performers and audience go back a long way. Try the established Urban Love Island Bar (*see p167*) or newcomer Seven Color (*see p167*) for a taster.

can speak English. The Salon is friendly but tipplers beware: it's booze free.

Like any other city with an expanding gay population, Beijing has its cruising spots. There's the infamous Dongdan Park, a mere condom toss from Tiananmen – watch out for the men with rolled up newspapers – or slightly classier are coffee shops in upmarket malls. Try the China Word Trade Center in Guomao or Oriental Plaza in Wangfujing.

INFORMATION

The government is still skittish about promoting gay venues and events in the press. While state-owned newspapers wax lyrical about how difficult it is to be homosexual, the censors get snippy about anything that overtly says 'gay Beijing', such as queer bar listings. Even so, *Time Out Beijing* magazine has a regular gay and lesbian page with events and features. There is some titillation on the newsstands. *Menbox* magazine pretends it's straight, but it's not fooling anyone with its cover to cover pictures of buff semi-naked men. The bolder *Visual Man* is an out and out gay rag, with more explicit pictures and articles in Chinese on homosexuality.

To make up for its fettered traditional media, China has a vibrant online gay community. Most gays and lesbians meet each other first over the internet. None, if any, of this is in English and a lot is just chatrooms and soft porn – or soppy poetry and cuddly toy pics in the case of the girls. However, there are two serious online resources – www.aibai.com for general news and www.lesplus.org, an online version of the free monthly lesbian magazine *Les+*. Pick up a copy at the Salon or West Wing dyke bar. Both websites are in Chinese only.

Of the English-language online resources, the biggest and best in the region is the Singapore-based www.fridae.com. As well as news and reviews, there is a personals section with tons of members – both boys and girls – from Beijing. www.utopia-asia.com is one the longest running websites and has good information on Beijing's queer nightlife while www.gaydar.co.uk has China-based profiles.

Bars & clubs

The Beijing scene is a little up and down – one month gay is in and clubs are scrambling over each other with pink tinsel, the next, they're all gone. **Destination** is the one gay club that is central and appears here to stay. On the fringes of town, there are a number of established drag and karaoke bars that are very popular with locals. The girls' scene is surprisingly steady with a quaint lesbian teahouse and a raucous Saturday night disco for the younger gals.

Destination

7 Gongti Xilu, Chaoyang (6551 5138/www.bjdestination.com). Metro Dongsishitiao. **Open** 9pm-late Tue-Sun. **Admission** RMB 30 (includes one drink). **No credit cards. Map** p244 N8.

In 2006, the city's only Western style gay club added a lounge café and restaurant. With its MTV screens, bouncy dance floor and cruising corridor, this place gets packed on weekends with locals, expats and the ever-hopeful money boys grinding to banging house. The DJs are pretty decent as are the drinks, and come 3am when you stagger out and fancy a bite to eat, there's Bellagio (*see p104*) a fag-friendly Taiwanese restaurant across the road. As the sole gay club in town it's also known as Desperation. **Photo** *p165*.

Pipe

Gongti Nanlu, Chaoyang (6593 7756). Metro Dongsishitiao. **Open** 8pm-late Sat only. **Admission** RMB 20. **No credit cards. Map** p244 N8.

Come Saturday nights the city's teenaged lesbians flock to Pipe for beer madness, dice games, some heavy petting, and a bop. From 9-10pm there's usually a drag show followed by some saucy dancing from a skinny lass in stockings. As midnight approaches and the girls go home to their parents, Destination (*see above*) is just around the corner.

Secret Garden

6 Sanlitun Nanjie, next to Pink Loft Thai restaurant, Chaoyang (6507 4890). Metro Dongsishitiao. **Open** 4.30pm-2am daily. **Admission** free. **No credit cards. Map** p245 O8.

Strictly speaking, Secret Garden is not a gay bar, but gay friendly. However, the fluffy decor and a crowd so flaming they're practically on fire, qualifies this for the list. Popular with would-be super boys, there's a small stage where you can do a turn.

Seven Color

Hua Tai Hotel, Jin Song Dong Kou, Chaoyang (8772 0166/www.7sebar.com). Metro Guomao. **Open** 5pm-6am daily. **Admission** free. **No credit cards. Map** p245 O12.

One of the newer additions on the drag circuit, this friendly bar has singing queens, boys dressed in thongs and stand up comedy. Unfortunately, with space a bit cramped, conversation is difficult against the racket from the amped up show or thumping techno. Décor is Chinese-style kitsch.

Urban Love Island Bar (Tsingtao)

6 Liulichang Dongjie, Xuanwu, Centre (8316 1284). Metro Hepingmen. **Open** 9pm-late daily. **Admission** free. **No credit cards. Map** p241 J11.

The top floor of this ramshackle bar at the end of a touristy antique street has weekend drag shows and Chinese stand up routines – lots of fake balloon breasts and skinny boys warbling love songs – which attract a steady following of older local gay men..

West Wing (Xixiangfang)

Deshengmen Tower, Xicheng, Houhai (8208 2836). Metro Jishuitan. **Open** 5pm-2am daily. **Admission** free. **No credit cards. Map** p242 J6.

This lesbian teahouse and bar has a fabulous location – inside the ancient city gate of Deshengmen. The owner undoubtedly has friends in high places. West Wing is a chilled out Chinese-style lounge with board games, fairy lights and, annoyingly, karaoke. Come summertime you can sit in the courtyard. This is a good place to find women in their late twenties and thirties. Beijing's 'civilised' lesbian hangout.

Saunas & massage

Beijing's men-focused saunas are little more than steamy cruising parlours. Be aware that because management is afraid of police raids, they never stock condoms – cartons of Jissbon and lube would be evidence of sex on the premises. Take your own supplies and store them in a box of cigarettes. Don't count on the locals – barebacking is all too common.

Club Oasis

Fuchengmen Nei, around the corner from Luxun Museum, Xicheng, Financial District (8740 0018/www.cluboasis.cn). Metro Fuchengmen. **Open** 24 hrs daily. **Admission** RMB 30-RMB 40. **No credit cards. Map** p240 G8.

This is Beijing's most popular gay sauna. There's something for everyone – a gym, karaoke room, movie lounge, internet café, massage parlour and even a bar. From the subway, head east, take the first left; after a while you'll pass the museum on your left and the sauna is at the end of a carpark on your right. Club Oasis is large, modern and brightly lit – a big step up from the world of disposable pants and grimy tiles common to Beijing's less salubrious saunas. Popular with gay locals and expats.

Manzluv Spa & Massage

Rm 1204, Building 12, Jianwai Soho, Chaoyang (5869 6450/http://en.nanzhilian.com). Metro Guomao. **Open** 24 hrs daily. **No credit cards. Map** p245 O10.

If it's a sultry Asian Adonis in a cowboy hat you're after, Manzluv is the place. This fancy spa in the Jianwai Soho business complex offers a plethora of treatments including a two-hour 'Trip of Romance' deep massage, a two-hour 'Genital Care' scrub and a two-hour 'Tibetan Medicine Butt Care' with essential oils. One-hour massage RMB 200 upwards.

Mind & Body

The *qi* to good health.

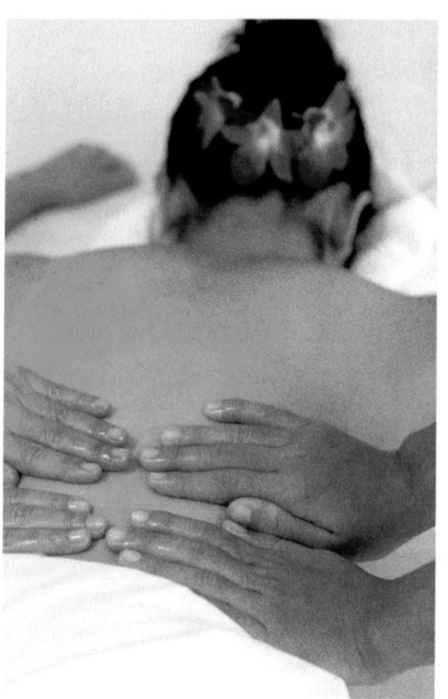

Chinese treatments with Thai touches at **I Spa**. *See page 169.*

Unwinding from a typically hectic Beijing day is considered a necessity by Chinese and expatriates alike. So it's just as well that, along with rip-off DVDs and *yang rou chuan'r* (lamb kebabs), massages, manicures and other self-indulgent delights are plentiful, reasonably priced if you know where to look and available around the clock. Whether it's a cheap-as-chips head massage at a local hair salon or a day spent luxuriating at a spa, Beijing's impressive selection of therapies and treatments will reignite any weary traveller's glow.

As you'd expect, most of the treatments are steeped in tradition, with Chinese massage or *tuina* the preferred antidote. *Tuina* has been used for over 2,500 years to adjust the body's *qi*, or vital energy, and thus keep it in tip-top shape. But now you'll find Westerners and Chinese alike making use of traditional local medicine, which has had the side effect of greatly increasing the number of English-speaking practitioners.

Plush day spas (usually housed in five-star hotels and international apartment complexes) are the newest edition to the pampering scene. **Touch Spa**, **Mandara Spa** and **I Spa** boast international quality and service standards, but without a Western price tag. Other traditional forms of therapy such as Japanese shiatsu, and Thai, Hawaiian and Swedish massage, are also becoming standard spa menu choices.

Massage

Whether you fancy a no-frills full body rub down at a blind massage parlour or an aromatically scented foot rub fit for an emperor, Beijing's massage joints are affordable and the ideal way to relax and wind down.

Aibosen Blindman Massage

11 Liufang Beili, Chaoyang (6465 2044/6466 1247). **Open** 10am-1am daily. **Treatment** *Chinese body massage* RMB 88/50mins; *foot massage* RMB 88/70mins. **No credit cards**. **Map** p243 N6.

Many dazed and drunk *laowai* have stumbled into Aibosen and promptly mistaken it for Shangri-La. And can you blame them? With its ungodly trading hours, free snacks, juices and late-night telly, and, of course, cheap foot massages Aibosen does at times seem like an oriental paradise. Staff unfortunately don't speak English, but are friendly and accustomed to interpreting foreigners' mimes.

Bodhi Therapeutic Retreat

2nd floor, 17 Gongti Bei Lu, Chaoyang (6417 9595). **Open** 11am-12.30am daily. **Treatment** *Chinese body massage* RMB 138/80mins after 5pm Mon-Thur, all day Fri-Sun; RMB 78/80mins before 5pm Mon-Thur. **Credit** AmEx, DC, MC, V. **Map** p244 N8.

This conveniently located oasis not only offers discounted Chinese massages before 5pm, but boasts an impressive selection of other massages such as Indian Ayurvedic and Thai. Polite, English speaking staff and tranquil atmosphere make for a pleasant experience. You'll even get to lounge around in a pair of cotton pyjamas.

Dragonfly Therapeutic Retreat

Ground floor of Eastern Inn, Sanlitun Nan Lu, Chaoyang (6593 6066/6593 6366). **Open** 11am-1am daily. **Treatment** *manicure* RMB 90; *pedicure* RMB 150. **Credit** AmEx, MC, V. **Map** p245 O7.

Can't decide between a foot massage and a manicure? Don't fret. Practically an institution in itself, the popular Dragonfly chain offers simultaneous massage and beauty therapy. Treatments cover almost every sin: had a boozy weekend? Try the two-hour-long Hangover Relief Massage (RMB 240); suffering a case of jet lag and one-too-many G&Ts on the plane? Then Happy Landing (RMB 300) is for you. Even the most seasoned spa-goer will be impressed with Dragonfly's set up; perhaps the only thing it can't cure is massage addiction.

I Spa

5th floor, Tower 2, Taiyue Suites, 16 Sanlitun Nan Lu, Chaoyang (6507 1517/www.ispa.cn). **Open** 11am-11pm daily. **Treatment** *massage* from RMB 398/hr; *facials* RMB 438/hr. **Credit** AmEx, DC, MC, V. **Map** p245 O7.

Beijing's only authentic Thai spa shimmers in all its lemongrass scented glory. Expect to be greeted by a smile and a heavenly ginger-infused tea. All staff speak English and are trained by Thai native and spa manager, Siriat. Rooms are elegantly presented with subtle touches of Thailand and a few of China, just to remind you where you are. When the treatment is over, take advantage of the shower facilities and fluffy white robes. **Photo** *p168.*

Other locations: Napa Club, 68 Shashun Lu, Xiaotangshan, Changping (6178 7795).

Mandara Spa

Palm Springs International Club, 8 Chaoyang Gongyuan Nan Lu, Chaoyang (6539 8888 ext 8080). **Open** 10am-midnight daily. **Treatment** *massage* from RMB 480/hr. **Credit** AmEx, MC, V. **Map** p244 O8.

This is hands-down the only Beijing spa that can turn its nose up at all the rest. And it's not because the Mandara group are seasoned experts with spas in the world's most exotic locations, it's because the company aimed to do something a little special in Beijing and succeeded. The spa takes you on a journey along the Silk Road with each room adopting a different theme, cleverly incorporating props to complete the look. There's even a hair salon, ensuring you leave the spa looking as well as feeling better than when you arrived.

Oriental Tai Pan Massage & Spa

1st floor, Xindong Lu, Chaoyang (8532 2177/ www.taipan.com.cn). **Open** 11am-12.30am daily. **Treatment** *foot massage* RMB 138/90mins. **Credit** AmEx, MC, V. **Map** p245 O7.

Tai Pan has been a hit with locals and expats since its opening and no wonder: with its stylish, private rooms, free snacks and juice, and considerate English-speaking staff what more could you want? The massages aren't bad either. Choose a traditional body massage or try an assortment of therapies including foot reflexology, Thai aromatic massage, hot stone and lymphatic therapy, ear candling and scrapping.

Other locations: 2nd floor, Block 9, Holiday Inn Lido Place, 2A Fangyuan Xi Lu, Chaoyang (6437 6299); Sunjoy Mansion, 6 Ritan Lu, Chaoyang (6502 5722).

Zen Spa. *See p170.*

Traditional Chinese Medicine glossary

Acupuncture

Acupuncture regulates the flow of *qi*, the body's vital energy, thus ensuring a harmonious balance between *yin* and *yang*, and better health. Fine needles (which have rounded ends) are inserted into acupuncture points in the body, along meridians or energy channels. The needles are then twirled and left in place for a few minutes (exact times vary depending on treatment). The twirling motion stimulates the flow of *qi* and removes blockages that cause pain and illness. Acupuncture has been used to treat various health problems, from headaches, insomnia, menstrual pain, and muscle cramps, to smokers wanting to kick the habit.

Cupping

Cupping is used as a way to 'draw out' and remove cold illnesses and get stagnant blood moving. In ancient times, bowls were heated on an open fire and then placed on the body. Modern treatment hasn't evolved much further: nowadays, glass cups are heated and then placed on the skin, thus causing a vacuum. The skin is 'sucked up' into the cup for ten to 15 minutes, thus encouraging the flow of *qi*, although a side effect is round bruises where the cup was, though the bruises heal within a few days. Sporting injuries, backache and frozen shoulders are most successfully treated with cupping. It is not suitable for children under 12 and the aged should also be cautious.

Ear candling

Dismissed by mainstream doctors as 'quackery', ear candling is still alive and strong in the Middle Kingdom. A hollow candle is placed in the ear canal with the other end lit in an effort to remove toxins from the patient's ear. The hot air is said to melt the ear wax and create a vacuum that draws toxins from the ear and nose.

Herbal medicine

There are over 5,000 herbal medicines listed in the Chinese *Materia Medica* – the bible of Chinese medicine – but only about 400 of these are commonly used today. Herbs primarily consist of dried plants and flowers, although exotic animal extracts are also used. Herbal concoctions are created by boiling and draining ingredients to form a tea, which can either be drunk or applied externally. While herbal medicine can give the impression of being a harmless, all-natural alternative to conventional Western medication, the opposite is true: patients need to be cautious when taking Chinese herbs – just as you would with any medicine.

Spa De Feng

Huaqing Jiayuan Buiding 18, Unit 1, Courtyard 1, Haidian, North-west (English 8286 3879/Chinese 8286 7369/www.linfengspa.com). Metro Wudaokou. **Open** noon-midnight daily. **Treatment** *massage* from RMB 180/50mins. House calls available; treatments are the same price plus 15% service fee. **No credit cards**. **Map** p249 F3.

Opened in 2006, Spa De Feng has a twist: it's for the boys. Facials, mineral baths and blissful massages will have even sceptical males returning.

Other locations: Sunshine 100 C306, 2 Guanghua Lu, Chaoyang (5100 1330).

Touch Spa

Holiday Inn Lido Plaza, 6 Jiangtai Lu, Chaoyang (6430 1072). **Open** 10am-3am daily. **Treatment** *body massage* from RMB 600/hr. **No credit cards**. **Map** p243 Q4.

Everything you'd expect to find at a hotel spa except that the ladies who lunch are mercifully missing. Instead, mild mannered staff fade into the tranquil surroundings – only to reappear with a telepathic sense of timing – to wait on equally well-behaved clients. Each room has its own shower facilities and treatments include Balinese, Hawaiian and Swedish massage and body wraps. The spa packages, which include a massage and wrap, are the best value.

Zen Spa

House 1, 8A Xiaowuji Lu, Chaoyang (8731 2530/ www.zenspa.com.cn). **Open** 11am-11pm daily. **Treatment** *massage* from RMB 450/hr; *facials* RMB 600/90mins. **Credit** AmEx, MC, V.

Zen is nestled in a traditional Chinese courtyard-style home and is so pleasing to the eye it regularly features in magazine spreads. Zen incorporates all that a spa should: attention to detail, striking interiors, knowledgeable therapists and impressive treatments. Overnight and weekend stays for couples are available. The only downside to Zen Spa is the out of the way location. **Photo** *p169.*

Chinese medicine

Traditional Chinese Medicine (TCM) is usually represented by two opposing but complementary forces known as yin (feminine and receptive) and yang (masculine and active).

A qualified and experienced TCM practitioner should prescribe and prepare mixtures to assure a standard of quality, rather than buying products off the shelf. Remember to tell them of any other herbs or medications you're taking to avoid harmful reactions.

Massage

Traditional Chinese massage (*tuina*) is a combination of brushing, kneading, rolling, pressing, and rubbing between the joints and acupressure points, known as the eight gates. It's through this stimulation that the stagnant *qi* is freed and distributed around the body. *Tuina* best treats stress related conditions and has been found to restore digestive, respiratory, and reproductive systems.

- The Chinese believe in the *yin/yang* complementarity of genders, so select a female therapist if you are male, and vice versa.
- Avoid having a massage immediately after a heavy meal. Wait at least an hour.
- Drink lots of water, preferably warm water, afterwards. This helps the detoxification process and stimulates the flow of *qi*.
- Do not allow heavy pressure to be applied to bones. An experienced or trained masseur or reflexologist will be well aware of this.

Moxibustion

One of the most reliable treatments in Chinese medicine, moxibustion is both inexpensive and effective. It is 2,000 years old and is used to improve blood circulation, relieve muscle tension and stiffness, and ease lower back pain. Moxa sticks are made from ground mugwort leaves, which are said to contain healing properties. A lit moxa stick is placed just above the acupuncture point but is removed before it burns the skin. Moxibustion can be used by itself or during acupuncture treatment where a burning moxa stick is placed gently on top of the needles.

Moxibustion can induce menstruation, making it dangerous for pregnant women, nor is it suitable for the elderly or diabetics.

Scrapping

Another member of the quack pack according to some of the more sceptical Western medical authorities, scrapping was originally used to treat fever caused by cholera. It involves repeated, pressured strokes over oiled skin with a rounded ceramic or metal spoon-like instrument. Maladies such as coughs, fatigue, headaches and sluggish *qi* are said to benefit from scrapping. As with cupping, scrapping can cause mild bruising, which fades in 2-4 days.

The relationship between these two elements is at the very heart of Chinese philosophy and affects every aspect of daily life – from beauty rituals and exercise routines to lovemaking conditions and dietary habits. When yin and yang are balanced, the body is healthy and functioning as it should. When there is internal disharmony, disease and illness follow. Chinese medicine seeks to bring the body back into equilibrium and thus, to a more healthy and disease-free state.

While many TCM clinics across the city treat foreign patients and have English-speaking doctors, it's wise to bring along a translator to avoid any misunderstanding if contemplating an in-depth medical assessment.

Don't expect instant diagnosis: complete assessment of your health involves the checking of all the component elements – the face, the tongue, pulse (all six of them), the eyes, bodily fluids and also your scent. These are evaluated as a group – in TCM they mean very little on their own – and are treated accordingly.

It's usual for the diagnosis to take place over a number of visits, as the patient's medical history, living habits and emotional well-being need to be taken into account.

For comprehensive TCM treatment, try one of the following.

Beijing Massage Hospital

7 Baochan Hutong, Xicheng, Financial District (6616 8880/www.massage-hospital.com). **Open** 7-11.45am, 1.30-10pm daily. **No credit cards. Map** p241 H7.

Beijing Tongren Tang Shi Xiaomo Traditional Chinese Medicine Clinic

15 Block, 7 Jianwai Soho, 39 Sanhuan Zhong Lu, Chaoyang (5869 1171/5869 1172). Metro Guomao. **Open** 8.30am-noon, 2-5.30pm daily. **No credit cards. Map** p245 O10.

Ping Xin Tang Clinic

4th floor, 218 Wangfujing Dajie, Dongcheng, Centre (6523 5566). Metro Wangfujing. **Open** 8.30am-5.30pm Mon-Fri; 8.30-11.30am Sat, Sun. **Credit** V. **Map** p244 L9. **Photo** *p172*.

T'ai chi

The centuries-old practice of t'ai chi, or *taijiquan*, remains a daily ritual for many Chinese elders and for good reason: the exercise's slow, careful movements offer a wealth of health benefits, from quieting a busy mind to relieving stress. Originally a form of martial art used for self-defence and combat, t'ai chi is now practised primarily for exercise and relaxation in parks, on the street and in apartment compounds. Through its graceful, structured movements, t'ai chi helps practitioners achieve a balance of yin and yang, thereby improving the flow of *qi*, or vital energy – considered in Chinese medicine as essential to good health. Witnessing or even participating in a class is a must: Ritan Park, Jingshan Park and Beihai Park are the most popular choices but be sure to arrive before 6am. For those after a more structured class try the following:

Jinghua Wushu Association

Kempinski Hotel, Liangmaqiao Lu, Chaoyang (135 2228 3751/www.jinghuawushu.com). **Classes** *adults* noon-1.30pm, 7-8.30pm Mon; 7pm Tue; 7-8.30pm Wed; 7pm Thur; 7.30-9pm Sat; *children* 5-6pm Thur; 4.30-5.30pm Sat. **Cost** call for price. **No credit cards**. **Map** p244 O7. **Other locations**: Ritan Park, Chaoyang.

Milun School of Traditional Kung Fu

Wangfujing, Dongcheng, Centre (139 1081 1934/ www.kungfuinchina.com). Metro Wangfujing. **Classes** 7-9pm Mon, Wed, Thur; 3-7pm Sun. **Cost** *individual class* RMB 150/class; *group class* RMB 400/month. **No credit cards**. **Map** p244 L9. **Other locations**: Ritan Park, Chaoyang.

T'ai Chi Workshop

1st floor, Health Club, CTS Plaza, Sanyuanqiao, Chaoyang (130 0103 9563). **Classes** 6.30pm Wed. **Cost** RMB 50. **No credit cards**. **Map** p243 O6.

Beauty

In Beijing it's still a pleasure to get spruced up: international hair stylists are setting up shop, manicurists are cheap and plentiful and, much to the delight of expats, Brazilian waxing, St Tropez spray tans and African hair braiding are rituals that no longer involve a plane ride 'home'. For overall cleanliness, efficiency and professionalism, middle-of-the-range to upper beauty salons are the best bet. For hair salons *see p142*.

Daisy's Beauty Salon

Room 301, Building B, Sunshine 100 International Apartments, 2 Guanghua Dong Lu, Chaoyang (5100 0556/57). Metro Yong'anli. **Open** 10am-8.30pm daily. **Treatment** *manicure* RMB 80; *pedicure* RMB 150; *leg wax* RMB 220. **Credit** MC, V. **Map** p245 O9.

Ping Xin Tang Clinic. *See p171.*

Daisy is the undisputed waxing queen of Beijing. Learning her trade in the States, this savvy Chinese returned to China to set up shop in 2005. Services have now extended to face and skin care, massage, intense pulsed light therapy, slimming treatments and nail care. All staff treat customers like friends and are confident, super friendly and speak English. **Other locations**: Rm 110, Building 7, MOMA Apartments, 1 Xiangheyuan Lu, Dongzhimenwai Dajie, Dongcheng, Chaoyang (8440 7728).

Frangipani Nail Salon

Shop 6, 30 Sanlitun Beijie, Chaoyang (6417 0889). **Open** 10am-7pm daily. **Treatment** *manicure* RMB 63; *pedicure* RMB 105; *foot massage* RMB 50/30mins. **No credit cards**. **Map** p245 O7.

After five successful salons in Shanghai, Frangipani opened its sixth in Beijing. It may be empty most days, but having something all to yourself in Beijing is a nothing short of a miracle. Services include manicures, pedicures, paraffin wax treatments, acrylic and gel nails, waxing and foot massage, as well as children's services. Little English is spoken.

Lovely Nails Salon

1st floor, Tongli Studios, Sanlitun Beijienan, Chaoyang (6417 5812). **Open** noon-7pm daily. **Treatment** *manicure* RMB 90; *pedicure* RMB 130; *eyebrow wax* RMB 100. **No credit cards**. **Map** p245 O7.

This New York-style nail salon is a perfect antidote for girls sick of the 20 kuai conveyer belt manicures on offer elsewhere. Each customer is looked after from start to finish: manicurists introduce themselves, tea is served and if you're peckish, staff are will order meals from the nearby European-style cafés. OPI products are used. Paraffin wax hand treatments, waxing and facials are also available.

Music

Folk tradition gives way to foreign fad.

All together now, at **D-22**. *See p175.*

Beijing has always been centre stage of China's live music scene as well as the place where first rock, then punk and now electronic music emerged. The popularity of the latter, combined with the rise of the nightclub, has dealt a blow to the live music scene and many young musicians have taken up the decks rather than the electric guitar. Despite this, rock has made something of a comeback (*see p174* **Rock revival**) and live music has expanded into other genres. Laptop rock (*see p175*) and folk rock are also very popular, and more recently there has been a slow but solid emergence of a crop of good local jazz acts.

WHERE TO BUY

It isn't hard to get hold of CDs in China – shops in most malls and markets have a range of chart-topping albums, genuine or otherwise. However if you are seeking something outside the mainstream you have to look that little bit harder. Many bands sell CDs at their concerts, and for the latest in Western releases, **Tom Shop** (2A, Hairun International Condominium, 2 Jiangtai Lu, Chaoyang, 5135 7487, 9.30am-11pm daily), hidden behind a screen and down the stairs of a paint shop, is probably the pick of the bunch. One of the biggest selections of quality CDs, including the latest Chinese releases, is at **Fusheng Records** (*see p135*). For fans of Chinese music **Sugar Jar** (*see p135*) offers unique, one-off, limited edition and other rare CDs that don't get a major release.

For those interested in picking up an instrument, anything from a classical Chinese *erhu* (traditional three-stringed instrument) to a Gibson Les Paul guitar is available around the Xinjiekou Nan Dajie area, where hundreds of musical shops are located. One of the best is Heng Yun Music (105 Xinjiekou Nan Dajie, Xicheng, Houhai, 6618 8745, www.hengyun.com, 10am-6pm daily).

Major venues

Many of the major venues in Beijing have been closed for refurbishment in the run up to the Olympics, meaning that big name international artists have bypassed Beijing on recent tours. But as of autumn 2007 most of these venues will be open again and Beijing will be able to accommodate the many superstars keen to add China to their tour diary. The biggest venue is the **Workers' Stadium** (Gongti Bei Lu, Chaoyang, 6501 6655) – Beijing's equivalent to London's Wembley Stadium. Next door to the Stadium is the **Workers' Gymnasium**

(Gongti Bei Lu, Chaoyang, 6501 6300), the largest indoor venue, with a smaller capacity than the stadium, but one that most visiting artists prefer. To the west of the city is **Beijing Exhibition Centre Theatre** (135 Xizhimenwai Dajie, near the Beijing Zoo, Xicheng, Financial District, 6835 4455). This stadium holds over 2,700 people and though it's all-seater, there are great views of the stage. Ticket prices range from RMB 100 all the way up to several thousand for VIP seats.

For information about classical music venues, *see p183* **Performing Arts**.

Pop, rock & electro

Canto pop – cheesy pop from Hong Kong and warbling Taiwanese singers and actors – became massively popular in the 1990s with manufactured stars such as Hong Konger Andy Lau bleating on about their disastrous love lives. A wonderful, but all too brief, era of mainland Chinese pop was spearheaded by Beijing babe Faye Wong, but little else happened until *Super Girl* arrived in 2005. China's version of *Pop Idol* or *American Idol*, it became the most popular show on TV with

Rock revival

Rock emerged in Beijing in the late 1980s with bands like Hei Bao (Black Panther), Tang Dynasty and Cui Jian – the much-lauded grandfather of Chinese rock who became the voice of the Tiananmen protesters with his song 'Nothing to My Name' – performing a mixture of Western inspired rock and Chinese political folk. Although the political undertones of the scene meant that rock was banned from being broadcast on state-controlled TV, the early '90s saw the underground subculture gravitate to the mainstream. However, tight restrictions by the government combined with an increase in commercially popular canto pop – specifically from Taiwan and Hong Kong – led to a major decline in rock by the mid-'90s.

By the late 1990 the dance clubs and DJ culture had begun to tighten their grip, forcing Beijing rock further underground. The demolition of some of the city's finest live music venues was the final nail in the coffin.

However, due to internet access, more foreign acts visiting the city, a rise in the number of international music festivals and a new generation of Chinese musicians whose lyrics are often social rather than political, the music has been quick to rise again. One sign that government restrictions have eased was the recent lifting of a ban on Cui Jian, allowing him to perform live in Beijing again.

In 2006 several Chinese bands, including Brain Failure (*pictured*), PK-14 and the Subs, toured the US and Western Europe, and 2007 saw Beijing bands Lonely China Day and Rebuilding the Rights of Statues play a US tour including the South by South West Festival in Austin. China's homegrown record label Modern Sky is also branching out Stateside to showcase Beijing rock to the American audience.

More and more rock festivals are springing up each year with huge attendances. In 2006 the Beer and Rock festival featured nearly all Beijing's best rock acts, including Second Hand Rose, AK-47, Reflector, Hang on the Box and New Pants, and the Beijing based Midi Music Festival (*see p147*) saw 60,000 visitors turn up over four days to hear dozens of up and coming bands perform. September 2007 brings the third Beijing Pop Festival produced by Rock For China, giving the best of Beijing the chance to share a stage with international acts such as Placebo and Supergrass. The number of live music venues almost doubled in 2006 with clubs of all sizes springing up across the city to cater to the ever-growing rock scene. It may be growing slowly, but it certainly is growing.

400 million viewers, and launched a group of averagely talented female singers to fame. China's version of Busted – rock boy band the Flowers – are also one of the more popular pop groups although shockingly derivative.

In the pop-saturated market it has been hard for alternative music to grow. Record companies won't invest and 90 per cent of all CDs sold are fakes. It has been almost impossible for musicians to make a career out of music, but things are looking up as more media attention is being given to the burgeoning underground scene.

As well as punk, rock and metal, a Chinese version of Brit Pop has been growing in many live music venues, and more recently there has been a wave of artists producing laptop music, some with more success than others. Neither dance music nor rock music, laptop music is a mish-mash of beats and erratic noises that enjoys quite a following. Shanshui are currently the most interesting and prolific band producing laptop music and several others such as former superstar rocker Wang Lei are giving the genre much-needed kudos. Yan Yun's Waterland Kwanyin evenings, performed regularly at venues around town, are a good opportunity to hear edgier takes on the music.

D-22

242 Chengfu Lu, Haidian, North-west (6265 3177/ www.d22beijing.com). **Open** 7pm-2am daily. **No credit cards**. **Map** p249 E3.

This experimental music joint, in the hub of student area Wudaokou, was opened in early 2007 by Michael Pettis who ran a club in New York before moving to China. The small venue packs a good crowd especially at weekends when local punk acts perform. With a wide variety of local and visiting international acts getting on the stage, D-22 has made a big name for itself in a very short time as the showcase for some of the most interesting acts that Beijing has to offer the discerning punter. **Photo** *p173.*

Mao

111 Guloudong Dajie, Dongcheng, Houhai (133 6612 1459). **Open** 10pm-late daily. **No credit cards**. **Map** p241 K7.

Opened in February 2007, this 500-capacity venue is hoping to take rock from small student bars on to a larger stage. The bar flanks the stage of the large open space and the grungy crowd creates a gig-friendly atmosphere. With local and international acts across all genres scheduled, Mao is expected to have a large impact on the music scene. However, the residential neighbourhood might cause problems.

Nameless Highland

Building 14, Area 1, Anhuili, Yayuncun (walk 200m north from the T-intersection with Yayuncun Hospital at the corner), Houhai (6489 1613). **Open** 8pm-late daily. **No credit cards**. **Map** p242 L3.

This well-hidden venue is in one of the larger pubs in town with two levels and a decent size stage. The cover charge – usually around RMB 30 – includes a beer and the music is usually heavy rock. Decorated in a rather obscure camouflage theme this is a favourite with the Chinese punk crowd.

South Gate Space

4 Jiuxianqiao Lu, 798 Art District, Chaoyang (6438 2797). **Open** for concerts. **No credit cards**.

Located in the trendy 798 Art District, the South Gate Space is a small theatre with a capacity for around 100 people. Located in one of the old outhouses of the factory area, the wooden beams give the place a character that is perfect for classical concerts. Folk, jazz and country music are also all mainstays, but expect anything to turn up.

Star Live

Top Floor, South Gate of Ditan Park, Dongcheng, Houhai (6425 5166/www.thestarlive.com). **No credit cards**. **Map** p242 L6.

With a capacity of up to 2,000 people, a large wide stage and two well-stocked bars, Star Live is by far the closest Beijing has to a Western gig venue. Most of Beijing's larger venues are all seated so the chance for a couple of thousand of people to mosh up the front provides an atmosphere almost unique in the city. The venue of choice for visiting bands such as Maximo Park, the Roots and Ziggy Marley it is also the place to catch the few Chinese bands that have risen to star status. Tickets range from RMB 30 to RMB 200 depending on the show, but with a great atmosphere, top-level balcony, and great sound and lighting this is the most professional live music experience in Beijing.

13 Club

161 Lanqiying (west side of Chengfu Lu, at Lanqiying East bus stop, look for the neon 13 light), Haidian, North-west (8262 8077). **Open** 8pm-2am daily. **No credit cards**. **Map** p249 E3.

13 Club is a student venue that leans heavily in the direction of serious punk. The very basic decor, consisting of cement floors and heavily graffiti-covered walls, proves it's all about the music, since there's precious little else to look at. With everything from death metal and rock to punk and ska, the 13 Club is the place to find the real heart of the metal scene.

2 Kolegas Bar

21 Liangmaqiao Lu (inside the drive-in cinema), Chaoyang (8196 4820). **Open** 9.30pm-late daily. **No credit cards**. **Map** p243 P6.

Unlike the cavernous underground dens of the West, music venues in Beijing are often little more than someone's front room – and 2 Kolegas is no exception. This compact venue has a bar that fits just one barman behind it and a bathroom that struggles to fit just one. However 2 Kolegas (or Liange Haopengyou) is one of the more interesting live music venues, with everything from laptop musicians standing in front of their computers to punk

Taking a break. **Yugong Yishan**.

bands bouncing around on stage. Look out in the summer for one of their outdoor parties, where bands play a mini-festival in the garden.

What? Bar

72 Beichang Jie (north of the West Gate of the Forbidden City), Xicheng, Centre (133 4112 2757). Metro Tiananmen West. **Open** 3pm-midnight Mon-Thur; 3pm-2am Fri-Sun. **No credit cards. Map** p241 J9.

Just to the west of the old Imperial Palace, the grammatically challenged What? Bar has a capacity of about 15. With three small tables, a tiny bar and a stage that forces a three piece to sit on each other's laps, cosy is an understatement. But with a mixture of jazz or blues and some very amateur rock, it's an interesting place in which to catch a glimpse of the underbelly of the Beijing music scene. The improvised jam sessions are great fun.

Yugong Yishan

1 Gongti Bei Lu (back of the car park, opposite the Workers' Stadium), Chaoyang (6415 0687). **Open** 6pm-2am daily. **No credit cards. Map** p244 N8.

The best dive bar in the city, Yugong has become the hub of the underground rock scene. Situated at the back of the Workers' Stadium car park, its frontage of broken neon lighting looks the part. Owner Lue Zhiqiang hand picks the best bands to perform at this straightforward, no glitz venue, which plays host to a wide variety of musical genres from blues, jazz, rock and punk to reggae, hip hop, live dance and DJ acts. International bands also take to the stage and the 300-capacity venue is regularly packed to the gills. Rumours of imminent destruction abound, but the owner has promised that Yugong will relocate if the bulldozers come calling. Let's hope the new venue will be able to recreate what has become a Beijing institution.

Jazz, blues & folk

Until recently, jazz in Beijing was generally only found in hotel bars being performed by foreign bands; but slowly an indigenous jazz and blues scene has emerged. Many of China's famous rockers from the heyday of the scene – the late-1980s – have turned in their later years to jazz, with the **CD Jazz Café** long being the venue where bands such as Du Yinjiao take to the stage. The latest addition to the scene has been the **East Shore Jazz Café** in Houhai where swing and jazz bands such as the Golden Buddha Jazz Unit and the Liu Yuan Jazz Band, perform regularly.

Blues, in the true sense of the word, is less prominent, but excellent local bands such as Sand, Confucius Says and Black Cat Bone play most weeks at venues across the city including **Yugong Yishan** and **2 Kolegas**. Folk music by local Chinese bands such as IZ and Xiao He, and Mongolian bands such as Hanggai, is popular across the city and live gigs can be caught in some of the smaller venues such as **Jiangjinjiu** and **What? Bar**.

CD Jazz Café

16 Nongzhanguan Lu, (beside the Agricultural Exhibition Hall), Dongsanhuan Bei Lu, Chaoyang (6506 8288). **Open** 3pm-late daily. **No credit cards. Map** p245 P7.

This large space is decorated with jazz memorabila. The large wooden tables allow the mainly Chinese listeners to sip coffee and chain smoke to their heart's content. With live jazz most weekends from local bands, the gigs are often the best in town.

East Shore Jazz Café

2nd Floor, Building 2, Qianhai Nanyuan, Di'anmenwai Dajie, Houhai (8403 2131). **Open** 2pm-2am daily. **Credit** AmEx, MC, V. **Map** p241 J7.

Situated on the east shore of the Houhai lake area this is a little gem. It is beautifully decorated with pictures of jazz greats collected by aficionado Liu Yuan. See if you can spot the photo of a jazz band playing in front of a Mao portrait c.1968 – this is perhaps China's first jazz band, with Liu's own father among the players. Jazz and swing groups perform most weeknights and every weekend and musician can head along on Mondays for a jam.

Jiangjinjiu

2 Zhongku Hutong, (courtyard between the Drum and Bell Towers), Dongcheng, Houhai (8405 0124). **Open** noon-2am Mon-Thur; noon-4am Fri-Sun. **No credit cards. Map** p241 K7.

This converted hutong home is just one small room with a bar in the corner and a fridge where you help yourself to RMB 15 beers. At weekends nearly all the wooden benches will be filled with locals and expats listening to sets of country and bluegrass, modern and classical folk, and blues and jazz bands.

Nightlife

Cut through the commercialism to find the people's party of your choice.

Babyface East. *See p178.*

Forget Mao suits and images of grey Beijing – the city's nocturnal entertainment scene is varied, vibrant and multi-hued: neon-lit KTV (karaoke TV) parlours filled with whisky-fuelled locals playing dice, and bumping and grinding to the latest pop and hip hop; upscale cocktail lounges frequented by ultra-rich glitterati; state-of-the-art danceclubs where *laowai* and local patrons rock to the dance beats of the world's top DJs.

While the current, highly commercialised entertainment scene renders a genuine underground virtually nonexistent, Beijing's nightlife has nonetheless come a long way since its inception a decade ago, when the first modest bars and clubs began to spring up in the Sanlitun precinct.

These days, revellers can choose from a number of districts in which to party. The Sanlitun strip still constitutes a mass of garish bars including one of the originals, Public Space – opened to near-hysterical acclaim in 1997, but now under new management and somewhat faded – while the nearby Gongti, or Workers' Stadium, strip is the location of many of Beijing's big-branded clubs, a trend started by **Babyface East** some years ago. The borders of Chaoyang Park are likewise emerging as a new clubbers' paradise, with several much-anticipated venues scheduled to open alongside one of Beijing's best-loved haunts, the infamous **World of Suzie Wong**; to the west, the Houhai area is home to scores of flashy, if occasionally rather tawdry, bars.

Beijing's best mixers use web-purchased vinyl in addition to downloaded music and DJ software, ensuring that the latest sounds are (mostly) played in clubs. It should be noted, however, that electronic music and dance clubs are targeted at a comparatively small audience

The best Clubs

To flaunt it alongside hipsters and billionaire boho babes
China Doll (*see p178*).

To hear cutting-edge producers
Cargo (*see p178*).

To hear the world's best DJs
Coco Banana (*see p179*).

To live out your popstar fantasy
Tango KTV (*see p180*).

To spot celebrities
The World of Suzie Wong (*see p180*).

– the great majority of the local Chinese population still prefer to bop about to hip hop and R&B American chart toppers.

Which is not to suggest that dance music is not a booming business: quite the opposite, as evidenced by the number of international DJs who flock to the city. While the rest of the world might have experienced a backlash against the superstar DJ phenomenon, China remains a lucrative market for these players. The capital is no exception, evidenced by the almost weekly appearances of the biggest names in the business. Thanks to the creativity and foresight of several promoters, the city is also increasingly playing host to a number of less hyped but quality electronic music acts from across the globe, creating a welcome diversity in Beijing's burgeoning nightlife.

Mingling at **Mix**. *See p179.*

Clubs

Babyface East

6 Gongti Xi Lu, Chaoyang (6551 9081). **Open** 8pm-4am daily. **Admission** free. **No credit cards.** **Map** p244 N8.

There's just no stopping this juggernaut. The nationwide Babyface brand is responsible for ODing Beijing on LED and UV, and for inspiring most of the other dance mega clubs in the city to set up shop. The two venues are, locale aside, virtually identical, boasting hi-tech sound, lighting and large dance floors for serious partying. While Babyface caters to a younger crowd of hyped-up revellers, there's no knocking their DJ policy: frequent 'top ten' DJs and quality, envelope-pushing acts. **Photo** *p177.*

Other locations: Babyface West, 1st Floor, Triumph Plaza, A143 Xizhimenwai Dajie, Xicheng, Financial District (8801 6848).

The Bank

9 Gongti East Gate, Chaoyang (6553 1998). **Open** 8.30pm-3am Mon-Thur, Sun; 8.30pm-5am Fri, Sat. **Admission** free. **Credit** AmEx, MC, V. **Map** p244 O8.

Opened in March 2007, on a prime location on the lake shoreline at the east gate of the Workers' Stadium, The Bank boasts a knockout locale. Steps lead from the ground-floor restaurant into a vast room where balconies command a sweeping view over the club. The large dancefloor is overseen by a deluxe DJ booth, where four local stars spin everything from house and breaks to eclectic party fare. A huge rooftop garden provides fantastic views for those who prefer cocktails under the stars.

Banana

1st Floor, Scitech Hotel, 22 Jianguomenwai Dajie, Chaoyang (6528 3636). Metro Jainguomen. **Open** 8.30pm-5am daily. **Admission** RMB 20-RMB 30. **No credit cards. Map** p244 N10.

Big, loud and the perfect venue at which to go off your – ahem – banana. A favourite of the local Chinese and one of the original dance clubs in Beijing (shown by the somewhat dated interior and furnishings), the dance floor still rocks – at ear-splitting volume – to the rhythm of hard house and NRG-fused dance, with top DJs making occasional appearances playing a range of hard-style genres including techno and trance. For a slightly classier experience, head upstairs to the small but sophisticated Spicy Lounge, where international and local DJs can be found spinning cool electro, house, minimal and everything in between.

Cargo

6 Gongti Xi Lu (in between Babyface and Angel), Chaoyang (6551 6878). **Open** 8pm-5am daily. **Admission** free Mon-Thur, Sun; RMB 50 Fri, Sat. **No credit cards. Map** p244 N8.

Introduced to the city's clubbers in 2006, Cargo is an expanse of intelligent sound and LED wall, popular with expats and locals alike for introducing some hip acts to the capital. The small dance floor has hosted seriously classy DJs including Felix Da Housecat and Superfreq Mr C.

China Doll

2nd Floor, Tongli Studios, North Sanlitun Lu, Chaoyang (6416 7968). **Open** 8pm-late daily. **Admission** free. **Credit** AmEx, MC, V. **Map** p245 O7.

This boutique dance club boasts a management team whose past successes include the infamous

Cloud Nine. The upfront music policy is presided over by Youdai – one of the city's best-known nightlife personalities – and delivered by up-and-coming local DJs spinning house, breaks and electro. Sexy underground styling, a slick drinks menu and chic decor make this tri-level warehouse the hottest new addition to the city's clubbing cohort.

Coco Banana

Gongti Xi Lu (in between Angel and the Green Tea House), Chaoyang (8599 9999). **Open** 8pm-4am Mon-Thur, Sun; 8pm-5am Fri, Sat. **Admission** free. **No credit cards**. **Map** p244 N8.

Smaller sibling of Banana, Coco offers the requisite Beijing Gongti clubbing experience – think ample LED lighting, UV galore and intelligent sound. The real drawcard for the wannabe-VIP set is the numerous – and expensive – private rooms available, replete with cowhide couches, large screen TVs and sound piped from the main room, ensuring one need not venture out for an authentic Coco clubbing experience. For mere mortals a Taiwanese resident DJ spins house and R&B in the mainroom to a compact dance floor surrounded by plenty of tables ready for some dice 'n' Chivas action.

Mix

Inside the Workers' Stadium, North Gate, Chaoyang (6530 2889). Metro Dongsishitiao. **Open** 8pm-6am daily. **Admission** free Mon-Thur, Sun; RMB 50 Fri, Sat. **Credit** V. **Map** p244 N8.

Mix is Beijing's own Ghetto Fabulous. A roster of international guest DJs and cheap drinks keep the large sunken dance floor pumping 'til the wee hours. The crowd comprises mainly youthful, largely foreign, clubbers presided over by wannabe B-Boys and their fly-girls. The music is a puzzle, however, with an in-house DJ crew of locals who play some upfront beats interspersed with dated '90s pop. With its cheap drinks and good vibe, Mix is worth a visit.

Tango

South Gate of Ditan Park (near Jindingxuan Restaurant), Dongcheng, Houhai (6428 2288). **Open** 8.30pm-3am daily **Admission** free. **Credit** AmEx, MC, V. **Map** p242 L6.

A mega club to rival the Gongti pack, Tango's main room is divided into a large dance floor, ample private booths and bar. Tango's recent renovations, a joint project between local and European design teams, have resulted in updated decor and sound, so

Clubbing Beijing style

Fancy yourself a hip, savvy clubber? You know the hottest underground producers, can tell the difference between electro and minimal, are able to out dance anyone else on the floor and have a wardrobe full of stylin' clubbing outfits... Abandon it all and enter the world of Beijing clubbing.

Get yourself some new duds

For males, anything that remotely resembles the latest Ja Rule or Sean Paul video clip is a good start. You know the score: B-Boy baggies, a cap (swivelled to the side) and super-sized T-shirt, preferably accented with some bling. Alternatively, don a suit and go triad style. Ladies: your motto is 'the smaller the better'. Sky-high heels and tiny everything, and ensure your thong is showing over the top of skin-tight pants/miniskirt.

Pick your club

Anything with an infantile name is a good start; try Babyface or Cutie. Also make sure the club plays R&B or hip hop – ideally with a live cover band that does Black Eyed Peas and Shakira impersonations.

Make an entrance

Preferably by having the driver drop you off at the door of the club in the Hummer. If that's not possible, at least make sure you have a very swanky sports car and that the door staff immediately wave you through in to the VIP area, where you can sit all night and watch the regular people through the one-way mirror windows.

Order your beverages

Every club in China has a sponsor. Usually, it's a big-name whisky brand. Make sure your club carries the brand you like, because drinking means copious jugs of whisky and green tea, all night long...

Brush up on your dice skills

Clubbing Beijing-style means long periods of time spent sitting at a tiny table, eating popcorn and fruit platters, and playing dice. It's a game of skill and cunning, and involves draining the loser of large amounts of money and sobriety.

Hit the dance floor

While Chinese nightclubs – for the most part – do not have a heavy emphasis on the dance floor (some nightclubs do not even have one), it's still important to know the rules: get in a big group of friends, lose all inhibition and bop around like an MTV popstar. Easy! Now, back to the dice.

The World of Suzie Wong.

expect more glitz and glam than ever before. Top floor Mango hosts bands and live acts while the basement carries on the KTV tradition. Tango has recently joined forces with Bedrock, ensuring that many producers and DJs from the seminal UK label frequently tour, playing every variety of progressive, house and techno.

The World of Suzie Wong

1A Nongzhanguan Lu, Chaoyang Gongyuan Ximen, Chaoyang (6593 6049). **Open** 7pm-late daily. **No credit cards. Map** p245 P7.

Suzie Wong's maintains its enduring tag of Beijing's most popular bar and club, and continues to pack the patrons in after three years in the business. The opulent surroundings suggest the opium-fuelled dens of the past while the music pumps up a small dance floor and floats over tables filled with suitably apathetic models. The in-house DJ trio of Bobby, Youdai and Chozie are among the city's best; combined with a good bar and balcony area, and an irrepressible party vibe, 'Suzie's' (aka 'the Wong's') is a guaranteed big night out, any night of the week.

Karaoke

Cashbox Party World

Side building of Tengda Plaza, Xizhimenwai Dajie, Xicheng, Financial District (8857 6566). **Open** 8am-2am daily. **Credit** MC, V. **Map** p249 E7.

Cashbox is aimed at party groups and offers an affordable range of rooms (RMB 165-RMB 235 per hour) for would-be pop superstars. The Chaoyang venue is immense, stretching out over some 130 rooms, while the Xicheng district complex caters for 100 separate groups. While the decor may be a little on the simple side, the choice of songs is extensive and offers a huge array of both Chinese and Western tunes to belt along to. Also included is a vast buffet all day, every day, so you can sate the hunger that only comes from flaunting your vocal prowess to the (Cashbox Party) world.

Other locations: 1st floor, Prime Tower, Chaoyangmenwai Dajie, Chaoyang (6588 3333 ext 9).

Party Life

Zhengren Plaza, 9 Chongwenmenwai Dajie, Chongwen, South (6708 6666). **Open** 24hrs daily. **No credit cards. Map** p244 L11.

Open 24 hours, Party Life is the location of choice for late-night revellers seeking refuge from a heavy evening of clubbing. The free buffet and drinks are a drawcard but it's the vast catalogue of sappy pop and movie tunes that appeals to crooners, although there are fewer western songs on offer than at other KTV joints. The rooms are nicely furnished and the price is competitive, with a small room setting patrons back a mere RMB 99, while a party room goes for RMB 119.

Regal

Building 22, 4 Gongti Bei Lu, Chaoyang (6500 1888). Metro Dongsishitiao. **Open** 24hrs daily. **No credit cards. Map** p244 O8.

Truly one for the must-be-seen-to-in-order-to-be-believed category, Regal is a four-storey fantasy world where visitors leaves a trail of projected flowers blooming from sensors in the floor, where twenty-foot Lalique crystal chandeliers hang from the ceiling and walls are made entirely from white feathers. The marble and granite levels contain numerous themed private KTV rooms (special mention to the black velvet wallpaper in room two and the crystal-encrusted tables in seven), which will set you back an hourly RMB 350 for a basic room, to a cool RMB 13,800, which secures an enormous private hall with remote-control mock Qin Dynasty brass-studded walls à la the Forbidden City, personal waiters and free-flowing Bollinger.

Tango KTV

79 Hepingli Xijie (South Gate of Ditan Park near Jindingxuan Restaurant), Dongcheng, Houhai (6428 2288). **Open** 24hrs daily. **Credit** MC, V. **Map** p242 L6.

Probably the hippest place in town in which to get caught singing Madonna, Tango (the club) now offers a large choice of KTV rooms to recline in after clubbing upstairs. A fantastic array of tunes and newly refurbished booths make this a good choice, and if your mates' crooning prove too much to bear, you can escape back to the nightclub. The free buffet also includes a huge spread of Western and Chinese dishes, with fresh juices, starters, mains and desserts to choose from. Room prices vary according to the time of night but expect to pay RMB 50-RMB 85 for a small room and RMB 80-RMB 215 for larger groups. For parties, there are an additional three larger room plans available.

Performing Arts

China's premier city for opera, acrobatics and Mandarin-language stand-up.

While not the richest, nor the most populous, city in the country, Beijing is the creative nerve centre for China's growing performing arts scene. Educated and reasonably cosmopolitan, Beijingers want their cultural taste to match their rising incomes, and visitors can come along for the ride. Beijing has played host to legends such as Jessye Norman, the Bolshoi Ballet and the Three Tenors. Second-tier touring ballet companies usually start and finish in the capital, which means plenty of *Swan Lake*s troll through town. International festivals are growing exponentially and artists such as conductor Richard Muti, soprano Eugenia Garza and the Teatro La Fenice are accepting invitations. Even better, more countries are sponsoring cultural/friendship years in China (2007 is the year of Spain, 2008 is Greece), which means high quality international acts will continue to grace the city.

As for homegrown talent, the world class **National Ballet of China** (NBC) has a wide and comparatively adventurous repertoire, and modern dance groups such as **Beijing Modern Dance Company** and **LDTX** are also making their international mark. While the choreography is still hit or miss, no one is afraid to experiment, and certainly pulling from the world's biggest talent pool should create strong companies in the long term.

China's classical music audience is small, but youthful and growing rapidly. Audiences may not always know what they're hearing, or may clap between symphony movements, but no one doubts that China will be a major player in the future. Beijing has a healthy number of orchestras, which range from good to inferior, mostly because of poor brass sections. This generation of musicians is growing up with summer music camps and better training – and these days, not everyone is learning the violin.

Sadly for Beijing, the age-old tradition of paying royal tribute did not die with the last emperor. Theatres routinely give out two-thirds of their tickets to government officials and 'encourage' local newspapers to write good reviews. This means the rest of us pay Broadway-style prices, usually between $20 and $150, a significant cost for most Chinese. For the 2001 visit of the Three Tenors the $2,000 tickets were the most expensive in the world. This prevents many ordinary people from building an arts education, and makes for bland programming, where a ballet isn't a proper ballet unless it has swans expiring gracefully somewhere in it, and every waltz is by Johann Strauss.

However, this is changing, and Beijingers are always open to sampling something new. In 2006, the Shanghai Opera Company brought Shostakovich's opera *The Nose* – based on a Gogol story about a man who discovers that his nose has not only gone missing from his face but is six feet tall and wandering around St Petersburg – to Beijing. At the intermission, the audience was stunned into silence; by the end they were standing and cheering.

Beijing Concert Hall. *See page 182.*

TICKETS AND INFORMATION

The not-for-profit mentality of the government-run theatres leads to some problems. That surly voice you finally hear after repeated phone calls may or may not know (or care) what is happening that night. Try going early and visiting the box office or speak to one of the many touts circling the theatres. Understand, however, that shows may be cancelled without notice – if the government wants a private performance, it gets one. Ticket websites are better for the big shows, try www.piao.com.cn, +86 10 6417 7845, or www.emma.cn, +86 10 6553 5699. Listings magazines are another source of information. Naturally, we think *Time Out Beijing* is the best, but there's also *City Weekend* and *That's Beijing*.

Venues

Beijing Concert Hall

1 Bei Xinhua Jie, Liubukou, Xicheng, Centre (6605 7006). **Tickets** vary. **No credit cards. Map** p241 J10.

With the best acoustics in town – though the sound engineers have yet to catch up – this newly refurbished hall concentrates on classical and Chinese traditional music. BCH's guests aren't generally as glamorous as those who waltz into the foyer at the Poly Theatre (*see below*), but there's plenty of spill-over during festival months. **Photo** *p181*.

Beijing Exhibition Theatre

135 Xizhimenwai Dajie, Xicheng, Financial District (6835 4455). Metro Xizhimen. **Tickets** vary. **No credit cards. Map** p249 F7.

This unremarkable venue focuses on some low-tier dance groups and Chinese music, but it is also the home for many blockbuster Western shows, such as *Rent* and *West Side Story*, and stars like the Black Eyed Peas.

Capital Theatre

22 Wangfujing Dajie, Dongcheng, Centre (6524 9847). Metro Wangfujing. **Tickets** vary. **No credit cards. Map** p244 L9

Beijing's centre for Chinese drama, showing anything from Cao Yu's classics to Taiwanese visionary Stan Lai's *Secret Love in Peach Blossom Land*, which was the theatrical highlight of 2006. Capital Theatre also has two smaller venues, the People's Art Experimental Theatre, and the People's Art Mini Theatre (6526 3337 for both), for shows slightly – but not radically – off the beaten path.

China Central Conservatory of Music

43 Baojiajie, Xicheng, Financial District (6642 5702). **Tickets** vary. **No credit cards. Map** p240 G10.

The no-frills hall of the best music conservatory in China hosts regular concerts from a number of international guests, established Chinese musicians playing both Chinese and Western instruments, and students. It's the ideal venue for a quick classical fix and you might spot a new virtuoso. CCCOM is also the home of the EOS orchestra (*see p185*).

Forbidden City Concert Hall

Zhongshan Park, Xichanganjie, Dongcheng, Centre (6559 8285). Metro Tiananmen West. **Tickets** vary. **No credit cards. Map** p241 K9.

Aesthetically Beijing's best theatre with gorgeous acoustics, the Forbidden City Concert Hall is in the heart of historic Zhongshan Park behind the Imperial Palace. They host some of the bigger names in classical and Chinese traditional music, and also run a lengthy and affordable summer concert programme, as well as some child-friendly events involving orchestras and puppets.

Great Hall of the People

West side of Tiananmen Square, Xichanganjie, Dongcheng, Centre (6406 8888). Metro Tiananmen West. **Tickets** vary. **No credit cards. Map** p241 K10.

China's seat of government by day, the Great Hall turns into an unlikely concert venue at night, hosting the biggest names in pop, classical and ballet. Unfortunately, the acoustics are terrible, seats are uncomfortable and tickets are hard to come by. If you want to see a performance here it's best to go through one of the ticket agencies.

National Grand Theatre

Chang'an Avenue, behind the Great Hall of the People, Dongcheng, Centre. Due to open July 2007. **Map** p241 K10.

Beijing's newest and most expensive addition to the theatre community has been plagued with controversy and financial woes since its drawing board days. The glass and titanium teardrop-shaped behemoth is surrounded by a moat, which seemed an odd design choice for one of the world's driest, dustiest and most polluted cities. Maintenance costs aside, the ultra-modern structure is a mere meander from the Forbidden City and the heart of historical Beijing. The 149,500 square metre (37 acre) building will have a 2,416-seat opera house, a 2,017-seat concert hall and a 1,040-seat theatre, with (reportedly) competitively priced tickets.

Peking University Century Hall

East gate of Peking University, 75 Haidian Lu, Haidian, North-west (6275 1278). **Tickets** vary. **No credit cards. Map** p248 D3.

Peking University sports a good selection of ballet and classical concerts, and is many touring companies' second run. Prices are reasonable but houses are packed and tickets go quickly.

Poly Theatre

1st floor, Poly Plaza, 14 Dongzhimen Nandajie, Dongcheng, Chaoyang (6506 5345). Metro Dongsishitiao. **Tickets** vary. **No credit cards. Map** p244 N8.

Losing the plot

Peking Opera (*jingju*) isn't for wimps. In fact, even the most ardent fans of Verdi and Puccini may discover in it a new definition of the word shrill, and the 'orchestra' is cacophony itself. Nevertheless, this is a cultural gem that has survived for over two hundred years, enchanting plebeians and royalty alike. Attention must be paid to such an art. Buy a ticket and prepare for an uncomfortable night – you'll be amazed at how much you enjoy yourself in the end.

Most Peking Opera stories are based on historic or legendary events and their corresponding characters. However, Westerners unfamiliar with the tales will still find much to wonder at in the art's complexity, beginning with the somewhat disturbing makeup. *Jingju* has a series of stock characters. The most elaborately painted face belongs to Jing, usually a warrior or an official, and the colour of his face indicates the content of his character. Red, for example, means goodness and courage, white signifies treachery and cunning, and black indicates brusqueness. The other characters are Sheng, male, Dan, female, and Chou, the clown, recognisable by the small patch of white on his face. Similar to the overly clever servants in Western operas, Chou is cunning, but not calculating. Sheng and Dan characters have a number of subcategories. For example, Xiao Sheng, is an adolescent, and must speak with his voice breaking. The Hua Dan (until 1949 played by men) is the flirtatious female of low social standing; naturally, she is chattier than the virtuous Qing Yi actress, and uses quicker (and less feminine) hand movements. Also interesting are the simple but effective props; savvy audiences understand that whips mean horses, paddles represent boats, and banners signify billowing waves.

Peking Operas can last over three hours with no intermission, and an audience that consists mainly of elderly Chinese cheerfully cracking sunflower seeds and chatting about the performance throughout the show. It's probably best for beginners to start with a foreigner-friendly highlight show, which is shorter and heavy on the martial arts. Alternatively, head for the Temple of Heaven (*see p76*) and watch committed amateurs and ex-pros doing opera improv sessions – just for the fun of it.

Peking Opera is an acquired taste, but you have to admire performers who can sing, act, dance, do martial arts and acrobatics. Imagine the Three Tenors trying that.

Li Yuan Theatre. *See p187.*

Beijing's acrobats defy gravity with parasols, push-bikes and poles...

Located in the Poly Hotel, the Poly Theatre has the city's biggest names, most festival acts and best mix of dance, theatre, Chinese and Western entertainment. Expect to see everything from Shaolin Monks to La Scala Ballet. Another plus is that besides being refreshingly convenient, it's the only theatre with both a coffee shop and a bar that stays open until 2am, making it good for a post-performance wrap up.

South Gate Space

4 Jiuxianqiao Lu, 798 Art District (8438 2797). **Tickets** vary. **No credit cards**.

The 798 Art District hosts a number of experimental theatre and dance pieces during festivals, but South Gate Space is the most reliable venue for anything off the beaten theatrical path, with a huge selection of both foreign and local groups doing dance, theatre and music.

Tianqiao Theatres

Tianqiao Theatre
30 Beiwei Lu, Xuanwu, South (8315 6300).
Map p246 K12.
Tianqiao Acrobatic Theatre
95 Tianqiao Market, Xuanwu, South (6303 7449).
Map p246 K12.
Tianqiao Le Cha Yuan
A1 Beiwei Lu, Xuanwu, South (6304 0912).
Map p246 K12.
For all: **Tickets** vary. **No credit cards**.

Located in the historic Tianqiao area, Tianqiao Theatre is the home of the National Ballet of China, but also features performers such as the Henri Oguike Dance Company and some Chinese theatre. Next door is the Tianqiao Acrobatic Theatre for nightly acrobatics and the Tianqiao Le Cha Yuan theatre for both *xiangsheng*, China's own version of stand-up (*see p186* **Gift of the gab**) and a Lao (Old) Beijing Variety Show with real local flavour.

Classical music

Melodious strings, fair winds and painfully amateur brass is a sadly accurate description of the vast majority of Beijing orchestras. Non-holiday programmes are refreshingly diverse, but Chinese musicians are trained in mechanics not interpretation, and taught to be stars, not team players – not to mention that many top musicians depart for foreign orchestras before the ink on their diplomas is dry.

The classical music scene, however, is expanding rapidly thanks to visionary Yu Long, the grand Pooh-Bah of China's orchestral music scene, who started both the China Philharmonic Orchestra (CPO) and the annual Beijing Music Festival (BMF), now in it's tenth year (*see p148*). Yu also arranged for Mozart's *Requiem* to be played in a downtown cathedral – a shocking but well-received first for a country where religion receives much official suspicion.

Major classical venues include the Beijing Concert Hall (1 Beixinhua Jie, Liubukou,

...at the **Tiandi Theatre**. *See p187.*

Xicheng, Centre, 6605 7006), the Forbidden City Concert Hall (inside Zhongshan Park, Xichangan Jie, Dongcheng, Centre, 6559 8285) and the Great Hall of the People (west side of Tiananmen Square, Xi Chang'an Jie, Dongcheng, Centre, info 6309 6156, tickets 6406 8888).

China Philharmonic

8838 4171/6551 8888/www.chinaphilharmonic.org.
Yu Long's elite group is by far the best choice for tonal quality, programme selection, and variety of guest conductors and soloists. These have included the likes of Sir Andrew Davis, Itzhak Perlman, Placido Domingo and Krzysztof Penderecki.

The China Philharmonic (CPO) – which usually plays the Poly Theatre or the Forbidden City Concert Hall, but occasionally turns up at the Beijing Concert Hall – is also the first choice for returning Chinese 'local boys made good', such as piano prodigies/bitter rivals Lang Lang and Yundi Li, violinist Li Chuanyun and cellist Wang Jian.

EOS Orchestra

6641 2017/http://eos.ccom.edu.cn.
A youth orchestra loosely affiliated with China's best music conservatory (CCCOM) this was started as an intensive three-year training programme for orchestral, not solo music. And intensive it is; EOS concentrates on 'all Mozart,' or 'all Beethoven' programmes, which may mean day-long concerts. Currently completely Chinese, EOS plans a pan-Asian selection process in the future.

Dance

Much has been made of China being the future of classical music, but crystal ball gazers shouldn't overlook its dance potential either. With their exceptional training programmes and technical skill, their naturally petite bodies, and the largest talent pool in the world, all that's missing is smooth-yet-adventurous choreography, and that's only a matter of time and confidence.

Meanwhile, glimpse the future with the following groups.

Beijing Modern Dance Company

6758 0922/6758 7161/www.bmdc.com.cn.
Beijing's most established modern dance group, BJMDC is the first stop for foreign groups looking for collaborators, from Norway's Teatre Ibsen to fashion designer Pierre Cardin. A courageous, talented company whose choreography ranges from the staid to the wild, their tours have swept over five continents, playing the Venice Biennale, Washington, DC's Kennedy Center and accompanying President Hu Jintao to Brazil.

LDTX

6405 4292/tickets 6405 4842/www.beijingldtx.com.
Born of a split that took place within BJMDC in 2005, the 14-strong company has already established itself as a serious contender. Founder Willy Tsao is draped in international awards, and he's gone on to create China's first modern dance company. Tsao gives his choreographers unlimited freedom regardless of their experience, creating some intriguing and well-received results.

Living Dance Studio (LDS)

6433 7243/6433 6143/www.ccdworkstation.com.
Founded in 1994 by life partners film director Wu Wenguang and dancer/choreographer Wen Hui, the Living Dance Studio (LDS) is Beijing's oldest dance troupe. Age does not mean complacency, however, and LDS creates multimedia productions using film, theatre and documentary-style interviews, as well as workshops where anything goes. LDS also founded the Crossing Festival (*see p187*), now in its third year.

National Ballet of China

8355 3737/www.ballet.org.cn.
The National Ballet of China (NBC) is consistently ranked fifth or sixth in the world, and was lauded by choreographic legend Roland Petit, who not only reworked his 1971 *Pink Floyd Ballet* specifically for the company, but took two dancers on his world tour. NBC has a range of standard favourites, such as *Swan Lake* and *Giselle*, but also experiments with more modern work by choreographers like Petit and John Cranko, and even collaborates with modern dance groups. NBC's signature work is *Raise the Red Lantern*, with a striking visual design courtesy of film director Zhang Yimou.

Theatre

English-language theatre is a rare treat for Beijing's expatriate community – the surtitle technology present in nearly every theatre is for Chinese only. European groups occasionally provide their own translations, but many local producers feel that Chinese theatre doesn't need Western audiences, who probably wouldn't understand the culture anyway. Even those that want to attract an expat crowd don't seem to grasp that language might be a good first step.

In the meantime, theatre buffs should look out for the National Theatre Company, which hosts such acclaimed directors as Lin Zhaohua and Wu Xiaojiang. Both featured heavily in the 2006 Year of Ibsen that marked the centenary of the great Norwegian playwright's death, and Wu is currently collaborating with Stanford University on a project about Martin Luther King. The most successful experimental group is Guan Haoyue's X2 Theatre Company, whose thirty-something comedy/dramas always have an extra dimension.

Gift of the gab

While acrobatics and Peking Opera have always held small but steady audiences, the traditional art of *xiangsheng* (cross talk) has suffered with the ill winds of politics. Rooted in satire, performers alternated between being starving artists, enemies of the state and tools of propaganda until nearly vanishing as pop music and action movies took hold. Lately, however, *xiangsheng* has made a startling revival, reaching a young audience with iPods and camera phones in a surprising leap across the Chinese generational chasm.

Legend has it that *xiangsheng* began in the Han Dynasty (206 BC-220 AD), but it wasn't until the Qing (1644-1911) that the skill was honed. At that time, Tianqiao, south of the city wall, was where acrobatics, street theatre and modern day *xiangsheng* all took root. *Xiangsheng* takes three forms: *dankou xiangsheng* is essentially a one-man stand-up act sometimes accompanied by a bamboo clapper (heard in Beijing taxis everywhere). The popular *dchu xiangsheng*, or cross talk, has one person talking and the other making comments. *Qunkou xiangsheng* needs three or more people, with one taking the lead and others making random comments while trying to steer him off the topic.

Modern performers use technology and current events, as far as the political climate will allow. The Tianjin group Haha Xiao won China's first internet xiangsheng competition in 2004, and scans the web for amateur works to perform, such as Western Food or Artificial Beauty. They also post recordings online, seeking comments from cyber fans. It is Guo Degang, however, who is the architect of xiangsheng's renaissance. A Tianjin native who was rejected from all the state-run troupes, 33-year-old Guo has achieved the unlikely status of xiangsheng rock star, and is its hip, fashionable, future, with an MP3 album, a website, a television career, and legions of fans and disciples.

Aspiring xiangshengers need clear enunciation, good stage presence and comic timing, as well as the ability to mimic local dialects, sound effects and opera melodies. Verbal acrobatic skills help too; performers have to foreshadow punch-lines with fakes, feints and teasers, such as misunderstandings, puns and coincidences, all peppered with local slang.

Even Westerners with fluent Chinese will have trouble following xiangsheng. Tickets are cheap but scarce, and three hours of sitting on cushion-free wooden chairs can be excruciating. For timely cultural entertainment, however, there's nothing better – and historic Tianqiao Le Cha Yuan theatre features Guo Degang every week. Pair after pair of mostly youthful performers dressed in Qing Dynasty garb deliver rapid dialogues, after which the MC selects certain acts to perform mysteriously determined encores. Those favoured bow, delivering self-effacing apologies for their poor work, and perform again to a rapt, multi-generational crowd drinking tea and scarfing down sunflower seeds. However, although it's Guo Degang who made the ancient hip again, xiangsheng was due a revival. In a nation with a long history of suppressed public opinion and tragic events, xiangsheng is welcome comic relief.

Tianqiao Le Cha Yuan

A1 Beiwei Lu, (near Tianqiao Theatre), Xuanwu, South. **Shows** *Lao (Old) Beijing Variety Shows* 7.30pm Mon-Wed; *xiangsheng* 7.15-10pm Thur-Sun. **Tickets** *Lao (Old) Beijing Variety Shows* RMB 150; *xiangsheng* RMB 20-RMB 60. **No credit cards**. **Map** p246 K12.

Festivals & events

May's Meet in Beijing Arts Festival (MIBJ) is the largest entertainment festival in Asia and is now entering its seventh year (*see p147*). Focusing largely on performing arts, MIBJ boasts a huge number of Chinese and international acts doing their various things in theatres, public squares and city parks. The avant-garde Dashanzi International Arts Festival (DIAF) overlaps MIBJ, carrying a balance of visual arts and cutting-edge performance groups. Busy May also sees the French Embassy's Croisements Festival, now in it's third year, and features French and Chinese groups collaborating in dance, theatre and music. After a long, bleak summer, festivals return with a vengeance in October, most notably the Beijing Music Festival (BMF), which is the best Beijing has to offer, and continues to improve. Also in October is the Crossing Festival, run by the Living Dance Studio, featuring both European and Chinese groups, and showcasing the winners of its annual choreography competition in May. In 2006 the Informal European Theatre Meeting (IETM) showcased experimental theatre and dance in conjunction with Crossing. Hopefully 2007 will see a repeat performance.

Chinese Arts

Acrobatics

With a history of over 2,500 years, acrobatics is China's most enduring and popular art. During the Qing Dynasty (1644-1911) when Beijing's conquering Manchu class enjoyed government subsidies, the Han Chinese underclass were pushed south into the Tianqiao area, which gave rise to modern acrobatics and street theatre. Today's acrobatic troupes come largely from poorer Sichuan province, acrobatics being more lucrative than farming or factory work. Beijing has four theatres running nightly acrobatics shows; Chaoyang Theatre's is the slickest and most professional, but Tianqiao Acrobatic Theatre (*see p184*), Tiandi Theatre and Beijing Workers' Club all have their own flavour, and equally gasp-worthy stunts.

Beijing Workers' Club

7 Hufang Lu, Xuanwu, South (6352 8910). **Tickets** vary. **No credit cards. Map** p246 J12.

Tiandi Theatre

10 Dongzhimen Nandajie, Chaoyang (6416 9893). **Tickets** vary. **No credit cards. Map** p244 M7. **Photo** *p184*.

Martial arts

Chinese call Kung Fu the 'father of all martial arts', insisting that the far inferior karate and tae kwon do are only more popular because of marketing. Maybe so, but the daily *Legend of Kung Fu* show at the Red Theatre is as commercial as they come – impressive stunts and creative staging tempered with overblown effects and a hyperactive fog machine.

Red Theatre

44 Xingfu Dajie, Chongwen, South (6710 3671). **Tickets** vary. **No credit cards. Map** p247 M12.

Traditional Chinese theatre

Many of China's provinces produce opera, but in Beijing, Peking Opera is king. It sprang up in 1709 when troupes from Anhui province performed for the emperor and never went home. Banned in Communist times, it still draws an audience of elderly fans. *See p183* **Losing the plot**.

Changan Grand Theatre

7 Jianguomennei Dajie, Dongcheng, Centre (6510 1308). **Tickets** RMB 60-RMB 180. **No credit cards. Map** p244 M10.

The centre of Chinese opera, running full-length daily Peking Operas and regular performances of Kun, Ping, Yue and other local operas, with the biggest names in the business. They also hold opera festivals several times a year.

Chaoyang Theatre

36 Dongsanhuan Bei Lu, Chaoyang (6507 2421/1818). **Tickets** RMB 120-RMB 200. **No credit cards. Map** p245 P9.

The only place to see both Peking Opera highlights and acrobatics on the same night, seven days a week. Come back the next day and see Muo Shu, traditional Chinese magic – with some startling tricks.

Hu Guang Hui Guan

Hu Feng Qiao, Shi Zhi Lu Kou, Shi Na Jiao, Xuanwu, South (6351 8284). **Shows** 7.30-8.40pm daily. **Tickets** RMB 150-RMB 280. **No credit cards. Map** p246 J12.

The 200-year-old teahouse theatre is the highlight of this rather tired show – which comes complete with complimentary snacks. Go for the decor, not the performance, which is far superior at Li Yuan Theatre.

Li Yuan Theatre

1st floor Qianmen Hotel, 175 Yongan Lu, Xuanwu, South (8315 7297). **Tickets** RMB 40-RMB 280. **No credit cards. Map** p246 J12.

The best place for Peking Opera highlights. Not only are the performers several cuts above the rabble, but the theatre sells glossy colour programmes in English. Come early and watch the actors putting on their elaborate makeup. **Photo** *p183*.

Sport & Fitness

There's more than just Olympic gold on offer in Beijing.

Dongdan PE Centre. *See p191.*

Beijing's infamous air quality has saddled it with a reputation as one of the worst places on earth to work up a sweat. It's true that running around gulping in smog during a pea-souper is daft, but on one of the capital's many clear days, Beijing is no worse than any other city when it comes to breathing. The city's Olympic chiefs are keen to calm pollution fears and, come the Games, a battery of cumulonimbus-busting cannons are on hand to clear the sky of the clouds which trap the emissions.

While it may not offer a huge range of spectator sports, Beijing's status does mean it plays host to many international sporting fixtures as well as the usual round of domestic competitions. Check ticket websites http://en.piaowutong.com and www.emma.cn for details of local sporting events.

Spectator sports

Athletics

The National Stadium and National Aquatics centre may have been purpose built to host the 2008 Olympic Games, but both will remain long after Beijing extinguishes its Olympic flame.

Basketball

Most people's knowledge of Chinese basketball probably starts and ends with Yao Ming, but domestically the sport is probably growing even faster than the Houston Rockets' centre did. The profile of the sport is huge, with all NBA games – especially those featuring Yao – screened live and the Beijing Ducks often playing to a packed house, despite being confined to the out-of-town **Shougang Basketball Centre**.

All teams in the China Basketball Association (www.asia-basket.com) are allowed to import two foreign players, usually US sportsmen on the way up or down, though only one non-Chinese player is allowed on the court at any one time in a bid to give domestic players more court time. The 2006 season was cut short to allow the national team to get together for the Asian Games, once again proving that profits come second to the quest for national glory.

Shougang Basketball Centre

159 Fushi Lu, Shijingshan (8829 6158). **Tickets** RMB 20-RMB 100. **No credit cards**.

This purpose built basketball arena atop a shopping mall is home to Beijing's best-supported team. Unlike the capital's soccer team, every fixture sees the mighty Beijing Ducks play to a packed house brimming with a family-friendly atmosphere.

Football

In September 2007 China hosts the Women's World Cup Finals and its team is currently ranked ninth in the world, considerably better than the men's side, whose sole appearance at a World Cup in 2002 can be described as, literally, pointless. The next generation of talent has been training together non-stop in preparation for the Olympics and – though they are an improvement – their best example of teamwork was getting involved in a 22-man brawl with Queens Park Rangers while on a visit to London. The Workers' Stadium will host the semi-finals and final of the Olympic football competition, as well as serving as home to China Super League outfit, Beijing Guoan and, occasionally, the national side.

The sport was dragged through the mud with the Black Whistle scandal that saw a referee sentenced to ten years in jail in 2002 for his part in a widespread match fixing scandal. Capital football fans often cite this scandal as the reason they hate the city's China Super League side, Beijing Guoan, who coincidentally have a reputation for being the most profane in the country. This has led Olympic chiefs to embark on a less than successful campaign to wash their mouths out with soap, lest they embarrass the city come 2008. For up to date football fixtures and transfer gossip, log on to www.sinosoc.com.

In a footie fairytale, the Beijing Institute of Technology's football team has won its way through to the Chinese second division and, as the only blemishes they're likely to have is a rash of teenage acne, these college kids will soon become the capital's clean alternative.

Golf

Whether or not it is Beijing's turn to host the Volvo China Open (www.volvochinaopen.com) on any given April, qualifying will be held at one of the city's golf clubs prior to the final, which rotates between Beijing, Shanghai and Guangdong. *See p191* for golf courses.

Martial arts

See p181 Performing Arts.

Motor sports

Beijing is definitely Shanghai's poor cousin when it comes to vehicles screaming around in circles. The A1 Grand Prix added Beijing to its

Beat or be beaten

The hardest part about developing athletic talent is finding the raw material in the first place. With over 3,000 sports schools nationwide, China is leaving no stone unturned in ensuring that would-be gold medallists take their first step towards a podium finish.

Shichahai Sports School on the banks of Houhai Lake trains nearly 600 gymnasts and table-tennis players between the ages of five and 16. With an Olympic record at Athens better than that of Canada, this nondescript school is considered a success by many in China. But in 2005 the school grabbed the headlines for all the wrong reasons when four-time Olympic rowing champ, Sir Matthew Pinsent, visited the school and, in a subsequent BBC report, detailed what he saw as routine beatings of the pupils. The oarsman's allegations caused little stir in China, where teachers are routinely tough on kids. The IOC responded by saying that what happened to China's young sports stars was no worse than the discipline meted out in British public schools 30 years ago.

The sports academies' tough approach may not be institutional practice, but with coaches due to pocket huge bonuses if their charges win gold, it is not surprising to find that they are pushing children to the limits. There have been some calls to reform the schools, not because of the things that are done to the children, but for what is not done for them. Ye Qiaobo, China's first Winter Olympics Gold Medallist, has been their highest-profile critic – pointing out that most athletes face financial insecurity after their career ends as the school system fails to provide aspiring stars with a real education, making them ill suited to a life outside sport should their dreams not come true. With China's one-child policy leaving parents all too aware that they have all their eggs in one basket, many are choosing to direct their children to more stable careers, a fact that Ye feels will ultimately harm China's sporting programme.

New Beijinger The snowboarder

Beijing changes every day. There are so many modern high-rise buildings being built these days, which is good, but it comes at a cost. We seem to be losing something of our history along the way, and some of the colour that made Beijing what it is. It's hard to support it 100 per cent. It's both sad and exciting at the same time.

My Chinese name is Huang Xuefeng, which means 'yellow snow mountain', so I was always meant to snowboard. I was one of China's first pro-snowboarders and was ranked third in the country, but now I've retired to become a judge.

What bugs me about Beijing is the traffic – it's getting worse and worse. The city's still nice though I would advise visitors to go shopping in Xidan and hang out in the park at the Temple of Heaven, though Houhai is my favourite place in the city. I love going on the boats in summer and skating there in winter.

When I was a kid I wanted to be a speed skater so I could wear a one-piece spandex suit. No joke. Thank God things have changed. Only the X-Men can get away with that!

Old Beijingers have a lot of enthusiasm, good humour and are very active, but they are also grumpy and stuck in their ways. I think it is both difficult and exciting for them to live in such a fast-changing city.

The younger generation is open minded, arrogant and lazy, yet also quite active. The one-child policy has produced a lot of spoiled kids. They also have to study all the time, so they can get into a good school but only play computer games to unwind.

My tip for tourists is to make a local friend, or get information from local people, so they see the real Beijing and not just touristy places like the Silk Market. They should try to get off the beaten track and see the unique areas of the city, the secret spots, check out a hutong or go to a small restaurant and eat with the locals.

If I had to sum up Beijing in 10 words it is big, dry, windy, hot, delicious, traditional, yet modern, safe, lively and sucks!

Marco Huang became a pro snowboarder by accident – he didn't return to his office job after a weekend on the slopes and his boss fired him. After winning everything he could in the fledgling Chinese snowboarding scene, he now judges competitions.

race calendar in November 2006, but after many complaints about the course, which ran through an unattractive industrial area, it is unclear if it will be an annual meet. See www.a1gp.com for more details. **Goldenport Motor Park** holds race events and expos as well as letting punters on the racetrack and 4WD assault course in their own cars.

Goldenport Motor Park 1

Goldenport Dajiw, Jinzhanxiang (follow signs from Airport expressway), Chaoyang (8433 3497/www.goldenport.com.cn). **Open** 8.30am-5.30pm daily. **No credit cards**.

Although a spin around the Second Ring Road may hint otherwise, Beijing doesn't have much in the way of motor sport. Goldenport hosts a few small events, but it was telling that when the A1 Grand Prix tour came to town, it raced through an industrial estate.

Snooker

China's love affair with snooker is growing as the local potting prodigy, Ding Junhui, climbs the world rankings, with the 2006/2007 table seeing him at number nine, although that represents a slight decline in his form of the previous year. With a handful of Chinese players now on the tour circuit expect to see the country start to challenge the Western dominance of the sport. The annual China Open is held in March or April at Peking University Gym, 11 Xi Lu, Sanhuan Bei Lu, Haidian, North-west. For tickets call 6553 5699 or visit www.emma.cn. See www.worldsnooker.com for exact tournament dates.

Tennis

Ping-pong was the only tennis most people thought China played until Zheng Ji and Yang Zi's women's doubles gold at the Athens Olympics. Now the China Open is a major stop on the ATP/WTA tour with a brand new venue and big prize purses and appearance fees. See www.chinaopen.cn for up to date schedule and Racquet sports (*see p192*) for venue details.

Participation sports

Basketball

The Overseas Student Basketball league has pick-up games mid-week and at the weekend in the north-west of the city. All players are welcome to turn up and join in a game. Those that want something more fluid, just show up at Dongdan and join the day long pick-up games for RMB 5-RMB 15 per person/hour all day, every day, indoor or out.

Dongdan PE Centre

108 Chongwennei Nandajie, Dongcheng, Centre (6512 9377). **Open** *Indoor* 8am-10pm daily; *Outdoor* 6.30am-10pm daily. **No credit cards. Map** p244 L10. **Photo** *p188.*

Overseas student basketball league

Main Gym, General Administration of Sport, 4 Tiyuguan Lu, Chongwenmen, Centre.
Games 6.30-8.30pm Wed.
Haidian Gymnasium, 12 Yiheyuan Lu, Haidian.
Games 2-4pm Sun. **Cost** RMB 30. **No credit cards. Information** Mr Ding 134 0103 6390.

Cricket

After watching Sri Lanka demolish Australia in the 1996 World Cup Final, Chinese sporting authorities started to take cricket seriously as a sport. Though the results will not be seen for a decade or more, in the meantime pad up with the **Beijing Cricket Club** (http://sports.groups.yahoo.com/group/beijingcricket/), which is made up of expat Brits, Aussies, Kiwis and subcontinentals as well as a growing number of Chinese players. The matches take place on different grounds every Sunday, moving indoors for the winter.

Dragon boat racing

Dragon boat racing fans across the world are petitioning Olympic chiefs to get the sport made an event at the 2008 Games. As far as participating is concerned, if there's not ice on Houhai then the **Beijing Dragon Boat Club** go for a paddle every Sunday, sometimes even on mid-week evenings. Contact Judy Xu on 139 1002 5251, jxu@vokdams.cn or bjdragonboatfans@yahoo.com for more details.

Football

Longer-term visitors to Beijing may want to join a team in one of the thriving International Friendly Football Club's four leagues (www.triggerfish.de/iffc). Red Ball runs 5-a-side leagues and, with a bar and its own pitches downtown, is ideal for a kickabout.

Red Ball Football Club & Bar

1 Gongti Bei Lu (at the back of the carpark opposite the North Gate of the Workers' Stadium), Chaoyang (6413 2848/www.redball.com.cn). **Open** 9am-midnight daily. **Map** p244 N8.

Golf

Beijing has lots of golf courses, most of them prohibitively expensive and not up to international standards. The Beijing Golf Club is the city's most established 18 holes and is to be found not far from the airport on the east bank of the Chaobai River, Shunyi (8947 0245, www.beijinggolfclub.com).

Despite being further downtown and cramped by comparison, Beijing CBD International Golf Club is the home to the China Open when it is the capital's turn to host the event (99 Gaobeidian Lu, Chaoyang, 6738 4801, www.h-cgolf.com).

Beijing Ladies Golf Club (beijingladiesgolf@yahoo.com) and Teetime Golf Club (139 0113 6379, www.teetimechina.com) provide opportunities to join capital golfers for a round mid-week and at the weekend, respectively.

Horse riding

The grasslands of Hebei are not far from the city, meaning horse trekking is an option. High Club (5166 8022, www.highclub.cn) runs trips throughout the year. Those passionate about horse riding might want to head to Inner Mongolia, China's big sky country (*see p205*).

Racquet sports

The city has a wealth of tennis courts for those wishing to emulate Zheng Ji and Yang Zi, running from the professional (International

Tennis Centre), to the indoor high end (Kerry Centre Gym), to weather-beaten outdoor courts (Workers' Stadium).

International Tennis Centre

50 Tiantan Dong Lu, Chongwen, Centre (6715 2532). **Open** 10am-10pm Mon-Fri; 8am-8pm Sat; 9am-9pm Sun. **Cost** RMB 300/hr. **No credit cards. Map** p247 M13.

Kerry Centre Gym

1 Guanghua Lu, Chaoyang (6561 8833). **Open** 6am-11pm daily. **Cost** free for hotel guests; RMB 16,000/year. **Credit** AmEx, MC, V. **Map** p245 O9.

Workers' Stadium

Gongti Bei Lu (Walk in North Gate and turn left and then head back towards road, behind Vics), Chaoyang (6501 6655). **Open** dawn to dusk daily. **Cost** RMB 60/hr. **No credit cards. Map** p244 N8.

Running

Starting in Tiananmen Square and finishing at the Olympic Stadium, the Beijing International Marathon is a truly capital affair. To join this October run register online by late September at www.beijing-marathon.com.

If fresh air is more your thing, then try the less-polluted, but far steeper, Great Wall Marathon; held every May; there are also half marathon, 10km and 5km races (www.great-wall-marathon.com). If that's all a bit much, there's always the Hash House Harriers' weekly run and Sunday social (8448 0896, www.hash.cn).

Rugby

With the number of corporate types flooding into the city, it is hardly a surprise to find that Beijing has a booming rugby scene. The Beijing Devils (www.beijingdevils.com) hold weekly games and mid-week training for full contact and touch rugby, as well as holding social events at team HQ, the Den (*see p124*).

Skiing & snowboarding

Every winter yet another ski resort opens in the suburbs, but be warned: all are overcrowded, have icy artificial snow and the facilities are not up to the standard most skiers are used to. Best of the bunch by a long way is Beijing Nanshan Ski Village. The ski season roughly runs from November to March.

Beijing Nanshan Ski Village

Shengshuitou Village, Miyun County (8909 1909/ www.nanshanski.com). **No credit cards.**

Around 60km (37 miles) north of Beijing, this resort is made all the more accessible by shuttle buses running directly to it in ski season. Though the resort does offer some summer activities, with 12 runs and a snowboard park, it comes alive in winter.

Swimming

All the city's big hotels have pools, the best of which is at the Kerry Centre (*see p39*).

Martial arts

Thanks in part to the crossover appeal of Hong Kong movie stars such as Bruce Lee and Jackie Chan, martial arts are one of China's most visible cultural exports. Though nearly every city across the world boasts kung fu and t'ai chi schools, many tourists want the added authenticity of being schooled in *wushu* (martial arts) while in the land of the tradition's birth and there are plenty of academies willing to teach them. Usually referred to under the umbrella terms kung fu or *wushu*, Chinese martial arts comprise hundreds of different individual disciplines.

Mastering their techniques takes years of painstaking practice. The listings below are aimed at beginners and are also a good starting point for the experienced martial artist to find exactly what he or she is looking for.

Experienced practitioners with time on their hands might want to opt for a residential course at the Beijing Sports University, which also runs Chinese language courses.

Baguazhang Wushu

Ritan Park, Chaoyang (Thomas 130 2106 9688). **Cost** RMB 60 (beginners); RMB 100. **No credit cards. Map** p244 N9.

This is a school for those who want a kung fu experience straight out of the movies – with Ritan Park's old mixture of lakes, pagodas and willow trees as a backdrop and a teacher who is well into his 70s. As authentic as they come.

Beijing Sports University

1 Yuanmingyuandong Lu, Haidian, North-west (6298 9570/www.bsu.edu.cn). **No credit cards.**

The foreigners' *wushu* club (call 6298 9634) runs short- and long-term training, all of which can be combined with Chinese language courses at the university. In fact, all of the university's other courses – from physiotherapy and sports medicine to advanced kung fu – are open to overseas students, but some may require basic Chinese-language skills (call 6298 9244 for details).

Jinghua Wushu Association

Kempinski Hotel, Liangmaqiao Lu, Chaoyang (hotel 6465 3388/Jinghua 135 2228 3751/131 4107 2677/www.jinghuawushu.com). **Cost** RMB 50/class. **No credit cards. Map** p245 O7.

After spending his early life at the punishing Shaolin academy, Liu Xiaoyan set up his own school and now teaches martial arts at venues across the city. The availability of English-speaking teachers make it the ideal choice for visitors.

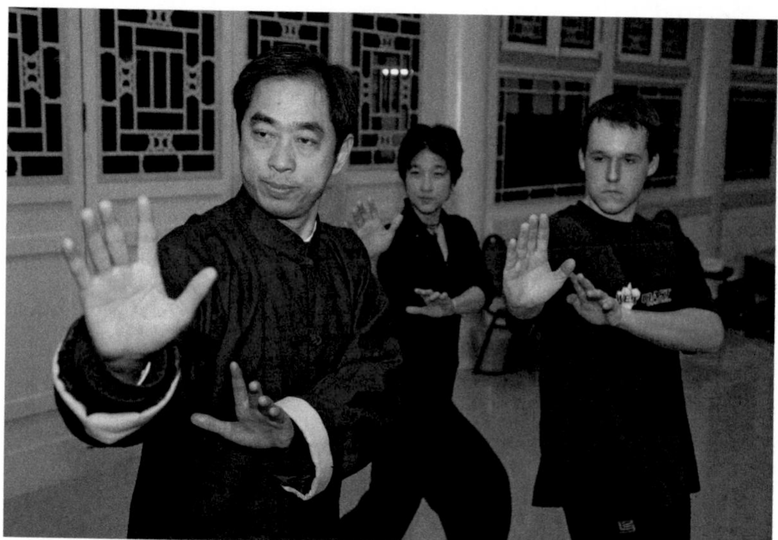

Follow the leader: expert coaching at the **Milun School of Traditional Kung Fu**.

Milun School of Traditional Kung Fu

Wangfujing, Dongcheng; Ritan Park, Chaoyang (139 1081 1934/www.kungfuinchina.com). **Cost** RMB 150/class. **No credit cards**. Map p244 L9.

A professionally run outfit, the Milun School of Traditional Kung Fu teaches *tai qi* and a range of kung fu styles in a hutong near Wangfujing. The school has an excellent website that is useful for helping those that are unfamiliar with the martial arts find just what they are looking for.

Tianyi Kung Fu Club

Beijing City International School, 77 Baiziwan Naner Lu, Chaoyang (130 5113 8804/www.tianyi culture.com). **Cost** first class is free. **No credit cards**. **Map** p245 O10.

Learn about traditional Chinese kung fu and the culture, history and philosophy behind them. Classes are taught by a seventh degree master and have English translation.

Fitness

Dance

If you're in the mood for a bit of a tango, your best bet is to head to Latinos (*see p125*) or Salsa Caribe (*see p127*); if your interest runs a little deeper, sign up with one of Beijing's affordable and professional modern dance companies. **Beijing Modern Dance Company** (*see p185*) runs hip hop, tap and modern dance classes, while with **LDTX** (*see p185*) you can dance with one of China's best modern companies.

Gyms

Those that want to fully engage with Beijing life may want to join the pensioners in using the brightly coloured street gyms that dot the city. If you really want to work up a sweat, head to any big hotel – all have good gyms with day rates negotiable. The best stand-alone gym is **Evolution Fitness**.

Evolution Fitness Center

Dabeiyao Dasha, Chaoyang (6567 0266/www.evolution-fitness.com). **Open** 6.30am-10.30pm Mon-Fri; 8am-9pm Sat, Sun. **Cost** RMB 800/mth; RMB 3,300/yr. **Credit** AmEx, MC, V. **Map** p245 O10. **Other locations**: Evolution Fitness Centre Blue Castle Center, 3 Xidawang Lu (300m north of Xiandaicheng Soho New Town), Chaoyang (8599 7650).

Hiking

The hills around Beijing offer some great hiking. More intrepid travellers might like to head to Huairou, from where you can get minibuses to Mutianyu and Huanghua sections of the wall (*see 201*). The Fragrant Hills north-west of the city also offer good accessible walking near the Summer Palace and the Botanical Gardens – *see p84* **The North-west**.

Those wanting something more organised should contact West China Adventure Tours (135 8168 2703, www.westchina.net.cn) or Beijing Hikers (139 1002 5516, www.beijinghikers.com).

Trips Out of Town

Features

Map

The Great Wall at Simatai. *See p203.*

Trips Out of Town
South-east Asia
BEIJING
Pyongyang
Seoul
Tokyo
Yellow Sea
Sea of Japan
CHINA
East China Sea
Shanghai
Taipei
Hanoi
Macau
Hong Kong
South China Sea
PACIFIC OCEAN
Vientiane
Bangkok
Manila
Ho Chi Minh City
Kuala Lumpur
Singapore
Magdagachi
Svobodnyy
Zavitinsk
Gora
Borzya
Hailar
Trans Manchurian Railway
Choybalsan
ULAANBAATAR
Tamsagbulag
Qiqihar
Jiamusi
MONGOLIA
Trans Mongolian Railway
Harbin
Jixi
Saynshand
Mudanjiang
Changchun
Jilin
Erenhot
Siping
Tumen
Inner Mongolia (p205)
Fusong
Fuxin
Shenyang
Fushun
Ch'ongjin
Jinzhou
Benxi
Hohhot
Zhangjiakou
Anshan
N. KOREA
Great Wall
Eastern Qing Tombs (p199)
Jinxi
Baotou
Ming Tombs (p199)
Sinuiju
The Great Wall (p201)
Datong
Qinhuangdao
Dandong
Hungnam
BEIJING
Tangshan
Korea Bay
PYONGYANG (p210)
Tianjin
Gulf of Chihli
Wuzhai
Baoding
Luda
Sea of Japan
Yinchuan
Cangzhou
Taiyuan
Shijiazhuang
Yantai
Inch'on
SEOUL
Handan
Jinan
S. KOREA
Yellow Sea
CHINA
Qingdao
Jining
Pusan
Zhengzhou
Kaifeng
Zaozhuang
Luoyang
Xi'an (p207)
Xuzhou
Fukuoka
Sundian
JAPAN
Bengbu
Nanyang
Nagasaki
Huainan
Nanjing
Hefei
Kagoshima
Suzhou
Wuhu
Shanghai
Yangtze
Yichang
Wuhan
Hangzhou
East China Sea
Ningbo
Zhuji
Nanchang
Quzhou
0
300 miles
Changsha
Wenzhou
0
300 kms
© Copyright Time Out Group 2007
Guiyang
Hengyang
Fuzhou

Getting Started

Climbing the Great Wall and other escapes.

Stepping out at **Simatai**. *See p203.*

Besides being the nation's cultural and political capital, Beijing is China's transport hub, and thus a great jumping off point to explore the north. Admittedly, this arid land isn't quite as picturesque as the soggy south, lacking water buffalo, verdant rice paddies and farmers in conical bamboo hats. However, as the first line of defence against the galloping hordes from the steppes, North China has been the base for numerous ruling dynasties, leaving an impressive number of world-famous relics. Not to mention that venturing outside grey Beijing is a welcome return to colour – the skies are brilliant blue, and farmers hang golden sheaves of corn outside their red brick houses.

Many Beijingers take weekend trips to the countryside to stay in village houses, breathe some fresh air and enjoy basic but hearty home cooking. Visitors may want to see some of China's treasures, too, and with a little planning, you can do both. Within easy reach are the **Ming Tombs** (*see p199*) and the far more impressive – and less popular – **Eastern Qing Tombs** (*see p200*). To balance the imperial narrative with some insights into how ordinary people lived, take a side-trip to **Chuandixia** (*see p200*), a crumbling little village full of courtyard houses with a population of no more than 80.

The best place to combine rural culture with ancient wonders is the **Great Wall of China** (*see p201*), a must-see for any visitor to East Asia. Avoid the tour-bus cacophony at Badaling (the closest location to Beijing) and hold out for sections of 'wild wall', particularly in Simatai, where the crumbling brick held together by rice paste remains unpaved and untouched, and the silent forest stretches out for miles. Local village houses offer meals and accommodation at reasonable rates, where guests can pile on to a *kang*, a hollow brick bed found in Northern China that is heated in winter. Other Westerners camp out in the guard towers, getting beer and firewood deliveries from local villagers. Great Wall camping is not technically legal, but not strictly prohibited either, and may be your best night in Beijing.

Xi'an (*see p207*) is practically a pilgrimage for the Chinese and a short, enjoyable visit for many Western visitors. An ancient walled city that was capital to eleven dynasties, Xi'an is most famous for its terracotta warriors, that were buried 2,200 years ago with emperor Qin Shi Huang. Discovered in 1974 by farmers drilling for water, these 8,000 earthenware warriors and horses with their distinct facial expressions fast became the archaeological marvel of the century. Xi'an is not a place to avoid crowds, at least around the warriors, but

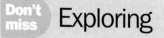

Don't miss Exploring

Chuandixia
For its cobbled streets and glimpses of an older China. *See p200.*

Inner Mongolia
You know you've always wanted to sleep in a yurt. *See p205.*

Pyongyang
And the writings of Kim Jong Il. *See p210.*

Simatai
The Wall at its wildest. *See p203.*

Xi'an
Buy your very own terracotta warrior. *See p207.*

Everyone's blown away by **The Great Wall**. *See p201.*

it is one of the most important cities of the ancient world, and a lap around the city on top of the wall is a good way to end the day.

If you've had enough of urban vistas, a trip to the grasslands of Nei Mongu or **Inner Mongolia** (*see p205*) will cure your crowd claustrophobia. Those expecting lush, rippling fields will be disappointed; for most of the year the grass is more like yellowed Astroturf, reaching 'healthy lawn' status only in summer. But gently sloping hills and the expanse of brilliant sky are greater rewards, and Mongolian festivities such as lamb roasts, horseback riding, copious alcohol and sleeping in a cosy yurt (Mongolian tent) make for a worthwhile trip.

For something completely different, try leaving China altogether and take a short flight into the surreal. **Pyongyang** in North Korea (*see p210*) will be an expensive weekend, but one you'll never forget. The most isolated country on earth and one of the few remaining police states, the city has a surprising amount of charm, mostly due to exceptionally warm people who, even though they have been indoctrinated against all things Western (American in particular), don't hold it against you.

TOURIST INFORMATION

For domestic trips, the China International Travel Service offices may be helpful – try their website at www.cits.com. For discounts on airline flights, go to www.elong.net, http://english.ctrip.com/, or www.flychina.com.

However, for Xi'an, Inner Mongolia and even Pyongyang, trains are the way. China has a beautiful landscape and Chinese trains are the warmest, friendliest conveyances around – the second class 'hard beds' are reasonably comfortable, and sitting in your mini-cabin with five Chinese people who give you food and cluck over your poor eating habits may be one of your better China experiences. If CITS can't help with tickets, you can go to the International Hotel (86 10 6512 6688), across from the Beijing Train Station; they will book and provide your tickets for a RMB 30 surcharge, which is easier than dealing with station hysteria, especially at Beijing West. Round trip tickets are not always available, so stay flexible.

Details for getting to the Great Wall and to Xi'an are given in those sections – as well as suggestions for bicycle and hiking trips.

BASICS

Like everywhere else, but especially in China, travel is easier during the off-season – try particularly to avoid the Chinese 'Golden Weeks' (New Year, May 1-7 and October 1-7, *see p149* **Golden weeks**), which see 1.2 billion people on the move, or at least so it seems. If you do have to travel at these times the pricier planes may be your only option, as train tickets will be impossible to find, and the crowds will defy physics (you may see passengers climbing in the windows to get to their seats).

As for accommodation, most prices are negotiable, but you'll need your passport everywhere you go. An overnight stay in a village may mean you have to be registered with the local police, but don't worry about it until they show up, as it's usually a simple process. And it's wise not to send the taxi away before you've confirmed where you're staying, since some low-rent guesthouses still refuse foreigners. This is a holdover from an old law (now changed) which held the guesthouse owner to blame if the guest got hurt.

Ming and Qing Tombs

Imperial bling.

The turbulence, not to say vandalism, of the last century destroyed much of China's past, but at least the tombs of the last two ruling dynasties survived, and conveniently they are within easy reach of Beijing. Thirty miles (45 kilometres) to the north are the Ming Tombs, the final resting place of 13 emperors, while some 125 kilometres (78 miles) east of the capital are the less heavily touristed Eastern Qing Tombs, with a mere five emperors, but a crown of spent queens and a positive harem of extinct concubines. But if you prefer your history alive rather than mouldering, head to Chuandixia, 90 kilometres (56 miles) north-west of the city, to see a cobblestoned Ming Dynasty village left bobbing in the wake of China's race to the future.

HISTORY

The Ming Dynasty ruled China from 1368 to 1644 and can count the Great Wall, unification of the empire and sea explorations – which may or may not have reached the United States – as some of its achievements. But all governments fall in the end and after a peasant uprising the final Ming Emperor, Chongzhen, hanged himself in Jingshun Park, behind the Forbidden City in Beijing. Ming gave way to Qing and the new ruling family consolidated its grip on China, bringing imperial influence to its height. But during the 1800s, faced with international pressure, massive rebellions and defeats in wars, the dynasty began its long decline. The Qing were finally overthrown when Empress Dowager Longyu abdicated on behalf of the last emperor, Puyi, on 12 February 1912.

Ming Tombs

Lying 50 kilometers (31 miles) to the north-west of Beijing are the Ming Tombs, the final resting place for 13 emperors. The complex has recently undergone considerable restoration work and at the time of writing only three tombs are open to the public. The highlight is Changling, Emperor Yongle's tomb. He found the peaceful spot early in the 15th century and decided that it was where he and his ancestors would lie. His complex is like a miniature Forbidden City, with dark crimson palaces and wooden halls.

Another mausoleum, Dingling, was the final home of Emperor Wangli: as you descend to the tomb, look out for his matching coloured spirit luggage to help him along his way. The final tomb open is Zhaoling, home to Emperor Zhu Zaigou. A few halls have been restored,

Eastern Qing Tombs. *See p200.*

Crumbling, quaint **Chuandixia**.

but the highlight here is wandering around the atmospheric ruins outside the tomb.

Getting there

Take tourist buses 1, 2, 3, 4 or 5 (RMB 50) from the Qianmen bus ranks. If time is tight a trip to the Tombs can be combined with a visit to the Badaling section of the Great Wall. Buses from Qianmen go to both destinations, but you could also ask your hotel to arrange a taxi for around RMB 400.

Eastern Qing Tombs

The Ming Tombs may be better known, but you get fewer tourists and more bodies for your buck at the Eastern Qing Tombs. Five emperors, 15 empresses, 136 concubines, three princes, and two princesses are here, all entombed between 1663 and 1935. The first to be buried was Emperor Shunzhi, and the last was an imperial concubine in 1935. The tombs are in a valley at the foot of Changduan Mountain, and their gold-tiled roofs surrounded by pine trees make an attractive picture. The highlight though is the atmospheric tomb of the Dowager Empress Cixi. Decades of work went into construction and when the Dragon Lady finally died, her coffin was overlain with a mattress of gold thread and pearls, and surrounded by 200 jewels and 108 precious images of the Buddha. The tomb has been plundered, but it remains an amazing sight.

Getting there

By public transport, catch a bus headed for Zunhua from the Sihui long distance bus station which is just south of the Sihui metro station. Get off at Shimen and then catch a taxi for RMB 10 to the tombs. Expect to pay around RMB 300 for a return taxi trip from Beijing.

Chuandixia

Chuandixia dates from the Ming Dynasty and was until recently virtually unknown. Now it attracts film crews and tourists looking for the charming China of days past. Chuandixia lies on an ancient trade route, and merchants used to rest in the village before continuing to Beijing. When the road became redundant in the 1950s, Chuandixia's fortunes declined – consequently, the village's 70 courtyards are near pristine. It is possible to make a single day trip of it, but better to stay overnight in a family home (don't worry about looking for a place: the locals will find you) for just RMB 20. You'll sleep on a traditional *kang* bed – toasty warm in winter as it's heated – and be fed all the fresh home cooked food you could possibly want.

Getting there

From Pingguoyuan metro station take bus 929 (RMB 8, 3 hours) to the village entrance. Alternatively, negotiate a taxi from the station for about RMB 100.

The Great Wall

There's no getting round it – this is a world-class attraction.

The view west from **Simatai**. *See p203.*

One of the Seven Great Clichés of the Modern World has to be that the Great Wall of China is visible from space. It was the lead off question journalists posed to China's first astronaut when he came back down to earth in 2003. 'The earth looked very beautiful from space, but I did not see our Great Wall,' lamented Yang Liwei, after 21 hours in orbit.

But you *can* see it from an aeroplane and if you're lucky and the day is clear you'll catch sight of the wall ten or 15 minutes before landing at Beijing international airport. From above you can see how it rises and falls with the contours of the hills to the north of the capital. If you flew the length of it – over 6,437 kilometres (4,000 miles) from Shanhaiguan on the coast to the Gobi Desert – you would see that there is no single continuous Great Wall but rather a series of ramparts.

HISTORY

From the 5th century BC on, northern China had defensive walls. Between the 3rd century BC and the 17th AD a succession of dynasties joined up huge sections to create a structure that had as much symbolic as military value.

However, it is the Ming Dynasty that is best known for constructing the Wall. After the Ming army's defeat by the fearsome Mongols in 1449, the Ming began building barriers along the northern border of China. Unlike earlier fortifications, the Ming construction was stronger and more elaborate, using bricks and stone instead of earth. Most of the sections near Beijing are Ming relics.

Since 1984, when Deng Xiaoping declared, 'Let us love our country and restore our Great Wall,' there has been much rebuilding and modifying of the extant structures: too much, some critics argue. While the renovated sections with their handrails and chairlifts make for easy treks and great photos, the rougher, run-down sections are more evocative and peaceful.

SIGHTSEEING

Well, there's only one sight – the Wall itself. The shops, museums and restaurants are just distractions. But on the right day, the Great Wall is one of those experiences – like Venice or the Iguazú Falls – that still can catch you unawares, no matter how many pictures and documentaries you've seen beforehand.

In winter, when the weather is crisp and the sky clear, the sight of the Wall against the parched mountains is extraordinary. Along some sections there are likely to be only a

Gate at **Shanhaiguan**, where the Wall begins its 4,000 mile journey. *See p201.*

handful of tourists out of season and you will hear birdsong and a whispering breeze. Modern Beijing's bustle and building boom seem a mere blip when considered from this lofty bulwark that has been here, in one shape or another, for 25 centuries.

From the capital there are four main options for one- or two-day trips to see the Wall: joining the crowds at Badaling or Mutianyu, both within a couple of hours of the capital, strapping on your walking boots for a climb at Huanghua, or travelling further afield to reach arguably the most striking section, Simatai.

Badaling

Mass tourism congregates at Badaling, 70 kilometres (44 miles) from the capital, where a restored section from the Ming period provides a grand – but perhaps too perfect – backdrop for photos, though it might be tricky to avoid having random tourists in your pics as it can get jam-packed. There is also the **Great Wall Museum** (entrance included in the ticket price) which has exhibitions on the history of the Wall, a look at the different dynasties connected with the structure and warfare on the Wall.

Badaling is the nearest section to Beijing and it can feel like everyone in the city has chosen the same day as you to visit. The government has developed this section into a full-on tourist destination and with its slide and fast-food outlets, this section is not for everyone. Having said that, if you are short of time and end up here, you can get a sense of the wonder of the Wall by walking as far east or west as your legs will take you and escaping the crowds.

Great Wall Badaling

Badaling Expressway, exit 17, Yanqing county (6912 1737/6912 2222/http://badaling.gov.cn/history/history.htm). **Open** 7am-6pm daily. **Admission** RMB 40; RMB 22.50 senior/student; RMB 20 child over 1.2m; free child under 1.2m; slightly higher in summer. **No credit cards**.

Where to eat & stay

There is a Starbucks and a California Beef Noodle King USA, a popular Chinese (despite the name) noodle fast-food restaurant. There are also many local restaurants at the entrance and parking lot area. Hotels include the luxurious Kempinksi managed **Commune by the Great Wall** (Badaling Exwy Great Wall exit (exit 16) at Shuiguan, 8118 1888, www.communebythegreatwall.com/en, doubles RMB 2,100) and the more affordable **Days Inn Beijing Rose Valley Hotel** (8 Sunshine Road, 8118 2300, www.daysinn.com, doubles RMB 300-RMB 500).

Getting there

By bus

By bus 919 from Deshengmen (RMB 12); tour bus 1 from Qianmen.

By car

By car Badaling Expressway to Badaling exit (exit 17), follow signs.

By taxi

By taxi approximately RMB 170 each way.

Mutianyu

To take some pressure off Badaling, the authorities have developed the Mutianyu section – 90 kilometres (56 miles) north-east of Beijing – into the second most visited part of the Wall. This section of restored wall dates from 1386 and was built on the foundations laid in the 6th century by the Qi Dynasty. The tourist junk available at the entrance can detract somewhat from the experience, but once you're on the Wall, it's easy to forget the tat. If you want to make the climb as easy as possible, chairlifts whisk people up to the watchtowers and you can whizz down on a slide, essentially little cars that let you twist and turn your way down the mountain if the mood takes you.

Great Wall Mutianyu

Mutianyu Town, Huairou county (6162 6505/6162 6022/www.mutianyugreatwall.com). **Open** 7am-6pm daily. **Admission** RMB 40; RMB 20 concessions. **No credit cards.**

Where to eat & stay

There are several local restaurants by the entrance. **Chang Cheng Shan Zhuang** (Mutianyu Town, 6968 6022, 6162 6395, doubles RMB 100-RMB 150) is a small Chinese hotel with restaurant, sauna and the inevitable karaoke equipment.

Getting there

By bus

Bus 916 from Dongzhimen to Huairou and then change to centre 8 minibus (*zhong ba*) to Mutianyu; tour bus 6 from Xuanwumen on weekends and holidays.

By car

From Sanyuan Qiao on 3rd Ring Road, take Jingshun Lu (which turns into National Road 101) to Huairou Qiao and turn toward Huairou. Follow signs to Qingchunlu Roundabout and turn to Huaisha Lu. Keep driving to Mutianyu Roundabout and follow signs to the Great Wall.

By taxi

Approximately RMB 230 each way.

Huanghuacheng

Just 60 kilometres (37 miles) outside Beijing, Huanghuacheng is a less developed part of the Wall. It is dangerously dilapidated in some sections, but that means less tourists and lots of empty, dramatic panoramas. In fact, the main danger at Huanghuacheng used to be from locals keen to extort money from visitors and not above carrying pitchforks to persuade unwilling tourists to part with the cash. But the government has stamped that out, and now everyone must pay a flat rate of RMB 25 before entering the area.

Great Wall Huanghuacheng

Chengguan Town, Huairou county (6165 1111/6165 1818/www.huanghuacheng.com). **Open** 8.30am-5pm daily. **Admission** RMB 25; RMB 12.50 students; free children under 1.2m. **No credit cards.**

Getting there

By bus

Catch bus 916 from Dongzhimen to Huairou which leaves every 20 mins from 5.30am to 6.30pm. When you arrive at the transit station, change to a minibus to Huanghuacheng or take a taxi for about RMB 30.

By car

Take Badaling Expressway and exit at Changping Xiguan and follow signs toward the Ming Tombs. Turn right when you reach Changling Tomb toward Jiuduhe. Turn left at the Jiuduhe intersection and continue to the Huanghuazhen intersection, then turn left. Once you reach the 'Y' intersection, bear right and continue until you reach the Wall.

By taxi

Approximately RMB 145 each way.

Simatai

For a more atmospheric experience, and a decent bit of trekking, head for Simatai, 110 kilometres (68 miles) out of town. The section is divided into two parts separated by a river and chain bridge. If you are on a day trip, visit the eastern section and walk up the steep but well preserved paths and turrets, passing through 15 watchtowers; there is also the option of a chairlift that takes visitors part-way up, cutting out most of the steeper climbs.

There are towers at regular intervals, providing natural rest- and photo-stops. For a major trek, head west and do a 10-kilometre (6-mile) walk along the ramparts to the village of Jinshanling, where you can spend the night.

Returning from either section, you can stroll back and let your knees take a kicking, or cut the journey short by using the flying fox zip-line which hurtles you over a river and down to the entrance area in a matter of seconds.

Great Wall Simatai

Gubeikou, Miyun county (6903 1051/8353 1111/www.simatai-greatwall.net/English.asp). **Open** 8am-5pm daily. **Admission** RMB 40; RMB 20 senior/student; RMB 20 child over 1.2m; free child under 1.2m. **No credit cards**.

Where to eat & stay

Apart from the usual slew of restaurants by the entrance to Simatai, there is a newly renovated hostel with private and shared rooms: **Simatai Great Wall International Youth Hostel** (Simatai Great Wall Scenic Area, 6903 5311, dormitory bed RMB 70).

Getting there

By bus

Bus 980 from Dongzhimen to Miyun Zhongdian station (terminal stop), then take a taxi from there; tour bus from Qianmen and Xuanwumen on weekends and holidays only.

By car

Take the Jingcheng Highway past Miyun. Turn right at Tanghe Bridge and follow signs to Simatai for 10 km (6 miles).

By taxi

Approximately RMB 700-RMB 800 round trip including 4-5 hr wait by driver.

Guided Great Wall tours

The following firms offer package-type trips to the Great Wall:

Beijing Xinhua International Tours

2001-1-1, Nanxiaojie, Guangqumen, Chongwen (6716 0201 ext 1006/1007/www.tour-beijing.com). **Rates** RMB 400-RMB 550/day. **Credit** MC, V.

The company offers private tours to Badaling or Simatai. Other tours available combine Badaling with the Ming Tombs or Forbidden City. The price includes transfer, guide, entrance ticket, pick up from hotel and lunch.

China Adventure Tours

5/F Elephant Plaza, A1 Dong Binhe Lu, Dongcheng (5109 9162/8621 6278/www.cnadventure.com). **Rates** RMB 420-RMB 500/day. **Credit** MC, V.

Hike across the Great Wall from Jinshanling to Simatai. The price includes transfer, guide, entrance ticket and pick up from hotel.

Gray Line

5/F Grand Rock Plaza, 13 Xinzhongxili, Dongcheng (5979 8038/www.grayline.com). **Rates** *Badaling* 370; RMB 290/child 3-11; *Mutianyu* RMB 263; RMB 220/child 3-11. **Credit** AmEx, MC, V.

Climb the Great Wall at Badaling and explore the Ming Tombs on a one day trip or spend half a day at Mutianyu with a stop at the Beijing Cloisonne Factory on the way back. Price includes transfer, guide, entrance ticket, pick up from hotel and lunch.

Commune by the Great Wall. *See p202.*

Inner Mongolia

Get in touch with your inner nomad.

'Your yurt is within spitting distance, sir!'

Horse riding through the green steppes, calling a yurt home for the night, or experiencing life on the grasslands is why tourists come to Hohhot, capital city of Inner Mongolia. But if you come expecting to find the descendants of the Golden Horde in all their legendary ferocity, that might prove difficult. Bows and arrows are definitely a thing of the past. Today, Hohhot is a bustling city with a mix of young adults blowing serious money at one of Zhongshan Xilu's clothing stores and old men trying to make some money selling roasted nuts and dried fruit on the street.

HISTORY

In the 13th century, the Mongolian people rose from the desert to form the second greatest empire in history (the British Empire was the biggest) and the largest continuous one. First, the Mongol army led by Genghis Khan (meaning 'Universal King' in Mongolian) charged through the Gobi Desert with one goal in mind: to take control of the capital of Northern China, Beijing.

The unwitting Chinese were unaware of what lay in store for them at the hands of the Khan. For years, the Great Wall – which was built with the sole intention of keeping the Mongols out – had protected the capital and its emperor. But for Genghis the Wall was nothing but a long fence. In 1215 Genghis Khan simply led his 50,000 strong army around it and took the city after a siege. With China – all 10 million square kilometres (3.9 million square miles) of it – under centralised rule, the great Khan was able to set his sights on conquering the world. Kublai, the last ruling Khan, died in 1294 and control slipped from the nomads.

By the end of the 14th century the Mongolians had reverted to their roots as roaming, warring tribes until Beijing gained complete control in the 18th century. Although he ruled nearly 800 years ago, Genghis Khan's legacy continues and he remains a hero in Mongolian eyes.

Sightseeing

The **Inner Mongolia Museum** (Hulunbeier Lu, 9.30am-4.30pm daily, RMB 10, free under-14s) provides a good introduction to the country through well-preserved artefacts, traditional costumes, farming and battle implements, and a dinosaur exhibit. An English-speaking history professor from the local university takes tours from RMB 80, but be sure to book ahead.

Activities

A trip to the grasslands is Hohhot's main attraction. Riding on the steppes and taking up residence in a yurt only takes place in the summer and even then you need to bring your winter woolies. **China International Travel Service** (CITS Inner Mongolia Hotel office, Wulanchabu Xilu, 047 1693 8888 ext 8123) conducts horse-riding and grassland tours. One-day tours cost from RMB 250 per person, two-days from RMB 300 per person.

Horse riding on the grasslands costs an extra RMB 50 per hour. It costs extra to stay overnight in a yurt and what you pay (which will include breakfast) depends on your bargaining skills; RMB 30-RMB 80 per person is the current rate. Taxi drivers and tour operators around the train station also provide private tours. Prices vary, though expect to pay anywhere from RMB 350-RMB 500 per person, and extra if staying overnight; just remember to smile while you bargain.

Where to eat & drink

During the summer months, Hohhot streets come alive: vendors set up small eateries complete with miniature tables and chairs, and serve tasty meat kebabs and local beer until the wee hours. Other food vendors follow suit, setting up nut and fruit stalls, and sell their goods by the *jin.*

Unfortunately, from October to April, it's a very different scene as everything moves indoors due to the unfriendly winter weather. Luckily the winter staple, Mongolian hot pot, will warm cold bones in no time and any of the small eateries near the train station do a good job in serving out generous helpings of meat, tofu and green veggies to add to seasoned broth.

For a more up-market sit-down affair (with less meat) try **Malaqin Fandian** (34 Xinhua Street, Hohhot, 047 1692 6685, 11.30am-5.30pm). Dishes are well presented and cooked to perfection. The impressive variety includes Peking duck, seafood, and plenty of vegetarian options; a meal for two costs around RMB 120. There's a pictured menu and staff are friendly but don't speak English.

Western food and coffee (at Western prices) can only be found at hotel restaurants; the best bet is the Holiday Inn Hohhot (*see below*).

Where to stay

A few years ago, Hohhot's accommodation ranged from filthy to passable. How times have changed. For those non-yurt nights, Hohhot now boasts plush 5-star accommodation, boutique-like hotels and even a Holiday Inn. Wedding receptions held at swish hotels are a regular feature on weekends so have your camera poised – the happy couple are more than obliging when it comes to posing for a pic.

Upgrading from three-star lodgings, the **Inner Mongolia Hotel** (Wulanchabu Xilu, Hohhot, 047 1693 8888, fax 047 1620 3511, www.nmghotel.com, doubles RMB 660) has recently reopened and let its new five-star status go to its head. The brochure reads, 'the civilized palace of Inner Mongolia grassland', and with ceiling to floor faux gold fittings, you might just have to agree.

Its next-door neighbour, the **Xincheng Guesthouse** (40 Hulun Nanlu, Hohhot, 047 1629 2288, doubles from RMB 350) is a comfortable retreat in a beautiful garden setting, but more tasteful in decoration and low-key without compromising on service or facilities. The **Holiday Inn Hohhot** (185 Zhongshan Xilu, Hohhot 047 1635 1888, fax 047 1635 1666, doubles from RMB 435) is a new addition, with all the services and comfort you'd expect from this chain.

Getting around

If you manage to get one, taxis are a cheap and a fuss-free way to explore the city. The city is quite compact so making your way around won't cost more than RMB 15-RMB 20. However, taxis are quite scarce; locals prefer getting around on zippy scooters, motorcycles and bicycles. Improve your chances of catching a cab by waiting at one of the yellow and red 'taxi stand' signs scattered around the city.

Public buses travel to most attractions and cost RMB 1, departing and terminating in front of the train station on Chezhan Xijie.

Getting there

By air

China Eastern Airlines, Air China and Hainan Airlines fly from Beijing to Hohhot daily from RMB 310 one way, depending on the season. Taxis from the airport to the city centre take around 20 minutes and cost approximately RMB 22.

By bus

There are 13 buses departing daily from Beijing's Liuliqiao Long Distance Bus Station to Hohhot Long Distance Bus Station. There are also 13 buses leaving Hohhot Long Distance Bus Station (front of the train station) to Liuliqiao; tickets RMB 130 one way.

By train

Trains to Hohhot depart from Beijing West train station daily. Train number 2085 leaves Beijing West at 8.46pm and arrives in Hohhot at 8.37am. Tickets are RMB 97 for a hard sleeper and RMB 156 for a soft sleeper.

A slightly faster train is the K89, leaving Beijing West at 9pm daily and arriving in Hohhot at 7.20am. Hard sleeper costs RMB 165 and RMB 254 for a soft sleeper. The fastest and most convenient train departing Hohhot for Beijing West is the K90 at 9.12pm daily, arriving in Beijing at 7.22am. Hard sleeper costs RMB 165 and RMB 254 for a soft sleeper. Alternatively, the K44 is the fastest morning train and departs at 8.52am and takes 10 hours and 28 minutes, arriving Beijing West station at 7.20pm.

When to go

The ideal time to visit Inner Mongolia is from May to September. Temperatures are pleasant during the day and the grasslands are at their greenest. In the evenings the temperature plummets and it's a good idea to pack warm clothes if staying overnight. It isn't fun venturing out in severe winter temperatures, so avoid visiting then, if you can.

Xi'an

Onward Xi'an soldiers, marching as to war.

The original capital of China, Xi'an is an archaeologist's dream. Take some rich clay soil, mix it with the ancient centre of the Chinese universe, toss in a Neolithic settlement, garnish with the start of the Silk Road, and you have some pretty magnificent history. And the city does a fine job in selling and telling its stories to tourists too.

The big draw of course is the **Army of Terracotta Warriors** – thousands of life-sized soldiers crafted more then 2,000 years ago to protect the ghost of China's first real emperor, Qin Shi Huang. Visitors can inspect them in their original ranks precisely where they were dug up. The city itself is ringed by spruced-up Ming Dynasty walls complete with watchtowers; its museums are full of treasures that beat anything Beijing can offer hands down; and there are the remains – including human skeletons – of a 6,000-year-old village at Banpo. Modern day Xi'an is not so bad either. Its Muslim Hui minority flavour the city with their spicy barbecue meats and their faith – the Great Mosque is China's biggest.

The big drawback is the pollution. The air can be so filthy it gets difficult to breathe. Plan a surgical trip, in and out in two or three days, and it won't be so bad. Because Xi'an is one of China's top tourist spots, arrange a visit during winter when the cold scares the crowds away. It's not too chilly for a Brit, though.

HISTORY

Xi'an is China's original capital and it's been the country's number one city for longer than any other Chinese urban centre, Beijing included. The Western Zhou Dynasty planted its roots in Hao, a stone's throw away, back in the 11th century BC. But the city proper was established around 200 BC under the Han Dynasty. They called it Chang'an, or city of perpetual peace. Ironic that, since it was torn apart in the first century AD. After a few hundred years or so of decline, Xi'an regained its former glory and then some, becoming a centre of Buddhist learning, thanks to its position as the eastern terminus on the Silk Road. By the Sui and Tang Dynasties (6th to 10th centuries AD) it was one of Asia's biggest and most important capitals. It was a city of more than a million people, with broad avenues, bustling with traders from Central Asia and the Far East. It lost out to Luoyang with the fall of the Tang Dynasty, but got some attention in the 14th century from the Ming who rebuilt the city walls and erected bell and drum towers. Both wall and towers still stand today.

The city would not hit the history books again until 1936 with the so-called Xi'an Incident, when KMT leader Chiang Kaishek was caught still in his pyjamas at a hot springs just outside the city. Chiang's own men forced him at gunpoint to sign a truce with the Communists so the two parties could unite against the Japanese invaders.

Nowadays Xi'an is a prosperous industrial city of over seven million people.

Sightseeing

It's one of history's little ironies that the **Army of Terracotta Warriors** (029 8139 9001, 8.30am-5.30pm daily; *photo p208*) attracts millions of tourists every year, yet it was designed to be a secret. The site was first discovered in 1974 by a group of farmers, 2,200 years after it was built and buried. There are three giant pits sheltered under hangars – visitors look down on the rows and rows of baked earth men, in battle formation, from above. Each life-sized figure – so far more than 8,000 have been scooped out of the clay – has a different facial expression. There are wise generals, angry officers, proud charioteers, and teenage foot soldiers. There are even some troops that look rather camp. It's worthwhile hiring an English-speaking guide (RMB 50) since the signs are not very helpful. Tickets cost RMB 90 (16 Mar-14 Nov) or RMB 65 (15 Nov-15 Mar). Note that flash photography is prohibited. Sadly, the Chinese tendency to add tack to everything has infiltrated even here. Visitors must walk through a wretched Qin Dynasty-themed shopping plaza to get to the real thing.

The army was built to protect China's first emperor, Qin Shi Huang – the main character in the epic film *Hero* – in his afterlife. His giant underground necropolis is about a mile away at the foot of an extinct volcano called Mount Li. According to records, his booby-trapped tomb complex is stuffed with palaces, treasures and a scale model of the universe with flowing mercury to represent water and pearls to stand in for stars. Unfortunately, you can't go into it as it hasn't yet been excavated – there are

Standing to attention forever. The **Army of Terracotta Warriors**. *See p207.*

technical problems to overcome – but you can potter about on a grassy mound on top of the necropolis. Tickets to the **Tomb of Qin Shi Huang** cost RMB 25; beware of ferocious souvenir sellers.

Down the road is **Huaqing Pool** (38 Huaqing Road, Lintong county, 029 8381 2004, Mar-Nov RMB 70, Dec-Feb RMB 40), a pretty palace and garden complex with hot springs at the foot of Mount Li. Emperors from as far back as the Western Zhou used to bathe here, but it was the Tang noblemen who went wild and turned it into a resort. But the pools have grown a little murky over the years.

On the way back into town are the remains of the Neolithic village of **Banpo**, thought to be home to a matriarchal settlement of farmers that flourished around 4500 BC. Visitors can look down on the fossilised imprints of huts. More eerie are the exposed graves complete with sleeping skeletons and the remains of pottery urns in which children were buried. Tickets go for RMB 20; English-language cassette guides cost RMB 10.

There is plenty to see in the town itself. Cop a low-flying, bird's-eye view of the city by cycling a full circuit on top of the city walls. Standing on the remains of Ming Dynasty fortifications, the 12-metre (39-feet) walls, recently refurbished and complete with impressive crenellations and watchtowers, encircle Xi'an's core. There is one gate in each of the four compass directions – the Silk Road would have passed through the westernmost archway. Entrance is RMB 40 (main access is via the South Gate). Bikes can be rented on top for RMB 20 for two hours – that's just enough time to pedal the 14 or so kilometres (nine miles) for one circumnavigation, pollution allowing.

Just north of the South Gate and standing in the middle of Xi'an's main crossroads is the three-eaved **Bell Tower** (Chang'an Lu Nan Dajie, 8.30am-5.30pm daily), which dates from the 14th century. It's more impressive from the outside; the inside is just souvenir shops and a limp display of ancient musical instruments. Its brother, the **Drum Tower**, squats about 100 yards away to the west. Entrance to each costs RMB 15, or RMB 25 will get you into both.

The Drum Tower's northern exit opens out into the Muslim quarter – a network of winding streets that lead to the **Great Mosque** (Huajue

Lane, 8am-6.30pm daily, RMB 15). Strolling around, it feels more like a Chinese imperial garden than a mosque. The few Islamic touches are confined to the occasional Arabic script, some pointed archways and a prayer hall of green and white cushions. Huajie Xiang, the small alleyway which curls south of the mosque, is filled with souvenir stalls – there's everything from embroidered Muslim caps to Mao memorabilia to fake Gore-Tex jackets.

A ten-minute walk east of the South Gate along Shuyuanmen, which is good for faux antiques and Chinese collectables, is the fabulous **Beilin Museum** (15 Sanxue Jie, 029 8725 8448, www.beilin-museum.com, Winter 8am-6pm, Summer 8am-6.45pm, RMB 30, RMB 15 concessions). This former Confucian temple is stuffed with thousands of man-sized stone tablets, or steles, that date back to the Han Dynasty. The forest of cracked grey-black stones is inscribed with stories, poems, texts, maps, even character primers all in beautiful calligraphy. Rubbings available.

There are a handful of sights just south of the city walls. The **Small Wild Goose Pagoda** (Youyi Xi Lu, 8am-5pm, RMB 15), a spindly 13-storey tower, was built back in the Tang Dynasty around AD 705 to store Buddhist sutras from India. An earthquake in the 16th century caused it to shrink from 45 metres (148 feet) to a little over 43 metres (141 feet). Its older and bigger brother, the **Big Wild Goose Pagoda**, sits in Dacien Temple, about four kilometres (2.4 miles) away. The tower, which dates back to AD 652, is more than 60 metres (197 feet) tall. Ticket: 25 RMB.

The **Shaanxi History Musuem** (91 Xiaozhai Dong Lu, 029 8521 9422, www.sxhm.com, Mar-mid Nov 8.30am-6pm, mid Nov-Feb 9am-5.30pm, RMB 35, RMB 17.50 concessions), a few streets away, puts everything in context. Its well-labelled galleries run from prehistory (over a million years ago) up to China's final Qing Dynasty (1911). There are tools, weapons, pots, statues, burial ogres, wine urns, art.

Further afield there is a smattering of imperial tombs – mainly of Han and Tang Dynasty emperors, their families, servants and concubines. The most famous of these are those of Han Dynasty emperor Mao Ling (40 kilometres, 25 miles, west of Xi'an) and at Qian Ling (80 kilometres, 50 miles, north-west of Xi'an), where China's only female ruler – Empress Wu Zetian – is interred.

Where to eat & drink

It's all hearty noodles, pork and mutton in Shaanxi. **Xi'an Fanzhuang** (2/F Xi'an Hotel, 298 Dong Dajie, 029 8768 0660), a ten-minute walk east from the main crossroads, is the place to eat traditional local food. **Laosunjia** (364 Dong Dajie, 029 8248 2828), a noisy, multi-storeyed Muslim palace, has been around for over a hundred years. There are also many places to eat along Huimin Jie, the main street in the Muslim quarter, running north from the Drum Tower.

Xi'an fancies itself as having something of a nightlife, but the clubs on offer are generally garish and lame. Head instead for **GZ** (just south of the Hyatt Hotel in an alleyway off Heping Jie, 013 4881 4907) which has live jazz and loungeable sofas.

Where to stay

Xi'an has more hotels than you can poke a stick at. The fanciest place in town is the **Hyatt Regency** (158 Dong Dajie, 029 8769 1234, fax 029 8769 6799, http://xian.regency.hyatt.com, RMB 900-RMB 1,400). You can't beat the **Bell Tower Hotel** (110 Nan Dajie, 029 8760 0000, fax 029 8727 1217, www.belltowerhtl.com, RMB 850-RMB 2,720) for either its rates or its location.

Getting around

Xi'an is arranged much like it was in the 8th century – a simple grid system bound by the city walls. The key point of reference is the Bell Tower which stands at the crossroads of the four main streets – Xi Dajie (West Street), Dong Dajie (East Street), Bei Daijie (North Street) and Nan Dajie (South Street). All the top tourist sights in town are walkable from here. Green taxis are cheap (flag fall RMB 5) and plentiful, but have your destination written in Chinese.

Getting there

By air

There are well over a dozen flights a day between Beijing and Xi'an. Tickets can go for as low as RMB 400 one way, and the flight takes about an hour and a half. Xi'an's airport, though, is a little out of the way, 50km (31 miles) north-west in the town of Xianyang. Expect to pay about RMB 200 for a taxi.

By train

Although it takes 12 hours by train, the journey is comfortable if you take a sleeper carriage. There are four daily overnight trains between Xi'an and Beijing. Tickets go for around RMB 300 one way. The station is next to the northern edge of the city wall, a RMB 10 ride by taxi to downtown

Tourist information

All the main hotels run full-day tours to see the out-of-town sights for around RMB 300 per person (including entrance fees), most leave by 9am. Or you can hire a car and driver for around RMB 500. There are two main routes – the popular eastern route usually takes in the Terracotta Warriors, Qin Shi Huang's tomb, Hua Qing Pool and Banpo. The less touristy western route covers the imperial tombs and Famen Si – a fancy Buddhist temple with some of the Buddha's finger bones. There's a lot of them about.

Pyongyang

House arrest has never been so much fun.

Dancing girls brighten up Kim Il Sung Square.

If market-hopping, Mao and the Mings all wear a bit thin, there's always a weekend excursion to the most secretive and mysterious nation on the planet. The 90-minute flight from Beijing to Pyongyang is a trip through the looking glass. To Westerners, it's the friendliest police state they have ever seen, while Chinese tourists shuffle uncomfortably and mumble about 1970s China. Someday, Pyongyang may look like Beijing, with neon lights, luxury cars and a gleaming financial district, but for now, you can experience the city Kim Il Sung had in mind.

The name Pyongyang means 'flat land', an ideal capital site in a nation that is over 70 per cent mountains. Picturesque it's not – there are no canals, no highways framed with maple trees, no striking night skyline. The dingy apartment blocks look like any small city in China, or the worst parts of Beijing. What it does have, however, are wide swathes of highway eerily free of cars, gleaming streets and squares, a surprising number of parks and towering monuments that defy imagination.

The drawback for the independent traveller is that you can only visit on a pre-arranged tour. Even solo visitors have to travel with two guides, a car and a driver, which can be prohibitively expensive. The bare minimum of pre-entry arrangements must include the services of a guide, meals, hotels, and itinerary for both international and domestic travel. Anyone who thinks they can book a tour and ditch their shackles later is sorely mistaken – meander one hundred yards away from your group and guides will call 'friend, friend, please come back'. Wander the hotel as you like, but sneaking out at night might get your guide in trouble with the authorities and is simply not worth the trouble.

However, being under house arrest has its benefits – namely, visitors can chat with their surprisingly accessible guides. Refrain from judging and criticising (particularly the Great and Dear Leaders) and they may open up about the housing shortage, or about the half-finished behemoth hotel that ran out of money. Photographing the locals is strictly prohibited, but waving and smiling goes over well with both civilians and soldiers – the children even shout hello. Go to a city park during national holidays, and families will invite you to their barbecues and ply you with homemade alcohol.

HISTORY

The Democratic People's Republic of Korea (DPRK) has many identities – North Korea, the 'Hermit Kingdom', 'Rogue Nation', card-carrying member of the Axis of Evil. However, just 60 years ago, it was part of a proud, if often victimised nation, with 5,000 years of history (if you're willing to count mythology about a bear and magic garlic) that had played reluctant host to China, Japan, the Mongols, the Manchus and various Western powers.

The US and USSR's 1945 'temporary' division and trusteeship of the peninsula was the final blow to a people who craved self-determination. In 1950, Kim Il Sung's army swept into the relatively impoverished south, and, after much bloody fighting, a 15-country UN force drove them back over the 38th parallel. A ceasefire (not a peace treaty) in 1953 ended the Korean War, but the uneasy coexistence has continued, exacerbated by bizarre northern incidents, such as the attempted assassination of the South Korean president (1968), the capture of the USS *Pueblo* (two days later), the assassination of South Korean officials in Burma (1983), kidnapping Japanese civilians (1970s) and shady doings over nuclear reactors (1980s-present), among others. Current leader Kim Jong Il's reign seems comparatively stable, but food shortages, refugee crises, and nuclear opportunism are still very real concerns, and for the most unpredictable, misunderstood regime on the planet, anything is possible.

Sightseeing

The sights and attractions below dispense with the usual listings as tourists have no telephone access and, given that it is impossible to visit any of the locations alone, addresses are superfluous.

Museums

The **Victorious Fatherland Liberation War Museum** will give you the 'real truth' about that unfortunate business over the 38th parallel. Here, a military guide takes you through rooms of captured US tanks, intricate dioramas, graphic war photos and selectively translated documents, all of which offer conclusive proof that the South Koreans and the Americans invaded North Korea, and that the north's rapid sweep across the peninsula was strictly a defensive measure. A museum staffer who formerly crewed the torpedo boat that sank the USS *Baltimore* may be on hand to tell the tale, which makes for an interesting story. However, the cruiser in question actually went on to survive the war and remained in active duty until 1971.

The USS *Pueblo* is equally surreal. Visitors are treated to a ship's tour, and a short film about the 'incident'. This hard-hitting documentary has the American hostages repeatedly admitting how they were being treated much better than they deserved considering their crime, while clearly the US protests illustrated how angry Americans were at the government's treatment of the innocent Korean people.

Then there's the 'apology letter' from the US. 'This proves that America sent a spy ship into Korean waters,' the guide says gravely, clearly disappointed when guests do not react with horror. **Kumsusan Memorial Palace** (Kim Il Sung's Mausoleum) is not open to American

Mass Appeal

Consider an elaborate Olympic Games Opening Ceremony, multiply it by one thousand, and you may have some idea what to expect from the Mass Games, or Arirang, where 100,000 athletes perform the ultimate salute to socialism. Each number sees thousands of performers working in perfect unison, doing complicated gymnastics, ethnic dance, battle scenes and veritable hymns to reunification, not to mention trapeze work *sans* net, and a dance of giant eggs to celebrate the bountiful North Korean agriculture. Even more startling is that the athletes exit the stage en masse, in total darkness, without incident.

Those lacking athletic prowess or innate grace can serve socialism as part of an enormous backdrop. 20,000 students hold books of coloured cards; by flipping pages at pre-arranged signals, they create smooth, uniform mosaics of the Korean countryside, various battles and reunification. Thirty minutes before the show, the students warm up with 'Socialist Slogans' flipped Mexican-wave-style, so praises to the government rapidly snake their way through the stands.

US tourists are only allowed into North Korea during the Mass Games, theoretically an annual event, but still staged/cancelled according to the whim of Kim Jong Il. Tickets are between €50 and €300 and the experience is unforgettable. Koreans agree. On the inbound plane, the flight attendants announce: 'Now you can see the real picture of our country, the Arirang performance proves our prosperity, you see our enjoyment to live a happy life without interference from outside sources'.

visitors. Other 'mourners' (in formal dress) travel on moving walkways and through a modified wind tunnel to remove dust, before joining crying Korean women in bowing to the embalmed Great Leader. Afterwards, the grief-stricken can visit Kim Il Sung's train carriage, his Mercedes and his many awards from other Axis-of-Evil hopefuls such as Robert Mugabe and Muammar Gaddafi.

Monuments

Pyongyang's many monuments are, in a word, big. First stop is the **Mansudae Grand Monument**; visitors express the appropriate reverence by bowing to the massive bronze figure of Kim Il Sung and can buy bouquets of flowers to lay at his feet. This is a serious business: taking partial body shots is forbidden and your guide will delete any photos that might be considered objectionable. The **Monument to Party Foundation** sports a mammoth hammer, sickle and calligraphy brush trio, representing the valued classes: worker, farmer and intellectual. The **Juche Tower** celebrates Kim Il Sung's policy of 'self-reliance' and affords a nice view of the grey, flat city, as well as a room of plaques from Juche Study groups around the world.

For off-the-beaten-track tourist sites, the **Kaeson Youth Funfair** has a Ferris wheel, roller coaster, and what visitors (and a few guides) affectionately call the 'wheel of death.' Those with weak grips will plunge to their ultimate demise; stronger riders may need several days worth of painkillers. To see public transport at its most glorious, visit the **Pyongyang Metro**, an extraordinary collection of chandeliers, mosaics and nearly vertical escalators. Besides lions, tigers and bears, **Pyongyang Zoo** has a fair selection of domestic cats, and the **Foreign Language Bookstore** sells airplane reading such as Kim Jong Il's *Great Teacher of Journalism* and *On the Art of Cinema*. Other titles include *The US Imperialists Started the Korean War*, and English-language texts, sporting useful sentences such as 'She is a native speaker of Esperanto.'

Outside Pyongyang:

A mere 168 kilometres (104 miles) south lies the **De-Militarised Zone** (DMZ), the world's most heavily guarded (and mined) territory. Until recently, propaganda messages emblazoned the surrounding hills and blared from speakers on both sides, but now all is quiet. Visitors can straddle the Korean border in the **Military Armistice Conference Hall**, where world leaders signed the ceasefire (technically the two nations are still at war). Nearby is **Kaesong**, a former capital of the Koryo Dynasty – also, the only place in North Korea with surviving pre-war architecture.

Mansudae Grand Monument.

Getting around

Tour operators will arrange either trains or Air Koryo Flights from Beijing. The only authorised reputable tour operator in Beijing is:

Koryo Tours

27 Beisanlitun Nan, Chaoyang (6416 7544/www.koryogroup.com). **Cost** from €1,390. Euro currency or Euro travellers cheques only. **No credit cards.**

Where to stay

Although solo travellers can make requests, generally meals, transportation and accommodation are arranged by either your tour or your guides, and foreign guests are 'encouraged' to stay either in the comfortable Yanggakdo or Koryo Hotels. Both have bars, revolving restaurants and karaoke parlours, but the Yanggakdo also has a casino, bowling alley, 'sauna' and a golf driving range.

Directory

Features

Peking University campus. *See p84.*

Directory

Getting Around

Arriving & leaving

By air

Beijing Capital International Airport (BCIA)

www.bcia.com.cn/en/index.jsp

Beijing Capital International Airport, fairly modest despite its grand name, is around 25km (15.5 miles) north-east of downtown. Thanks to the new Airport Expressway which empties right into the heart of the city, a taxi takes around 30-40 minutes and costs RMB 80-RMB 100 (and that's including the RMB 10 road toll). The airport used to have a big problem with touts whose unmetered taxis were definitely a bad deal. Make sure you head to the official taxi queues – they are signed – and insist on the meter.

Roomy airport shuttle buses leave every 15 to 30 minutes and take around an hour. There are three different routes, stopping at some of the major hotels. The stop is directly outside arrivals; tickets cost RMB 16 and the service runs from 8am to 10.30pm daily. The route that ends at Beijing International Hotel just across from the Beijing Train Station runs until the last flight.

Beijing plans to have a metro line linking the airport with downtown by April 2008.

Duty free and banking facilities (including money changing) are open 24 hours; ATMs accept Visa, MasterCard, Maestro, Plus and Cirrus; there's a small post office and foot massage parlour; China Mobile has dozens of counters selling pre-paid SIM cards; and while the Chinese restaurants are a rip-off there are regularly-priced Starbucks and KFC in the arrivals hall and terminal. Left-luggage counters (6459 8151) are near gate 9 in arrivals and gates 8 and 10 in departures; charges are between RMB 20 and 30 per day depending on the size of the bags. The lost luggage office (6459 9523) is opposite carousel number 8 in the luggage collection hall. There are several tourist advice counters (6459 8145) in arrivals. They are not much good on advice, but they can help book hotel rooms and rustle you up a map.

Elong (400 810 1119, www.elong.net) and Ctrip (800 820 6666, www.ctrip.com) have good deals on international and domestic plane tickets. They can deliver the ticket to your hotel so long as you can pay the courier cash on delivery. They also have hotel deals.

> All numbers starting with '800' are toll free from a land line. Numbers starting with '400' are free from mobile phones.

Airlines

More than 50 international airlines fly into BCIA. Air China and British Airways are the only airlines which fly non-stop between London and Beijing.

Air Canada

Rm C201, Lufthansa Center, 50 Liangmaqiao Lu, Chaoyang (6468 2001/www.aircanada.com).

Air China

15 Changan Xijie, Xidan, Xicheng, Centre (400 810 0999/www.airchina.com.cn).

Air France

Rm 1606-08, Kuntai International Mansion, 12A Chaoyangmenwai Dajie, Chaoyang (400 880 8808/ www.airfrance.com.cn).

British Airways

Rm 2112, Kuntai International Mansion, 12A Chaoyangmenwai Dajie, Chaoyang (400 650 0073/ www.ba.com).

Northwest Airlines

Rm 501 West Wing, China World Trade Center, Chaoyang (400 8140 0814/www.nwa.com/cn/ en/home). Metro Guomao.

United Airlines

Rm C, 15/F, Gateway, Tower A, 18 Xiaguangli, North Road, East Third Ring, Chaoyang (800 810 8282/www.cn.united.com).

By rail

Beijing has four stations, but the two main ones are **Beijing Station** (5182 1114, 6512 8930) in the centre of town for trains to Shanghai, Hong Kong, Pyongyang and Russia, and **Beijing West Railway Station** (5182 6253) for most provincial capitals including Xi'an and Lhasa in Tibet. Tickets are only sold four days in advance or less – note during national holidays, and on popular routes (eg Beijing-Shanghai, Beijing-Xi'an) throughout the year, tickets sell out quickly. You can get tickets at the stations, but it's far less hassle to buy them from an agency for a small surcharge of RMB 5-RMB 10. Try the ticket agency near the City Hotel (A15 Gongti Donglu, Chaoyang, 6509 3783, 8am-9pm). You can also buy tickets online from www.piao.com or www.51piao.com and get them delivered to your hotel for an extra RMB 10. Many hotels will also help with buying tickets, but you will pay a hefty commission for this service. Beijing Station has its own subway stop, while Beijing West Railway Station is a short taxi ride from the Military Museum subway stop. A high-speed rail link between the two stations is under construction – and is due to be finished sometime in 2007.

For overnight journeys, a hard sleeper (*ying wo*) is a berth on a three-tier bunk open to the corridor. The slightly plusher soft sleeper (*ruan wo*) is a bed on two double-decker bunks in a private room. Soft sleeper berths are usually twice as expensive as hard sleepers, and can often cost about as much as a plane ticket to the same destination.

Public transport

Beijing's public transport system is pretty dire. Roads are congested, buses pack their passengers in like sardines, and the subway system is not very comprehensive.

The city, though, pre-Olympics, is scrambling to get the metro up to scratch, and there's a slew of new routes which are either being built or on the drawing board. See the current Beijing metro map on page 256.

Plans are afoot to build 260 kilometres (162 miles) of new urban track by 2015, costing more than RMB 100 billion. Until then, though, taxis are the way to go. As long as you're not travelling during rush hour, cabs are also relatively inexpensive.

Metro

Look out for the big blue signs with 'Beijing Subway' written in Chinese and English next to a white D with a circle around it. Inside announcements, subway maps and station names are in Chinese and English. Navigating your way underground is not difficult, but be prepared to battle with the crowds. Most stations have toilets; you can generally smell them. Services run from around 6am until 11pm.

Currently there are four subway lines. Line 1 runs west to east from Pingguoyuan to Sihui. You will need this line if

Slow berth to China

If you think you know what a sleeper carriage is, then try the long-haul rail journey between Europe and Beijing. Between vodka parties, cold fish suppers and those long bouts of *Oblomov* or *The Brothers Karamazov*, you're bound to get some zeds – not least because everyone else is dozing too – and when they're not they're probably speaking either Mandarin or Russian.

Which train?

The Moscow-Beijing services use branches of the Trans-Siberian network. There are two main options, the 7,620-kilometre (4,735-mile) Trans-Mongolian, which takes six nights and passes through Ulan Bator; and the 8,986-kilometre (5,623-mile) Trans-Manchurian, which takes an extra night and allows you to make a stop in Harbin (famous for its Winter Ice Festival). Ulan Bator has a certain caché with Westerners, so you are more likely to meet tourists on that service. Both services fill up a month or more before departure so book ahead. Neither is specifically aimed at tourists, so you may well pass through say, the Great Wall, in the dark.

How much?

Plenty of tour operators across Europe and North America offer packages on the Trans-Siberian, and will help with accommodation, visas and the complex business of arranging stopovers in the more interesting towns. These might include Ekaterinburg for the Ural mountans; Perm 2 for photos of abandoned tank factories; and Novosibirsk for a stroll round the former Soviet science academy town, Akademgorodok. If you only have time for one stop, get off at Irkutsk and head for Lake Baikal, the huge, beautiful, impossibly deep freshwater inland sea in the heart of central Siberia. Package tours with stops cost anything from $2,400 (£1,200) and upwards, not including flights to Moscow and from Beijing.

If you insist on going it alone, then you will have to arrange for an 'invitation' to Russia or, at least, proof that you have accommodation booked wherever you plan to stay. A single Moscow-Beijing ticket costs between $350-$450, depending on the class of journey – there are two classes of four-berth sleeper compartment and a first-class two-berth option. You will pay more if you employ a Russian tour firm to purchase the ticket, but it will be speedier that way. For tickets out of Beijing go to a travel agent or, if you fancy a queue and a long chat in Mandarin, the main railway station.

Further information

See Trailblazer's *Trans-Siberian Handbook* for general information and historical and cultural anecdotes about the stops on the line; see also www.seat61.com/Trans-Siberian.htm for details about planning and buying tickets. And for information about visas see www.russialink.org.uk/embassy.

you take the subway to Tiananmen Square, Wangfujing or Silk Street (Yong'anli Station). Line 2 or the circle line does a loop around the centre of the city. You can use this line to go to the Lama Temple (Yonghegong station), the Bell Tower (Gulou dajie station) and Liulichang antiques alley (Hepingmen Station). These two lines intersect at Fuxingmen and Jianguomen stations. Line 13 is an overland route in the north of the city which connects downtown with Haidian District (for all the major universities and the jumping off point for the Summer Palace). There's an interchange station with Line 2 at Xizhimen and Dongzhimen stations. Finally the Batong Line connects Sihui station to a residential suburb in the south-east of the city. Every station has a ticket counter – fares are RMB 3 on Lines 1 and 2, and RMB 5 if you're travelling out to a station on Line 13. There are no ticket machines.

Buses

Most bus journeys cost between RMB 1 and RMB 2; passengers usually pay a conductor who roams up and down the aisle. Buses are generally crowded and not a good idea unless you speak Chinese or know where you are going. www.bjbus.com/english/tour/default.htm has a good map of Beijing's urban bus routes. Buses run from around 6am to 10pm, with a handful of night buses.

There are a few very useful buses that serve as cheap-rate tour buses. Catch the No.1 at Beijing Railway Station to expore the central business district The No.5 can be picked up at Zhongshan Park, from where it meanders around the tree-lined streets behind the Forbidden City; hop off anytime to see the hutongs. The No.10, from Beijing Railway Station, goes past Tiananmen Square, up Chang'an Jie and into the Muslim quarter. Tickets cost RMB 1.

Taxis

Visitors to the city tend to plump for cabs – they're inexpensive, plentiful (except during rush hour and major rainstorms) and, provided you have the destination written down in Chinese (few cabbies speak English), fairly stress free. It's not usually a problem, but make sure the driver uses the meter. Flag fall is RMB 10 for the first three kilometres (two miles), and then RMB 2 for each kilometre thereafter. Waiting time is also added to the bill. After 11pm, flag fall rises to RMB 11. All drivers should offer you a receipt at the end of the journey. Call 6835 1150 to complain about a taxi (take down the driver's number – it's written on the large card with the driver's photo on the dashboard).

Many cab drivers don't know their way around the city, although that doesn't stop them picking you up and then asking random pedestrians for directions. Unless your destination is well known, take a map with you and point it out to the driver. While most cabs are honest, it is not uncommon for the unsuspecting tourist to be taken for a lap around a Ring Road before being dropped off only several hundred metres from where he started. Some dodgy cab drivers use tourists to part with fake banknotes, so check your change. If the driver refuses a note saying it is fake be warned – a sleight of hand may have replaced your genuine RMB 100 with a fake. Many cabs don't have seatbelts. Feel free to refuse to take a cab if it doesn't have seatbelts, another will be along immediately after.

Driving

Without a Chinese driving licence you won't be able to hire a car in Beijing. To get the necessary permit you will need residence papers, an international driver's licence, to undergo a medical exam and pass a written test. FESCO (8561 6663, 8651 2228, www.fescochina.com.cn) will ease foreigners through the hoops for an all-in-one charge of RMB 800. The whole caboodle takes about a month to process. And even with your licence, you can't drive outside Beijing. And to cap it all, the city's drivers are some of the world's most dangerous.

It's more practical to hire a car and a driver: your hotel can help you negotiate a day rate with a cabbie – budget around RMB 400-RMB 600/day.

Cycling

Beijing used to be full of bicycles. Nowadays there are a lot more cars on the road, but the cycle lanes remain and as the city is dead flat, biking's a good way to get around. It's especially fun to cycle around Houhai and the hutongs. Watch out for the world's most dangerous drivers, though – owners of new cars have zero respect for cyclists.

Most of the youth hostels hire bikes for around RMB 20-RMB 50/day depending on quality, see the Where to Stay chapter for details.

Walking

Apart from strolls around the hutongs and embassy district, Beijing's not great for walking. The pollution can be bad, cyclists career on to the pavement at will, and everything's spread out. That said, the city's central core is fairly grid-like and easy to navigate on foot. Take a good map – *see pp238-249.*

Resources A-Z

Addresses

Street signs are in Chinese characters, with pinyin underneath. Most street names end with *jie* or *lu* (*jie* means street, *lu* road), *dajie* (avenue), *dalu* (main road) or hutong (lane). Beijing is laid out like a grid and since streets are fairly long, the compass direction – north (*bei*), east (*dong*), south (*nan*) or west (*xi*) – is often added to the name to identify which end of the street you are on. Until the 1950s Beijing's central core was bounded by an ancient city wall, about 18 metres (60 feet) thick at its base. In a bid to eradicate China's imperial past, the Communist government tore it down, so that by the 1960s nothing was left except a few gates, such as Deshengmen and Qianmen (*see p55*). Streets that cross this wall still reflect in their name whether they were outside (*wai*) or inside (*nei*) the boundary, eg Dongzhimenwai Dajie, which is outside the wall changes its name to Dongzhimennei Dajie once it crosses the boundary of the old road, now marked by the Second Ring Road.

Although addresses have street numbers, taxi drivers tend to go by the name of the building (if it's big enough) or the name of a landmark nearby, such as a mall, hotel, bridge or crossroads.

Age restrictions

You have to be at least 14 years old to have sex in China, although to get married the groom has to be at least 22 and the bride, 24. There is no minimum age of consent for homosexual sex. It is illegal to sell alcohol or cigarettes to the under-18s, although the law is not enforced – the old folk grumbled it was unfair if they couldn't send their grandchildren out to buy them the odd carton or flagon of rice wine. China's minimum age for driving a vehicle is 18.

> All numbers starting with '800' are toll free from a land line. Numbers starting with '400' are free from mobile phones.

Attitude & etiquette

See p219 **Etiquette and customs**.

Business

While doing business in China is all about *guangxi* (connections), that doesn't mean you can skip the official hoops. The local government has set up the Beijing Investment Promotion Bureau (3/F, Building F, Fuhua Mansion, 8 Chaoyangmen Bei Dajie, Centre, 6554 3149, http://www.investbeijing.gov.cn) to help overseas entrepreneurs invest in the city. Beijing Foreign Enterprise Human Resources Service Co (FESCO), whose logo should be a dead ringer for supermarket giant, Tesco, can help with the human resources side of things. FESCO is at 14 Chaoyangmen Nan Dajie, Centre, 8561 6663, 8651 2228, www.fesco.com.cn.

Business cards

These are always offered and accepted with both hands. It's customary to have one side printed in English and the other in Chinese. You can get a box of 100 cards printed up for around RMB 30 at any of hundreds of printing shops all over the city. The word *fuyin*, meaning photocopy, is usually somewhere in the sign. Else try Kinko's Copies (1/F Focus Plaza, 19 Financial Street, Xicheng, Financial District, 6657 3215, www.kinkos.com.cn).

Convention centres

Beijing is no Shanghai, but it's beginning to attract its fair share of conventions and exhibitions these days. The big boys generally hold their business in one of the following venues.

Beijing Exhibition Center

135 Xizhimenwai Dajie, Xuanwu, Financial District (6835 4455). **Map** p240 F7.

Beijing International Convention Center

8 Beichendong Road, Houhai (6491 0248/8498 5588/ www.bicc.com.cn/english/index.asp). **Map** p243 N5.

China International Exhibition Center

6 East Beisanhuan Road, Chaoyang (8460 0223/ www.ciec-expo.com/cms/template/ index_en.html). **Map** p243 N5.

China World Trade Center

1 Jianguomenwai Dajie, Chaoyang (6505 2288/www.cwtc.com). **Map** p245 O10.

Couriers & shippers

Express mail services (*kuaidi*) are dirt cheap if you use one of the local Beijing firms – around RMB 10 for a package delivery inside Beijing.

Beijng Zhaijisong Express

11/F Zhaowei Tower, 14 Jiuxianqiao Lu, Chaoyang (400 678 9000/www.zjs.com.cn). **Open** 8.30am-5.30pm Mon-Fri. **No credit cards**.

DHL

1/F, COFCO Plaza, Tower B, 8 Jianguomen Neidajie, Dongcheng, Centre (800 810 8000/400 810 8000/ www.cn.dhl.com). **Open** 8.30am-6.30pm Mon-Fri. **No credit cards. Map** p244 N10.

FedEx

Room 101, Tower C, Lonsdale Center, 5 Wan Hong Road, Chaoyang (800 988 1888/400 886 1888/www.fedex.com/ cn_english/). **Open** 9am-8pm Mon-Sat; Closed Sun. **No credit cards.**

Office hire & business centres

Beijing is now bristling with companies offering business services, and virtual and serviced office apartments.

Servcorp

6/F, Tower W2, Oriental Plaza, 1 Dong Chang'an Jie, Dongcheng, Centre (8520 0500/www.servecorp.net). **Open** 8.30am-5.30pm Mon-Fri. **No credit cards. Map** p244 L10.

Translators & interpreters

Herald Translation

Room 2007, Beijing Silver Tower, 2 Dongsanhuan Beilu, Chaoyang (6410 7126/www.herald-ts.com). **Open** 8.30am-5.30pm daily. **No credit cards. Map** p243 O6.

Chambers of commerce

American Chamber of Commerce in China

Rm 1903, China Resources Building, 8 Jianguomenbei Dajie, Dongcheng, Centre (8519 1920/ www.amcham-china.org.cn). **Map** p244 M10.

British Chamber of Commerce in China

Rm 1001, China Life Tower, 16 Chaoyangmenwai Dajie, Chaoyang (8525 1111/ www.pek.britcham.org). **Map** p244 N9.

Canada China Business Council

Suite 18-2, CITIC Building, 19 Jianguomenwai Dajie, Chaoyang (8526 1820/www.ccbc.com). **Map** p244 N10.

Consumer

China is not that hot on consumer rights. However, most reputable stores will exchange faulty goods if you have the receipt and return the item within a few days. Beijing Tourism Administration (6512 6688, 8515 7055, http://english.bjta.gov.cn) takes complaints from tourists, but don't hold your breath. Chinese only.

Customs

Visitors are limited to 400 cigarettes or 100 cigars, and 1.5 litres of alcohol. You also can't bring in more than one camera, one video camera and one computer. Be careful with printed matter. Don't carry more than, say, one Bible and certainly no material on sensitive subjects such as the Tiananmen Square massacre or the Falun Gong banned spiritual sect. There is no limit on foreign currency, but there is a RMB 6,000 cap on renminbi either in or out. Saying that, Chinese customs officials take very little interest in Western tourists.

Disabled

Beijing may be hosting the 2008 Paralympics but the city is ill equipped for disabled travellers. Some modern shopping plazas and five-star hotels have wheelchair ramps, but taxis, the metro and many public buildings do not. Pavements on major streets have ridges to guide the blind but few road crossings have audio alerts at traffic lights. Beijing eTours (http://beijing.etours.cn/disabled_travel/index.jsp, Jia 23, Fuxing Lu, Haidian, North-west, 6716 0201) offers special city tours for people in wheelchairs.

Drugs

Beijing's youth are experimenting with recreational drugs, usually in nightclubs, but much of what passes around is of dubious purity and quality. China takes a dim view of illegal substances. Smugglers can get the death penalty; users are forced into rehabilitation centres. Best to steer clear.

Electricity

China runs on 220 volts, 50 Hz. Four different kinds of sockets are typically used – three-pronged angled (the most common), three-pronged round, two-pronged flat, and two-pronged round. Adapters are widely available from electronics markets and stores.

Embassies

Australia

21 Dongzhimenwai Dajie, Chaoyang (5140 4111/ www.austemb.org.cn). **Open** 8.30am-4.50pm Mon-Fri. **Map** p244 N7.

Canada

19 Dongzhimenwai Dajie, Chaoyang (6532 3536/ www.beijing.gc.ca). **Open** 9am-11am, 1.30-3pm Mon-Thur; 9am-noon Fri. **Map** p244 N7.

New Zealand

1 Ritan Donger Jie, Chaoyang (6532 2731/www.nzembassy.com/china). **Open** 8.30am-5pm Mon-Fri. **Map** p244 N9.

Republic of Ireland

3 Ritan Dong Lu, Chaoyang (6532 2691/www.embassyofireland.cn). **Open** 9am-12.30pm; 2-5pm Mon-Fri. **Map** p244 N9.

South Africa

5 Dongzhimenwai Dajie, Chaoyang (6532 0171). **Open** 8am-4.30pm Mon-Fri.

Etiquette and customs

About face

Beijingers are ludicrously, agonizingly generous. No matter the relationship, the chances that your dinner companion(s) will are as slender as a rice pancake. Pushing the issue will damage face, a concept that is almost incomprehensible to Westerners but is intrinsic to Asian culture. Chinese want you to love China, and they wave off their generosity, explaining that 'Chinese people are very kind.' Criticising China or the Chinese government is like insulting a family member, and will not be forgiven. However, the better you know people, the more this veneer starts to slip. Close friends allow you to alternate lunch treats, and may spew vitriol about their home country. Try to reassure them that it's the same everywhere; they'll insist you don't understand China. As for heated confrontations, avoid them in any potentially valuable situation or relationship. However, sometimes a display of temper is the only thing that moves truculent salespeople or shady taxi drivers, so don't be afraid to raise your voice once in a while.

Greetings

The Chinese name game is a tough code to crack. Xu Xiaomei could be Miss Xu, Xu Jingli (manager), Xu Laoshi (teacher) Lao Xu (older person) or simply Xu Xiaomei. She is Xiaomei only to very close friends and family. It's better to simply ask 'What shall I call you?' and let them guide you through the myriad of monikers (there are nicknames too!). As for international introductions, some visitors feel uncomfortable about calling a junior in age and position 'Miss Li' while she refers to them as 'Bob' or 'Mary.' There is no disrespect intended here; Chinese believe Westerners prefer being addressed by their given names. Confusion also arises when a man introduces himself and then says succinctly, 'This is my wife.' Chinese women retain their own names upon marriage, so you can't even take a stab at her name. Again, asking is the only way around this – they'll be touched at your concern.

Conversation

Most Chinese insist that 'rude' personal questions about age and especially income are things of the (globally isolated) past, but you'd be surprised at how many taxi drivers, neighbours and random strangers inquire about your rent or salary. Being evasive or pretending not to understand is effective. However, explaining that Western people dislike talking about money goes down surprisingly well. More educated Chinese may avoid even innocuous inquiries such as 'are you married?' for fear of cultural insensitivity. Break the ice and ask them first.

Gestures

A gesture that will raise gasps of delight among your hosts is the knuckle 'thank you.' Legend has it that popular Qing Dynasty Emperor Qianlong ventured out incognito to see how the other half lived, and since his attending officials couldn't kowtow to him without revealing his identity, they rapped their bent forefingers and middle fingers on the table, which symbolised their knees. Today this is sometimes abbreviated to fingertips, but it's a nice way to thank tea servers, and one that Chinese are particularly happy to see.

Booze

Brutal winters and ample leisure time led north China to develop a strong alcohol culture. Even Western women, falling conveniently into that 'third gender', will be expected to partake in what their Chinese sisters modestly refuse. Cite ideological objections or a medical condition. In Beijing, people will understand – further north, temperance is viewed with suspicion, since only people with secret agendas remain sober. Paradoxically, feigning intoxication may be the best way to gain trust.

Gifts

To southern Chinese, gift giving is quid pro quo; to northerners, it shows a 'warm heart.' Northerners give gifts or buy dinners to ensure that visitors leave China waxing poetic about the kindness of the Chinese; your immediate reciprocation can be a loss of face. While there are gift idiosyncrasies having to do with language homonyms (shoes represent evil, for example), Chinese are generous with Westerners' lack of cultural knowledge, and will overlook many slights – especially if the present has cultural significance to you. As for basic gifts, however, such as visiting someone's home, fruit (even in plastic bags) is always welcome.

United Kingdom

21/F, North Tower Kerry Centre, 1 Guanghua Lu, Chaoyang (8529 6600/www.uk.cn). Metro Yong'anli. **Open** 8.30am-4.30pm Mon-Fri. **Map** p245 O9.

USA

3 Xiushui Beijie, Jianguomenwai Daijie, Chaoyang (6532 3831/ http://beijing.usembassy-china.org.cn). **Open** 8.30am-noon; 2-4pm Mon-Fri. **Map** p244 N10.

Emergencies

See also **Health** and *p223* **Police**.

Useful numbers

Ambulance 120
Directory assistance 2689 0114 (English)
Fire services 119
IDD help 115
Police 110
English-speaking police 8402 0101
Time 117
Tourist information 6513 0828
Weather 121

Gay & lesbian

See the **Gay & Lesbian** chapter, *pp165-167*.

Health

China does not have reciprocal healthcare agreements with other countries, so it is wise to take out private insurance before you come. Western-standard hospitals are pricey, so it's worthwhile getting a policy that is not stingy with in-patient costs. Some private clinics accept international insurance including BUPA and TIECARE. Check with your insurance provider before you travel.

Beijing is rated as one of the world's worst for air pollution. Sufferers of asthma or other respiratory problems may find the city's air exacerbates their condition. Do not drink water straight from the tap, bottled water is cheap and can be bought almost everywhere.

Vaccinations against Hepatitis A and B, polio, tetanus, flu (for the over-50s), chickenpox, and typhoid are generally recommended. Japanese encephalitis vaccinations are also advised for travel to remote rural areas.

Hospitals

The better public hospitals have 'VIP' foreigners' wings where the doctors speak English, and some have medical training overseas. Expect to pay around RMB 200-RMB 500 for a consultation with an English-speaking doctor, and around RMB 800 a night for a bed in a ward. Beijing also has a number of much pricier international-standard private clinics including the Beijing United Family Hospital network.

Many doctors over-prescribe since hospitals make a lot of their money through drugs sales. Make sure you understand what medications you are taking.

China-Japan Friendship Hospital

Yinghua Dongjie, Heplingli, Hepingjie Beikou, Houhai (6422 2952/English 8420 5121/24hr emergency line 6422 2969/www.zryhyy.com.cn). **Open** *Clinic* 8am-noon, 1-5pm Mon-Fri; 8am-noon Sat. *Emergencies* 24hrs daily. **Credit** MC, V. **Map** p243 M5.
Most staff speak some English, but some have not had overseas training; beds for foreigners.

Peking Union Medical College Hospital

1 Shuaifuyuan, Wangfujing (foreigner wing is south of the in-patient building), Dongcheng, Centre (6529 5284/www.pumch.ac.cn). **Open** *Clinic* 8am-4.30pm Mon-Fri. *Emergencies* 24hrs daily. **No credit cards. Map** p244 L10.
This is one of the most popular clinics in a public hospital for expats. Traditional Chinese Medicine is also available. Many of the doctors were trained overseas and speak good English.

Private clinics/ doctors

Beijing International SOS Clinic

Building C, BITIC Jingyi Building, 5 Sanlitun Xiwujie, Chaoyang (6462 9112/24hr call centre 6462 9100/www.internationalsos.com). **Open** *Clinic* 8am-9pm daily. **Credit** AmEx, MC, V. **Map** p245 Q7.
The clinic of choice for most expats on insurance packages. Consultations start at RMB 1,000 with an overseas doctor. Call-out service available.

Beijing United Family Hospital

2 Jiangtai Lu, Lido, Chaoyang (6433 3960/24hr emergency hotline 6433 2345/www.unitedfamilyhospitals.com). **Open** *Clinic* 9am-5.30pm Mon-Fri; 11.30am-4.30pm Sat. *Emergencies* 24hrs daily. *Pharmacy* 24hrs daily. **Credit** AmEx, MC, V. **Map** p243 Q4.
This state-of-the-art private hospital is out by the airport. All the staff speak English and many are from overseas.

Contraception & abortion

Thanks to its one-child policy, China has some of the most accessible contraceptive and abortion facilities in the world. Contraception can be bought over the counter at most pharmacies – the RU-486 abortion pill, which has been legally available for around a decade, should only be taken with a doctor's prescription. Abortions are available at the hospitals above and at the American-Sino OB/GYN Service (218 Xiaoguan Beili, Anwai, Houhai, 6496 8888, www.asog-beijing.com). Note that doctors will generally not perform abortions on women more than ten weeks pregnant.

Dentists

Since dental treatment is expensive some expats prefer to head over to Thailand – for the same price, you can have a beach holiday thrown in. If you find yourself caught short, the following clinics have English-speaking staff.

Arrail Dental Clinic

Rm 208, CITIC Building, 19 Jianguomenwai Dajie, Chaoyang (6500 6472/www.arrail-dental.com). **Open** 9am-8pm Mon-Sat; 9am-5pm Sun. **Credit** AmEx, MC, V. **Map** p245 O10.
Check-up is RMB 100. Offers full-range of non-surgical treatments including cosmetic dentistry.

SDM Dental

NB210 China World Trade Center, 1 Jianguomenwai Daijie, Chaoyang (6505 9439/www.sdmdental.com). **Open** 9am-8pm daily. **Credit** MC, V. **Map** p245 O10.

Opticians

The Chinese like to wear glasses and they know all about them. Opticians are everywhere. They will give free eye exams and grind lenses in a few hours for upwards of RMB 100.

Pharmacies & prescriptions

Most hospitals and clinics have onsite pharmacies. There are also chemists all over town that sell both Chinese and Western medicines. Many of these are 24 hours. Staff are unlikely to speak English, so try to find out the generic name of the medicine in Chinese. Stick to chain pharmacies such as Golden Elephant Medicine or Watsons to avoid the danger of buying counterfeit pills – head for the major malls to locate the major pharmacies and health stores. Note you can no longer purchase antibiotics over the counter. *See p143.*

STDs, HIV & AIDS

Treatment is available at the hospitals and clinics listed on page 220. However, be aware that if you test positive for HIV while you are in China you will be deported. The Chinese Chaoyang AIDS Volunteer Group gives free anonymous tests for STDs including HIV at the Chaoyang District Chinese Centre for Disease Control, Rm 1003, 25 Huawei Li, Panjiayuan, Chaoyang, South, 8778 9709.

Hongshulin

6329 6183.
A support group for those diagnosed with HIV.

Helplines

Alcoholics Anonymous

139 1138 9075/ www.aabeijing.com.

ID

Foreigners should always carry their passport or a photocopy of their passport and Chinese visa.

Insurance

Make sure you have adequate health and travel insurance before travelling to Beijing, as China has no reciprocal medical agreements with other countries.

Internet

Beijing is very definitely wired, but do note that many websites that the government considers sensitive – including BBC News Online and Wikipedia – are blocked. This filtering software tends to slow down the internet.

Most five-star hotels have free broadband access for guests with their own laptop. Otherwise, there are tons of internet cafés – look for the *wangba* signs – around town. They're super cheap, around RMB 2-RMB 5 per hour, but are usually jammed with spotty smoking teens addicted to online gaming.

As well as all branches of Starbucks, a growing number of funky cafés, restaurants and bars now carry free wireless. Check www.chinapulse.com/wifi/ for an updated list of Wi-Fi joints. In fact, Beijing is far better than London for wireless: everywhere has it, even the smallest joint.

Language

China has hundreds of dialects, but the standard version of Chinese, which everyone on the mainland should speak, is called *Putonghua* (common language) or Mandarin. Beijingers are inexplicably proud of their accent – thick and liberally mixed with a heavy 'er' sound – and consider themselves to be speaking the Chinese equivalent of the Queen's English. The romanisation of Chinese is called *pinyin*.

English is not widely understood outside hotels, Western restaurants and bars so if you're travelling by taxi get your address written down in Chinese – namecards and magazine listings are good for this.

Left luggage

There are left luggage counters at Beijing Capital International Airport (*see p214*) and Beijing train stations (*see p214*). Hotels will generally allow you to store luggage on their premises if you have been a guest.

Legal help

Foreign law firms are not able to litigate personal cases in China, so if you get in trouble with the law, you need to hire a Chinese lawyer. Contact your embassy (*see p218*) if you need to find an attorney.

Libraries

The Bookworm (*see p134*) has a big library of English-language fiction – now about 16,000 books. RMB 300 makes you a member for a year.

National Library
33 Zhongguancun Nandajie, Haidian, Financial District (8854 5593/www.nlc.gov.cn). **Open** 9am-9pm Mon-Fri; 9am-5pm Sat, Sun. **Map** p249 E7.
Foreigners may not borrow books but can read from a huge range of English-language editions in the reading rooms.

Lost property

If you've left something in a taxi, you can probably kiss it goodbye. On the off chance it's been handed in, call the taxi firm and ask them to trace the driver. The driver's number and the taxi firm number will both be printed on your receipt. Contact your embassy (*see p218*) in the case of a lost or stolen passport. Beijing Capital International Airport has a lost property office (6459 8333).

Media

Magazines

Beijing is bursting with free entertainment and listings magazines with information on the latest shows, concerts and DJs, as well as restaurant and bar reviews. The best, of course, is *Time Out Beijing*, which is a free monthly and is always available at Starbucks. Also available are *That's Beijing* (www.thatsbj.com) and *City Weekend* (www.cityweekend.com.cn). Find them at Western-style bars and clubs.

You can buy Western magazines such as the *Economist*, *Cosmopolitan* and *Esquire* at a substantial mark-up at the Bookworm and Chaterhouse (*see pp134-135*) and some five-star hotels.

Newspapers

The *China Daily* is a daft, English-language newspaper with about 10 pages of dry news. The website (www.chinadaily.com.cn) is more fun – there's usually some semi-naked celebrity shots in their photo gallery. *Beijing Today* (http://bjtoday.ynet.com), which is associated with the relatively bold *Beijing Youth Daily*, sometimes has challenging stories. It comes out every second Friday.
As state-owned newspapers, both are muzzled by self-censorship and are, in essence, government mouthpieces.

You can buy major international newspapers, such as the *International Herald Tribune*, the *Financial Times*, the *Wall Street Journal* and Hong Kong's *South China Morning Post* at bookshops in five-star hotels.

Radio

To find the correct frequency for BBC World Service (www.bbc.co.uk/worldservice/) or Voice of America (www.voanews.com/) broadcasts log on to their websites.

China Radio International (CRI) has an English-language service on 91.5 FM. There's the usual stodgy state-controlled news, but also lifestyle programmes including a radio cookery show.

Television

There are dozens and dozens of Chinese-language TV channels all showing the same bland pop shows or epic dramas with flying kung fu masters and teary women. CCTV 9 is an English-language channel that has (fairly lame) news broadcasts, pretty much on the hour.

Most top-end hotels have BBC World, CNN, ESPN and HBO. If the screen suddenly goes dark and silent, it's probably because there's a news report that implies some kind of criticism of the Chinese government.

Money

China's currency is the RMB (*renminbi*), also known as the *yuan* or *kuai*. Bills come in denominations of RMB 100 (red), 50 (green), 20 (beige), 10 (blue), five (purple), two (dark green) and one (green). There are 10 *mao* or *jiao* in one RMB. These are your shrapnel.

The *renminbi* is allowed to trade narrowly relative to a basket of currencies, one of which is the US dollar. It is currently trading at around RMB 7.8 to the US dollar.

As few countries recognise the RMB, and you are limited to exporting a maximum of RMB 6,000 out of the country, you should change all your left over cash before you leave (Hong Kong will change RMB). You will need to bring the receipts of when you bought your RMB to sell back your Chinese currency.

ATMs

Where there is a bank, there is usually an ATM. There are banks all over town and they are easy to spot as the signs will also be in English. ATMs generally accept foreign cards connected to Cirrus, Plus, AmEx, Visa and MasterCard – those in touristy districts, such as Wangfujing, around Silk Street, and close to five-star hotels are your best bet. Your bank back home will charge a small fee for the transaction, but some Chinese banks may add on a small charge. The Bank of China charges RMB 25 for each withdrawal.

Banks

Most banks are open 9am to 5pm every day, including Saturday and Sunday. There are dozens of different banks in the country, but these are the big Chinese ones.

Bank of China
Yatai Dasha, 8 Yaobao Lu, Chaoyang (95566/www.bj.bank-of-china.com). **Open** 9am-5pm daily. **Map** p244 N9.

China Construction Bank
160 Fuxingmennei Street, Xicheng, Financial District (95533/www.ccb.com/portal/en/home/index.jsp). Metro Fuxingmen. **Open** 9am-4.30pm daily. **Map** p241 H10.

Industrial & Commercial Bank of China (ICBC)
55 Fuxingmennei Dajie, Xicheng, Financial District (95588/www.icbc.com.cn). **Open** 9am-5pm daily. **Map** p240 G10.

Overseas banks with a presence include:

Citibank
16/F Tower 2, Bright China Changan Building, 7 Jianguomennei Dajie, Dongcheng, Centre (6510 2933/www.citibank.com). Metro Jianguomen. **Open** 9am-4.30pm Mon-Fri; 10am-3pm Sat. **Map** p244 N10.

HSBC
G/F, Block A, Beijing COFCO Plaza, 8 Jianguomennei Dajie, Dongcheng, Centre (6526 0668/www.hsbc.com.cn). Metro Jianguomen. **Open** 8.30am-4.30pm Mon-Fri. **Map** p244 N10.

Bureaux de change

You can change cash or travellers' cheques at the airport and all major banks. Hotels also change money for guests, but the rates they give are not as competitive, so use in need only. Because of long queues and commission charges it may just be easier to withdraw cash from an ATM using your bank card. Check with your bank, but most ATMs will only let you withdraw a maximum of RMB 3,000-RMB 5,000 each day.

There is a black market in Beijing, but because of the problem with counterfeit money it's best to avoid it. Since it's difficult to exchange your left over RMB when you leave, try not to change too much cash.

Credit cards

Although the infrastructure for credit card transactions is improving, you won't be able to use your card in many places, just top-end hotels and swanky shopping plazas.

Lost/stolen credit/debit cards

American Express
10 800 744 0106

MasterCard
10 800 711 7309

Visa
10 800 711 2911

Tax

A 15 per cent tax is added to four- and five-star hotel bills, while some restaurants slap on a ten per cent service charge.

Natural hazards

Beijing's biggest problem is pollution. Coal-fired power stations, factories just outside the city limits and a massive increase in cars have made the city one of the filthiest cities in the world.

On top of this, every spring is sandstorm season, when heavy winds whip in blankets of sand from the encroaching Gobi desert. Denuded grasslands in Inner Mongolia are the main culprit behind the worsening storms. On bad sandstorm or pollution days, it is best to stay indoors.

The English-language weather forecast hotline is 121. You can access the day's air quality reading on the website of the State Environmental Protection Administration of China (http://english.sepa.gov.cn).

Opening hours

Banks, museum and shops are usually open 9am to 5pm every day, including the weekend. Shops are also open every day but they close a bit later, around 8 or 9pm.

Police

Public Security Bureau (PSB) officers wear a dark navy blue uniform. All police stations have a blue sign marked 'police station' in Chinese and English with the PSB's gold, red and blue crest. If you have to make a phone call, they are often accommodating.

They are highly unlikely to speak English, but many are nonetheless friendly. Call 110 in an emergency.

Beijing Municipal Public Security Bureau
9 Dongdajie, Qianmen, Dongcheng, South (8402 0101/www.bjgaj.gov.cn/epolice/index.htm). **Map** p241 K10.

Postal services

The Chinese mail service is erratic; usually it takes about a week for a letter from Beijing to arrive in the UK, but sometimes it can take up to two months.

There are post offices all over town that allow you to post letters overseas, but if you want to send a package you should go to the international office on Jianguomenwai (*see p224*).

Postcards to Europe and America cost RMB 4.50; letters under 20g cost only RMB 6. Note, the package contents are inspected and you may not be able to post large numbers of CDs or DVDs overseas – especially if they are pirated copies.

See also p217 Couriers.

Post offices

Beijing International Post & Telecommunications Office

Jianguomenbei Dajie, Yabao Lu, Dongcheng, Chaoyang (6512 8114). **Open** 8am-6.30pm daily. **Map** p244 M10.
You can get post mailed here – bring your passport.

Property

Finding a home

There's plenty of choice on the house front. If you've got the money you can settle in a serviced apartment, a villa in suburbia, a luxury self-contained apartment complex, or a refurbished courtyard home – think faux Qing Dynasty. Monthly rents for any one of these are anything upwards of RMB 8,000; although small two-bedroomed courtyard houses go for as low as RMB 5,000 a month. Those less well off can choose from a regular flat to a homestay with a Chinese family (expect to help little Wang with her homework). Local apartments vary according to the district, but are generally around RMB 3,000-RMB 4,000 a month for two-bedroomed flats, while a homestay costs around RMB 1,500-RMB 2,000 a month.

There is an army of pushy estate agents out there ready to help you find a home. The websites below are also good starting places to finding an apartment (note many ads are posted by agencies).

www.thatsbj.com
Apartments for all budgets, as well as ads for flatshares.
www.wuwoo.com Bilingual site with interactive map.
www.chinahomestay.org Helps place students with Chinese families.
www.home007.cn Rental and sales across China.

If you fancy an apartment complex you can walk into its management office and ask them to show you any empty flats. This way you can deal directly with the landlord.

Foreigners are free to rent property in Beijing – the only requirement is that you and your landlord register with the local PSB station on the day you move in.

Real estate agents

The commission that goes to the agency is almost always paid by the landlord. If they insist that you pay, change your agency.

Century 21

1725 Hanwei Plaza, 7 Guanghua Lu, Chaoyang (6561 7788/www.century21cn.com). **Open** 9am-5pm daily. **Map** p244 O9.
International property agents

Golden Keys

D24 Wanda Plaza, 11 Langjiayuan, Jianguo Lu, Chaoyang (6226 9900/www.zdhouse.com). **Open** 8.30am-9pm daily.
One of Beijing's biggest agencies with more than 300 offices.

Religion

Capitalism is China's newest religion. The Communist Party outlawed all faiths when it came to power except for five state sanctioned beliefs – Buddhism, Catholicism, Islam, Protestantism and Taoism, with Judaism inhabiting something of a grey area. Each officially sanctioned 'church' has to operate under the government's direction.

Buddhist

Guanji Si (Temple of Great Charity), Fuchengmennei Dajie, Xicheng, Financial District (6616 0907). **Open** 9am-10.30pm daily. **Map** p241 H8.

Jewish

King's Garden Villa D5A, 18 Xiao Yun Road, Chaoyang (8470 8239/www.chabadbeijing.com). **Open** 8.30am-6pm daily. **Kabbalat Shabbat** *Winter* 20min after candle lighting Fri; *Summer* 5min after candle lighting Fri. **Torah class** 10.15am Sat. **Shach/Mussaf** 11am Sat. **Mincha** 1hr before end of Shabbat, Sat. Shabbat meals served after services on Fri, Sat.

Islamic

Niujie Mosque, 88 Niuwujie, Xuanwu, South (6353 2564). **Open** 8am-6.30pm daily. **Map** p246 H11.

Roman Catholic

St Joseph's, 74 Wangfujing Dajie, Dongcheng, Centre (6524 0634). Metro Wangfujing. **Mass** 6.30am, 7am Mon-Sat; 6.15am, 7am, 8am Sun. **Map** p244 L9.

Safety

Keep a close eye on your belongings and the worst thing that is likely to happen is a taxi driver gives you fake money in your change. Lower the likelihood of this happening by always carrying small bills on you – lots of tens and 20s. Beijing is a relatively safe city, but take care of pickpockets in crowded bus and train stations.

Avoid accepting invites from locals that hang around tourist areas. Common scams include posing as a 'struggling art student' to wheedle tourists into buying prints at inflated prices. A request to practise English at a teahouse can turn sour when the manager in collusion with the 'language student' offers up a bill for hundreds of RMB. The rickshaw drivers around Tiananmen Square have a bad rap for being duplicitous; the ones around Houhai are generally trustworthy; just make sure you agree on the final price before you set out.

Smoking

China is the world's biggest manufacturer of cigarettes and the biggest consumer – one of every three cigarettes smoked in the world is smoked in China. Cigarettes are cheap too, at around RMB 12 for a pack of imported cigarettes – but beware of counterfeits. However, even here the non-smoking brigade is gaining ground – Beijing has banned lighting up in many offices and public places, including cinemas, the subway and some shopping plazas.

Study

Language classes

Chinese is the number one reason for expats to come to Beijing – tens of thousands arrive here every year to enroll in a Mandarin course. You can study formally at a university or take private classes. The latter is more expensive – around RMB 100 an hour for one-on-one – compared to around RMB 20,000 a year for an average of 18 hours of class a week. Some private schools offer group classes which work out super cheap – less than RMB 20 an hour.

Beijing Language & Culture University (BLCU)

15 Xueyuan Lu, Haidian, North-west (8230 3821/www.eblcu.net). Metro Wudaokou. **Rates** RMB 23,200/yr. **No credit cards. Map** p249 F2.

BLCU accepts the biggest intake of foreign students, with around 6,000 new freshmen enrolling every year. It's rumoured to be the 'party' choice.

Beijing Normal University (BNU)

19 Xinjiekou Dajie, Xicheng, Financial District (6220 8305/ www.bnu.edu.cn). **Rates** RMB 22,400/yr. **No credit cards. Map** p249 H5.

As BNU is outside the university district of Haidian, there are fewer foreigners around, and more chances to practise Chinese. Since it's a teacher training college, its staff have a good reputation.

Frontiers

3/F, 30 Dongzhong Jie, Dongzhimenwai, Dongcheng, Chaoyang (6413 1547/www. frontiers.com.cn). Metro Dongzhimen. **Rates** *Group classes* RMB 2,000/44hrs. *Individual tuition* RMB 70/hr. **No credit cards. Map** p244 N7.

This is a laid-back school, with a cosy lounge, social events and friendly teachers. It's useful for those who just want a grounding in useable Chinese, serious students should look elsewhere.

Other locations: Rm 1403, Entrance 1, Huaqiao Village, 24 Jianguomenwai Dajie, Chaoyang (6515 8278).

Global Village

Chengfu Lu, Haidian, North-west (6253 7737). Metro Wudaojou. **Rates** *Group classes* RMB 240/20hrs. **No credit cards. Map** p249 F2.

This school is custom run for Korean students, but anyone can take classes. At RMB 12 an hour, it's one of the cheapest options. Former students give it a good rap – rigorous teaching, albeit big classes, and flexible schedules.

Taipei Language Institute

3/F, Room 312, InterChina Commercial Building, 33 Dengshikou Jie, Dongcheng, Centre (6525 5761/www. tli.com.tw). **Rates** *Individual tuition* RMB 110/hr. **No credit cards. Map** p244 L10.

Expensive, but its teachers have a good reputation for being hard core. Students recommend it as the serious choice for those committed to learning Chinese.

Telephones

Dialling & codes

The country code for China is 86 and the area code for Beijing is 010; drop the prefix zero when calling from overseas. If you are in Beijing, you do not need the area code.

Once inside China, to phone overseas dial 00, followed by the country code, the area code, then the telephone number. The US and Canada country code is 1; the UK 44; Australia 61; and New Zealand 64.

If you're phoning Shanghai from Beijing, add 021 to the front of the number. For toll free numbers *see p217*.

Public phones

Chinese public phones take pre-paid phone cards; they come in units of RMB 20, RMB 30, RMB 50 and RMB 100.

Operator services

Local directory assistance (English) 2689 0114
International enquiries 115
Collect/credit card calls 108 + country code
AT&T 108 888
MCI 108 712
Sprint 108 16

Phonecards

Internet Protocol (IP) cards are available from newsstands and phone shops. The cards are always heavily discounted – eg a RMB 100 face-value card should cost around RMB 35. Different IP cards have different rates. They can be used with landlines and mobiles. A RMB 100 China Unicom '17910' card lasts for about 27 minutes to the UK.

Mobile phones

China uses the GSM 900/ 1800 systems for its mobile networks. The two operators are China Mobile and China Unicom. China Mobile is generally recognised to have the better coverage.

You can sign up with your home operator for roaming, provided your phone is GMS 900/1800 compatible. A cheaper option is to buy a pre-paid SIM card (RMB 100) in Beijing and use it in your phone. Local calls cost around 6 mao a minute incoming and outgoing. You can buy top-up cards – in units of RMB 50 and

RMB 100 – at newsstands and phone shops.

Mobiles are inexpensive in Beijing. You can pick up a new model for as little as RMB 500 or a second-hand phone for as low as RMB 200 (*see p129* shopping/markets).

Pay-as-you-go plans are only available for Chinese customers or foreigners with a local guarantor.

Faxes

Most hotels will accept incoming faxes for their guests for a small charge.

Time

Beijing is in the same time zone as Hong Kong and Singapore – GMT+8. The country does not change over to daylight savings time.

Tipping

It is not customary to tip in Beijing. Be careful giving tips to staff in small local restaurants as they may be searched and accused of stealing if found with cash at the end of a shift. However, taxi drivers who go out of their way to help will be happy to receive a couple of RMB, although they won't expect it. Only in five-star hotels and top-end restaurants would a tip be expected, although these places usually include a service charge as well. Tour guides also expect to be tipped.

Toilets

Beijing has just about got the toilet thing covered and, with the Olympics coming, the city has been at pains to make them look good (although smelling good seems to have been bypassed). There are plenty of public toilets around the city, most shopping plazas will have toilets, and restaurants and bars won't mind if you pop in just to use their washroom. Streetside public lavatories are generally of the squat variety, don't always have cubicles, and almost never have toilet paper.

Tourist information

Beijing's tourist offices are pretty lame – they cater to domestic holidaymakers rather than foreigners. The most convenient office is a couple of blocks east of the north gate of the Workers' Stadium. There is a 24-hour tourist hotline (6513 0828) with some English-speaking operators if you're lucky. Your hotel is probably a better source of information.

Beijing Tourist Information Center

11-12 Gongti Bei Lu, Chaoyang (6417 6627/http://english.bjta.gov.cn/). **Open** 9am-5pm daily. **Map** p244 N8.

Visas & immigration

All visitors to China need a visa. Obtain this before you travel from a Chinese embassy or consulate. Most tourists are given a 30-day single entry visa, called an L visa. From the UK, a tourist visa costs £30, and takes four working days to process. A double entry visa costs £45. A one-day express service costs an extra £20. Business visas require a letter of invitation from a Chinese organisation. Once inside China, it is easy to get a one month's extension to an L visa from the Foreign Affairs Office of the Public Security Bureau (2 Andingmen Dongdajie, Dongcheng, 8402 0101, 8.30am-4.30pm Mon-Sat). It takes about five days to process. For updated information on current visa regulations and application procedures check the following websites:

Canadian citizens

www.chinaembassycanada.org/eng

UK citizens

www.chinese-embassy.org.uk/eng/

US citizens

www.china-embassy.org

Weights & measures

China uses the metric system.

1 kilometre = 0.62 miles
1 metre = 1.09 yards
1 centimetre = 0.39 inches
1 kilogram = 2.2 pounds
1 gram = 0.035 ounces
1 litre = 1.76 pints
0° Centigrade = 32° Fahrenheit

What to take

Beijing is a modern metropolis and anything you'll need is probably on sale somewhere, although overseas brands and imported goods are more expensive than back home. To be on the safe side, you should, however, bring any prescription medicine you might need. If you're travelling to rural areas you should also take your own syringes.

Some products which are hard to find include deodorant, antacids, tampons with an applicator, sunblock and moisturiser – Beijing is super dry in the winter and you'll need to slather lots of this on. If you are heading out to the country (especially Inner Mongolia, *see p205*) you will need even more. The white skin fashion fad in Asia means moisturisers and suntan lotion here often include bleaching agents.

Some expats also recommend you bring your own condoms. Brands on sale here tend to be a little, shall we say, 'snug'.

When to go

Beijing is at its best in autumn (September and October). Temperatures have simmered down from the scorching summer, light breezes often clear the skies of smog, and the evenings are pleasantly cool. While the snow in winter can make visiting the Summer Palace magical, you'll need to swaddle yourself in warm clothing – temperatures regularly sink below zero. With few winds, pollution reaches killer levels and the atmosphere is so dry, skin becomes prune-like. Spring is another good time to come – temperatures are buoyed up to a British summer standard and there is a good chance of catching a blue sky day as this is the windy season. Unfortunately, if the wind is in the wrong direction, you'll be caught in a sandstorm when the sky turns orange and your mouth fills with dust. Summers are cooking with the mercury seldom below 30 degrees. But when Beijing lies drenched after an August rainstorm, it's the only time the city feels clean.

If possible, you should avoid visiting Beijing during one of the national holidays (*see p149* **Golden weeks**) when the whole country is on holiday. Hotel rooms, flight and train tickets are at a premium, and tourist sites swell with sightseers. The crowds are suffocating.

Public holidays

New Year's Day 1-2 January
Lunar New Year three days in January/February (depending on lunar calendar). *See p228.*
May 1 Labour Day 1-3 May
October 1 National Day 1-3 October

Women

While you might get stared at in Beijing, the attention is usually not sleazy, unless you're in a bar or club. Even so, it is sensible to be cautious. Sit in the back seat of a taxi if you're alone and avoid travelling by yourself at night. Under Mao, China enjoyed a measure of sexual equality – women, said the Great Helmsman, hold up half the sky. Since the reforms females have been petted and teased by media-induced trends into becoming petulant little empresses. China celebrates International Women's Day on 8 March – the date in Chinese (*san ba* or three eight) has become synonymous with the word 'bitch'.

Working in Beijing

There are plenty of opportunities from teaching English, freelance editing and writing, to working for one of the growing number of multinationals. If you speak good Chinese, your employment prospects are much rosier. Casual jobs usually pay between RMB 100 to RMB 300 an hour.

If you're looking for a fatter pay packet, apply for a job within your profession before coming to China. Internships are a good way to get your foot in the door; many lead to a paid position.

Work permits

Many foreigners live and work in Beijing on six-month F (business) visas. These are easy to buy from visa brokers in Hong Kong or Beijing itself, although officially you need a letter of invitation. *That's Beijing* and *City Weekend* carry dozens of adverts placed by visa brokers. It's illegal to

Climate

Month	Temperature (centigrade/fahrenheit)	Relative humidity	Rainfall (mm/inches)	Sunshine (hrs/day)
Jan	-10 to 1/14 to 34	50	4/0.1	7
Feb	-8 to 4/17 to 39	50	5/0.2	7
Mar	-1 to 11/30 to 52	48	8/0.3	8
Apr	7 to 21/45 to 70	46	17/0.7	8
May	13 to 27/55 to 81	49	35/1.4	9
June	18 to 31/64 to 88	56	78/3	9
July	21 to 31/70 to 88	72	242/10	7
Aug	20 to 30/68 to 86	74	141/6	7
Sept	14 to 26/57 to 79	67	58/2	8
Oct	6 to 20/43 to 68	59	16/0.6	8
Nov	-2 to 9/28 to 48	56	11/0.4	6
Dec	-8 to 3/17 to 37	51	3/0.1	6

What's your animal?

鼠 Rat	1924	1936	1948	1960	1972	1984	1996	2008
牛 Ox	1925	1937	1949	1961	1973	1985	1997	2009
虎 Tiger	1926	1938	1950	1962	1974	1986	1998	2010
兔 Rabbit	1927	1939	1951	1963	1975	1987	1999	2011
龍 Dragon	1928	1940	1952	1964	1976	1988	2000	2012
蛇 Snake	1929	1941	1953	1965	1977	1989	2001	2013
馬 Horse	1930	1942	1954	1966	1978	1990	2002	2014
羊 Sheep	1931	1943	1955	1967	1979	1991	2003	2015
猴 Monkey	1932	1944	1956	1968	1980	1992	2004	2016
雞 Rooster	1933	1945	1957	1969	1981	1993	2005	2017
狗 Dog	1934	1946	1958	1970	1982	1994	2006	2018
豬 Pig	1935	1947	1959	1971	1983	1995	2007	2019

work on this kind of visa, but the authorities generally turn a blind eye. If you get a full-time job with a Chinese or overseas company in Beijing they will help you arrange a work visa, which also gets you a residence permit. Your company will guide you through the lengthy process but briefly you will need to provide about ten passport photos, sign a contract with the firm, and pass a rudimentary medical exam which includes HIV and STD tests and a chest X-ray. Your company should cover all associated costs.

Useful addresses

Once in Beijing, the best way to find work is to search the classified pages of www.thatsbj.com, or ask around at expat hangouts around Sanlitun. Many jobs are found by word of mouth.

You can also contact companies directly – there is considerable demand for English teachers.

Also check:

www.chinahr.com China's branch of www.monster.com.

www.jobsdb.com Jobs around south-east Asia including China and Hong Kong.

www.danwei.org For work in media and PR.

Vocabulary

Beijingers think they're the bee's knees because standard *putonghua* is largely derived from the Beijing dialect. Although the two languages are very close, the Beijing accent is marked by a very liberal use of the 'er' sound – linguists call this a rhotic vowel – and Beijingers have a tendency to slur their words together and exaggerate their tones. This makes Beijing *hua* (the Beijing dialect) almost incomprehensible to foreigners learning Chinese if the accent is very strong.

On a basic level, Chinese is easier than many languages. There are no tenses – Chinese words have only one form. Suffixes are used instead to denote tenses. There are no comparative adjectives. The most challenging part of learning Chinese is often the tones, as each sound has four different inflections, each of which can change the meaning of a word. In the written language, characters take the place of an alphabet.

A character can be a word or part of a word, but normally a word consists of two or more characters. There are about 20,000 characters in a normal Chinese word processor. For those who do not read characters, there is a romanised alphabet called *pinyin*. However, Chinese rarely understand it when spoken by non natives. Not all consonants in *pinyin* are pronounced as in English:

c	like the 'ts' in 'hits'
q	like the 'ch' in 'chase'
r	like the 's' in 'measure'
x	like the 'sh' in 'shop'
z	like the 'dz' in 'duds'

Pronouns

I/me *wo*	Us	*women*
You *ni*	You	*nimen*
He *ta* She *ta*	They	*tamen*

Smalltalk

My name is... *Wo jiao...*
My surname is... *Wo xing...*
(I am) American *Wo shi meiguo ren*
British *yingguo ren*
Canadian *jianada ren*
Australian *aodaliya ren*
European *ouzhou ren*

Hello *Ni hao*
Goodbye *Zai jian*
Thanks *Xie xie*
How are you? *Ni zenme yang*
I'm fine *Hai keyi*
Sorry *Duibuqi*
You're welcome *Bu keqi*
Please speak more slowly *Qing shuode man yidian*
I don't understand *wo bu mingbai*

Negatives

The word *bu* in front of a verb/adjective makes it negative.

I want – *Wo yao*
I don't want – *Wo bu yao*
I know – *Wo zhidao*
I don't know – *Wo bu zhidao*
I understand – *Wo mingbai*
I don't understand – *Wo bu mingbai*
That's right – *dui*
That's not right – *Bu dui*

Asking questions

To ask a question you say the positive and negative forms of the verb:
Do you any have any…? *Nei you meiyou …?*
(literally you have, not have …)
What *shenme?*
What's your name? *Ni jiao shenme?*
What do you want? *Ni yao shenme?*

Getting around

Can we take this taxi? *Keyi ma?*
I want to go to (the)… *Wo yao qu…*
Use the meter please *Qing da biao*
Turn left *Zuo guai*
Turn right *You guai*
Go straight *Yizhi zou*
Stop the car *Ting che*
Hotel *Da jiu dian*
Airport *Feiji chang*
Train station *Huoche zhan*
Metro *Ditie zhan*
This place … *Zhe ge difang...*
I want to go home *Wo yao hui jia*

Shopping

How much is it? *Duoshao qian?*
That's too expensive *Tai gui le*
It's too big *Tai da*
It's too small *Tai xiao*
Please give me a receipt *Qing gei wo fapiao*

Eating & drinking

Can I have the menu *Qing gei wo caidan*
Do you have an English menu? *Ni you meiyou yingwen caidan?*
I want a... *Wo yao …*
Can I have the bill *Maidan*
Bar *Jiuba*
Café *Kafei guan*
Restaurant *Fandian*

Days

Monday *Xingqi yi*
Tuesday *Xingqi er*
Wednesday *Xingqi san*
Thursday *Xingqi si*
Friday *Xingqi wu*
Saturday *Xingqi liu*
Sunday *Xingqi tian*
Morning *Zaoshang/shangwu*
Afternoon *Xiawu*
Evening *Wanshang*
Today *Jintian*
Tomorrow *Mingtian*
Yesterday *Zuotian*
What's the time? *Xianzai…jidian?*

Numbers

Zero *ling*
One *yi*
Two *er*
Three *san*
Four *si*
Five *wu*
Six *liu*
Seven *qi*
Eight *ba*
Nine *jiu*
Ten *shi*
Twenty *er-shi*
Twenty-one *er-shi-yi*
100 *yi bai*

Emergencies

Help! *Jiuming a!*
Fire! *Zhao huo le!*
Police! *Jingcha!*
Call an ambulance *Qing jiao yi ge jiuhuche*
I need to see a doctor *Wo yao kan bing*
I've lost my passport *Wo de huzhao diule*
Please can you help me? *Ni neng bu neng bang wo?*

Further Reference

Books

Non-fiction

Michael Aldrich
The Search for a Vanishing Beijing (2006)
Historian Aldrich explores what's left of the rapidly disappearing imperial past of China's greatest city.

EN Anderson
The Food of China (1990)
Intelligent account of the fascinating history of Chinese food and its role in the general affairs of the nation.

Jung Chang
Wild Swans: Three Daughters of China (2003)
The ultimate China memoir, describing three generations of Chinese women and their struggles throughout the 20th century. It's also worth reading her biography of Mao for an insight into the man responsible for the deaths of millions.

Rachel DeWoskin
Foreign Babes in Beijing (2006)
Amusing, huge-selling account of the author's experiences as a token American in a Chinese TV serial.

Will Hutton
The Writing on the Wall (2006)
Subtitled 'China and the West in the 21st Century' this primer provides a handy summary of the facts and figures behind the economic boom and the possible future scenarios.

James Kynge
China Shakes the World (2006)
Recent winner of the Goldman Sachs Business book of the year award. Ex-*Financial Times* correspondent Kynge discusses China's future in a globalised economy in erudite, well researched, journalistic fashion. A must-read for China-watchers.

Julia Lovell
The Great Wall: China Against the World 1000BC-2000AD (2007)
Accessible, entertaining account of the history and significance of China's most famous landmark from Cambridge Professor of Chinese history, Dr Julia Lovell.

James McGregor
One Billion Customers (2005)
The definitive account of China's exploding consumer market, and its impact on the global economy.

Anchee Min
Empress Orchid (2005)
A compelling, vivid account of life in the Forbidden City on the eve of the collapse of imperial China.

Fiction

Chun Sue
Beijing Doll (2004)
Racy title, originally banned in China for its frank exploration of the sexual awakening of a Beijing girl.

Geling Yan
The Uninvited (2006)
A downtrodden young man finds he can keep his family in pocket and his stomach full by posing as a journalist. A well-crafted comic analysis of the duplicities of modern China.

Ha Jin
The Crazed (2004)
Award-winning author Ha Jin winds a tale of intrigue, set during the Tiananmen protests in 1989, around an ailing professor and a hapless student who becomes his caretaker.

Lin Yutang
Moment in Peking (1980)
A beautifully written narrative that follows a prominent Chinese family from the beginning of the Boxer Rebellion through the Japanese Invasion. The fictional story gives a great feel for the culture and feel of 'old Beijing'.

Music

Cui Jian
Rock and Roll on the New Long March
Cui Jian is the 'father of Chinese rock', and has fallen in and out of political favour since the launch of this, his first album, all the way back in 1987.

Ruins
Glide Like a Leaf
Spacey rock with a Radiohead feel.

Second Hand Rose
Second Hand Rose
Perhaps Beijing's best traditional/contemporary rock combo.

Subs
Down
Screaming garage punk from Beijing's sexiest quartet.

Wild Children
Zhouyu
Beijing folk at its finest, featuring traditional instruments in a contemporary setting.

Film

Beijing Bicycle
dir Wang Xiaoshuai (2000)
Violence, gang warfare and teenage angst over a stolen bicycle in this affecting snapshot of contemporary Beijing life.

Beijing or Bust
dir Hao Wu (2005)
Documentary featuring six American-born Chinese who opt to throw everything in and head for Beijing.

The Last Emperor
dir Bernardo Bertolucci (1987)
Luscious, visually striking portrayal of the fall of China's last imperial dynasty. Bertolucci does the extraordinary story justice.

Shower
dir Zhang Yang (1999)
Sharp portrait of family life in contemporary China as a successful businessman returns to his Beijing home under the impression his father has died.

Waiting Alone
dir Dayyan Eng (2004)
Set in the haunts of Beijing's new generation of clubbers and misfits, *Waiting Alone* garnered a string of awards and nominations on its release. Fresh and lively.

Websites

www.chinadigitalnews.net
Useful, critical and up-to-date – and the fact that it's blocked by the Chinese state's great internet firewall is proof of credibility.

www.chinaexpat.com
Listings and city information for the expatriate living in China.

www.crienglish.com
Website for China's biggest English-language radio station. All the news from a Chinese perspective, with archived radio programmes.

www.danwei.org
Sharp, witty, English-language media-monitoring site with all the latest from across the media.

www.ewsn.com
Prolific Hong Kong site translating Chinese news and media for the benefit of English speakers.

www.zhaopin.com
Searchable China jobs database, in Chinese and English.

Index

Note: page numbers in **bold** indicate section(s) giving key information on a topic; *italics* indicate photos.

Index

n

o

p

Accommodation

Bars & pubs

Restaurants